Penguin Educat

Early Lear

Edited by W. S

Penguin Modern Psychology Readings

General Editor
B. M. Foss

Advisory Board
Michael Argyle
Dalbir Bindra
P. C. Dodwell
G. A. Foulds
Max Hamilton
Marie Jahoda
Harry Kay
S. G. M. Lee
W. M. O'Neil
K. H. Pribram
P. L. Reid
Roger Russell
Jane Stewart
Anne Treisman
P. E. Vernon
Peter Warr
George Westby

Early Learning and Early Experience

Selected Readings
Edited by W. Sluckin

Penguin Books

Penguin Books Ltd, Harmondsworth,
Middlesex, England
Penguin Books Inc., 7110 Ambassador Road,
Baltimore, Md 21207, U.S.A.
Penguin Books Australia Ltd,
Ringwood, Victoria, Australia

First published 1971
This selection copyright © W. Sluckin, 1971
Introduction and notes copyright © W. Sluckin, 1971

Made and printed in Great Britain by
C. Nicholls & Company Ltd
Set in Monotype Times

This book is sold subject to the condition that
it shall not, by way of trade or otherwise, be lent,
re-sold, hired out, or otherwise circulated without
the publisher's prior consent in any form of
binding or cover other than that in which it is
published and without a similar condition
including this condition being imposed on the
subsequent purchaser

Contents

Introduction 9

Part One Early Conditioning 15

1 Einar R. Siqueland and Lewis P. Lipsitt (1966)
Conditioned Head-Turning in Human Newborns 17

2 J. Koch (1968)
Conditioned Orienting Reactions to Persons and Things in Two- to Five-Month-Old Infants 23

3 D. F. Caldwell and J. Werboff (1962)
Classical Conditioning in Newborn Rats 35

4 Walter C. Stanley, Anne Christake Cornwell, Constance Poggiani and Alice Trattner (1963)
Conditioning in the Neonatal Puppy 39

Part Two Imprinting 49

5 W. Sluckin and E. A. Salzen (1961)
Imprinting and Perceptual Learning 51

6 P. P. G. Bateson (1964)
Changes in Chicks' Responses to Novel Moving Objects over the Sensitive Period for Imprinting 71

7 E. A. Salzen and C. C. Meyer (1967)
Imprinting: Reversal of a Preference Established during the Critical Period 93

8 Howard S. Hoffman, John L. Searle, Sharon Toffey and Frederick Kozma, Jr (1966)
Behavioural Control by an Imprinted Stimulus 97

Part Three Learning and Development 101

9 D. O. Hebb (1949)
The Relation of Early to Later Learning 103

10 M. A. Vince (1961)
Developmental Changes in Learning Capacity 112

11 J. P. Scott (1968)
Early Development 136

12 Bettye M. Caldwell (1967)
The Optimal Learning Environment for the Young Child 149

Part Four
Restriction and Enrichment of Early Experience 169

13 William R. Thompson and Woodburn Heron (1954)
The Effects of Restricting Early Experience on the Problem-Solving Capacity of Dogs 171

14 Ronald Melzack and T. H. Scott (1957)
The Effects of Early Experience on the Response to Pain 189

15 Seymour Levine, Jacques A. Chevalier and Sheldon J. Korchin (1956)
The Effects of Early Shock and Handling on Later Avoidance Learning 202

16 Victor H. Denenberg (1964)
Critical Periods, Stimulus Input and Emotional Reactivity: A Theory of Infantile Stimulation 210

Part Five **The Development of Special Traits** 235

17 J. McV. Hunt, Harold Schlosberg, R. L. Solomon and Eliot Stellar (1947)
The Effects of Infantile Experience on Adult Behaviour in Rats 237

18 J. P. Scott, Sherman Ross, Alan E. Fisher and David J. King (1959)
The Effects of Early Enforced Weaning on Sucking Behaviour of Puppies 257

19 Lorna Smith Benjamin (1961)
The Effect of Bottle and Cup Feeding on the Non-Nutritive Sucking of the Infant Rhesus Monkey 280

20 Gene P. Sackett (1967)
Some Persistent Effects of Different Rearing Conditions on Pre-Adult Social Behaviour in Monkeys 298

Part Six Parental Deprivation in Infancy 305

21 Bill Seay and Harry F. Harlow (1965)
Maternal Separation in the Rhesus Monkey 307

22 R. A. Hinde, Y. Spencer-Booth and M. Bruce (1966)
Effects of Six-Day Maternal Deprivation on Rhesus Monkey Infants 320

23 Leon J. Yarrow (1961)
Maternal Deprivation: Towards an Empirical and Conceptual Re-Evaluation 328

Part Seven
Early Socialization in Animals and Man 331

24 K. F. Taylor and W. Sluckin (1964)
Flocking of Domestic Chicks 333

25 Robert B. Cairns and Donald L. Johnson (1965)
The Development of Inter-Species Social Attachments 337

26 J. P. Scott (1958)
Critical Periods in the Development of Social Behaviour in Puppies 343

27 H. R. Schaffer and Peggy E. Emerson (1964)
The Development of Social Attachments in Infancy 365

28 H. R. Schaffer (1966)
The Onset of Fear of Strangers and the Incongruity Hypothesis 387

Further Reading 405

Acknowledgements 406

Author Index 407

Subject Index 413

Introduction

What happens early in the individual's life may profoundly influence his psychological development. This could be as true for animals as for man. The theme is an old one, reflected in the writings of churchmen, empiricist philosophers, Marxists, psychoanalysts, learning theorists and others. At a more practical level, the workings of the early influences have been inquired into by child psychologists, by educationalists and by animal trainers. More recently, a new element has been brought to bear upon the debate, and that is the findings of experimentalists. As years go by, there are more and more such findings about the lasting effects of one or another kind of early experience.

This is not to say that theoretical discussion has died down. On the contrary, it is as alive as ever; but it is now becoming better informed. Both the empirical studies and theorizing about the nature of early influences are the concern of developmental psychology; indeed, it is a fast developing sector of developmental psychology. The aim of this book of Readings is to put the student in direct contact with research endeavour in this sector. At a time when books of Readings are being compiled in various fields of psychology, there appears to be a growing gap in the Readings literature in the area of early experience, and especially early learning. The present book is an attempt to remedy this situation.

The term 'early experience' refers customarily to all effects of stimulation in infancy, whether immediate or long lasting. 'Early learning' is a narrower concept, for not every kind of early experience can be regarded as learning. But which type of experience early in life *is* or *is not* learning is often difficult to decide. This is partly because the concept of learning is not susceptible to a sharp definition; see, for example, Hilgard and Marquis (1961) and Hinde (1966). But even if it were, we should still have some difficulty in assigning the label 'early learning' to certain cases simply because of our ignorance of the actual results of stimulation in those cases; that is, it is not always clear whether early stimulation makes its impact on later behaviour with or without the mediation of learning.

Consider, for example, the possible effects of exposure early in life to cold. Such early experience could have various physical repercussions; and the physical effects could have some behavioural concomitants. The psychological effects of exposure to cold could stop there, in which case it would be out of place to describe such early experience as early learning. However, experience of this kind could involve learning also. For the infant could in some situations have scope for acquiring ways of acting to keep warm, it could develop preferences for perceptual cues associated with slight temperature rises, and so on. Whether and when early-experience effects involve early-learning effects is thus, in a large measure, a matter of empirical knowledge, sometimes depending on the results of complex experimental investigations.

The distinction, however, between early experience and early learning must not be over-stressed. Although not always clear-cut or important, it may have convenient classificatory value. Thus, we can place at one end of the continuum those studies which are obviously concerned with learning, for example, conditioning experiments. At the other end will be studies which investigate how the organism is affected by simply being exposed to sensory stimuli of various kinds; but even here an element of learning cannot be ruled out.

The material in the present book is grouped in such a way that the early parts are devoted to what is clearly early learning, while the more general heading of early experience would fit the later parts better. This sequence is reflected in the title of the book, where early learning comes before early experience. But, as with many titles, ours is only a rough-and-ready indication of the contents. In fact, the last section, Part Seven, which logically follows from Part Six ('Parental Deprivation in Infancy'), reverts to the theme of early learning by dealing with early socialization in animals and man.

To return to the beginning, Part One gives a sample of research papers in the field of early conditioning. The smallness of the sample precludes the inclusion of many important research reports. As far as the conditioning of very young babies is concerned, the reader may wish to acquaint himself additionally with the work of Papousek: this he may do by looking up Ambrose (1970) and Stevenson, Hess and Rheingold (1967). Work concerning learning in the first year of life is surveyed and discussed by L. P. Lipsitt, who is himself a notable research worker in this field, in Lipsitt and Spiker (1963). Conditioning of very young animals is reviewed in Sluckin (1970). It will be seen that Readings 3 and 4 concern early conditioning of rats and dogs; but, of course, the young of many other species have been studied – examples are domestic chicks (James and Binks, 1963) and infant monkeys (Mason and Harlow, 1958).

It is partly a matter of definition of terms as to whether imprinting, dealt with in Part Two, is or is not a form of conditioning. It is certainly early learning *par excellence*, although at one time imprinting tended to be regarded as primarily a manifestation of instinctive behaviour. Four papers cannot, of course, adequately represent research in this area, but there are critical reviews to which the reader may turn such as those by Bateson (1966) and Sluckin (1964). Examples of other experimental studies in the field which may be described as classical imprinting are those of Hess (1964), Klopfer (1967) and Schutz (1965). Whether imprinting occurs in mammals, including human beings, is a highly debatable issue; experimental reports and discussions in this area may be exemplified by the papers of Sackett, Porter and Holmes (1965), Salzen (1967) and Sluckin (1968).

What the infant learns depends both on his learning capacity and on the opportunity for learning provided by the environment. The Readings in Parts Three and Four shed light on both these factors and on their interaction. Pioneering thinking here was that of Hebb (1949). It will be seen that some of the Readings selected are particularly concerned with long-term effects of both relatively stimulating and relatively restricted environments; perhaps of greatest interest is the influence of early experience upon the individual's later learning abilities. The question of sensitive or critical periods in the early development of behaviour is at once important and controversial. Some salient findings, and the nature of the controversy, may be gleaned from the papers of Ambrose (1963), Schneirla and Rosenblatt (1963) and Scott (1962).

The various lasting effects of early experience taken together have, of course, to do with personality development. The latter, conceived very broadly, may be studied in animals as well as in persons. Early influences upon behavioural development are the subject matter of Parts Five and Six. The reader interested in the subject of emotional growth may look up Denenberg (1963). The question of the effects of parental deprivation and separation looms large in psychological literature. The basic references in this field are the two World Health Organization monographs by Ainsworth *et al.* (1962) and by Bowlby (1951); See also Bowlby (1965) with appendix by Ainsworth. The study of maternal deprivation may be balanced and broadened by the study of the development of attachment behaviour; for this purpose Bowlby (1969) should be consulted.

Lastly, Part Seven is specifically concerned with early experience as a socializing agent. Again, our approach is one that typifies comparative psychology; that is, the development of social behaviour is seen as a process which is characterized by certain features irrespective of species. The ethological approach to the social behaviour of animals is at its best displayed in Tinbergen (1953). Aspects of the development of social behaviour in animals, and the human implications of this, are treated in Dimond (1970). A thorough review of our knowledge of the socializing processes in human beings, together with extensive theoretical discussion of the issues involved, will be found in Goslin (1969).

References

AINSWORTH, M. D. *et al.* (1962), *Deprivation of Maternal Care*, World Health Organization.

AMBROSE, J. A. (1963), 'The concept of critical period for the development of social responsiveness in early human infancy', in B. M. Foss (ed.), *Determinants of Infant Behaviour*, vol. 2, Methuen.

AMBROSE, J. A. (1970), *Stimulation in Early Infancy*, Academic Press.

BATESON, P. P. G. (1966), 'The characteristics and context of imprinting', *Biol. Rev.*, vol. 41, pp. 177–220.

BOWLBY, J. (1951), *Maternal Care and Mental Health*, World Health Organization.

BOWLBY, J. (1965), *Child Care and the Growth of Love*, Penguin.

BOWLBY, J. (1969), *Attachment and Loss*, vol. 1, Hogarth Press.

DENENBERG, V. H. (1963), 'Early experience and emotional development', *Sci. Amer.*, vol. 208, pp. 138–46.

DIMOND, S. J. (1970), *The Social Behaviour of Animals*, Batsford.

GOSLIN, D. A. (ed.) (1969), *Handbook of Socialization Theory and Research*, Rand McNally.

HEBB, D. O. (1949), *The Organization of Behavior*, Wiley.

HESS, E. H. (1964), 'Imprinting in birds', *Science*, vol. 146, pp. 1128–39.

HILGARD, E. R., and MARQUIS, D. G. (1961), *Conditioning and Learning*, 2nd edn, Methuen.

HINDE, R. A. (1966), *Animal Behavior*, McGraw-Hill.

JAMES, H., and BINKS, C. (1963), 'Escape and avoidance learning in newly hatched domestic chicks', *Science*, vol. 139, pp. 1293–4.

KLOPFER P. H. (1967), 'Stimulus preferences and imprinting', *Science*, vol. 156, pp. 1394–6.

LIPSITT, L. P., and SPIKER, C. C. (eds.) (1963), *Advances in Child Development and Behavior*, Academic Press.

MASON, W. A., and HARLOW, H. F. (1958), 'Formation of conditioned responses in infant monkeys', *J. comp. physiol. Psychol.*, vol. 51, pp. 68–70.

SACKETT, G. P., PORTER, M., and HOLMES, H. (1965), 'Choice behavior in rhesus monkeys: effect of stimulation during the first month of life', *Science*, vol. 147, pp. 304–6.

SALZEN, E. A. (1967), 'Imprinting in birds and primates', *Behaviour*, vol. 28, pp. 232–54.

SCHNEIRLA, T. C., and ROSENBLATT, J. S. (1963), '"Critical periods" in the development of behavior', *Science*, vol. 139, pp. 1110–15.

SCHUTZ, F. (1965), 'Sexuelle Prägung bei Anatiden', *Z. Tierpsychol.*, vol. 22, pp. 50–103.

SCOTT J. P. (1962), 'Critical periods in behavioral development', *Science*, vol. 138, pp. 949–58.

SLUCKIN, W. (1964), *Imprinting and Early Learning*, Methuen.

SLUCKIN, W. (1968), 'Imprinting in guinea-pigs', *Nature*, vol. 220, p. 1148.

SLUCKIN, W. (1970), *Early Learning in Man and Animal*, Allen & Unwin.

STEVENSON, H. W., HESS, E. H., and RHEINGOLD, H. L. (eds.) (1967), *Early Behavior: Comparative and Developmental Approaches*, Wiley.

TINBERGEN, N. (1953), *Social Behaviour in Animals*, Methuen.

Part One Early Conditioning

Improvements in experimental methods have made it possible to condition younger and younger individuals in a variety of ways. Early learning of this kind, however, is always more evident in precocial species (in which the newborn young have fully developed sense organs and are capable of locomotion) than in altricial species (in which physically the young are relatively immature at birth). Human beings may be placed in the altricial region of the continuum, although nowhere near the extreme end. Conditioning of human neonates has only recently been achieved experimentally. Siqueland and Lipsitt (Reading 1) report three successful experiments in which sweet liquid was used for reinforcement. Koch (Reading 2) worked with very much older infants and showed how at a later stage of development new reinforcing agents, namely access to novel stimuli, become effective. Animals such as rats, cats and dogs are clearly altricial and their neonates are not capable of much learning. Yet Caldwell and Werboff (Reading 3) succeeded in training newborn rats by means of a typical classical-conditioning procedure. Stanley, Cornwell, Poggiani and Trattner (Reading 4), using much ingenuity, brought about both appetitive and aversive conditioning in three-day-old puppies. This suggests that it would be rash to assume the absence of conditionability in the newborns of any species of placental mammal.

1 Einar R. Siqueland and Lewis P. Lipsitt

Conditioned Head-Turning in Human Newborns

Excerpts from Einar R. Siqueland and Lewis P. Lipsitt, 'Conditioned head-turning in human newborns', *Journal of Experimental Child Psychology*, vol. 3, 1966, pp. 356–76.

Introduction

Recent conditioning studies with human newborns (Lipsitt and Kaye, 1964; Papousek, 1961) suggest that, with increasing refinement of experimental techniques, analyses of learning processes are now possible in young organisms whose immature neuromuscular status has been a barrier previously to extensive behavioral study. Such investigations have shown that certain behavior patterns of human newborns can be viewed as learning phenomena, and traditional learning concepts such as reinforcement, conditioning and extinction are useful in the analysis of infant behavior. It was the purpose of the present studies to explore the usefulness of a special form of instrumental conditioning in newborns. As yet, there has been little experimental data clearly demonstrating that some environmental events may act as reinforcing stimuli to shape or selectively strengthen responses in the behavioral repertoire of the newborn (Lipsitt, 1963). The present study sought to increase the probability of occurrence, through reinforcement consequences, of an elicited response in the behavior repertoire of the newborn. Thus the present procedure capitalized upon a response which at the outset is an elicited response, but which gains in response-strength through reinforcement of that elicitation. The response selected for study was that of head-turning to tactile stimulation of the face.

A number of investigations have focused on parameters of head movement in infants as an unconditioned response (e.g. Blauvelt and McKenna, 1961; Gentry and Aldrich, 1948; Peiper, 1963; Pratt, Nelson and Sun, 1930; Prechtl, 1958; Turkewitz, Gordon and Birch, 1965). These investigators have studied the influence of such parameters as duration and intensity of stimulus, deprivational state, arousal level, age of infant and medication of mother during delivery. Prechtl (1958) has provided the most complete description of head movement in the human newborn.

Clinical observations of the initial feeding interactions between the mother and newborn (Blauvelt and McKenna, 1961; Gunther, 1961) have also resulted in the observation that the head-turning response may serve an important function in the early feeding history of the infant and also in speculation as to the role of learning on subsequent behavior in the feeding situation. Such observations suggest there may be conditions under which environmental consequences of this response alter the likelihood of the response. Gewirtz (1961) has in fact suggested that instrumental or operant learning concepts are useful in understanding behavior of young organisms in which specific components of unconditioned responses are shaped or strengthened by environmental consequences functioning as reinforcers.

The focus of the present investigation was to evaluate the cumulative effect of reinforcement operations on the response of ipsilateral head movements to tactile stimulation of the face. These experiments investigated whether, under certain reinforcement conditions, the likelihood of this response in newborns can be altered, a response which is considered by many to be in fact a reflex. The first experiment studied the effect of experimentally pairing reinforcement with the occurrence of ipsilateral head movements to tactile stimulation. The effect of reinforcement parameters on probability of response occurrence over successive presentations of the tactile stimulus was assessed; thus the data were evaluated for evidence of instrumental conditioning in the first days of human life. [...]

Summary of experiments

Three experiments demonstrated learning in human newborns with techniques involving the strengthening of a head-turning response through reinforcement contingencies. The first study demonstrated that administration of a dextrose–water solution contingent upon an ipsilateral response to tactile stimulation of the cheek increases the frequency of such responding. A second study presented the tactile stimulus on the opposite cheeks on alternate trials, right- and left-handed stimulation being paired with differential auditory stimuli. Reinforcement was given differentially with ipsilateral responding to the two 'eliciting' stimuli, and learning was revealed through increased occurrence of the reinforced response, in contrast to habituation of the nonreinforced response. In the final experiment, involving tactile stimulation on only one side, the two auditory stimuli served as positive and negative cues. Ipsilateral turns to right-sided stimulation in the presence of one cue were reinforced, while such turns in the presence of the other cue were not. Infants acquired the discrimination and demonstrated reversal behavior when the cue-reinforcement contingencies were reversed. All subjects in these studies were under four days of age and all experimental treatments were given in one session lasting no longer than one hour. No major effect of age was obtained, nor did amount of time since previous feeding within the range studied exert any effect. [...]

General discussion

These experiments show that, under certain experimental conditions, environmental events can function as reinforcing stimuli to shape or selectively strengthen components of 'unconditioned responses'. The results indicate that presentation of dextrose via nipple can function as a positive reinforcing stimulus for head movement responses in human newborns. Bilateral head movements, of the amplitude observed and quantified in these studies, were brought under the control of instrumental reinforcement contingencies. It is suggested that the rapid acquisition effects demonstrated in these experiments may reflect the immediate temporal relationship between response occurrence and the reinforcing event. Head rotations of a specified response class were followed immediately by presentation of a stimulus event which provided infants with both oral-tactile and taste stimulation.

In the first experiment the effect of reinforcement was to produce stable responding to a stimulus (tactual stimulation of cheek) which functioned initially as a 'low-level elicitor' of the to-be-reinforced response class. For control Ss, response habituation (response decrement below base line) occurred over successive presentations of the eliciting stimulus. For experimental Ss, reinforcement resulted in a reliable acquisition effect and termination of reinforcement resulted in extinction. One interpretation of this acquisition effect suggests that the 'low-level eliciting stimulus' acquired discriminative cue value for the reinforcement of turning responses. This suggestion implies that some stimuli may have complex functions, reflecting interactions and summations of eliciting and discriminative properties.

It should be noted that the initially low probability of response elicitation obtained in the present series of experiments may reflect the specific, and somewhat arbitrary selection of experimental stimulation parameters. Turkewitz, Gordon and Birch (1965) have reported higher probability of response elicitation with newborns using experimental procedures quite different from those employed in the present study. Other investigators (Blauvelt and McKenna, 1961; Prechtl, 1958) have reported inter- and intrasubject variability in response elicitation and have indicated that the response may be influenced by such factors as food deprivation, age, arousal level and medication during delivery. Comparison between base line response measures among studies is difficult because of differences in experimental procedures such as response criterion, preparation and positioning of Ss during testing, arousal effects of testing procedures, intertrial interval and parameters of the tactile stimulus. Papousek (1967), with procedures similar to those used here, reported comparable base line responding in his newborn population. He also reported a shaping procedure with milk reinforcement prior to obtaining stable turning to tactile stimulation in the newborn population.

Our second experiment suggests a type of learned discrimination in newborns, in that responding to two different eliciting stimuli, in the context of differential reinforcement, was brought under control of these reinforcement contingencies. Individual infants demonstrated not only a decrement in the nonreinforced response (habituation), but also showed increased occurrence of the reinforced response (acquisition). Reliable extinction effects were demonstrated after termination of reinforcement.

Evidence of an acquired stimulus discrimination was seen in the last experiment. When response to a tactile stimulus was differentially reinforced in the presence of two auditory stimuli, newborns showed increased responding to tactile stimulation in the presence of the positive auditory cue, but response to the same tactile stimulus in the presence of the negative auditory cue did not change.

Possibly the type of learning experiences provided for newborns in the normal feeding situation may not be too different from the experimental prototypes investigated in these experiments. Stimuli that function as low-level elicitors in the initial feeding situation may acquire discriminative function because they provide cues for reinforcing environmental consequences. The breast-fed infant may demonstrate a higher probability of ipsilateral turning to tactile stimulation when held in feeding position at the mother's breast than when lying supine on the mother's lap. This suggests that infants may readily learn to turn differentially to the tactile stimulus when it is presented in the context of complex visual and postural cues signaling that reinforcement or nonreinforcement will follow occurrence of the turning response.

It is difficult to specify clearly the type of learning processes involved in these experiments. The distinction between respondents and operants as labels for response classes in the newborn becomes somewhat blurred and may be cumbersome and arbitrary. Furthermore, in the immature organism there may be interactions between these response classes (Bijou and Baer, 1961, pp. 71–3). It was observed in the course of these experiments that marked increases in spontaneous turning responses occurred during the intertrial intervals after a few trials of reinforced responding. A similar observation has been reported by Papousek (1967). The only quantitative data on this observed increase in intertrial turning was provided by the third experiment. Examination of the analog records indicated that infants showed a marked increase in spontaneous turning over the first blocks of training trials, reaching asymptote by the fourth and fifth blocks of trials. They subsequently showed a gradual decrease in spontaneous turning over the last five blocks of training trials. It is not possible to determine from these results whether the observed increase in spontaneous head movements reflected a general arousal effect or whether it specifically reflects the reinforcement of the response class.

It is clear from these results that head turning to tactile stimulation in newborn infants may be influenced by environmental events which function as reinforcers. It is suggested also that some environmental stimuli may under certain conditions have complex functions for the human newborn's behavior and very early in the history of the organism begin to reflect interactions between eliciting and learned cue functions.

References

BIJOU, S. W., and BAER, D. M. (1961). *Child Development: Vol. 1. A Systematic and Empirical Theory*, Appleton-Century-Crofts.

BLAUVELT, H., and MCKENNA, J. (1961), 'Mother–neonate interaction: capacity of the newborn for orientation', in B. M. Foss (ed.), *Determinants of Infant Behavior*, Wiley, pp. 3–20.

GENTRY, E. F., and ALDRICH, C. A. (1948), 'Rooting reflex in newborn infant: incidence and effect of it on sleep', *Amer. J. Dis. Child.*, vol. 75, pp. 528–39.

GEWIRTZ, J. L. (1961), 'A learning analysis of the effects of normal stimulation privation and deprivation on the acquisition of social motivation and attachment', in B. M. Foss (ed.), *Determinants of Infant Behavior*, Wiley pp. 213–90.

GUNTHER, M. (1961), 'Infant behavior at the breast', in B. M. Foss (ed.), *Determinants of Infant Behavior*, Wiley, pp. 37–40.

LIPSITT, L. P. (1963), 'Learning in the first year of life', in L. P. Lipsitt and C. C. Spiker (eds.), *Advances in Child Development and Behavior*, vol. 1, Academic Press, pp. 147–95.

LIPSITT, L. P., and DELUCIA, C. A. (1960), 'An apparatus for the measurement of specific response and general activity in the human neonate', *Amer. J. Psychol.*, vol. 73, pp. 630–32.

LIPSITT, L. P., and KAYE, H. (1964), 'Conditioned sucking in the human newborn', *Psychonom. Sci.*, vol. 1, pp. 29–30.

PAPOUSEK, H. (1961), 'Conditioned head rotation reflexes in infants in the first months of life', *Acta Pediat.*, vol. 50, pp. 565–76.

PAPOUSEK, H. (1967), 'Experimental appetitional behavior in human newborns and infants', in H. W. Stevenson, E. H. Hess and H. L. Rheingold (eds.), *Early Behavior*, Wiley, pp. 249-77.

PEIPER, A. (1963), *Cerebral Function in Infancy and Childhood*, trans. B. Nagler and H. Nagler, Consultants Bureau, New York.

PRATT, K. C., NELSON, A. K., and SUN, K. H. (1930), 'The behavior of the newborn infant', *Ohio State Univ. Stud. Contr. Psychol.*, no. 10.

PRECHTL, H. F. R. (1958), 'The directed head turning response and allied movements in the human baby', *Behaviour*, vol. 13, pp. 212–42.

SIQUELAND, E. R. (1964), 'Operant conditioning of head turning in four-month infants', *Psychonom. Sci.*, vol. 1, pp. 223–4.

TURKEWITZ, G., GORDON, E. W., and BIRCH, H. G. (1965), 'Head turning in the human neonate: effect of prandial condition and lateral preference', *J. comp. physiol. Psychol.*, vol. 59, pp. 189–92.

2 J. Koch

Conditioned Orienting Reactions to Persons and Things in Two- to Five-Month-Old Infants

Excerpt from J. Koch, 'Conditioned reactions to persons and things in two- to five-month-old infants', *Human Development*, vol. 11, 1968, pp. 81–91.

Introduction

One of the earliest and most basic reactions of the young infant to the objects in its environment is the optic orientation to them. In the first month of life the infant is able to fixate an attractive object if it appears in its visual field. Very soon the infant learns to follow moving objects with its eyes and later to find them among other objects. This following and searching for attractive objects is realized through a turning of the eyes and the head. In two-month-old infants it is possible to establish conditioned head-turning to a sound reinforced by showing an attractive object: a conditioned reaction based on the orienting reflex.

A problem for investigation is which objects are more attractive for the orienting reflex of an infant and which are less. Is the human adult the strongest stimulus influencing the behavior and the whole mental development of the child? Does the human adult represent the strongest stimulus acting on the child as early as the first days of its life or does this relation develop in the course of life as a result of repeated contacts between the child and the adult? When the adult is the strongest stimulus influencing the mental development of the child, does it mean that he is also the most attractive stimulus evoking the strongest orienting reactions in the infant?

From these very complicated questions and complexes of problems we have selected one aspect: the development of conditioned head rotation in infants reinforced by an adult in an experimental situation. Our aim was to study the conditions which enable the development of conditioned orienting responses on the basis of social reinforcement. For this purpose we used different variations of social reinforcers and according to the course of the development of conditioned orienting responses we drew conclusions as to the relative strength of these reinforcers for the orienting response.

Method
Subjects

The subjects were 110 healthy, normal infants at the end of their second, third, fourth and fifth month of life. They lived with their mothers in the Institute for the Care of Mother and Child in Prague-Podolí or with families in the nearby surroundings of the Institute.

Apparatus

During the experiment the child was placed in a cabin (100 cm × 60 cm × 60 cm) with the head in a simple apparatus for the registration of the child's head-turning. On each side of the child's head was a window (on the left side 30 cm × 30 cm, on the right side 50 cm × 50 cm, both 30 cm from the baby's eyes) where the reinforcing stimulus appeared. Both windows could be opened and closed by a curtain. The source of the sound signals used for the conditioned stimulus was in a midline position near the feet of the child.

Procedure

A conditioned head-turning to a sound was established in the infant. Conditioned responses were reinforced by one of three types of reinforcers: (a) presentation of the face and voice of the mother, (b) presentation of the face and voice of a stranger and (c) presentation of different noise-making toys. After the presentation of the conditioned stimulus – a sound signal – the child could respond in one of three different ways: (a) by turning the head within eight seconds to the side on which the reinforcer appeared: this was considered to be a *conditioned response*; (b) by turning the head only after the eighth second when the side window was illuminated and a human face calling the child or a toy emitting a sound appeared: this was called a *primary response*; (c) by not turning the head even to the reinforcing stimulus or by turning the head to the opposite side: this was a *zero or a negativistic reaction*. At this point the experimenter turned the child's head to attain reinforcement. Each child received ten sessions of the same type. Each session consisted of ten trials in which the stimulus and the reinforcer were paired. A session lasted twelve to fifteen minutes and each child had only one session a day.

Results

In each of the following figures the change of the mean percentage of conditioned and primary responses during the ten sessions in ten infants is shown. The changes in the percentage of the conditioned orienting responses are demonstrated by full-line curves; the dashed-line curves show the changes of the combined percentage of the primary and conditioned responses (the difference between the two curves indicates the percentage of primary responses).

The two-month-old infants

Figure 1 shows the change of the percentage of orienting responses reinforced by the appearance of the face and the voice of the mother in two-month-old infants. In these children it was difficult to establish a conditioned reaction in these conditions. In the seventh and eighth sessions only 10 per cent of the conditioned signals were followed by a conditioned response and in the following sessions the percentage of conditioned responses had a tendency to drop. The disappearance of the conditioned and also of the primary responses in some infants was very remarkable. These children reacted in the eighth to tenth session in a negativistic way: they didn't turn their head toward the mother and even turned their head away from her. They actively resisted the attempt of the experimenter to turn their head toward the mother, they were restless and cried.

Figure 2 demonstrates the results of ten other two-month-old infants in whom the orienting head-turning was reinforced by the appearance of the face of a stranger speaking kindly to them. The percentage of conditioned orienting responses had a monotonically increasing tendency and by the tenth session 20 per cent of the conditioned stimuli evoked a conditioned response. The percentage of conditioned responses with this type of reinforcement

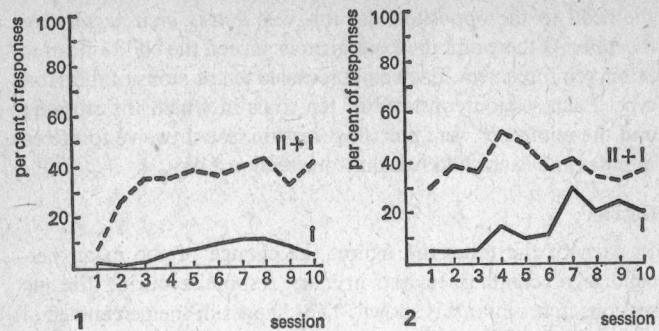

Figure 1 The course of conditioning of orienting reactions in two-month-old infants reinforced by the face and the voice of the mother. (I = curve of conditioned responses, II + I = curve of primary and conditioned responses)

Figure 2 The course of conditioning of orienting reactions in two-month-old infants reinforced by the face and the voice of a stranger. (I = curve of conditioned responses, II + I = curve of primary and conditioned responses)

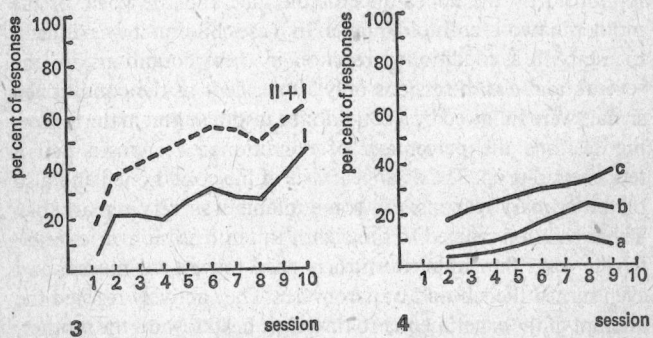

Figure 3 The course of conditioning of orienting reactions in two-month-old infants reinforced by various toys. (I = curve of conditioned responses, II + I = curve of primary and conditioned responses)

Figure 4 Comparison of the conditioning-course of orienting reactions in two-month-old infants reinforced by (a) the mother, (b) a stranger and (c) different toys. (Smoothed average of percentage of conditioned responses)

increased faster than in experiments in which the reactions were reinforced by the appearance of the mother.

Figure 3 indicates the change of orienting responses reinforced by showing different types of toys. Conditioned responses appeared sooner and increased faster than reactions always reinforced by the same person. In the tenth session the children reacted correctly to 40 per cent of the conditioned stimuli.

In Figure 4 the three main curves are compared (smoothed average of percentage of conditioned responses). In this study the mother was the weakest reinforcer for establishing a conditioned, orienting response, the stranger was a stronger reinforcer and continually changing toys were the strongest reinforcer.

The three-month-old infants

Figure 5 shows the change of percentage of orienting responses reinforced by the presentation of the face and the voice of the mother. The percentage of conditioned responses increased at the start, reached their maximum in the third session (over 30 per cent) and then gradually decreased. In comparison with the two-month-old infant, in the three-month-old infant the percentage of conditioned orienting reactions increased in the first sessions quicker, attained the maximum sooner (third session: seventh session) and the maximum had a higher level (40 per cent: 10 per cent). But after the maximum the three-month-old infants also had a decrease in the percentage of conditioned responses.

Figure 6 demonstrates the change of the percentage of orienting responses reinforced by the presentation of the face and the voice of a stranger. The percentage of conditioned responses increased at the beginning of the conditioning process faster than those reinforced by the mother, attained in the third session a maximum of nearly 60 per cent and in the following sessions the percentage did neither increase nor decrease.

Figure 7 illustrates the change of the percentage of orienting reactions reinforced always by the same toy. The percentage of conditioned reactions increased steadily, attained in the eighth session a maximum of nearly 60 per cent and during the following sessions the percentage had a declining tendency.

Figure 8 gives a picture of the change of percentage of orienting responses reinforced by showing different toys. The percentage of conditioned responses had a steadily increasing tendency with no drop; in the tenth session nearly 80 per cent of the conditioned stimuli were followed by a conditioned response.

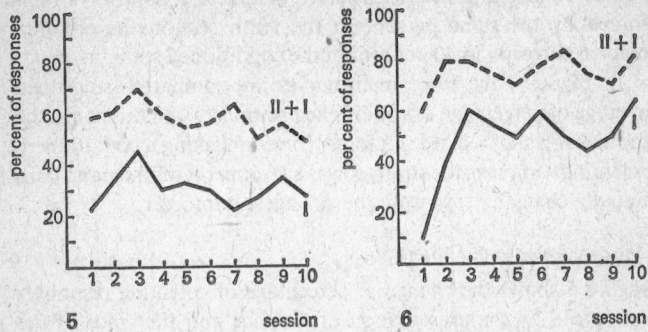

Figure 5 The course of conditioning of orienting reactions in three-month-old infants reinforced by the face and the voice of the mother. (I = curve of conditioned responses, II + I = curve of primary and conditioned responses)

Figure 6 The course of conditioning of orienting reactions in three-month-old infants reinforced by the face and the voice of a stranger. (I = curve of conditioned responses, II + I = curve of primary and conditioned responses)

In Figure 9 all four curves are compared. The mother – a well-known object which always appears in the same manner – was a weak reinforcer for the conditioning of orienting responses. The stranger and always the same toy have two common characteristics: they are new to the child, but they are the same at each appearance. Therefore their reinforcing power was nearly the same: they were stronger reinforcers than the mother but not as strong as continually changing toys.

The four- and five-month-old infants

In four- and five-month-old infants we can at this time show only the results of experiments from establishing a conditioned orienting response reinforced by the appearance of a stranger and of different toys.

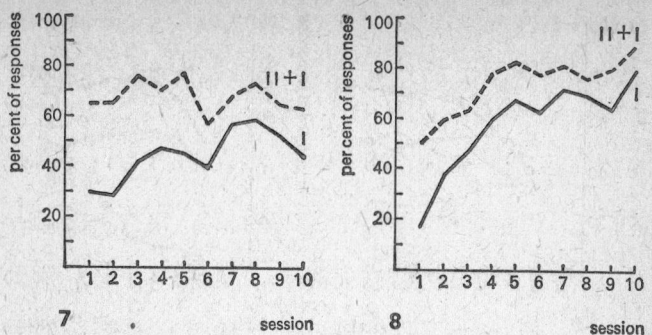

Figure 7 The course of conditioning of orienting reactions in three-month-old infants reinforced always by the same toy. (I = curve of conditioned responses, II + I = curve of primary and conditioned responses)

Figure 8 The course of conditioning of orienting reactions in three-month-old infants reinforced by different toys. (I = curve of conditioned responses, II + I = curve of primary and conditioned responses)

Figure 10 demonstrates the smoothed average of the percentage of correct conditioned orienting head-turnings reinforced by a stranger in the course of ten sessions in four groups of infants of different age, i.e. in the second, third, fourth and fifth months. The curves of two- and three-month-old children were shown above. The percentage of correct conditioned orienting responses in four-month-old infants increased in the first to sixth sessions, the infants reacted in the sixth session to 75 per cent of the conditioned stimuli correctly and in the following sessions the percentage of these responses decreased. In five-month-old infants the percentage of responses increased in the course of the first to fourth sessions, attained a maximum of nearly 80 per cent and after the fifth session the percentage of the conditioned responses dropped very rapidly.

If the results for all age groups are compared the following conclusions can be drawn: the older the infant (a) the higher the percentage of correct responses at the beginning of the conditioning procedure, (b) the faster the conditioning process and (c) the more precipitous the decreasing tendency.

J. Koch

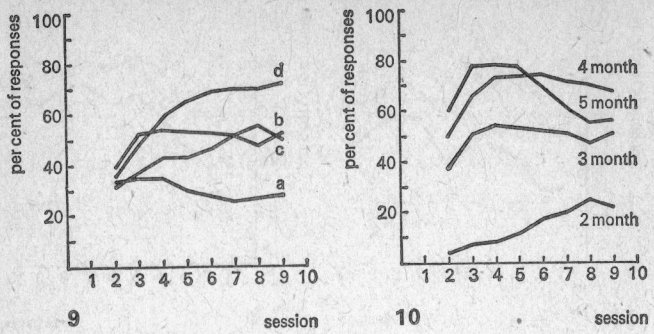

Figure 9 Comparison of the conditioning-course of orienting reactions in three-month-old infants reinforced by (a) the mother, (b) a stranger, (c) the identical toy and (d) various toys

Figure 10 Comparison of the conditioning-course of orienting reactions reinforced by the presentation of the face and the voice of a stranger in two-month-, three-month-, four-month- and five-month-old infants

Figure 11 represents the smoothed average of the percentage of conditioned responses reinforced by showing different toys during the conditioning process in four age groups. The courses of conditioning in two- and three-month-old infants were shown above. The four-month-old infants reacted correctly in the fourth session to more than 80 per cent of the conditioned signals and in the course of the following sessions the percentage of the conditioned orienting head-turning attained nearly 90 per cent. The five-month-old infants reacted in the third session to more than 90 per cent of the conditioned signals. In the following sessions they reacted to more than to 95 per cent of conditioned stimuli with a conditioned response. The comparison of the results of all four age groups leads to the following conclusions: the older the infant (a) the better the performance at the beginning of the conditioning procedure and (b) the earlier the best performance level is attained. When the reactions are reinforced by showing different toys, no decreasing tendency in the course of ten sessions appears.

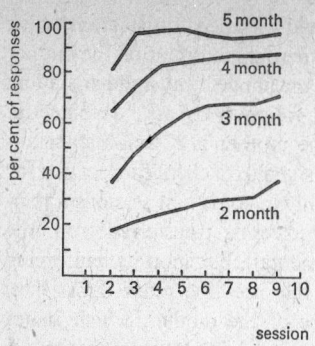

Figure 11 Comparison of the conditioning-course of orienting reactions reinforced by the presentation of different toys in two-month-, three-month-, four-month- and five-month-old infants

Discussion

Our aim was to find out how conditioned orienting responses, reinforced by the presentation of social and nonsocial reinforcers, develop in an experimental situation. Our results enable us to draw conclusions about the properties of the orienting reflex, but about the properties of social relationships we may judge only indirectly and with the greatest precaution.

The establishment of conditioned reactions with the orienting head-turning reinforced by the presentation of the face and the voice of the mother was very difficult. In our experimental conditions these reactions extinguished after a short time and the child was very soon oversatiated through this reinforcing stimulus. How can we explain this discrepancy of these findings and the common belief that the mother is the strongest reinforcer?

The orienting reflex has other characteristics and obeys other laws than other basic reflexes. One special characteristic of the orienting reflex is that it extinguishes very rapidly if evoked or reinforced by a stimulus which doesn't change itself or which doesn't signalize a change somehow important for the child. Therefore the main reason for the discrepancy of our findings with the common statement was probably the unnatural experimental situation. In natural conditions the mother always appears in other situations and is associated with need satisfaction which evokes pleasant feelings. In the experimental situation the mother appeared always in the same and unchanged way and her smiling appearance and talking was not followed by need satisfaction. In the experimental situation the mother is a well-known unchanging stimulus which doesn't signalize a change important for the child. Such a stimulus had only in some first sessions a reinforcing effect (this reinforcing power is transferred from the natural situation into the experimental), but soon its reinforcing and even its eliciting power on the orienting reflex diminishes, because the repeated appearance of the mother, which is not accompanied with anything else, is an extinction situation. A further application of this stimulus in the same manner evokes oversatiation which reveals itself in aversive behavior. This holds good only for the experimental situation; if the child leaves the situation in which it refuses to look at the mother and if it returns to the natural situation, it begins to respond with fixation and smiling responses toward the mother immediately.

The stranger as a reinforcer also appeared in the experimental situation always in a similar manner, but he is an unknown and new object for the child. The fact that the stranger appeared only in the experimental situation caused him to have a larger reinforcing strength than the mother notwithstanding that he also appeared always in the same way. In three-month-old infants in whom the orienting reaction was reinforced always with the same toy, the percentage of conditioned orienting reactions increased during the conditioning process in the same manner as when reinforced always by the same stranger. Both reinforcers – the stranger and the same toy – possess in relation to the orienting reflex two common properties: both are in the experimental situation a new, but reiterating object. Notwithstanding that both stimuli have a stronger reinforcing effect than the mother, they are not able even in five-month-old infants to influence the conditioning process so that the infant reacts to all conditioned stimuli. In experiments with the stranger as a reinforcer, the older the infant, the higher was the rate of conditioned stimuli to which the infant responded in a correct manner at the beginning of the conditioning process, and the earlier he attained the maximal rate of responses, the higher was the level of performance. The maximal rate of responses didn't cross even in five-month-old infants the level of 80 per cent. In all age groups the maximum of performance was followed by a decrease in the percentage of responses and the older the infants, the earlier the decrease began and the more precipitous it was. This means that in this experimental situation the older infant learns more quickly to turn the head to the person after a signal, but that he is earlier satiated with this play and the state of oversatiation appears sooner.

The strongest reinforcing effect on the conditioning process was when different toys were used as reinforcers. Each toy was something new in the experimental situation and it never appeared again during the same session. This kind of reinforcement influenced the behavior of the children so intensively that from the third session the five-month-old infants reacted correctly to nearly 100 per cent of the conditioned stimuli. Notwithstanding the continuous uninterrupted regular reinforcement schedule, the conditioning procedure produced a great resistance to satiation and, therefore, the percentage of conditioned responses steadily increased in all age groups.

Conclusions

1. If a stimulus with which the child is acquainted in other situations is used always in the same manner and always in the same situation as a reinforcer for the establishment of a conditioned orienting response, then this stimulus becomes in this situation a successively weaker reinforcer. Eventually the orienting reaction extinguishes to this stimulus. If we continue to use this stimulus in this situation, an aversive behavior against this stimulus is elicited.

2. If a new, hitherto unknown stimulus appears in a certain situation repeatedly it has a stronger reinforcing effect in establishing a conditioned orienting response than a stimulus known from other situations. But also a new stimulus appearing always in the same manner loses its reinforcing strength after some time and the orienting reaction formerly elicited by it extinguishes.

3. The strongest reinforcer for the establishment of conditioned orienting responses is a new, constantly changing stimulus. It

produces conditioned behavior with a great resistance to satiation.

4. The older the infant, the faster the establishment of a conditioned orienting reaction and the earlier the rise of a state of satiation when a weak orienting stimulus is used as a reinforcer.

3 D. F. Caldwell and J. Werboff

Classical Conditioning in Newborn Rats

Excerpt from D. F. Caldwell and J. Werboff, 'Classical conditioning in newborn rats', *Science*, vol. 136, 1962, pp. 118–19.

There is a paucity of experimental evidence demonstrating learning in newborn animals. In the experiment reported here we undertook to determine the ability of newborn rats to learn a simple conditioned response. The time intervals between presentation of conditioned and unconditioned stimuli were varied to determine whether the performance of the newborn rats is similar to that of older animals.

Newborn albino rats of the Sprague–Dawley strain[1] were tested on an apparatus for measuring delayed conditioned leg flexion. The animal was suspended in a harness to immobilize it in a nontraumatic manner. The conditioned stimulus was a vibrotactile stimulus delivered to the animal's chest by a glass rod attached to a speaker cone. The vibration of 128 cps was produced by an audio oscillator set at an amplitude just sufficient to cause the rod to vibrate. No sound was emitted at these values. The unconditioned stimulus was delivered to the right foreleg by means of saline-saturated felt electrodes. This stimulus, of 50 ms duration, was a direct-current electric shock of 1 mA delivered through a current-regulating device which insured a constant current value regardless of the change in the animal's body resistance. All time intervals were controlled by electronic timers. Leg flexions were recorded by means of a microtorque motion-displacement transducer connected to the animal's leg by a fine thread. Spring tension on the transducer arm made it possible to record the leg movement. The output of this transducer, fed into an Offner (model A) electroencephalograph, was recorded, together with the time of presentation of the conditioned stimulus.

1. The test animals were the offspring of first-conception gravid animals purchased from Dawley Farms, Plymouth, Michigan, and shipped a distance of thirty miles at sixteen to twenty days of gestation.

All animals received initial training with the conditioned stimulus only, within a period of from 1 to 8 hours after parturition, to insure that the stimulus would not elicit a leg-flexion response. The criterion for completion of this phase of training was ten consecutive presentations (conditioned stimulus only) without leg movement. Immediately after this, eight blocks of ten trials were presented, with random intertrial intervals of either 10, 15, 30, 45 or 50 s and an interblock interval of 3 min. Four groups of animals ($n =$ nine per group, randomly divided between males and females) were given paired conditioned and unconditioned stimuli on four different schedules, with intervals between the stimuli of 300, 600, 1200 and 2400 ms, respectively. For each experimental group a control group ($n =$ four per group) was tested in a pseudoconditioning situation, with the same conditioned- and unconditioned-stimulus parameters, but with the order of the stimuli randomly varied.

The data presented in Figure 1 demonstrate that newborn rats are capable of learning a simple conditioned response. Data for males and females within each of the experimental and control groups were combined when analyses for sex differences in conditioning proved nonsignificant. Furthermore, data for the four control groups were combined, since no statistical differences were found for these groups.

The performance of the four experimental groups was significantly superior to that of the control groups ($p < 0.002$ in a two-tailed Mann–Whitney U Test for all comparisons). There were no significant differences in levels of performance of the 600, 1200 and 2400 ms groups. However, the performance of these groups did differ significantly from that of the 300 ms group, as indicated by an analysis of variance ($p < 0.01$, two-tailed test). The highest level of performance attained was 32 per cent for the 1200 and 2400 ms groups. This level of performance is below that traditionally reported in the literature on classical conditioning of adult rats (Hilgard and Marquis, 1961). However, in another investigation (Biel and Wickens, 1941) a maximum performance of 39 per cent was reported for classical conditioning; this is similar to the performance of the 2400 ms group. In the study reported here, the optimum interstimulus intervals for learning were found to be between 600 and 2400 ms, with the 1200 ms group manifesting the highest mean percentage of conditioning. This is in contrast to the finding, reported in the experimental literature (Hilgard and Marquis, 1961), that the best interstimulus interval for learning in adult animals is between 300 and 600 ms. The higher percentage of learning found with longer intervals in the newborn rat may be due, in part, to the lack of maturation in neural development at this age, as compared to development in the older animal, and is probably related to the low degree of myelinization and the low speed of neural conduction concomitant with this stage of neural development. On the basis of this interpretation, a linear relationship between total mean percentage of conditioning and length of interstimulus interval would be expected – the longer the interval, the larger the mean percentage of conditioning. It should be noted, however,

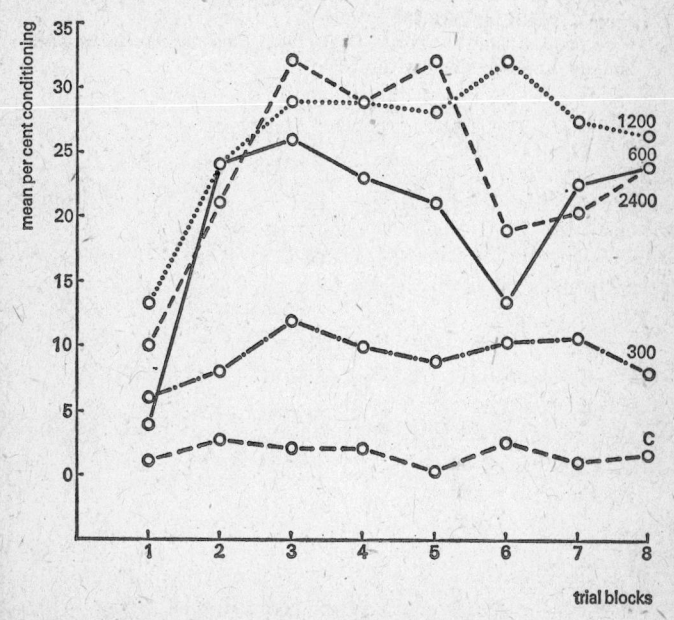

Figure 1 Mean percentages of conditioned responses for newborn rats trained according to classical conditioning procedure with intervals between conditioned and unconditioned stimuli of 300, 600, 1200 and 2400 ms, respectively

that the experimental data show a curvilinear relationship for the four stimulus conditions, with the 1200 ms interval resulting in the greatest amount of conditioning. Such a curvilinear relation is similar to that reported in the literature for classical conditioning in the adult, but it differs markedly in that the peak is shifted to a longer interstimulus interval. The performance decrement found for the 300 ms group during the fifth trial block and for the 600 and 2400 ms groups during the sixth trial block may represent a fatigue reaction resulting from the massed presentation of stimuli. The need for additional research on the learning capacities of the newborn organism is clearly indicated.

References

BIEL, W. C., and WICKENS, D. D. (1941), 'The effects of vitamin B_1 deficiency on the conditioning of eyelid responses in the rat', *J. comp. Psychol.*, vol. 32, pp. 329–40.

HILGARD, E. R., and MARQUIS, D. G. (1961), *Conditioning and Learning*, 2nd edn, Appleton-Century-Crofts.

4 Walter C. Stanley, Anne Christake Cornwell, Constance Poggiani and Alice Trattner

Conditioning in the Neonatal Puppy

Excerpt from Walter C. Stanley, Anne Christake Cornwell, Constance Poggiani and Alice Trattner, 'Conditioning in the neonatal puppy', *Journal of Comparative and Physiological Psychology*, vol. 56, 1963, pp. 211–14.

The purpose of this experiment was to determine whether the neonatal puppy, that is, one less than two weeks of age, can be appetitively and aversively conditioned. Doubt and disagreement exist concerning the existence of conditioning in the neonatal puppy. It has been concluded (Scott, 1958) on the basis of naturalistic observation (Scott and Marston, 1950) that neonatal puppies give no indication that they learn as adults do, but Volokhov (1959) presents a table in which food-reinforced conditioning is said to occur at one day of age. Some aversive conditioning has been found at about two weeks of age (Cornwell and Fuller, 1961; Volokhov, 1959) and stable appetitive and aversive conditioning has been obtained in fifteen-day-old puppies (Kliavina, Kobakova, Stel'makh and Troshikhin, 1958), but, in so far as the authors are aware, no evidence has been published to show that aversive conditioning occurs in the neonatal puppy.

To maximize the probability of finding both appetitive and aversive conditioning, the present experiment (a) used stimuli and measured or rated responses well within the sensorimotor abilities of the neonatal puppy, (b) deprived Ss of food to increase their sensitivity to tactile and liquid stimuli injected into their mouths and (c) used a classical conditioning procedure which assured objectivity in E's handling and stimulating Ss, but was 'impure' in that it contained components of operant conditioning so that a variety of the parameters known to affect conditioned behaviour could be operative.

Method

Subjects

The *S*s were twenty-one Shetland sheepdog puppies and five cocker spaniels, the progeny of stock maintained at Hamilton Station of the Jackson Memorial Laboratory. Their mean age on the first day of training was three days, range one to five days; their mean age on the seventh and last day of training was ten days, range seven to thirteen days.

Apparatus

The apparatus consisted of a bellows manometer with a pointer that rode over Teledeltos paper moving at a constant speed. One end of a flexible tubing was attached to the manometer. The other end had a glass tube covered with soft rubber – a simulated bitch's nipple. Soft rubber, identical in size and shape to that on the manometer tube was put on the glass ends of two ordinary eye droppers used for injection of milk and quinine solution. The *E* timed his actions by a stop watch. A one cps time marker rode on the Teledeltos paper. The marker served as a check on *E*'s timing and also provided a base for counting individual sucks on the record.

Procedure

Twenty-four *S*s were divided into eight trios, whose members were matched as to sex, breed and litter in so far as possible. The members of each trio were then randomly assigned to one of three groups: a positive group to receive milk, a neutral group to receive no liquid and a negative group to receive a quinine solution. The remaining two cocker spaniel *S*s were randomly assigned to the neutral and the negative groups.

Each trial was conducted as follows: the *S* was picked up and held for 10 s. Then the motor drive of the recorder was started, and 5 s later the manometer nipple (conditioned stimulus) was inserted into *S*'s mouth and kept there for 5 s. Five seconds after removal of the manometer nipple, the *S* in the positive group was dropper-fed for 15 s with 0·5 cc of milk made from Esbilac (a powdered simulated bitch's milk sold by the Borden Company) and water. Thus, the unconditioned stimulus was dropper nipple plus milk in the mouth. The timing of this procedure was a classical conditioning one. But since S could suck prior to the delivery of milk, the procedure, temporally, contained elements of instrumental conditioning.

The timing of events was exactly the same in all three groups. Neutral group Ss, however, received no liquid. Instead, the manometer nipple was simply reinserted in their mouths for 15 s. Negative group Ss were dropper-'fed' for 15 s with 0·5 cc of quinine hydrochloride solution – 500 mg/100 cc of water.

Using a nontoxic bitter-tasting substance, sucrose octa-acetate (Warren and Pfaffmann, 1959) instead of quinine hydrochloride was considered but rejected since the latencies of response both by several puppies and by Es seemed slow, being as long as 5 to 10 s. It was assumed that the quantity of the quinine solution which might be ingested would be too small to produce any significant toxicity and, in fact, negative group Ss' weight gains were quite comparable to those of Ss in the other two groups.

On each day of training, the Ss were separated from the dam in the morning five to six hours prior to the start of the afternoon conditioning session. The Ss received ten trials per day, eight paired CS–US presentations and two CS-alone presentations, for seven days, with at least ten minutes between successive trials within a session. Scheduling difficulties required that occasionally less than ten trials be given on a particular day and that up to two days occasionally intervene between successive training days.

Sucking behaviour, as recorded on the Teledeltos paper by the manometer pointer, was the index of positive or appetitive conditioning; vigor of struggling by S as rated by E on a nought- to three-point scale was the index of negative or aversive conditioning.

Results

Positive or appetitive conditioning

Sucking records were examined in two ways: first, in terms of mean number of sucks per trial or CS presentation, the most sensitive measure available; second, in terms of percentage of trials during which measurable sucking behavior occurred, a less sensitive but common measure of conditioning.

Figure 1 shows mean number of sucks per trial plotted on days of training. The curves diverge as expected from the conditions of reinforcement, the positive group improving, the neutral group declining and the negative group being markedly suppressed in performance. Friedman's nonparametric test performed on days 2 to 7 data of the eight trios of Ss yielded a p less than 0·01. The ps on two-tailed Wilcoxon Paired Replicates Tests for all the two-group comparisons were 0·01 or less.

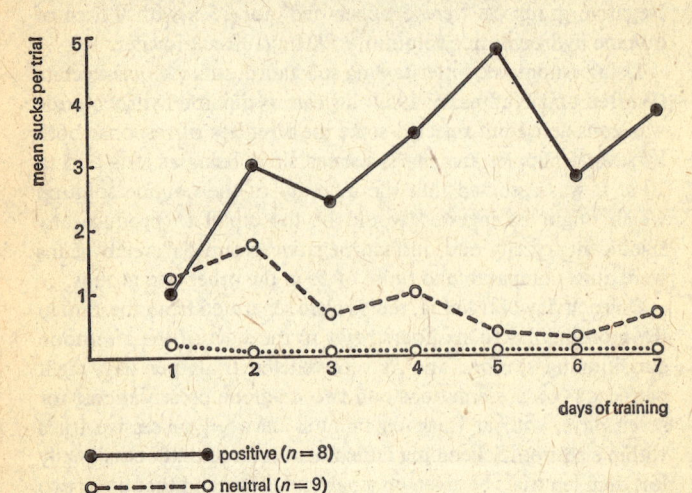

Figure 1 Mean number of sucks per trial during CS presentation, as a function of days of training

A comparable and reliable divergence in performance occurred with the percentage trials measure, the positive group responding on 45 per cent of the trials on day 7, the neutral group on 12 per cent and the negative group on 0 per cent. On day 1 the overall percentage of responding was 16.

The most convincing evidence for learning, however, comes from an analysis of the responding during the CS trial 1 of each session after day 1 because such data cannot be confounded by possible arousal or suppressive effects of stimulation perseverating from one trial to the next within a session. Mean number of sucks per day were 2·0, 0·1 and 0 for the positive, neutral and negative groups, respectively. The corresponding means for number of days on which sucking occurred were 1·8, 0·4 and 0. For mean number of sucks per trial, the Friedman p was less than 0·01, and the positive group is markedly superior to the other two groups, the p for each comparison being 0·02. For number of days on which sucking occurred, the less sensitive measure, the Friedman p was greater than 0·05. However, if one makes the further reasonable assumption that all that needs to be demonstrated is superiority of the positive group over the other two groups, and directly calculates Wilcoxon two-tailed ps for these two crucial comparisons, the p for the positive–neutral difference is 0·05, and that for the positive–negative difference is 0·02.

Negative or aversive conditioning

The ratings of vigor of struggling were examined in the same ways as were the records for sucking behavior. In terms of both measures, the negative group improved in performance, the neutral group stayed about the same and the positive group showed increasing impairment. Friedman test ps were less than 0·01 for days 2 to 7 and all two-group comparison ps were less than 0·02.

Mean figures of struggling per trial appear in Figure 2. Performance expressed by percentage of trials on which some struggling occurred was 99 on day 7 for the negative group, 66 for the neutral group and 41 for the positive group. On day 1 the overall percentage of responding was 79. The mean rating per trial for the vigor-of-struggling data (four-point scale) for first trials only on days 2 to 7 of training was 0·8, 1·3 and 2·1 for the positive, neutral and negative groups, respectively. For mean rating per trial, the more sensitive measure, the Friedman p is 0·01, and the negative–neutral and the negative–positive differences each have a p of 0·01. The number of days on which struggling occurred, the less sensitive measure, was 3·8, 5·2 and 5·9 for days 2 through 7 for the positive, neutral and negative groups, respectively; the Friedman p is 0·05. The negative–positive difference p is 0·01; the neutral–positive difference p is 0·05.

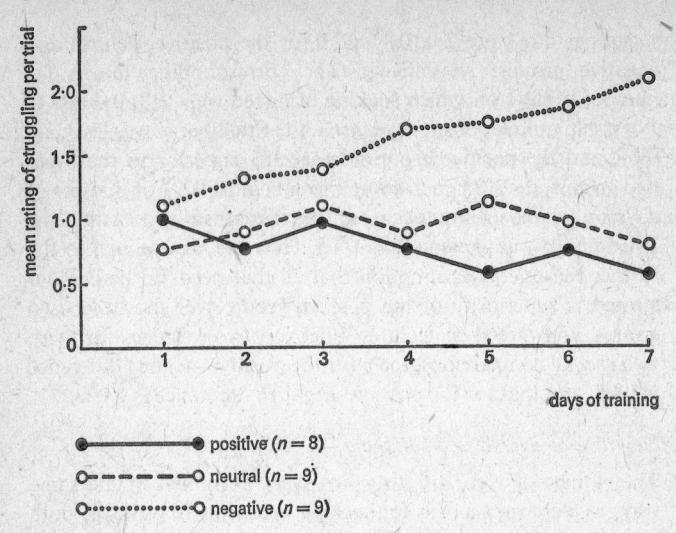

Figure 2 Mean rating of vigor of struggling per trial during CS presentation, as a function of days of training

Discussion

The most sensitive and crucial measures of appetitive and aversive conditioning in the present experiment are mean number of sucks per trial and mean rating of vigor of struggling per trial, on first days, days 2 to 7. Both these measures were statistically significant for the most relevant comparisons, positive–neutral and positive–negative for sucking and negative–neutral and negative–positive for struggling. These findings, plus the fact that all other group differences are as would be expected from the conditions of reinforcement and are also statistically reliable in the great majority of instances, provide convincing proof that both appetitive and aversive conditioning occurs in the neonatal puppy.

The findings are obviously contrary to any contention that the neonatal puppy cannot learn and, further, mean that previous failures to obtain aversive conditioning (Cornwell and Fuller, 1961; Fuller, Easler and Banks, 1950; James and Cannon, 1952; Volokhov, 1959) may be attributed to the specific conditioning techniques used rather than the lack of conditionability in the neonatal puppy.

The second important feature of the data is the degree of stability of conditioned behavior which was found. Ordinarily in classical conditioning, the criterion of stability is 80 to 100 per cent occurrence of conditioned responses. The present findings fulfill this criterion in two ways. Sucking behavior was 100 per cent suppressed, and near 100 per cent struggling occurred in the negative group. Thus, not only the first occurrence of conditioning but the degree of stability of the conditioned behavior achieved at a particular age may be attributed to the specific conditioning procedure used, not necessarily to relative unconditionability of the Ss used.

How, then, might we interpret both the first occurrence and the attainment of a particular degree of stability of conditioned behavior at different ages when different conditioning procedures are used? We suggest that the different procedures reflect different fulfilment of the conditions required for the acquisition and the maintenance of conditioned behavior. By 'conditions' we mean the temporal and quantitative properties of variables which affect conditioned behavior, as drive, modality, and intensity of stimuli, class of response required and measured, temporal and quantitative parameters of reinforcing stimuli, etc. In the present experiment, for example, drive was present because Ss were food-deprived; the specific cs, tactile stimulation of the buccal cavity, was distinctive and functional; the responses measured or rated were within the behavior repertory of the neonatal puppy; and the reinforcing stimuli, milk and quinine solution, appeared to elicit responses with a reasonably high probability in most Ss.

These variables by no means exhaust the list of variables known to affect performance during conditioning. Yet, even these were apparently neither maximally effective nor maximally adapted to our specific Ss. For example, although some hunger drive was clearly present in all Ss, it appeared markedly lower in the cocker spaniel than in the Shetland sheepdog Ss. The one cocker spaniel in the positive group was seldom observed to suck even when milk was injected into its mouth. Second, the specific cs, the manometer nipple, was not procedurally always equitable in the three groups. After some trials had ensued, the struggling of the negative Ss became pronounced, and at times the five seconds allowed for the insertion of the manometer nipple would terminate without such insertion being possible. This observation, in turn, suggests that the total functional stimulus pattern in our procedure probably included tactual, kinesthetic and vestibular components correlated with picking S up and holding it during each trial.

Third, although the temporal aspects of procedure were classical, it is possible to interpret the findings as being largely due to operant conditioning components of the procedure. The struggling behavior of negative Ss could avoid briefly the manometer tube, the stimulus most closely associated with aversive stimulation from quinine; hence, struggling could have been maintained by a Sidman (1953) avoidance schedule. The sucking in positive Ss could be followed by milk injection, but since milk injection was not contingent on sucking, there would be only accidental or adventitious reinforcement of sucking by milk. It is precisely such adventitious reinforcement which can produce drifts from one class of responding to another, rather than stable maintenance of one class of response (Skinner, 1948).

In general, the present findings show that both appetitive and aversive conditioning is possible in the neonatal puppy and that the resultant behavior can be reasonably stable when conditioning procedures are specifically adapted to the neonatal puppy.

References

CORNWELL, A. C., and FULLER, J. L. (1961), 'Conditioned responses in young puppies', *J. comp. physiol. Psychol.*, vol. 54, pp. 13–15.

FULLER, J. L., EASLER, C. A., and BANKS, E. M. (1950), 'Formation of conditioned avoidance responses in young puppies', *Amer. J. Physiol.*, vol. 160, pp. 462–6.

JAMES, W. T., and CANNON, D. J. (1952), 'Conditioned avoiding responses in puppies', *Amer. J. Physiol.*, vol. 168, pp. 251–3.

KLIAVINA, M. P., KOBAKOVA, E. M., STEL'MAKH, L. N., and TROSHIKHIN, V. A. (1958), 'K voprosu o skorosti obrazovaniia uslovykh refleksov u sobak v ontogeneze', *Zh. vyssh. nervn. Deiatel'*, vol. 8, pp. 929–36. (See *Psychol. Abstr.*, vol. 34, p. 838.)

SCOTT, J. P. (1958), 'Critical periods in the development of social behavior in puppies', *Psychosom. Med.*, vol. 20, pp. 42–54.

SCOTT, J. P., and MARSTON, M. V. (1950), 'Critical periods affecting the development of normal and maladjustive behavior of puppies', *J. genet. Psychol.*, vol. 77, pp. 25–60.

SIDMAN, M. (1953), 'Avoidance conditioning with brief shock and no exteroceptive warning signal', *Science*, vol. 118, pp. 157–8.

SKINNER, B. F. (1948), '"Superstition" in the pigeon', *J. exp. Psychol.*, vol. 38. pp. 168–72.

VOLOKHOV, A. A. (1959), 'Comparative-physiological investigation of conditioned and unconditioned reflexes during ontogeny', *Pavlov J. higher nerv. Activ.*, vol. 9, pp. 49–60.

WARREN, R. P., and PFAFFMANN, C. (1959), 'Early experience and taste aversion', *J. comp. physiol. Psychol.*, vol. 52, pp. 263–6.

Part Two Imprinting

Unlike classical or instrumental conditioning, imprinting is most in evidence in neonate animals, but mainly in those of precocial species. What is nowadays often described as classical imprinting occurs in nidifugous birds, that is, those whose young leave the nest soon after hatching; our Readings are all concerned with classical imprinting. From the start there has been some uncertainty, and much debate, about the characteristics of imprinting. Initially, knowledge was based on field observations, but laboratory experiments were soon begun in the hope of providing a clearer understanding of the imprinting phenomena. Some early experiments are reported by Sluckin and Salzen (Reading 5), together with some germane theorizing. From the start the question of the sensitive period for imprinting has been the subject of a great deal of research. An example of such research is the study by Bateson (Reading 6). The question of reversibility of imprinting is closely tied up with that of the critical period. It is tackled experimentally by Salzen and Meyer (Reading 7). The reader may note that we shall return to the intriguing problem of critical periods – albeit in a much wider context – in the later parts of the book (see Readings 17 and 26). As a further example of research in the field of imprinting we have the paper by Hoffman, Searle, Toffey and Kozma (Reading 8); this is concerned with the control of the animal's activity based on providing the animal with, or withholding from it, the stimulus-figure to which it is imprinted. This type of experimental work represents a fresh and important development in the study of early imprinting attachments.

5 W. Sluckin and E. A. Salzen

Imprinting and Perceptual Learning

Excerpt from W. Sluckin and E. A. Salzen, 'Imprinting and perceptual learning', *Quarterly Journal of Experimental Psychology*, vol. 13, 1961, pp. 65–77.

Introduction

Following responses of newly hatched nidifugous birds have been used by many workers to investigate imprinting, especially since Thorpe (1956) surveyed the subject and emphasized the importance of such studies. These responses have been employed in two ways. In one type of study (e.g. Fabricius, 1951; Guiton, 1959; Hess, 1957; Jaynes, 1956, 1958b; Ramsay and Hess, 1954), the birds were required to discriminate between objects by approaching and following one object rather than another. In the second type of study (e.g. Jaynes, 1957, 1958a; Moltz and Rosenblum, 1958a), the birds were required to respond repeatedly to a single object, and the degree of attachment to that object, that is, imprinting, was presumed to be indicated by the occurrence, latency and strength of the following response. As originally stated by Lorenz (1937), imprinting involves the discrimination of species characteristics, which implies the production of different response patterns to different patterns of movement, form, colour and sound. It could be argued, therefore, that studies of the second type were not studies of imprinting but simply studies on the development and establishment of the approach and following responses, and that discrimination experiments were required to determine whether these responses had become attached to a specific object.

There is no doubt, however, that the occurrence and establishment of the following response is important in imprinting studies since this is the response required in the discrimination tests. Salzen and Sluckin (1959) attempted to investigate the incidence and duration of following responses in domestic chicks without reference to imprinting. The present paper contains observations and experiments on both the following response and imprinting.

The first occurrence of the following response will be considered by reference to the stimulus situation in which it occurs, the differences in its incidence among individuals, and the differences in its incidence with age. Subsequent occurrences of the following response will be considered in terms of the effects of earlier experience of the object, and the effects of the act of earlier following. Finally, imprinting will be considered in terms of the stimulus situations which elicit following in experienced birds, and in terms of the extent to which such responses may be elicited by new stimulus situations.

The original stimulus situation

It is clear from the work of Fabricius and Boyd (1954) and Hinde, Thorpe and Vince (1956) that a wide variety of moving objects may elicit the following response in birds. Fabricius (1951), after a careful study with ducks, concluded that the movement of parts of the body were of great importance in the release of the following response. Since then Smith (1960) has shown that movement in one plane in the form of a distant rotating black and white disc is an adequate stimulus to cause chicks to approach and give contentment calls. Further, both James (1959) and Smith have shown that a flashing light will also serve as a stimulus for this response. Collias (1952) has reported that certain repetitive sounds with low-frequency components will evoke the approach response. Fabricius (1951) and Weidmann (1958) have observed that short repeated calls will produce following in ducks. We have found that knocking, tapping, rustling of paper and clucking will make some chicks approach. It seems likely, therefore, that a wide variety of moderately intense visual or auditory disturbances of the environment that are brief and repetitive in character are capable of eliciting filial responses in chicks and ducklings.

In an earlier paper (Salzen and Sluckin, 1959) we reported, among other things, upon the incidence in domestic fowl of the following response to a moving box. We did not in that paper concern ourselves with the responsiveness of chicks to sound. However, in the course of our work we had collected data on the chicks' responsiveness to sound and on its relationship to the chicks' previous visual experiences. The method used in our experiments is described in detail in the earlier paper mentioned above. Very briefly, the behaviour of 450 chicks of a Rhode Island Red flock was observed individually from eighteen to thirty hours after hatching: the following responses of each chick to a red box 8 in × 6 in × 6 in high, suspended 2 to 4 in above the floor, were tested in an alley 10 ft × 2 ft 6 in × 2 ft high. Each chick was so placed at the start that it could either run away from the box or follow it when the box was moved with a jerk away from the chick. The box was moved every ten seconds; a responsive chick would move up to the box and then the box movement would be repeated; when a chick did not follow, the box was returned to its earlier position. Chicks in one group were exposed individually to fifty movements of the box, in another group to ten movements and in a third group to no movements, spending one minute beside the stationary box. Our earlier paper is concerned with the responses of these birds to the movements of the box on later occasions. Here we report on the chicks' responsiveness to sound which was tested in each case by tapping on the side of the runway immediately after the chick had experienced fifty, ten or no movements of the box. Chicks tended either to ignore the noise or respond to it by approaching its source. Those that appeared to attend to the noise but failed to run to it were regarded as not responding.

Table 1 shows that responsiveness to this second stimulus was related to previous experience of box movement. The results as set out indicate that experience of the moving box tended to facilitate responsiveness to the second stimulus complex. Smith, in a personal communication, has also reported a facilitation effect in that a small-diameter patch of flashing light evoked more approach responses from chicks that had previously experienced a large circle of flashing light than from those that had not had such an experience. In view of this facilitation effect, measures of the initial responsiveness of chicks to a moving object may vary considerably with their visual experience. Part A of the table shows that greater experience of the moving box resulted in a greater proportion of the birds responding to sound. Part B of the table shows that birds that had followed the box were more responsive to sound than were those that had not previously followed the box.

Table 1 Results of Sound Tests Carried Out on Day-Old Chicks Immediately after They Had Been Exposed to the Moving-Box Test

A

Number of movements of the box seen by the chicks in the visual test	0	10	50
Proportions of chicks that responded to sound after the visual test	$\frac{37}{150}$ (25%)	$\frac{58}{150}$ (39%)	$\frac{76}{150}$ (51%)
Probabilities of the indicated differences being chance occurrences, as determined by the Brown (1956) test.	←—— $p<0.05$ ——→	←—— $p<0.05$ ——→	
	←————————— $p<0.01$ —————————→		

B

Number of movements of the box seen by the chicks in the visual test	Proportions of chicks that responded to sound among those that in the visual test had:		Probabilities of the differences between columns being due to chance occurrences as determined by the Brown test
	followed the box at least once	not followed the box	
10	$\frac{45}{86}$ (52%)	$\frac{13}{64}$ (20%)	$p<0.01$
50	$\frac{73}{120}$ (61%)	$\frac{3}{30}$ (10%)	$p<0.01$

Variability in responsiveness

There is some evidence of constitutional differences in sensitivity to a moving object even within one breed of domestic chicks. Hess (1957) has claimed that imprintability, which may be related to this responsiveness, is inherited in domestic fowl and can be bred into or out of a strain, and that it is probably sex-linked in Cochin Bantams. Klopfer (1956) has also suggested a genetic explanation of reported differences in sensitive periods and imprintability. Table 2 shows inter-batch variations in responsiveness encountered by us. Guiton (1959) found that visually

Table 2 The Incidence of Following in Different Batches of Chicks During a Test with a Moving Box, as Described in the Text, Lasting Three Minutes

Source and nature of batches of chicks	Numbers of chicks tested for 3 min with a moving box	Numbers of chicks that responded by following the box	Percentages of followers in the different batches
1st experiment (1959)			
1st supplier:			
RIR laboratory hatch	159	73	46
RIR commercial hatch	96	49	51
2nd experiment			
2nd supplier:			
RIR laboratory hatch	88	24	27·5
BL×LS laboratory hatch	103	19	18·5

The differences between either hatch of the first experiment and either hatch of the second experiment are significant beyond the 1 per cent level of confidence according to the Brown (1956) test.

isolated chicks followed better than socially reared ones and that a few hours of social experience preceding a period of isolation resulted in greater responsiveness to a moving object than did complete isolation. In an experiment summarized in Table 3 we gave three pre-test treatments to Brown Leghorn × Light Sussex chicks. Our results tend, on the whole, to confirm Guiton's findings.

The influence of some social experience upon later responsiveness may account for the apparent rise in 'imprintability' recorded by Jaynes (1957) for the first half of the critical period, since his birds had been kept in groups before testing. The same

Table 3 The Effects of Social Life on the Responsiveness of Chicks

Pre-test treatment of batches of chicks	Tested when 1 day old batch A	batch B	batch C	Tested when 5 or 6 days old batch D
Isolation (each chick was kept in a separate cage and could see no moving objects between hatching and test)	$\frac{4}{10}$ (40%)	$\frac{10}{24}$ (42%)	$\frac{20}{41}$ (49%)	$\frac{5}{15}$ (33%)
Social (groups of chicks were kept in enclosed cages between hatching and test)	$\frac{8}{14}$ (57%)	$\frac{8}{24}$ (33%)	$\frac{6}{41}$ (15%)	$\frac{0}{13}$ (0%)
Social for the first 6 hr and then isolation			$\frac{28}{41}$ (68%)	

The entries in the table are the proportions of birds that followed a moving box in the course of a three-minute test. The proportions of isolated and social birds that responded were not significantly different in batches A and B, but were significantly different in batch C at the 0·01 level of confidence using the Brown test and in batch D at the 0·05 level using the Fisher test. In batch C six hours of social life followed by eighteen hours of isolation resulted in a greater proportion of followers than did complete isolation (although the difference in the proportions was not quite statistically significant at the 0·05 level).

may apply to Hess's similar results with mallards (1957) and chicks (1959a), since although they were reared in darkness they could hear one another, and sound was used in both the imprinting and the testing situations; it should be noted that although the sounds on the two occasions were different, Guiton's generalization-through-isolation theory would predict that the difference would not prevent the test sounds from being effective. This explanation is not unlikely in view of the facilitation effect described in the previous section of this paper.

Loss of sensitivity – the critical period

The work of Fabricius (1951), Ramsay and Hess (1954), Weidmann (1958), Hess (1957) and Jaynes (1957) has shown that ducklings and chicks will not follow a moving object if exposure to that object is delayed for some two or three days. This early period has been called the 'sensitive' or 'critical' period and in general it is clear that ducklings and chicks are most easily imprinted during the first day or so after hatching. In our 1959 paper we noted that in individual cases chicks remained responsive for as long as five days. Guiton (1958) has shown that isolated chicks remain responsive to a moving object after three days by which time most socially reared chicks failed to respond. In a subsequent study Guiton (1959) concluded that socially reared chicks become imprinted to one another and that when subsequently exposed to a moving object they show 'searching' behaviour and 'distress' rather than strong and fearful avoidance of the moving object itself. Table 3 shows our own results for the responsiveness of socially reared chicks and isolated chicks to three-minute exposure to a moving box under our standard testing conditions as described in our 1959 paper. It can be seen that in one out of three experiments twenty-four hours of social life was sufficient experience to reduce significantly responsiveness compared with isolates, and that in a fourth experiment only isolated birds remained responsive after five days. On another occasion three birds that had been isolated for six days responded vigorously within three minutes of exposure to the moving box. There is support, therefore, for Guiton's contention that the end of the critical period results from the increasing selectivity of responsiveness with experience or, in other words, that imprinting brings about its own end.

An earlier explanation that the loss of responsiveness was due to the development of fear was first proposed by Hinde, Thorpe and Vince (1956) and it was supported by Hess (1957) on the basis of drug experiments. More recently Hess (1959a) has claimed that all his chicks showed fear, i.e. distress notes and avoidance by thirty-three to thirty-six hours, and that this corresponds with the loss of the following response. Jaynes (1957) has recorded that weak flight begins to appear at thirty to thirty-six hours and strong flight begins to appear at fifty-four to sixty hours and he suggests that fear of strange moving objects in chicks reared socially may rise to a maximum in the first week of life and decrease thereafter. Guiton (1959) has stated that fear is developed sufficiently to interfere with following at four days whereas most socially reared birds are imprinted by three days. It is possible, therefore, that fear responses, at least in the form of avoidance, are the responses that imprinted birds make to strange objects, i.e. to objects to which they are not imprinted.

Fabricius (1951), Guiton (1959), Jaynes (1957), Weidmann (1958) and no doubt other workers, too, have all observed that birds may show fear and avoidance of a moving box at first, yet may subsequently come to follow the box most strongly. We have observed this. On three occasions we selected a chick that showed extreme avoidance of a moving box, isolated it and exposed it to the moving box for three minutes every day. These chicks finally began to follow and in this way we have had a chick responding for the first time when over two weeks old. On another occasion a similar procedure was used with three chicks that had remained 'frozen' and three that had shown active avoidance of the box selected from a batch of chicks first tested when one day old. The former three followed well after a few days but the latter three had not begun to follow when the experiment ended after twelve days. It is possible that further treatment would have induced these birds to follow as in the previous experiment. Similarly we have isolated chicks for two or three days before exposing them to a moving box. At first some of these birds have shown avoidance and fear of the box but in all (six) cases prolonged exposure has resulted in following usually within the first hour. Jaynes (1957) has reported a similar observation with chicks five and six days old that had been reared socially, and Fabricius (1951) earlier recorded a similar experience with ducks but attributed it to feeding conditioning rather than to imprinting.

It seems, then, that habituation to the strange object may cause the avoidance response to disappear and the following response, and presumably imprinting, to occur. Hess (1959b) has claimed that birds that are induced to follow objects in this way do not in fact become imprinted to these objects. Following similarly takes place under the influence of a tranquillizing drug, chlorpromazine (but not meprobamate) (Hess, 1957, table 1, item 4), and in this particular instance Hess seems to consider that imprinting did occur after the end of the critical period as judged by the performance of his control group.

Guiton (1959) has reported that although avoidance is most marked in isolated birds, experience of the moving object usually reduces fear and results in following. In socially reared birds avoidance or crouching also disappears due to habituation but in most cases this does not result in following. Instead these birds show 'searching' behaviour with distress calls and the model is ignored, i.e. true habituation to the model has taken place. We feel, therefore, that the evidence is against fear being the cause of the end of the sensitive period, and that imprinting can end only as a result of its own action in increasing the selectivity of the animal's responses.

The effect of experience

In the work considered here the following response has been used as an indicator of the development of filial responsiveness. This development is shown both by the bird's immediate response to experience of a moving object and by its performance after a time interval, i.e. by the amount of retention of responsiveness. In a study of this kind Jaynes (1958a) has shown that under his particular experimental conditions ten minutes' experience of a moving box was sufficient to induce following in some day-old chicks, but that forty minutes' experience was required before all his chicks responded. Furthermore this experience was effective whether given on the first day or spread over the first four days and the greater the amount of experience the greater was the probability of a response thirty and seventy days later. Jaynes used six chicks for each condition in his experiment. In a similar study (1959) we found that the percentage of chicks that followed a moving box on the first day after hatching was approximately proportional to the amount of experience of that box, so that after ten movements of the box 50 per cent of the chicks had begun to follow and after fifty movements 80 per cent were following. Under test conditions similar though not identical to those of Jaynes we could detect a significant difference between the chicks that had received these two amounts of experience which approximated to two and eight minutes' exposure. We also recorded a considerable variability in the responsiveness of chicks within and between batches and therefore felt that further data were desirable.

In Table 4 are the results of an experiment carried out by us in which chicks from a Brown Leghorn × Light Sussex cross were subjected to one or other of three treatments. Using the experimental procedure described in our previous paper, chicks were given three minutes' or thirty minutes' experience of a moving box at one day of age, or six minutes' experience on each of the

Table 4 The Effects in Socially Reared Chicks of the Amount and Distribution of Experience of a Moving Box on Subsequent Responsiveness to this Stimulus

Amount of experience of a moving box	3 min	30 min	30 min
Distribution of this experience	One session of 3 min on the first day	Three sessions of 10 min on the first day	One session of 6 min on each of the first 5 days
Proportions of birds that responded to the moving box in a 3 min test on sixth day after hatching	$\frac{3}{16}$ (19%)	$\frac{6}{14}$ (43%)	$\frac{6}{11}$ (55%)

The probability that the difference between the first and third columns was a chance occurrence is $p = 0.032$, as determined by the Fisher Exact Probability Test.

first five days after hatching. The only difference from our previous procedure was that chicks that failed to respond within the first three minutes were rejected. All the chicks were tested for three minutes in the same situation on the sixth day. The results in Table 4 confirm Jaynes's claim that within these conditions the degree of imprinting is proportional to the amount of experience of the moving object. Further, the fact that we were able in our previous experiment to detect the effect of ten movements of a box on subsequent responsiveness of chicks suggests that the mechanism is extremely sensitive but requires strengthening by repetition.

The effect of effort

The experiments described in the last section did not separate the effects of visual experience of the moving object from the effects of the act of following. Hess (1957) attempted to do this by running ducks at different speeds for the same length of time; he found that the longer distance resulted in better imprinting as judged by responsiveness in discrimination tests. It could be, however, that the faster-moving object is a more potent stimulus than the slower-moving one. In our own work (1959) we were unable to find any relation between the distance run by chicks on first exposure to a moving box and their performances on subsequent occasions. Hess's (1957) results with drugs appeared to lend support to his assertion and he suggested that meprobamate, being a muscle relaxant, prevented imprinting by interfering with the 'muscular tension or other afferent consequences' of following. Yet at the same time he stated that this drug did not interfere with motility or coordination either in the training or test sessions. It is difficult to see how these two claims can be reconciled. In the same experiment chlorpromazine gave good imprinting under all conditions, yet Ryall (1958) and Taeschler and Carletti (1959) have reported that chlorpromazine simultaneously reduces emotional behaviour and motor activity in rats and mice. Hess (1958) has found that obstructions in the runway resulted in stronger imprinting because of the greater effort required in following, and this is perhaps the strongest evidence for the effect of effort. In a more recent paper Hess (1959a) showed for chicks that the ability to run improved over the first sixteen hours during which time 'imprintability' showed a corresponding improvement. A correlation of this kind does not prove the causal relationship between effort and imprinting. In any case chicks that cannot run may make considerable efforts to follow, and so the relationship must be between running and imprinting, in which case the result of the obstruction experiment remains unexplained.

Jaynes (1957) has also found that although the percentage of chicks responding decreased throughout the critical period the strength of imprinting judged by retention tests tended to increase during the first day, i.e. as locomotory ability increased. Poor locomotory ability does not necessarily mean poor locomotory effort, but in both Jaynes's and Hess's experimental circumstances it may well result in the chick spending very little of the training time near to the box and as a result obtaining very little experience of the box. In our own experimental circumstances (1959), where the box was never more than twelve to eighteen inches from the chicks, we found that very good runners often failed to respond in the later tests whereas some non-runners subsequently performed very well. Unlike Hess's chicks, however, all our birds had social experience between the tests and this may have affected their responsiveness in the second test. In a recent study Baer and Gray (1960) allowed chicks to see but not to follow or contact a white or a black guinea-pig during one of the first four days after hatching. At seven days the chicks were tested in a choice situation with black and white guinea-pigs. They spent significantly more time near the familiar than near the unfamiliar guinea-pig, and this effect was strongest when the previous experience of the guinea-pig had been on the second day after hatching. It would seem, therefore, that there is evidence that some imprinting can occur without the act of following, and that the evidence concerning the role of the effort of following is not yet convincing.

Later stimulus situations

As imprinting progresses so the bird becomes less likely to respond to stimuli other than the experienced one or ones. The extent to which a bird will generalize is, therefore, an inverse measure of the degree of imprinting. The first effect of experience appears to be one of facilitation of responsiveness to stimulation, as has been described earlier. Further experience restricts this responsiveness to an increasingly well defined stimulus pattern, as has been suggested by the individual recognition of two humans by chicks reported by Gray and Howard (1957). In Guiton's (1959) study, after two or three days of social life chicks had become imprinted specifically to chicks in that they would not follow other objects which they could thus discriminate from chicks.

Repeated presentation of the imprinted stimulus may lead to an apparent loss of the following response. Thus, Moltz and Rosenblum (1958a) have reported that with repeated daily experiences of a moving box the following response of Peking ducks wanes. We observed that when chicks were exposed singly to an intermittently moving box (in a mechanized version of our standard imprinting runway with a suspended white cylindrical box which travelled up and down the centre of the ten-foot alley in alternating half-minute periods of rest and movement), they all began to follow within the first hour and stopped following after several hours. A warm cover with food and water was situated to one side of the alley and the chicks spent progressively more time in their vicinity. In the experiment of Moltz and Rosenblum it could be said that the birds had become habituated to the stimulus situation, and in our experiment they had become at least temporarily satiated with the stimulus. However, the box had not ceased to be a stimulus to the chicks, for very strong and close following could be produced simply by the experimenter appearing and waving his arms, shouting, clapping and stamping his feet. When then left undisturbed the chick would gradually cease following the box once more.

This last observation is particularly interesting in view of Hess's (1959a) suggestion that fearfulness stops the following response from appearing. Moltz and Rosenblum (1958b) have shown that if ducks are first habituated to the testing enclosure, then they are less responsive to a moving box than birds not so treated.

Moltz, Rosenblum and Halikas (1959) have shown that electric shock treatment given inside the testing enclosure also increased the level of responsiveness of ducks. The differences in responsiveness of birds treated in these ways have been ascribed by these workers to the effect of anxiety.

In further observations on six chicks that had become satiated with and had ceased to follow the intermittently moving box as previously described, we found that following may be restored in two ways. Firstly, by introducing a second moving object (a red duster) and, secondly, by quietly and surreptitiously introducing strange static objects into the alley. In each case as soon as the chick noticed the strange objects it began to follow the moving box with 'anxious' chirps. These observations provide a possible solution to the apparent contradiction between the effects of 'anxiety' in facilitating following and 'fearfulness' in inhibiting following. If fear is taken to be the avoidance of a stimulus situation, then there may be avoidance of a fluctuating stimulus pattern (figure) and avoidance of the environment or stable stimulus situation from which the figure is differentiated (ground). Filial responses are to the figure, and fear of a figure thus prohibits such responses. We have suggested in an earlier section that fear is simply the response that birds make to objects to which they are not imprinted. Thus the imprinted bird not only goes to the figure to which it has become attached, but also avoids the strange figure. The establishment of the attachment of a bird to its environment is not so easily revealed in the way that attachment to a figure is revealed by the following response. In our experiment, however, the relationship was revealed when the satiated birds avoided the strange features of the environment by resuming their approach and following responses to the familiar moving box. Thus it is clear that filial responses can be restored by making some change in the environment and that birds come to discriminate by approach and avoidance responses both between familiar and unfamiliar moving objects and between familiar and strange environments. It is not clear whether both processes are imprinting, but Thorpe (1956) has already suggested that an exclusive attachment to an environment may be a form of imprinting.

If changes in the environment or ground will restore responsiveness to the imprinted moving object or figure, it is possible that there is also some loss of discrimination, i.e. increased responsiveness is accompanied by increased generalization. This might account for the response of social chicks to a moving object after they have been isolated for a time. We have tried taking a chick that had been with the white cylinder for several hours out of the runway, substituting a red duster for the cylinder and immediately replacing the chick. If 'anxiety' caused by this procedure resulted in generalization (and this treatment certainly causes chicks that have ceased following to resume following the familiar box) then such a chick should have followed the duster. We found that in all of four cases the chick showed avoidance of the duster. We feel, therefore, that anxiety effects cannot explain the generalization phenomena found by Guiton (1959) and that some process of forgetting must be involved. The anxiety effect, however, may explain why Hinde, Thorpe and Vince (1956) could not get any waning of responses to the figure in coots, since at the end of each run the birds were chased, caught and handled. Yet these workers found that responses to moderately strange objects waned gradually, suggesting that the discriminatory ability asserted itself over anxiety. These same workers tried the familiar objects in strange environments with mixed results: moorhens did not follow and coots followed less well. Clearly, further research is needed in this field.

Reversibility

Thorpe (1956) has already quoted several observations that suggest that imprinting is not irreversible. It is apparent from a previous section that attachments can be induced after the end of the so-called critical period provided that the bird has not been previously exposed to moving objects. Guiton (1959) has shown that socially reared birds become imprinted to one another in that they will not respond to a moving box. If such birds are isolated for a time they may subsequently respond to other objects. Table 5 shows our own results for experiments of this kind. It can be seen that day-old socially reared chicks did not respond to a moving box until they had been isolated for three hours. In another experiment chicks reared socially for two days would not respond after three hours' isolation but would do so after twenty-four hours' isolation. If, as has been suggested in an earlier section of this paper, the strength of social attachment is proportional to the amount of experience, then it might be expected that the reversibility could be similarly affected so that the longer the social experience, the longer the isolation required before responses to strange objects can be obtained. In this case the removal of the familiar objects and habituation to new objects might well produce the kinds of behaviour reported by Goodwin (1948), Steven (1955) and perhaps even the case of the Muscovy ducks reported by Lorenz (1937). Goodwin's birds responded sexually to the species with whom they were reared and not to their parent species with whom they had spent only the first

Table 5 The Effect of a Period of Isolation on the Responsiveness of Socially Reared Chicks to Three Minutes' Experience of a Moving Box

Batch of chicks	Pre-test treatment of newly hatched chicks	Proportions of birds that responded to the 3 min experience of a moving box by following	
E	21 hr social life followed by 3 hr isolation	$\frac{7}{8}$	probability of this difference being a chance occurrence is $p = 0.0023$
	24 hr social life	$\frac{0}{6}$	
F	48 hr social life followed by 3 hr isolation	$\frac{0}{8}$	probability of this difference being a chance occurrence is $p = 0.054$
	48 hr social life followed by 24 hr isolation	$\frac{2}{3}$	

The table also indicates that the length of the isolation period necessary to produce this effect may be related to the amount of social experience of the chicks. The probabilities recorded in the table were determined by the Fisher Exact Probability Test.

week or so of their lives. Lorenz's ducklings were reared for nearly seven weeks with Greylag geese before being removed and it is, therefore, not impossible that one of them should subsequently still prefer geese. It may be that the reversibility of imprinting involves the acquisition of new objects but not necessarily the loss of old ones. There is evidence in the reports of Fabricius (1951), Guiton (1959), Hinde, Thorpe and Vince (1956), and Jaynes (1957) that birds may become attached to several objects. In view of the relation between amount of experience and strength of attachment one might expect that the birds' preferences for objects would be related to the relative amounts of previous experience of these objects. In this respect, therefore, Lorenz's observation is still a remarkable one.

Imprinting and perceptual learning

As implied in the introduction, it is probably best to restrict the term 'imprinting' to those experimental situations in which the 'imprinted' bird is required to discriminate between patterns of movement, form, colour, sound, etc., and not simply to repeat earlier responses to the same stimulus pattern or object. The development of the imprinting process, or attachment to a class of stimuli, consists of a sharpening of discrimination between this and other classes. It would appear that this view of imprinting conforms to the criterion of perceptual learning put forward by Wohlwill (1958). As perceptual learning takes place, 'each stimulus to be discriminated must be classifiable, *qua* physical stimulus, into the class of stimuli to which the corresponding differential response is preattached'. As Wohlwill points out, 'paired-associate learning and similar tasks are left outside the province of perceptual learning situations'.

The development of attachment to environmental stimuli, or imprinting, seems to fit in with the progress of perceptual learning, as outlined by Gibson (1959). He has suggested that a distinction may be made between the environment and the social components of the environment in terms of the nature of the physical stimulation which they provide. Briefly, in the case of vision, the environment is one of surfaces, whereas the social or animal environment is one of movement and deformation of surfaces. Gibson contends that these are the kinds of information that the organism receives and has to differentiate. We suggest, therefore, that the process of which imprinting is a part may be considered in these two divisions, i.e. perception of the inanimate environment and perception of the animate environment, and that the development of social responses is part of the second of these two categories. In the course of the development of their social responses, the chicks have first to discriminate the moving surfaces from the static. The progress of discrimination may be revealed by the chicks' contentment calls and their approach and following responses. As the chicks' percepts of the stimulus situation become further differentiated with respect to movement, form, colour and sound, so discrimination in the form of choice of object-following will occur and this is the process of imprinting as originally conceived.

If 'imprinting' is extended to cover the development of the tendency to orientate social responses to moving or changing stimulus patterns, such as a flashing light, a source of intermittent sound or a moving object, then the concept becomes identical with that of the development of perception of the animate or social environment. If 'imprinting' is also to cover the development of perception of the inanimate environment, then the discussion by Thorpe (1956) of cases of attachment to environments and our own observations of the effect of changes in the static environment on the chick's following response become relevant. The imprinting process, then, could be regarded as part of a process of developing perception resulting from repeated stimulation. Gibson (1959) in considering this type of phenomenon, has asked, 'Do the qualities of a thing emerge from repeated impressions of the same thing or only by contrast with different things?' He considers that existing evidence on the perception of unfamiliar objects in laboratory situations favours the latter, but he points out that the former possibility has not been studied. Some of our studies on the following response are, however, a step in this direction. 'Repeated impressions of the same thing' occur when a chick is exposed for a time to a moving object. In one of our experiments we exposed chicks individually for a few hours to a moving white cylinder. These chicks then discriminated between the moving white cylinder and a similarly moving red duster, either when the two were presented together or when they were presented consecutively. It would seem, therefore, that in imprinting the view that the qualities of an object may emerge simply from continued impressions of it must be seriously considered.

References

BAER, D. M., and GRAY, P. H. (1960), 'Imprinting to a different species without overt following', *Percept. mot. Skills*, vol. 10, pp. 171–4.

BROWN, J. (1956), 'A modified significance test for the difference between two observed proportions', *Occup. Psychol.*, vol. 30, pp. 169–74.

COLLIAS, N. E. (1952), 'The development of social behaviour in birds', *Auk*, vol. 69, pp. 127–59.

FABRICIUS, E. (1951), 'Zur Ethologie junger Anatiden', *Acta zool. fenn.*, vol. 68, pp. 1–175.

FABRICIUS, E., and BOYD, H. (1954), 'Experiments on the following reactions of ducklings', *Wildfowl Trust Annual Report, 1952–3*, pp. 84–8.

GIBSON, J. J. (1959), 'Perception as a function of stimulation', in S. Koch (ed.), *Psychology: A Study of a Science*, McGraw-Hill, pp. 456–501.

GOODWIN, D. (1948), 'Some abnormal sexual fixations in birds', *Ibis*, vol. 90, pp. 45–8.

GRAY, P. H., and HOWARD, K. I. (1957), 'Specific recognition of humans in imprinted chicks', *Percept. mot. Skills*, vol. 7, pp. 301–4.

GUITON, P. (1958), 'The effect of isolation on the following response of Brown Leghorn chicks', *Proc. Roy. Phys. Soc. Edin.*, vol. 27, pp. 9–14.

GUITON, P. (1959), 'Socialization and imprinting in Brown Leghorn chicks', *Anim. Behav.*, vol. 7, pp. 26–34.

HESS, E. H. (1957), 'Effects of meprobamate on imprinting in water-fowl', *Ann. N.Y. Acad. Sci.*, vol. 67, pp. 724–32.

HESS, E. H. (1958), '"Imprinting" in animals', *Sci. Amer.*, vol. 198, pp. 81–90.

HESS, E. H. (1959a), 'Two conditions limiting critical age for imprinting', *J. comp. physiol. Psychol.*, vol. 52, pp. 515–18.

HESS, E. H. (1959b), 'Imprinting', *Science*, vol. 130, pp. 133–41.

HINDE, R. A., THORPE, W. H., and VINCE, M. A. (1956), 'The following response of young coots and moorhens', *Behaviour*, vol. 9, pp. 214–42.

JAMES, H. (1959), 'Flicker: an unconditioned stimulus for imprinting', *Canad. J. Psychol.*, vol. 13, pp. 59–67.

JAYNES, J. (1956), 'Imprinting: the interaction of learned and innate behavior: I. Development and generalization', *J. comp. physiol. Psychol.*, vol. 49, pp. 201–6.

JAYNES, J. (1957), 'Imprinting: the interaction of learned and innate behavior: II. The critical period', *J. comp. physiol. Psychol.*, vol. 50, pp. 6–10.

JAYNES, J. (1958a), 'Imprinting: the interaction of learned and innate behavior: III. Practice effects on performance, retention and fear', *J. comp. physiol. Psychol.*, vol. 51, pp. 234–7.

JAYNES, J. (1958b), 'Imprinting: the interaction of learned and innate behavior: IV. Generalization and emergent discrimination', *J. comp. physiol. Psychol.*, vol. 51, pp. 238–42.

KLOPFER, P. (1956), 'Comments concerning the age at which imprinting occurs', *Wilson Bull.*, vol. 68, pp. 320–21.

LORENZ, K. Z. (1937), 'The companion in the bird's world', *Auk*, vol. 54, pp. 245–73.

MOLTZ, H., and ROSENBLUM, L. A. (1958a), 'Imprinting and associative learning: the stability of the following response in Peking ducks (*Anas platyrhynchos*)', *J. comp. physiol. Psychol.*, vol. 51, pp. 580–83.

MOLTZ, H., and ROSENBLUM, L. A. (1958b), 'The relation between habituation and the stability of the following response', *J. comp. physiol. Psychol.*, vol. 51, pp. 658–61.

MOLTZ, H., ROSENBLUM, L. A., and HALIKAS, N. (1959), 'Imprinting and level of anxiety', *J. comp. physiol. Psychol.*, vol. 52, pp. 240–44.

RAMSAY, A. O., and HESS, E. H. (1954), 'A laboratory approach to the study of imprinting', *Wilson Bull.*, vol. 66, pp. 196–206.

RYALL, R. W. (1958), 'Effect of drugs on emotional behaviour in rats', *Nature, Lond.* vol. 182, pp. 1606–7.

SALZEN, E. A., and SLUCKIN, W. (1959), 'The incidence of the following response and the duration of responsiveness in domestic fowl', *Anim. Behav.*, vol. 7, pp. 172–9.

SMITH, F. V. (1960), 'Towards a definition of the stimulus situation for the approach response of the domestic chick', *Anim. Behav.*, vol. 8, pp. 197–200.

STEVEN, D. M. (1955), 'Transference of "imprinting" in a wild gosling', *Brit. J. anim. Behav.*, vol. 3, pp. 14–16.

TAESCHLER, M., and CARLETTI, A. (1959), 'Differential analysis of the affects of phenothiazine-tranquillizers on emotional and motor behaviour in experimental animals', *Nature, Lond.*, vol. 184, p. 823.

THORPE, W. H. (1956), *Learning and Instinct in Animals*, Methuen.

WEIDMANN, U. (1958), 'Verhaltenstudien an der Stockente (*Anas platyrhynchos*. L.): II. Versuche zur Auslösung und Prägung der Nachfolge und Anschlussreaktion', *Z. Tierpsichol.*, vol. 15, pp. 277–300.

WOHLWILL, J. F. (1958), 'The definition and analysis of perceptual learning', *Psychol. Rev.*, vol. 65, pp. 283–95.

6 P. P. G. Bateson

Changes in Chicks' Responses to Novel Moving Objects over the Sensitive Period for Imprinting

Excerpt from P. P. G. Bateson, 'Changes in chicks' responses to novel moving objects over the sensitive period for imprinting', *Animal Behaviour*, vol. 12, 1964, pp. 479–89.

The apparent restriction on imprinting to a sensitive period in the life-cycle was regarded by Lorenz (1935) as one of the special characteristics of the learning process. Modern workers are more inclined to treat it as a feature of the context in which imprinting occurs than as a feature of the process itself. Nevertheless the concept remains an important one since a special situation is as interesting as a special process.

Evidence for the sensitive period is derived from descriptions of the extent to which birds can be imprinted with a standard object at different ages. These descriptions do not, on their own, explain the changes in sensitivity. What then are the causes? Gottlieb (1961b) has found that the period can be more satisfactorily measured in terms of age from the beginning of embryonic development than in terms of post-hatch age. The onset of the sensitive period would not therefore appear to be greatly affected by experience after hatching. By contrast the end is determined by such experience (Moltz and Stettner, 1961). As a consequence of learning the characteristics of an object in their rearing pens, the birds begin to respond differently to novel moving objects (Bateson, 1964a; Guiton, 1959; Salzen, 1962; Sluckin and Salzen, 1961). These changes, which are used as indirect evidence for the sensitive period and may be regarded as proximate causes of its end, have been broadly characterized by previous workers (e.g. Gottlieb, 1961a; Hess and Schaeffer, 1959; Jaynes, 1957). However, the picture is far from complete because only a limited number of measures have been used and these have frequently been dependent on one another; furthermore little attempt has been made to establish the relationships between them. The results described below fill in some of the missing detail for the changes in the responses to novel stimuli of isolated domestic chicks.

Methods

Subjects

Fertile Rhode Island Red × Light Sussex eggs were obtained from a commercial hatchery four days before the eggs were due to hatch. Incubation was completed in an electrically operated, still-air incubator. At four to eight hours after hatching the chicks were transferred in darkness to the pens in which they were to be reared.

Rearing conditions

Each chick was kept in visual but not in auditory isolation in a triangular pen each side of which was approximately one foot long and nine inches high. Pens were formed by partitioning cylinders of hardboard into six sectors. Each group of six pens was heated by one centrally placed 150W infra-red lamp. The pens were supplied with bowls of chick mash and with automatic watering cylinders; they were continuously illuminated except for the occasions when a chick was removed from or returned to its pen.

Apparatus

The testing apparatus was similar in design to that used by Hess (1959). The circular runway was eighteen inches wide with an outside diameter of nine feet. The outer wall was eighteen inches high and made of unpainted hardboard and the inner wall was made of semi-transparent 'Window-lite'. The runway floor consisted of unpainted wooden boards. The moving model was a hardboard box (ten inches long, five inches wide and seven inches deep) suspended by nylon threads from a beam which was thirty-two inches above the floor; the bottom of the model was two-and-a-half inches above the floor. The beam was attached to a central shaft which could be rotated by a partially silenced electric motor. When the electric motor was switched on, the moving model took approximately sixty-five seconds to complete one revolution of the runway; its speed was therefore a little over four inches per second. The apparatus was illuminated by twelve 60W bulbs and the temperature was maintained at 70°F.

Observations and control of the lights and apparatus were conducted from behind one of the walls of the room in which there was a small glass panel about five feet from the ground. Mirrors were arranged in the room so that all points of the runway could be observed from behind the glass panel.

Procedure

All the results are based on the scores of chicks which were tested individually and once only. The birds were tested in order of hatching. All lights in the rearing and testing rooms which adjoined each other were turned off when a chick was transferred from its pen to the runway for testing. The chick was placed in the runway at the opposite side to where the model was situated. When the door to the testing room was closed and the experimenter behind the observation panel, the lights were turned on again. One and a half minutes later the electric motor driving the model was started; this meant that approximately two minutes after the lights had been turned on the model was presented to the chick for the first time. The test was begun when the model was two feet away from the chick and ended exactly twenty minutes later. The model moved continuously round the runway during this period. After the test was over the lights were turned off and the chick was returned to its pen.

The first and second groups of results are based on the scores of 229 birds all of which were tested on the third day after hatching. The mean age of these birds was 73·7 hours (standard deviation=2·9) and the range was from sixty-six hours to eighty-one hours. The birds were reared in pens painted with one of a number of different patterns and tested on one of a number of differently painted models. In lumping their scores it has been assumed that the different rearing and testing conditions did not affect the *relations* between the measures.

The third group of results is based on the scores of chicks of which about a half were reared in pens painted with yellow and red horizontal stripes and tested on a model painted with black and white vertical stripes. The other half were reared in pens painted with the black and white pattern and tested on a model painted with the yellow and red pattern. Thus all the chicks were exposed to a model which differed from the rearing pens in pattern. The number of chicks tested on each day and the average age of each group are shown in Table 3 (page 86).

Measures

Avoidance responses. When the chicks were within two feet of the model, any movement directed away from it, other than movements involved in pecking at the runway floor or walls, was termed avoidance. 'Freezing' in response to the model was also classed as an avoidance response although avoidance does not very aptly describe such behaviour. The crudest measure was the *percentage of birds which avoided*. The time from the beginning of the test to the end of the minute in which avoidance responses were last recorded was called the *persistence of avoidance*. The *strength of avoidance* was measured by recording the amount of time spent moving away from the model on a cumulative stopwatch. This measure included the amount of time spent attempting to escape from the runway since it was often not possible to determine when this activity began and avoidance of the model ended. During the course of a test a note was made of the stopwatch reading at precise minute intervals.

Positive responses and following. Any movement directed towards the moving model when it was within two feet of the chick was termed a positive response. Furthermore the 'twitter' call or 'contentment tone' given in the presence of the model and pecks or nestling movements which brought the bird in contact with the model were called positive responses. The least sensitive measure of positive responses was the *percentage of birds which responded positively* to the model. Following, which was one of the positive responses, was defined as any movement in the same direction as the model when the chick was immediately in front, on either side or within two feet of the trailing edge of the model. The times from the beginnning of the test to the ends of the minutes in which the first positive response and the first following response were given were termed the *latency of positive responses* and the *latency of following* respectively. The *strength of following* was measured by recording the time spent following the model on a cumulative stop-watch. Readings were taken from the stop-watch at precise minute intervals after the beginning of the test.

Vocalizations. The calls of the domestic chicken were first described in detail by Collias and Joos (1953). The two commonest calls of the chick are the 'distress call' and the 'contentment tone'. Andrew (1964) has used the neutral terms, 'peep' and 'twitter' respectively, for these two calls and his usage will be followed here. The peep is loud, falls in pitch, lasts for rather more than one-tenth of a second and may be given at a rate of up to three a second. By contrast the twitter is softer, tends to rise in pitch, lasts for less than one-tenth of a second and is given at slightly more than four a second. Intermediate calls do occur but generally peeps can easily be distinguished from twitters by ear alone.

The peeps were recorded automatically by means of a machine which consisted of a microphone, suspended above the runway, an amplifier and an electro-mechanical counter positioned so that readings could be taken from it during the course of a test. The amplifier had a control by which the amplitude threshold could be altered. Since the chick's calls could be heard, the loud twitters or intermediate calls could be quickly excluded by raising the threshold, if the counter began to record them.

No attempt was made to record the number of twitters although a note was made of when these calls were given.

Results

Changes in behaviour within the test

The quantitative data presented in this section are all based on the scores of chicks which were tested on the third day after hatching; however, the changes in behaviour occurring within the test were broadly similar for all the other age groups except the one-day-old birds which showed very little avoidance of the model.

Within the two-minute period between the lights being turned on and the first presentation of the model the great majority of the chicks stood up and began to cheep. Of these a few began to walk about but most remained where they had been placed in the runway. Apart from the one-day-old birds the majority of the

Table 1 Scatter Diagram Showing the Relationship between Persistence of Avoidance and Latency of Positive Responses

Persistence of avoidance	\	Latency of positive responses																				
		1	2	3	4	5	6	7	8	9	10	11	12	13	14	15	16	17	18	19	20	>20
0		18			1	1																
1		3	2	3	1	1	2															1
2		4	9	1	2		1	1														
3		1	1	3	4				1													3
4			1	2	1	2			1		1		1									
5			1	3	2		1															
6		1				2	3	1	1		1											1
7					4	3	2															
8			1		1	2	1			1		1				1	1					
9							1	1	1							1						

10		1	3	1			2
11			1		2	1	1
12				1	1	1	
13	1		1	1	1	1	4
14		1		1	2		
15				1	1	3	1
16					1	1	2
17				1		1	1
18					1	1 2	2
19							3
>19	1					1	62

Both measures are expressed in minutes after the beginning of the test. The figures in the diagram refer to the number of chicks obtaining the scores denoted by the position of these figures.

chicks avoided the moving model for at least part of the test. The initial reaction ranged from a slight turning away of the head to running wildly away from the model and emitting peeps continuously. In between these extremes birds attempted to jump out of the runway, walked a short distance in front of the model or ran past it. Some birds 'froze' on the first presentation of the model but this posture was rarely held for very long and was almost invariably succeeded by active avoidance.

Many of the chicks avoided for the whole of the twenty-minute test. The mean percentage time spent avoiding in each minute of the test is shown in Figure 1. The decline after the fifth minute was almost perfectly linear; the decrease from the sixth to the twentieth minute was highly significant ($d=3·61, p < 0·001$). The increase over the first five minutes of the test was primarily due to many birds 'freezing' on their first few encounters with the model. However, a contributory factor might have been that the birds had had little experience of walking or running before the tests.

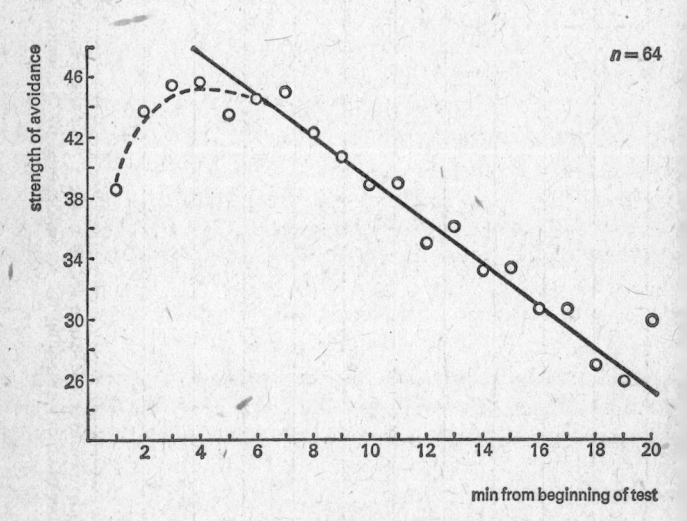

Figure 1 The mean strength of avoidance in each minute of the test. Only the scores of the chicks which avoided for the whole test have been used. The strength of avoidance is expressed as the percentage of each minute spent avoiding

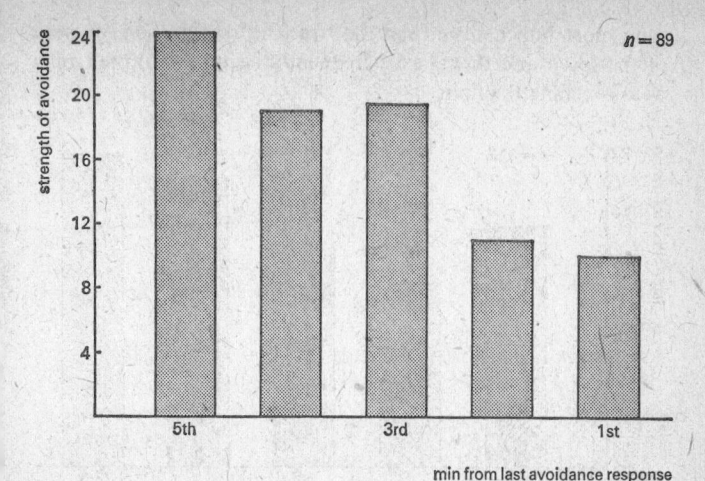

Figure 2 The mean strength of avoidance in each of the last five minutes before avoidance ceased. Only the scores of chicks which ceased to avoid during the test have been used. The strength of avoidance is expressed as the percentage of each minute spent avoiding

The chicks which did stop avoiding the model during the test spent less and less time avoiding before ceasing to do so altogether. The mean percentage time spent avoiding in each of the last five minutes before avoidance ceased is shown in Figure 2. The decline from the fifth to the first minute was highly significant (Wilcoxon Matched Pairs Test: $z = 4.58$, $p < 0.0001$). It should be stressed here that the measure of strength of avoidance included the time spent attempting to escape from the runway; this activity, which was not necessarily given in the presence of the model, is presumably what Guiton (1959) called 'searching behaviour'.

A few of the chicks that ceased to avoid the model during the course of the test became unresponsive to it and an occasional bird was unresponsive from the beginning of the test. While these unresponsive birds often sat down they differed from the 'freezing' birds in several respects. They peeped spasmodically or even continuously and were not always immobile; when sitting they were more hunched up than the 'freezing' birds, the eyes were often closed and their heads frequently sagged until their bills were touching the floor.

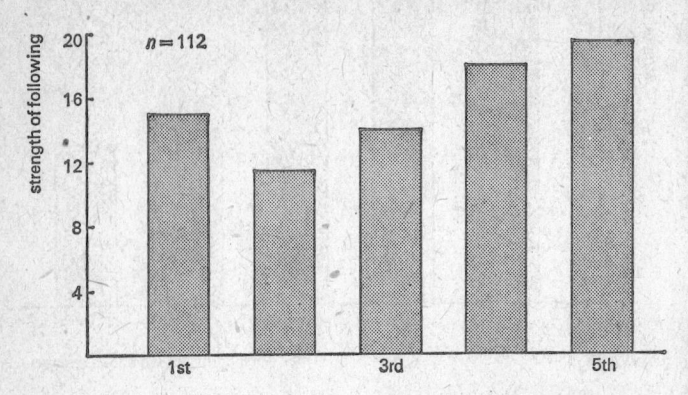

Figure 3 The mean strength of following in each of the first five minutes after following began. The strength of following is plotted as the percentage of each minute spent following

The majority of the chicks that stopped avoiding during the course of the test subsequently gave a positive response to the model. Sometimes the switch from avoidance to positive responses was dramatic, taking place within a few seconds. In such cases the switch was usually signalled by the chick giving the model a violent peck. Other chicks took many minutes to change over from one response to the other. The strength of avoidance declined until the bird was motionless whereupon it began to look at the model and perhaps give the twitter; on each successive presentation of the model the chick would make stronger and stronger approach intention movements until finally it made contact with the model by pecking or nestling against it. After a chick had made a positive response it tended, on subsequent presentations of the model, to approach from greater and greater distances and follow for longer and longer periods. The mean percentage time spent following the model in each of the first five minutes after following began is shown in Figure 3. The decline from the first to the second minute was statistically significant (Wilcoxon Test: $z=3.97$, $p < 0.0001$) as was the increase from the second to the fifth minute (Wilcoxon Test: $z=3.45$, $p < 0.0001$); there was no obvious event which would account for the initial decline.

Once a positive response had been given it was unusual for a bird to give another avoidance response. Occasionally, however, birds remained ambivalent and tended to avoid the model as it approached and follow as it went away; in such cases calls intermediate between the peep and the twitter were commonly given. Chicks which were not overtly ambivalent almost invariably gave the twitter as they approached and nestled against the model, but frequently gave the peep as they followed behind.

Relations between some of the measures

The chicks whose scores were used for calculating the relations between some of the measures were all tested on the third day after hatching.

The correlation between the persistence of avoidance and the latency of positive responses was so strong that it is best demonstrated in a scatter diagram. Table 1 shows how few chicks responded positively before ceasing to avoid altogether; it also shows that the majority of the chicks gave a positive response very shortly after ceasing to avoid.

In Table 2 the persistence of avoidance is plotted against the latency of following. Here again the correlation was very strong but comparison between this table and Table 1 shows that following responses were usually not given as promptly as the other positive responses on the cessation of avoidance. Even so, the persistence of avoidance, the latency of positive responses and the latency of following may be treated as one variable representing the point at which avoidance changed to following. The persistence of avoidance has been arbitrarily used as the change-over point for the purposes of establishing the relations between this point and the measures of strength of avoidance and following.

When the strength of avoidance over the *first* five minutes of the test is plotted against the persistence of avoidance, a positive correlation is obtained (Spearman Rank Correlation Coefficient

Table 2 Scatter Diagram Showing the Relationship between Persistence of Avoidance and Latency of Following

Latency of following	1	2	3	4	5	6	7	8	9	10	11	12	13	14	15	16	17	18	19	20	>20
Persistence of avoidance																					
0		6	8	3	1		2														1
1		3	1	2	1	1	2		1												2
2		5	7	2		2	1	1													3
3			1	1	5	1							1	1							2
4				2	1	1	1	1													1
5					1	1	2	2													1
6			1			3	2	1				2	1								1
7							1	2	1	1		1	1	1	1						1
8							2	1		2	1	1		1	1		1				2

Time (min)							Total
9		1			1	1	1
10	1 2	1			1		2
11	1 1						4
12		1			1		1
13	1	1		1 1			7
14	1		1 1 1				4
15		1	1		1		4
16							4
17			1				2
18				1			5
19							3
>19							64

Both measures are expressed in minutes after the beginning of the test. The figures in the diagram refer to the number of chicks obtaining the scores denoted by the positions of these figures.

$= 0.431$, $t = 3.93$, $p < 0.0001$). This relationship is to be expected in view of the linear decline in the strength of avoidance during the course of the test. When the strength of avoidance over the *last* five minutes before avoidance ceased is plotted against the persistence of avoidance, neither a positive nor a negative correlation is obtained.

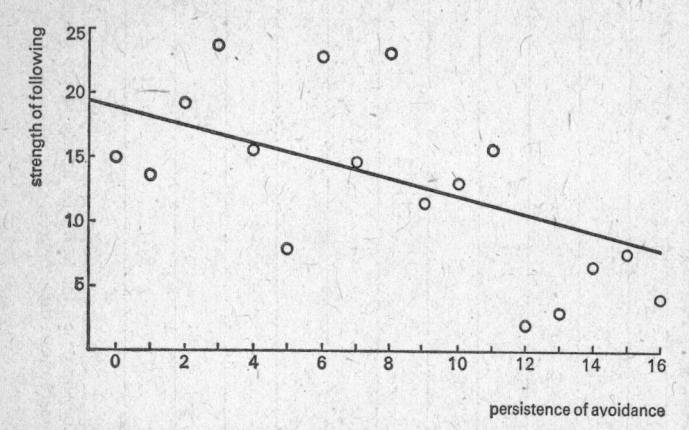

Figure 4 The mean strength of following plotted against the persistence of avoidance. The strength of following is expressed as the percentage of the five-minute period after following began spent following. The persistence of avoidance is expressed in minutes after the beginning of the test

In Figure 4 the mean strength of following over the first five minutes after following began is plotted against the persistence of avoidance. A negative relation between the two measures exists. A regression line with the following equation was fitted to the data:
$$y = 19.28 - 0.725\,x \pm 0.309.$$

The gradient of this line is significantly less than zero ($p < 0.01$).

In Figure 5 the strength of avoidance over the last five minutes before avoidance ceased is plotted against the strength of following over the first five minutes after following had begun. Since five minutes was considered the minimum period over which a reliable score of the strengths of avoidance or following could be

obtained and since the two activities did not overlap, none of the chicks whose scores are given in Figure 5 stopped avoiding before the fifth minute of the test or started following after the sixteenth minute. The scatter of points can be conveniently separated about the mean strength of avoidance of 19 per cent. A positive correlation exists between the strength of avoidance values of less than 19 per cent and the strength of following. A regression line was fitted to the data with the following equation:
$y = 5.67 + 0.771x \pm 0.273$.

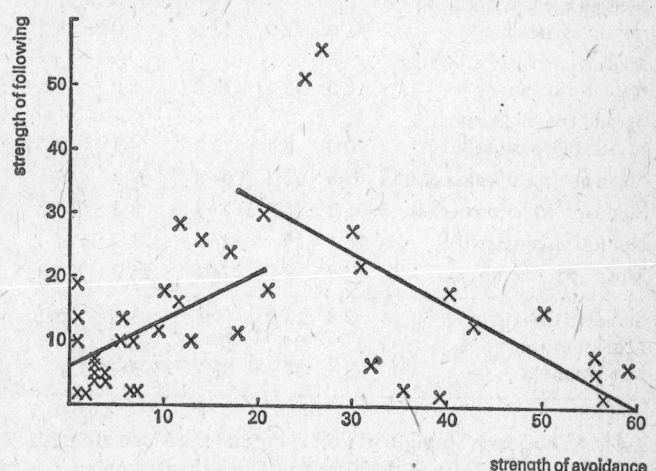

Figure 5 The strength of following plotted against the strength of avoidance. The strength of avoidance is expressed as the percentage of the five-minute period before avoidance ceased spent avoiding and the strength of following as the percentage of the five-minute period after following began spent following

The gradient of this line is significantly greater than zero ($t = 2.81$, $p < 0.01$). A negative correlation exists between the strength of avoidance values of more than 19 per cent and the strength of following. The equation of the regression line fitted to these data is:
$y = 46.8 - 0.773x \pm 0.244$.

The gradient of this line is significantly less than zero ($t = 3.42$, $p < 0.01$).

Table 3 The Percentage of Birds Responding Positively, the Median Latency of Positive Responses, the Median Latency of Following Response, the Percentage of Birds neither Avoiding nor Responding Positively, and the Rate of 'Peep' Calling on Each of the First Five Days after Hatching

Day after hatching	1	2	3	4	5
Responding positively	100·0	65·2	66·7	78·3	70·8
Median latency of positive responses in min	1·0	12·0	13·0	8·0	8·5
Median latency of following response in min	6·5	12·0	13·0	8·0	10·5
% neither avoiding nor responding positively	0·0	8·7	0·0	4·3	0·0
Mean no. 'peep' calls per min	65·8	75·3	64·8	69·5	59·3
Standard deviation of calls	25·3	16·1	27·8	8·3	8·2
Number of birds tested	16	23	27	23	24
Mean age in hours	24·7	49·7	74·4	96·0	124·8
Standard deviation	2·8	3·7	4·8	3·3	5·2
Minimum age	19	45	67	92	116
Maximum age	28	57	81	103	131

Table 4 The Mean Strength of Following and the Mean Strength of Avoidance on Each of the First Five Days after Hatching

Day after hatching	1	2	3	4	5
Mean strength of following	6·2	15·6	16·3	16·3	11·7
No. obtaining strength of following score	11	12	16	16	14
Mean strength of avoidance	—	13·8	25·3	34·6	33·5
No. obtaining strength of avoidance score	0	13	12	15	6

Changes in behaviour with increasing age

The values of the measures which were based on the scores of all the chicks are shown for each of the first five days after hatching in Table 3 or in Figure 6.

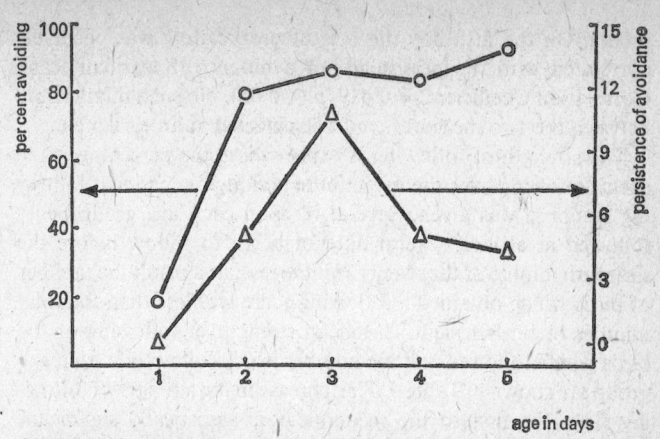

Figure 6 The percentage of chicks which avoided the model at any time and the median persistence of avoidance on each of the first five days after hatching. The persistence of avoidance is expressed in minutes after the beginning of the test

The proportion of birds which responded positively declined significantly from the first to the second day ($p < 0.01$) and there was a concomitant increase in the latency of positive responses over the same period (Mann–Whitney U: $z = 3.62$, $p < 0.001$) but not in the latency of following. These trends reversed after the third day but the changes are not significant.

The proportion of birds avoiding increased significantly from the first to the second day ($p < 0.001$) as did the persistence of avoidance (Mann–Whitney U: $z = 3.74$, $p < 0.001$). However, the apparent positive relationship between the two measures broke down after the third day (see Figure 6); the proportion avoiding continued to increase up to the fifth day but the persistence of avoidance of the *birds which avoided* declined significantly from the third to the fourth day (Mann–Whitney U: $z = 1.77$, $p < 0.05$). The proportion of birds which neither avoided the model nor gave a positive response remained at a low level over the first five days after hatching.

The rate of 'peep' calling declined significantly from the fourth to the fifth day ($t = 4.14$, $p < 0.001$) and the variance declined significantly from the third day to the fourth day ($F = 11.13$, $p <$

0·001). On the fifth day the rate of peep calling was positively correlated with the persistence of avoidance (Spearman Rank Correlation Coefficient = 0·479, $p < 0·05$). No such relationship between the two measures could be detected at an earlier age.

The strength of following is expressed as the percentage time spent following over the five-minute period after the first following response was given. Several birds in each age group never followed at all and several did not begin to follow before the sixteenth minute of the twenty-minute test; as a result the number of birds which obtained a following score was less than the total number of birds tested. The mean strength of following of the birds which followed and the number which followed in each age group are shown in Table 4. The increase in the strength of following from the first to the second day is statistically significant (Mann–Whitney $U = 32·5$, $p < 0·05$).

The strength of avoiding is expressed as the percentage time spent avoiding over the period of the test in which avoidance responses were given. The scores of birds which avoided for less than five minutes have not been used. The numbers in each group for which a strength of avoidance score was obtained were further reduced because the measure had not been devised when the first batches were tested. The mean strength of avoidance for each group is shown in Table 4. The increase from the second to the fourth day was statistically significant (Mann–Whitney $U = 40·5, p < 0·01$).

Discussion

Under the conditions of this experiment the most marked changes in behaviour occurred from the first to the second day after hatching. The majority of the day-old birds did not avoid the model at all and responded positively at once. By the second day the proportion of birds which avoided had increased significantly and the proportion of birds which responded positively had correspondingly declined. These changes reflected the significant increases in the closely correlated measures of persistence of avoidance and latency of positive responses. The latency of following response did not increase significantly over the same period because many of the day-old chicks were inactive and appeared to be incapable of locomotion. In another study the persistence of avoidance and the latency of positive responses were found to be shorter for chicks exposed to a model which resembled the pens in which they had been reared than for chicks exposed to a dissimilar model (Bateson, 1964a). Thus many of the changes in behaviour occurring over the first few days after hatching were probably the consequences of the process by which the birds learn the characteristics of their immediate environment.

The rate of 'peep' calling declined significantly from the fourth to the fifth day after hatching. This result confirms one of the findings of Kaufman and Hinde (1961) who showed that at 60°F the rate of calling of experimentally naïve chicks declined with age. This drop was presumably due to the increasing ability of the birds to regulate their own temperature. In the experiments reported here the birds less than five days old stopped peeping momentarily as they gave a positive response; however, they did not do so for very long and consequently the rate of peeping over the whole test was not related to any of the other measures. However, on the fifth day, when the rate of peeping was less affected by temperature, this measure was positively correlated with the persistence of avoidance. This demonstrates, albeit crudely, that the rate of peep calling declined once avoidance of the model had ceased.

While the proportion of birds which gave positive responses declined from the first to the second day, the strength of following of the birds which followed increased significantly over the same period. This apparent paradox, which has been previously reported by Guiton (1958) and Jaynes (1957), arose because the strength of following measured locomotive ability as well as the readiness to follow. The strength of avoidance was also a measure of locomotive ability which explains why the lower values of this measure were positively correlated with the strength of following.

The higher values of the strength of avoidance were negatively correlated with the strength of following as was the persistence of avoidance. These negative relations were to be expected, for in the imprinting situation birds follow less strongly objects which differ from the one whose details they have learned (Cofoid and Honig, 1961; Jaynes, 1958; Moltz, 1960) and may also avoid unfamiliar objects (Bateson, 1964a; Gottlieb, 1961a; Guiton, 1959; Jaynes, 1956, 1958; Moltz, 1960). In other words the greater the difference between a novel object presented to a bird and the one on which it was trained, the less strongly that object will be followed and the more likely it is to be avoided.

By definition, following and avoidance could not have been performed simultaneously, but of course the two activities could have been given alternately. In fact the relations between them are more organized. Not only was there a strong correlation between the point in the test at which avoidance responses ceased and the point at which positive responses were first given, but also the strength of avoidance declined steadily before avoidance ceased and the strength of following increased after the first following response had been given. There was, however, a significant decrease in the strength of following from the first to the second minute after following began. This suggests that the steady change from strong avoidance to strong following is less regular about the moment of change-over. It is perhaps worth noting that aggressive responses were also given at this point. The well-organized relationship between avoidance and positive responses suggests that a single mechanism controls the occurrence of both forms of behaviour. If there were not such an arrangement, stimuli which were subsequently explored or became associated with such activities as feeding would be responded to socially as well.

The persistence of avoidance, the latency of positive responses the strength of avoidance and the strength of following reached peaks around the third or fourth day after hatching and thereafter declined. For the most part the downward trends were not statistically significant but the persistence of avoidance of the birds which avoided declined significantly. Previously Jaynes (1957) had suggested that 'fear' in chicks rises to a maximum in the first week of life and thereafter declines; Gray and Howard (1957) also observed that the 'fearfulness' of chicks increased up to the fourth day after hatching and then decreased. In a more recent study Salzen (1962) found little difference between the responses to a novel moving object of day-old and seven-day-old isolated chicks, apart from an 'initial shock fear reaction' on the part of the older birds. Unfortunately he did not measure the responses of isolated birds of intermediate age so a direct comparison with his results cannot be made. Nevertheless all these results taken together suggest an overall decline in responsiveness over the second half of the first week. Salzen's (1962) results indicate that week-old socially reared chicks are more responsive to moving objects than isolated chicks. Thus a cause of the change in behaviour of the isolated birds after the third or fourth day may have been prolonged exposure to an unchanging environment. The results of measuring the activity of isolated chicks are described by Bateson (1964b); the purpose of these experiments was to determine whether the chicks' activity changed over the period in which their responsiveness declined.

References

ANDREW, R. J. (1964), 'Vocalization in chicks, and the concept of "stimulus" contrast', *Anim. Behav.*, vol. 12, pp. 64–76.

BATESON, P. P. G. (1964a), 'Effect of similarity between rearing and testing conditions on chicks' following and avoidance responses', *J. comp. physiol. Psychol.*, vol. 57, pp. 100–103.

BATESON, P. P. G. (1964b), 'Changes in the activity of isolated chicks over the first week after hatching', *Anim. Behav.*, vol. 12, pp. 490–92.

COFOID, D. A., and HONIG, W. K. (1961), 'Stimulus generalization of imprinting'. *Science*, vol. 134, pp. 1962–4.

COLLIAS, N., and JOOS, M. (1953), 'The spectrographic analysis of sound signals of domestic fowl', *Behaviour*, vol. 5, pp. 175–87.

GOTTLIEB, G. (1961a), 'The following-response and imprinting in wild and domestic ducklings of the same species (*Anas platyrhynchos*)', *Behaviour*, vol. 18, pp. 205–28.

GOTTLIEB, G. (1961b), 'Developmental age as a baseline for determination of the critical period in imprinting', *J. comp. physiol. Psychol.*, vol. 54, pp. 422–7.

GRAY, P. H., and HOWARD, K. I. (1957), 'Specific recognition of humans in imprinted chicks', *Percept. mot. Skills*, vol. 7, pp. 301–4.

GUITON, P. (1958), 'The effect of isolation on the following response of Brown Leghorn chicks', *Proc. Roy. Phys. Soc. Edin.*, vol. 27, pp. 9–14.

GUITON, P. (1959), 'Socialization and imprinting in Brown Leghorn chicks', *Anim. Behav.*, vol. 7, pp. 26–34.

HESS, E. H. (1959), 'Imprinting', *Science*, vol. 130, pp. 133–41.

HESS, E. H., and SCHAEFFER, H. H. (1959), 'Innate behaviour patterns as indicators of the "critical period"', *Z. Tierpsychol.*, vol. 16, pp. 155–60.

JAYNES, J. (1956), 'Imprinting: the interaction of learned and innate behavior: I. Development and generalization', *J. comp. physiol. Psychol.*, vol. 49, pp. 201–6.

JAYNES, J. (1957), 'Imprinting: the interaction of learned and innate behavior: II. The critical period', *J. comp. physiol. Psychol.*, vol. 50, pp. 6–10.

JAYNES, J. (1958), 'Imprinting: the interaction of learned and innate behavior: IV. Generalization and emergent discrimination', *J. comp. physiol. Psychol.*, vol. 51, pp. 238–42.

KAUFMAN, I. C., and HINDE, R. A. (1961), 'Factors influencing distress calling in chicks, with special references to temperature changes and social isolation', *Anim. Behav.*, vol. 9, pp. 197–204.

LORENZ, K. Z. (1935), 'Der Kumpan in der Umvelt des Vogels', *J. Ornithol.*, vol. 83, pp. 137–213, 289–413.

MOLTZ, H. (1960), 'Imprinting: empirical basis and theoretical significance', *Psychol. Bull.*, vol. 57, pp. 291–314.

MOLTZ, H. and STETTNER, L. J. (1961), 'The influence of patterned-light deprivation on the critical period for imprinting', *J. comp. physiol. Psychol.*, vol. 54, pp. 279–83.

SALZEN, E. A. (1962), 'Imprinting and fear', *Symp. Zool. Soc., Lond.*, vol. 8, pp. 199–217.

SLUCKIN, W., and SALZEN, E. A. (1961), 'Imprinting and perceptual learning', *Q. J. exp. Psychol.*, vol. 13, pp. 65–77.

7 E. A. Salzen and C. C. Meyer

Imprinting: Reversal of a Preference Established during the Critical Period

E. A. Salzen and C. C. Meyer, 'Imprinting: reversal of a preference established during the critical period', *Nature*, vol. 215, 1967, pp. 785–6.

Two distinctive features of 'imprinting' originally emphasized by Lorenz (1937) were that there was a critical period in which the preference for a particular species was established and that the preference established during this period was permanent and could not be changed by subsequent experience. These two features have been reiterated by Hess (1959a), who has added a primacy–recency feature, claiming that the first imprinting experience has priority over a subsequent one. These features of imprinting have been questioned by Sluckin and Salzen (1961), who treated imprinting as a perceptual learning phenomenon in which the sensitive period is experience-dependent and the stability of an imprinted preference is dependent on the amount of experience. More recent reviews by Sluckin (1964) and Bateson (1966) have supported this view. In particular the perceptual learning view of imprinting has been developed into a neuronal model hypothesis of imprinting by Salzen (1962) and it predicts that object preferences established by the imprinting process should be subject to reversal given sufficient exclusive and enforced experience of new objects after the end of the so-called critical period. The present experiment demonstrates a reversal of this kind.

The experiment used Cornish × White Rock chicks hatched in separate boxes and transferred when twelve to eighteen hours old to isolation rearing cages. In the centre of each cage separate from the sources of food, water and heat, there was either a dark blue or a green cloth covered paper ball about 5 cm in diameter and hanging approximately 3 cm above the floor. The chicks quickly became strongly attached to the balls, spending much time beside them, and interacted with the balls by pushing, pulling and pecking them. After three days (twelve hours light/dark cycle) the chicks were tested for their preference between blue and green balls. The balls were hung midway on opposite long sides of a box (45×90 cm). The chick under test was placed in the dark at the mid-point of a short side, a lamp was switched on above the box, and the chick was given two minutes in which to go to and stay with one of the balls. A preference was recorded if the chick after reaching a ball either contacted it, pecked and pulled it, and/or gave pleasure calls, or stayed close (one inch) beside the ball and was silent or pleasure calling. The trial was ended when either of these criteria was reached or at the end of two minutes. The light was switched off, the chick was returned to a holding box and the positions of the objects were reversed ready for the next trial. Ten trials were made with each chick. After testing the chicks were returned to their cages and the balls exchanged so that each chick now had a new and different coloured ball. The chicks began to respond to the new balls on the same day. Three days later the chicks were again tested for their preferences between green and blue balls. Then they were returned to their cages for a further three days but this time without any balls present. Finally, a third preference test was given. In this way twelve chicks were imprinted with a blue ball and then given reversal training with a green ball, while ten chicks were tested in the opposite manner.

The results are shown in Figure 1 in terms of the mean number of responses made by the chicks to each ball in each preference test. The two colour treatments are combined because they were nearly balanced and gave similar results. The results show that at the end of the first three days the chicks had an almost exclusive preference for their familiar coloured ball ($p < 0.01$, Wilcoxon Test). After the second three-day period, this preference had been reversed ($p < 0.01$, Wilcoxon Test). At the third test the new preference was maintained or even slightly increased because the responding to the preferred ball had increased significantly since the second test ($p < 0.02$, Wilcoxon Test). Twenty-one of the twenty-two chicks made more responses to their familiar ball on the first test. On the second and third tests eighteen and seventeen of these twenty-one chicks made more responses to the newly experienced ball.

There can be no doubt that the period in which the first ball

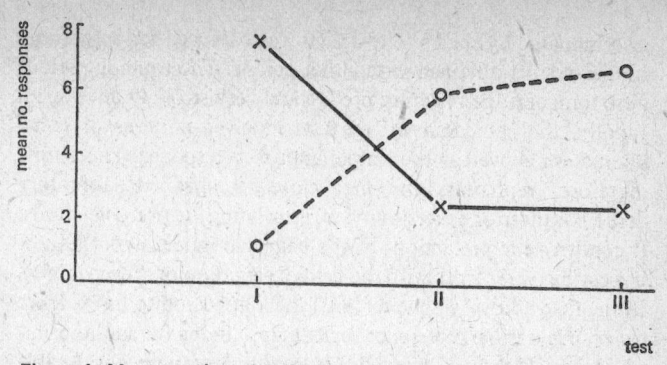

Figure 1 Mean number of responses to the first-learned (x) and second-learned (o) coloured balls in the two-choice discrimination test. Each of the twenty-two chicks had ten two-minute trials in each of three tests which were given at intervals of three days

was experienced included any possible critical period for imprinting in chicks. The experience began eighteen hours after hatching and Hess (1959b) has claimed that this period reaches its peak at this time for chicks. Furthermore, the second ball was experienced well after the end of the critical period of twenty-four hours determined by Hess. Many studies (e.g. Bateson, 1966; Sluckin, 1964; Sluckin and Salzen, 1961) have shown that domestic chicks imprint with objects when exposed to them within the first three days after hatching. Thus the experiment shows that a strong preference established during this imprinting period can be completely reversed by subsequent experience. It also shows that this reversal was maintained intact after a period in which forgetting of both objects could have occurred. It cannot be said, therefore, that learning which takes place after the imprinting period is more rapidly forgotten than the learning during the imprinting period. Thus it would seem that the most recently learned preference predominated, contrary to Hess's (1959a) claim of a primacy effect in imprinting. The recent test by Kaye (1965) of a primacy effect gave an equivocal result, probably because of the very short training periods involved. The present test used stimulus objects that differed only in colours that were known from pilot studies to be equally easily learned and discriminated by chicks. The design was balanced for colour and similar results obtained with either colour. The training periods were long and the resulting preferences very strongly developed. Finally, the behaviour in the tests involved patterns of social interaction as well as the simple approach response. This study, therefore, represents the first closely controlled laboratory demonstration of reversibility of imprinting in precocial birds. It confirms the predictions of the neuronal model hypothesis of imprinting and agrees with the field observation of Steven (1955). In the field study by Schein (1963) there appeared to be evidence for an irreversible preference for humans among human-imprinted turkeys. It should be noted that these turkeys were always able to see humans as well as their later flock companions. Under these circumstances the neuronal model hypothesis would not necessarily predict a change in preference. The present demonstration of reversibility of imprinting in chicks agrees with the demonstration of a reversible social attachment in lambs (Cairns and Johnson, 1965). Similar results have been obtained with a shape discrimination and a full account will be published elsewhere.

References

BATESON, P. P. G. (1966), 'The characteristics and context of imprinting', *Biol. Rev.*, vol. 41, pp. 177–220.

CAIRNS, R. B., and JOHNSON, D. L. (1965), 'The development of interspecies social attachments', *Psychonom. Sci.*, vol. 2, pp. 337–8.

HESS, E. H. (1959a), 'Imprinting', *Science*, vol. 130, pp. 133–41.

HESS, E. H. (1959b), 'Two conditions limiting critical age for imprinting', *J. comp. physiol. Psychol.*, vol. 52, pp. 515–18.

KAYE, S. M. (1965), 'Primacy and recency in imprinting', *Psychonom. Sci.*, vol. 3, pp. 271–2.

LORENZ, K. Z. (1937), 'The companion in the bird's world', *Auk*, vol. 54, pp. 245–73.

SALZEN, E. A. (1962), 'Imprinting and fear', *Symp. Zool. Soc., Lond.*, vol. 8, pp. 199–217.

SCHEIN, M. W. (1963), 'On the irreversibility of imprinting', *Z. Tierpsychol.*, vol. 20, pp. 462–7.

SLUCKIN, W. (1964), *Imprinting and Early Learning*, Methuen.

SLUCKIN, W., and SALZEN, E. A. (1961), 'Imprinting and perceptual learning', *Q. J. exp. Psychol.*, vol. 13, pp. 65–77.

STEVEN, D. M. (1955), 'Transference of "imprinting" in a wild gosling', *Brit. J. anim. Behav.*, vol. 3, pp. 14–16.

8 Howard S. Hoffman, John L. Searle, Sharon Toffey and Frederick Kozma, Jr

Behavioural Control by an Imprinted Stimulus

Excerpts from Howard S. Hoffman, John L. Searle, Sharon Toffey and Frederick Kozma, Jr, 'Behavioral control by an imprinted stimulus', *Journal of the Experimental Analysis of Behavior*, vol. 9, 1966, pp. 177–89.

Introduction

The present experiments sought to employ imprinting as an avenue for research into the responses of young organisms to a parental figure. With the exception of Harlow and Zimmerman's (1958, 1959) pioneering work with infant monkeys, previous investigations of these responses have been largely limited to collecting and integrating clinical observations (Bowlby, 1958, 1960) or to analysing ethological information (Hafez, 1962; Gottlieb, 1963; Sluckin, 1965). Many investigators have obtained data relevant to the interpretation of the parent–offspring relationship (Sluckin, 1965) but, in general, such data have been collected while investigating other issues.

In the work reported here, laboratory techniques were developed to investigate directly the affiliative relationship. The basic approach applied the analytical tools of operant conditioning to elucidate the duckling's behavioral responses to an imprinted object. Presumably by experimentally elaborating the factors involved in these reactions it will be possible to understand better imprinting and the implications of imprinting for the interpretation of the primary social bond between the young organism and its parent.

Summary of experiments

Newly hatched ducklings were exposed to imprinting procedures and subsequently trained to peck a key by presenting the imprinting stimulus as the reinforcing (response contingent) event. It was found that the key peck was learned only when imprinting procedures were initiated during the first six to eight hours after hatch. Additional studies revealed that: (a) the duckling's distress vocalizations were reduced in the presence of the imprinting stimulus and enhanced in its absence; (b) when the ducklings had constant access to the imprinted stimulus (via a key peck), pecking responses occurred in bursts and relatively few distress vocalizations occurred; (c) the initial effect of extinction procedures was an increase in key peck rate. When, however, repeated key pecks failed to produce the imprinted stimulus, distress vocalization ensued and peck rate declined; (d) both the presentation of an unfamiliar mechanical figure and delivery of electrical shock enhanced distress vocalization and key pecks; (e) for some ducklings, certain familiar objects in the environment influenced distress calls in a manner comparable to the imprinted stimulus in that distress calls increased when these objects were removed. [...]

Conclusions

These findings indicate that the behavioral control exerted by the imprinted stimulus is a product of imprinting *per se* and that the imprinted stimulus more or less continuously regulates behavior. Apparently it does so in somewhat the same way that food influences behavior. When, for example, an organism is deprived of food, food-directed behavior increases in probability. A similar enhancement of behavior directed toward an imprinted stimulus occurs when the imprinted stimulus is withheld. Moreover, when the subject has free access to food, eating is not continuous but occurs in bursts. A comparable pattern emerges when the subject has free access to the imprinted stimulus. There is, however, one important difference between behaviors controlled by the imprinted stimulus and those controlled by food. Aversive stimulation enhances behavior directed toward the imprinted stimulus, whereas food-directed behavior is typically suppressed by aversive procedures.

At present, little is known about the dynamics of the behavioral control exerted by an imprinted stimulus, but the close correspondence between distress calls and the presence or absence of the imprinted stimulus suggests that responses which produce the imprinted stimulus probably serve to terminate aversive conditions which develop when the imprinted stimulus is withdrawn.

Apparently, aversive stimuli such as electrical shock or novel objects, facilitate responses which produce the imprinted stimulus by enhancing the aversive conditions on which these responses are based. The present work also reveals that for some ducklings a similar dynamics may operate with certain familiar objects (e.g. the key and/or the brooder box) in that the withdrawal of these objects generates an aversive condition which enhances both distress vocalization and approaches to the imprinted stimulus via the key peck. Even less is known about the variables responsible for this last effect.

References

BOWLBY, J. (1958), 'The nature of the child's tie to his mother', *Inter. J. Psycho-anal.*, vol. 39, pp. 1–24.
BOWLBY, J. (1960), 'Separation anxiety', *Inter. J. Psycho-anal.*, vol. 41, pp. 89–113.
CAMPBELL, B. A., and PICKLEMAN, J. R. (1961), 'The imprinting object as a reinforcing stimulus', *J. comp. physiol. Psychol.*, vol. 54, pp. 592–6.
CHURCH, R. M. (1963), 'The varied effects of punishment on behavior', *Psychol. Rev.*, vol. 70, pp. 369–402.
ESTES, W. K., and SKINNER, B. F. (1941), 'Some quantitative properties of anxiety', *J. exp. Psychol.*, vol. 29, pp. 390–400.
GOTTLIEB, G. (1963), 'A naturalistic study of imprinting in wood ducklings (*aix sponsa*)', *J. comp. physiol. Psychol.*, vol. 56, pp. 86–91.
HAFEZ, E. S. E. (1962), *The Behaviour of Domestic Animals*, Ballière, Tindall & Cox.
HARLOW, H. F., and ZIMMERMANN R. R. (1958), 'The development of affectional responses in infant monkeys', *Proc. Amer. Phil. Soc.*, vol. 102, pp. 501–9.
HARLOW, H. F., and ZIMMERMANN, R. R. (1959), 'Affectional responses in the infant monkey', *Science*, vol. 130, pp. 421–32.
HESS, E. H. (1964), 'Imprinting in birds', *Science*, vol. 146, pp. 1128–39.
JAYNES, J. (1957), 'Imprinting: the interaction of learned and innate behavior: II. The critical period', *J. comp. physiol. Psychol.*, vol. 50, pp. 6–10.
KOVACH, J. K., and HESS, E. H. (1963), 'Imprinting: effects of painful stimulation upon the following response', *J. comp. physiol. Psychol.*, vol. 56, pp. 461–4.
MOLTZ, H. (1960), 'Imprinting: empirical basis and theoretical significance', *Psychol. Bull.*, vol. 57, pp. 291–314.
MOLTZ, H., ROSENBLUM, L., and HALIKAS, N. (1959), 'Imprinting and level of anxiety', *J. comp. physiol. Psychol.*, vol. 52, pp. 240–44.
PETERSON, N. (1960), 'Control of behavior by presentation of an imprinting stimulus', *Science*, vol. 132, pp. 1295–6.

SIDMAN, M., HERRNSTEIN, F. J., and CONRAD, D. G. (1957), 'Maintenance of avoidance behavior by unavoidable shocks', *J. comp. physiol. Psychol.*, vol. 50, pp. 553–7.

SLUCKIN, W. (1965), *Imprinting and Early Learning*, Aldine.

TAYLOR, K. F., and SLUCKIN, W. (1964), 'An experiment in tactile imprinting', *Bull. Brit. Psychol. Soc.*, vol. 17, no. 54, 10A.

Part Three Learning and Development

Interest in the study of early learning was enormously stimulated by Hebb (Reading 9). He attempted to achieve an understanding of the development of learning from early to later stages. The theme was taken up by Vince (Reading 10) who considered at length the evidence from her own experiments, and much other work besides, for her view of the developmental changes in learning capacity. A survey from a comparative angle of behavioural development in general, and learning in particular, is presented by Scott (Reading 11). Given certain characteristics of early learning, we may ask what the conditions conducive to efficient learning early in life are. Caldwell (Reading 12) expresses some views on the subject as far as the young child is concerned. The student will note that this last Reading ties up with the topic of Part Six and especially Reading 23.

9 D. O. Hebb

The Relation of Early to Later Learning

Excerpts from chapter 6 of D. O. Hebb, *The Organization of Behavior*, Wiley, 1949, pp. 109–16.

In this section I shall bring together the behavioral evidence on the relationship between learning in infancy and that of the normal adult animal. [...]

It is proposed that the characteristics of learning undergo an important change as the animal grows, particularly in the higher mammals; that all learning tends to utilize and build on any earlier learning, instead of replacing it (Mowrer, 1941), so that much earlier learning tends to be permanent (Hunt, 1941; Tinbergen, 1942); and, finally, that the learning of the mature animal owes its efficiency to the slow and inefficient learning that has gone before, but may also be limited and canalized by it.

The general proposition

It is, of course, a truism that learning is often influenced by earlier learning. Innumerable experiments have shown such a 'transfer of training'. Learning A may be speeded up, hindered, or qualitatively changed by having learned B before. The question for debate is how great the effect may be in general behavioral development (as distinct from the effect of some one specific habit on some other) and what theoretical use is to be made of it.

McGeoch (1942, pp. 445–6), for example, has said:

After small amounts of learning early in the life of the individual, every instance of learning is a function of the already learned organization of the subject; that is, all learning is influenced by transfer....

The learning of complex, abstract, meaningful materials and the solution of problems by means of ideas (reasoning) are to a great extent functions of transfer. Where the subject 'sees into' the fundamental relations of a problem or has insight, transfer seems to be a major contributing condition. It is, likewise, a basic factor in originality, the original and creative person having, among other things, unusual sensitivity to the applicability of the already known to new problem situations. Perceiving, at whatever level, is probably never free of its influence; and there is no complex psychological event which is not a function of it.

Those are strong words and I propose that they must be taken literally – as presumably they were meant to be taken. Unless we are to regard them as just a lip service to logic and the known facts of behavior, they must influence general psychological theory profoundly. If the learning we know and can study, in the mature animal, is heavily loaded with transfer effects, what are the properties of the original learning from which those effects came? How can it be possible even to consider making a theory of learning in general from the data of maturity only? There must be a serious risk that what seems to be learning is really half transfer. We cannot assume that we know what learning transfers and what it does not: for our knowledge of the extent of transfer is also derived from behavior at maturity, and the transfer from infant experiences may be much greater and more generalized.

An example, in itself important for the theory of learning, will also show the dangers of generalizing from adult to infant behavior with regard to transfer. A student once pointed out to me that James's famous experiment on memorization begged the question. James wanted to see if practice in memorization would increase the ability to memorize. He found it did not, and later writers have found the same thing. As a result, it has been concluded that practice *per se* has little or no transfer value, without instruction as to better methods of learning. But all this is done with adults who have had long practice already, and the student pointed out that the transfer effects *must have been complete before the experiments began*, and could not be demonstrated by the method used. James (1890) used highly educated adult subjects, Woodrow (1927) college sophomores. What would have been the result with subjects who had done no memorization before? We do not know, but it is certainly quite illogical to conclude that undirected practice has no transfer value because we find no evidence of it where there is no reason for expecting it. Above all, it would be illogical to conclude from this sort of evidence that the incidental learning of infancy has a negligible effect on later learning.

It has already been emphasized that perception is affected by past experience (Carmichael, Hogan, and Walter, 1932; Gibson, 1929; Krechevsky, 1938; Leeper, 1935; Zangwill, 1937). What is learned is in terms of what is perceived: what is not perceived can hardly be remembered. Koffka (1935) has emphasized that patterns may be seen and remembered by the arousal of 'older trace systems'; Woodworth (1938) says that all perceiving is 'schema with correction', that is, in terms of earlier perceptual habits. How do these habits get established in the first place? What are the properties of the learning that sets up the 'older trace systems', of learning in its first stages, before there are any earlier habits to help it along? These questions cannot be completely answered at present, but even the skimpy evidence we have is enough to reorient the whole problem of learning.

The first learning of primates is extremely slow and very different from that at maturity

There are two kinds of learning. One is that of the newborn infant, or the visual learning of the adult reared in darkness or with congenital cataract; the other that of the normal adult. I have repeatedly cited the behavior of the patient born blind and given his sight after motor (and speech) development was well along, to show that the first learning is extremely inefficient as far as detectable effects on behavior are concerned, despite the completion of physical maturation (von Senden, 1932). Here it is referred to once more, partly to show that the early inefficiency is not due to poor motivation and partly to make a comparison of man with other species.

Von Senden reports a serious disturbance of motivation, apparently in all cases, at one stage of learning. But this cannot be the main cause of the slowness of learning, for two reasons.

1. Motivation is not disturbed in the first stage, immediately upon beginning to use the eyes. At first there is a period of delight, particularly in colors, and apparently a complete preoccupation with the new experience.

Before long, the patient finds out how hard it is to get an

effective use of pattern vision. The 'crisis' of motivation then ensues. Until that point there is interest and application; things that are easy to learn are learned and not forgotten; color names are readily remembered, but it takes a long apprenticeship before any useful or demonstrable learning occurs in pattern vision.

Learning is evidently going on in this period, as long as the patient continues to keep his eyes open and makes any effort, but it can hardly be demonstrated except in the later increase of efficiency.

2. The second reason for denying that poor motivation explains the poor learning of man, in his first visual experience, comes from the observations of Riesen (1947). His chimpanzees, reared in darkness, were certainly motivated: both by hunger and by their strong drive to find and cling tightly to an attendant when they were out of their living cages. Yet there was no sign that either hunger or the desire to cling had taught them, in forty to fifty hours' visual experience, how to discriminate the white-clad attendant from any other part of the environment. Astonishing as it was, the chimpanzees appeared to be completely avisual at this stage of the experiment.

Moreover, in further tests, a strong electric shock failed in a dozen trials to set up any avoidance whatever of a large, distinctive stimulus object. After a single trial, normal animals of the same age and in similar circumstances showed violent avoidance of the object with such painful properties. In the slowness of their first visual learning, man and chimpanzee are in the same class. The human slowness is not due to defects of motivation, but points to some fundamental property of the learning process in primates.

Relationship of learning to phylogenesis

The conclusion that the first learning differs radically from the later one needs most important qualification: the difference depends on phylogenetic level.

The evidence so far has been for the higher primates only. Training in pattern vision is slower for the rat reared in darkness than for normal rats, but the difference is not nearly as great as for chimpanzee or man. The rat reared in darkness is capable of a selective visual discrimination, definitely learned, after a total visual experience of less than fifteen minutes (Hebb, 1937, pp. 113-115). He requires six times as many trials as the normal to learn a discrimination of horizontal from vertical stripes, and twice as many for erect versus inverted triangles, but within an hour or so his behavior cannot be distinguished from that of normal animals. As we have seen, the corresponding time for primates is a matter of weeks or months.

There are no comparable data for other species, but some insect behavior suggests strongly that the first learning of the invertebrate is still quicker and much prompter in reaching full efficiency than the rat's. What learning ability there is seems to appear fullblown, with little or no apprenticeship needed. The bee, for example, on first emerging from a completely dark hive flies off and is able to find the entrance to the hive again. We know also that finding the hive depends on vision. The behavior indicates that the insect's learning starts out, from the very first, at the mature level of efficiency. [Much that we attribute to instinct, because no *prolonged* learning is evident, might thus be due to learning that needs only a few seconds for its completion. The associations that are formed may be only certain ones to which the nervous system is especially adapted (Tinbergen, 1942, p. 82): heredity would still have an overmastering importance, but learning may nevertheless be essential to some apparently instinctive acts.]

As we go up the phylogenetic scale, then, we find in mature animals an increasing ability to learn complex relationships, but also, surprisingly, a slower and slower rate of learning in infancy.

This does not refer merely to the fact that higher animals have a longer period of physical maturation. We have always known that a rat grows up and develops whatever capacities the adult rat has, in three months – or a dog in six months, whereas a chimpanzee takes ten years and a man twenty years. We have thought, I suppose (if the question ever came up at all), that this longer period of behavioral development meant only that maturation takes longer in the primate and that with less instinct he has more to learn. But the clinical and experimental evidence points to an additional factor. Given a really new and unfamiliar set of sensations to be associated with motor responses, selectively, the first definite and clearcut association appears sooner in rat than in man and apparently sooner in the insect than in the rat.

We commonly regard quick learning as the main distinction of higher species and in certain conditions this is true. Normal man can glance once at a face and remember it for years. The chimpanzee Bimba was pricked once with a lancet and never again would permit it to be brought near her – but with no avoidance of other objects of the same size or roughly the same proportions (Finch, 1940).[1] This is something completely outside the rat's scope. We think of it as intelligent learning and are prone to regard it as an innate property of the primate brain. It cannot be innate, however, as Riesen's evidence shows. So also with the ability to remember faces: Miner's (1905) patient, described as exceptionally intelligent despite her congenital cataract, two years after operation had learned to recognize only four or five faces and in daily conferences with two persons for a month did not learn to recognize them by vision. The human baby takes six months, the chimpanzee four months, before making a clear distinction visually between friend and enemy. Evidently, this is a period of learning as well as of maturation: not just a matter of waiting until certain neural structures are fully grown, with learning then at a typical adult rate.

There have been, in general, two schools of thought concerning the rate of learning. The configurationists, stressing the importance of insight, have been inclined to hold that learning occurs as a single jump, an all-or-none affair proceeding by discrete steps ('noncontinuity theory'); their opponents, that learning is graded in amount, built up steadily by small increments and typically independent of any special factor of insight ('continuity theory').

But it is impossible to avoid the conclusion that both types of learning occur and that one is characteristic of the mature animal, the other mainly of the infant. There *is* insightful, single-trial, all-or-none learning – in the mature animal, but never in the in-

1. It is relevant here, in discussing the nature of learning in higher species, to add a reference also to the remarkable learning capacity of rhesus monkeys that Harlow (1949) has demonstrated in a long series of experiments. Harlow's whole argument, showing how the learning capacity may be changed out of all recognition by prolonged experience, is a powerful reinforcement of the position adopted in these pages.

fant of a higher species. There *is* a slow-increment learning in the infant, in which no trace of insight whatever can be found, and in the mature animal also when he has been reared in darkness and is learning to use vision. It is reasonable to suppose in general that the less familiar the situation or the task to be performed, the more important slow-increment learning becomes. But it seems also that few situations can be set up in which there is nothing familiar, so that it would be very hard to find an instance of learning in the mature animal in which there is not some effect of insight.

We are now in a position to define the relationship of the learning capacity to phylogenetic level. There is no evidence to support the idea that learning *in general* is faster in higher species – even at maturity. In the infant, the evidence is conclusive that the rate of the first learning is slowest in the highest species, quite apart from slowness of maturation. The distinctive characteristic of learning in higher species is the ability to handle complex relationships and handle them as quickly as lower species can handle simpler ones. Man can learn to unfasten a latch quicker than the chimpanzee, the chimpanzee quicker than a rat; but, if we take the learning at which each species is most efficient, there is no good evidence that one is faster than another.

Lashley (1929) has made this point effectively. After discussing an experiment by Pechstein in which rats and human subjects learned mazes of identical pattern and in which the rats showed to rather good advantage – in one respect their scores were better than those of the human subjects – Lashley goes on to point out that with simple enough habits lower species and the feeble-minded learn about as fast as normal man. Such habits are not retarded, in rate of formation, by extensive brain damage. There is also reason to think that immediate incidental memory occurs in lower species, and Lashley concludes:

> The comparative study of learning in different animals gives little evidence that evolution has brought any change in the rate of formation of the simpler habits. On the other hand, there is a fairly consistent rise in the limits of training and in the formation of complex habits with ascent in the phylogenetic scale.

In summary, then, the phylogenetic changes in the learning

capacity are as follows: (a) more complex relationships can be learned by higher species at maturity; (b) simple relationships are learned about as promptly by lower as by higher species; and (c) the first learning is *slower* in higher than in lower species.

References

CARMICHAEL, L., HOGAN, H. P., and WALTER, A. A. (1932), 'An experimental study of the effect of language on the reproduction of visually perceived form', *J. exp. Psychol.*, vol. 15, pp. 73–86.

FINCH, G. (1940), 'Diary of Bimba', Yerkes Laboratories of Primate Biology, Florida.

GIBSON, J. J. (1929), 'The reproduction of visually perceived forms', *J. exp. Psychol.*, vol. 12, pp. 1–39.

HARLOW, H. F. (1949), 'The formation of learning sets', *Psychol. Rev.*, vol. 56, pp. 51–65.

HEBB, D. O. (1937), 'The innate organization of visual activity: I. Perception of figures by rats reared in total darkness', *J. genet. Psychol.*, vol. 51, pp. 101–26.

HUNT, J. McV. (1941), 'The effects of infant feeding-frustration upon adult hoarding in the adult rat', *J. abnorm. soc. Psychol.*, vol. 36, pp. 338–60.

JAMES, W. (1890), *The Principles of Psychology*, Holt, Rinehart & Winston, 1910.

KOFFKA, K. (1935), *Principles of Gestalt Psychology*, Harcourt, Brace & World.

KRECHEVSKY, I. (1938), 'An experimental investigation of the principle of proximity in the visual perception of the rat', *J. exp. Psychol.*, vol. 22, pp. 497–523.

LASHLEY, K. S. (1929), 'Nervous mechanisms in learning', in C. Murchison (ed.), *The Foundations of Experimental Psychology*, Clark University Press, pp. 524–63.

LEEPER, R. W. (1935), 'A study of a neglected portion of the field of learning – the development of sensory organization', *J. genet. Psychol.*, vol. 46, pp. 41–75.

McGEOCH, J. A. (1942), *The Psychology of Human Learning*, Longman.

MINER, J. B. (1905), 'A case of vision acquired in adult life', *Psychol. Rev. Monogr. Suppl.*, vol. 6, no. 5, pp. 103–18.

MOWRER, O. H. (1941), 'Motivation and learning in relation to the national emergency', *Psychol. Bull.*, vol. 38, pp. 421–31.

RIESEN, A. H. (1947), 'The development of visual perception in man and chimpanzee', *Science*, vol. 106, pp. 107–8.

TINBERGEN, N. (1942), 'An objectivistic study of the innate behaviour of animals', *Bibl. Biotheoret., Leiden*, vol. 1, pp. 39–98.

VON SENDEN, M. (1932), *Raum- und Gestaltauffassung bei operierten Blindgeborenen vor und nach der Operation*, Barth, Leipzig.

Woodrow, H. (1927), 'The effect of type of training on transference', *J. educ. Psychol.*, vol. 18, pp. 160–71.

Woodworth, R. S. (1938), *Experimental Psychology*, Holt, Rinehart & Winston.

Zangwill, O. L. (1937), 'A study of the significance of attitude in recognition', *Brit. J. Psychol.*, vol. 28, pp. 12–17.

10 M. A. Vince

Developmental Changes in Learning Capacity

M. A. Vince, 'Developmental changes in learning capacity', in
W. H. Thorpe and O. L. Zangwill (eds.), *Current Problems in Animal
Behaviour*, Cambridge University Press, 1961, pp. 225–47.

Introduction

The way in which an animal's learning capacity develops with age is not yet understood. It is difficult to decide from the work published in this field whether there are developmental changes in learning separate from the effects of growth or of changes in neuromuscular coordination, experience and motivation; or whether indeed the problem has ever been satisfactorily formulated. An early attack on this question was made in 1903 with J. B. Watson's work on 'The development of the psyche in the white rat', and in 1929 the question was to some extent diverted by C. P. Stone's monographs on 'The age factor in animal learning'. Stone came to the conclusion that age differences appearing in animal learning experiments could be attributed solely to motivational change.

More recently work on children and some on birds, and also work on the effects of early experience on mammalian behaviour, suggest that although Stone's conclusions are important, there are developmental changes in the behaviour underlying learning which cannot be understood in motivational terms. The purpose of this chapter is to examine some of this work and discuss its significance as well as some of the experimental difficulties inherent in it.

The work on birds will be considered first.

Some developmental changes in birds

In all the work described in this section an attempt was made to keep motivation, in Stone's sense of a hunger 'drive', at a low level by allowing the birds to feed normally throughout the testing.

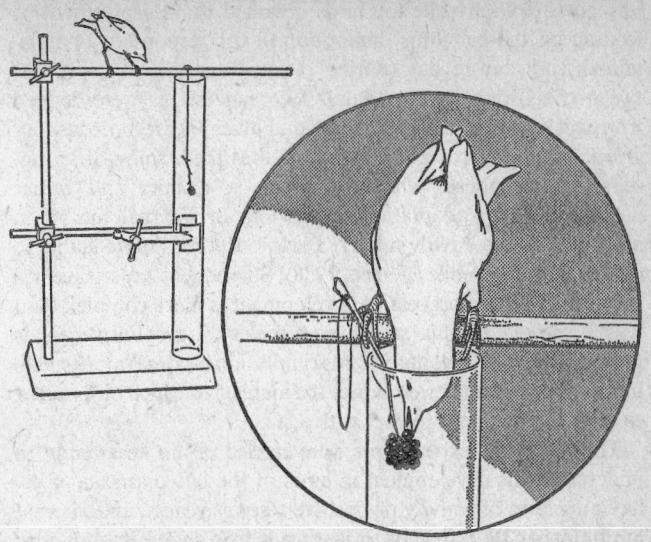

Figure 1 Left: 'string-pulling' situation. Right: a canary reaches for the bait while holding a pulled-in loop of string with one foot

In the first experiment a clear-cut difference was found between juvenile and adult finches in a simple learning situation. This situation has been described in detail by Thorpe (1956). The birds were fed at intervals with a certain type of food on a particular perch. Later the food was suspended from this perch on the end of a string which had to be pulled up and held before the bait could be eaten, as the string was suspended inside a glass cylinder (Figure 1). In this situation some juveniles were successful within the test period of twelve half-hour trials but all adults failed. Records of the birds' behaviour while they were being tested showed that success was related to the length of time spent responding in the experimental situation: the young birds were more continuously engaged in pulling at the string and so on, and spent less time in each trial in such irrelevant activity as preening, feeding, sleeping and bathing than the adults. In respect to the experimental situation the young birds thus appeared to be more responsive than adults of the same species. In addition the records showed that whereas the response of all birds waned during any unsuccessful trial while the birds obtained no reinforcement by feeding on the bait, this diminution in the response was maintained from day to day (during twenty-four-hour intervals between trials) only in the adults. Two suggestions were derived from this experiment. The first was that juveniles are more responsive than adult birds and the second that the waning of an unreinforced response, which represents a distinct and rather delicate form of adaptation (extinction, or internal inhibition according to the Pavlov theory: Pavlov, 1927), is more stable in adults than in juveniles (Vince, 1958). Subsequent experience has suggested that the process of development is more complex than was suspected at this stage; nevertheless if responsiveness is greater in the juveniles and internal inhibition becomes more stable in the adults, we may well expect the manner in which birds adapt to their surroundings to vary with age.

The remaining experiments were carried out in an attempt to understand the development in birds of these two aspects of behaviour: level of activity or positive responsiveness, and internal inhibition or the capacity to learn not to respond in situations where a response is not reinforced.

The second point will be dealt with first.

The development of internal inhibition in birds

The test situation used in the next two experiments was the same and was very simple. The results of the previous experiments suggested that internal inhibition is weak in young birds. According to Pavlov's theory, internal inhibition is the basis not only of extinction but also of a differentiation: the capacity to respond differently to similar stimuli some of which are and some of which are not reinforced. The birds were trained to remove a white cardboard lid from a dish containing food (Figure 2). When the lid-removing response had become stable, they were presented in random order either with the dish containing food and covered with a white lid or with the same dish, empty and covered with a black lid. A bird responding adaptively in this situation continued to feed by pulling off white lids and after pulling off the black lid a few times gradually ceased to respond to this negative stimulus, indicating as it did an empty dish. In this situation, therefore, the time taken by the bird to remove the black lid (negative latency), or the number

Figure 2 A hand-reared great tit removes white lid from dish containing food. Differentiation situation

of correct negative trials when the black lid was not removed at all, was a measure of internal inhibition.

In the next experiment (Vince, 1959) twenty positive and twenty negative trials were given in random order to five groups of finches; a group of adult canaries and a group of juvenile canaries; also three groups of greenfinches – wild adults, hand-reared juveniles and aviary-reared juveniles.

The results of this experiment were, at first sight, confusing. The aviary-reared juvenile greenfinches achieved by far the highest proportion of correct negative responses: they gave up removing the black lid after very few trials and did not touch it again. The other juveniles gave results which were on the whole weaker than adults of the same species. This latter difference was not, however, entirely clear-cut. The hand-reared greenfinches and juvenile canaries actually made correct negative responses sooner than the adults and their performance was superior in the first ten trials, but it appeared that the task was easier for the juveniles as their responses to the black lid were weaker initially, giving longer latencies. Also in the second half of the experiment the adults of both species put up the best performance: they were slow to give up responding to the black lid but once they had done so they were able to ignore it

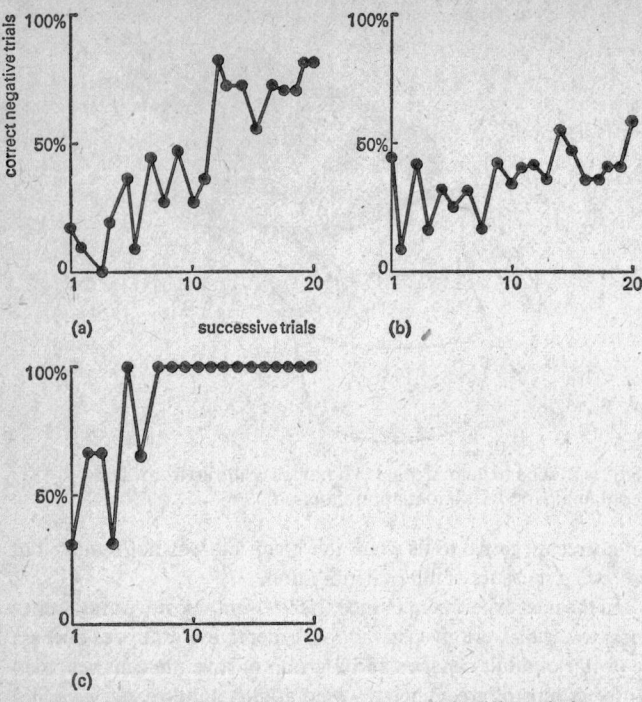

Figure 3 Mean number of correct negative trials in differentiation experiment with finches (from Vince, 1959). (a) Adult canaries and adult greenfinches, (b) juvenile canaries and hand-reared juvenile greenfinches and (c) aviary-reared juvenile greenfinches

more consistently than the juveniles, whose early differentiations tended to break down (Figure 3).

Although the results obtained from wild adult and hand-reared greenfinches and from adult and juvenile canaries confirm the view that there is an improvement with age, those obtained from the aviary-reared juveniles do not, and it is clear that these results are not consistent with any hypothesis that internal inhibition develops as a function of age alone; in greenfinches the best and worst performances were obtained from the two juvenile groups, the hand-reared and aviary-reared birds. The results can, however, be understood if a second variable is considered, that of individual experience or conditions of rearing. The canaries had all been reared and kept under comparable, rather restricted conditions and in this, as in the previous experiment, there was evidence of an improvement with age in this species. If variety of early experience is a factor affecting development, then the aviary-reared juvenile greenfinches, given their richer experience, may be supposed to represent a later stage of development than their hand-reared contemporaries, and if this is so we have again an indication of improvement which would normally occur with age. However, the performance of the adult wild greenfinches, although superior to that of the hand-reared birds, was inferior to that of the aviary-reared birds. It seems likely that the adults will have been through the stages of development represented first by the hand-reared and secondly by the aviary-reared birds. These results, therefore, led to the suggestion that the process of development of internal inhibition, if considered as a function of age, must be represented by a curve which rises to its maximum in the juveniles and later falls slightly; and also that a richer or more varied experience may well change the slope of the curve, giving a sharper rise possibly to a higher level.

These suggestions have received some confirmation in experiments carried out on the great tit (Vince, 1960). Here the birds were originally all wild, but some were taken as nestlings, reared by hand and subsequently kept and tested indoors. The others were taken as juveniles, having been reared in the wild, and were tested under the same conditions as the first group. The hand-reared birds were tested at ages ranging from four and a half to seventy-three weeks from the date of fledging. Only two groups of wild-reared birds, those whose ages can be assessed with some confidence, will be considered here. These were tested at approximately eight and twenty weeks after fledging. These birds were all given the same task as the finches in the previous experiment, that of differentiating between a dish containing food and covered with a white lid, and an empty dish covered with a black lid. But they were given up to forty instead of twenty positive and negative trials.

The level of performance achieved by each individual tested is indicated in Figure 4. Here the individual performances were assessed by counting the number of negative trials before the bird achieved the criterion of two successive correct trials, when the black lid was not touched at all. Individual records giving the latency in successive positive and negative trials and showing (a) a good performance and (b) a poor performance are given in Figure 5. Here short negative latencies indicate that the bird failed to make the differentiation, continuing to pull off black as well as white lids, while longer negative latencies indicate that the bird was able, to some extent at least, to ignore the negative stimulus.

The individual scores given in Figure 4 suggest that, although there are large individual differences, there was in fact some improvement with age in the capacity to learn not to respond, followed by a decrease in this capacity in the hand-reared adults. Although the wild-reared birds were few, there are indications that a similar curve might be expected from them and, as predicted, their performance is considerably superior to that of the hand-reared birds. There are, however, great difficulties in comparing the performance of animals reared under different conditions. These are discussed elsewhere in relation to the present work (Vince, 1960) and in more general terms have been set out by Beach and Jaynes (1954) and by King (1958).

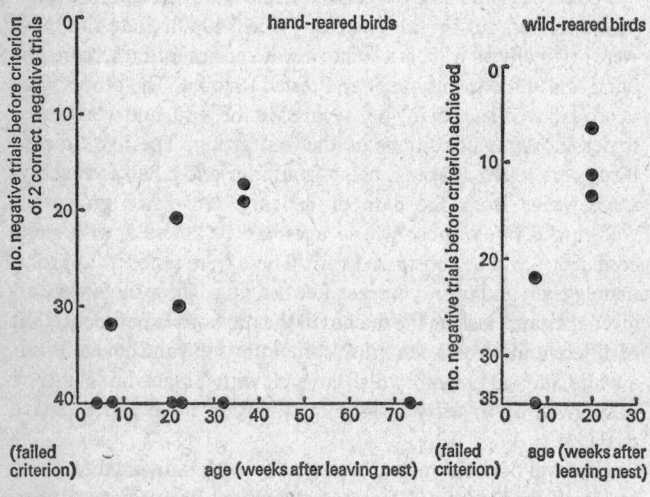

Figure 4 Performance of individual hand-reared and wild-reared great tits in differentiation experiment (from Vince, 1960)

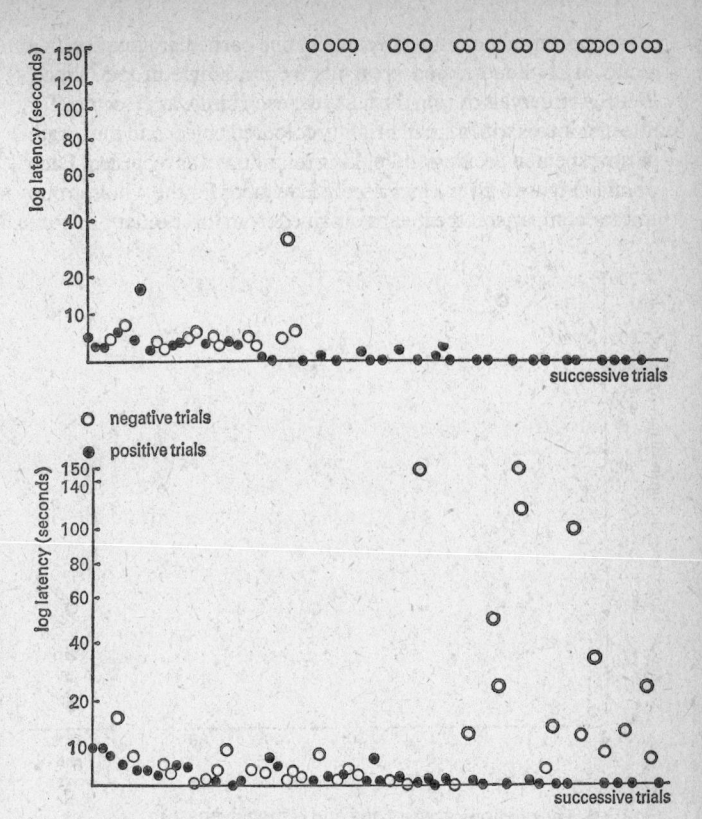

Figure 5 Individual records from differentiation experiment. Top record: wild-reared great tit, approximately twenty weeks after leaving nest; lower record: wild-reared great tit, approximately eight weeks after leaving nest (from Vince, 1960)

The development of positive responsiveness in birds

The first experiment described suggested that juvenile finches were more responsive than adult finches; the question which now arises is whether there are changes in responsiveness or level of activity which, if plotted against age, will provide a curve similar to that of internal inhibition.

Such curves can certainly be obtained. Figure 6 shows the

changes with age in responsiveness in one particular situation in a group of six hand-reared great tits from a single brood (Vince, 1960). At intervals during the first year each bird was presented for fifteen minutes with a small brightly coloured object and the length of time spent in pecking and pulling this about was recorded. Each point in Figure 6 gives a mean score in seconds for the whole group and for comparison the means obtained from three older birds are

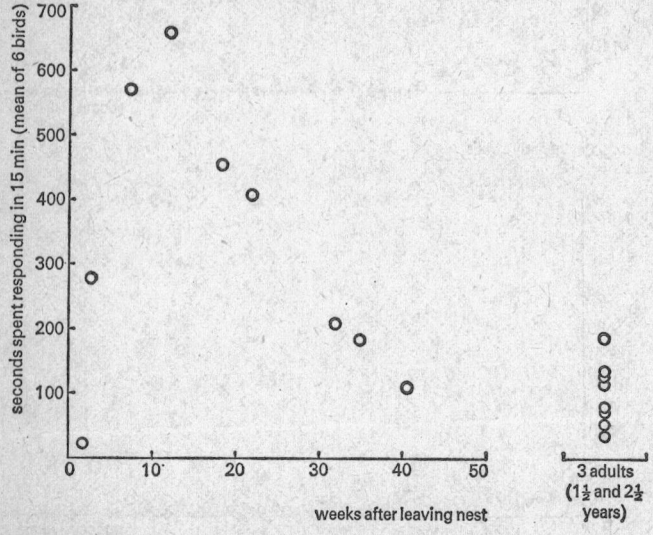

Figure 6 The relation between age and responsiveness in hand-reared great tits (from Vince, 1960)

also shown. In this situation responsiveness increased from a very low level when measured at two weeks after leaving the nest, to a maximum between ten and twenty weeks. It then fell off rather rapidly and soon after thirty weeks reached the level achieved by a group of adults similarly tested. No data of this kind are yet available for the wild-reared birds.

If, therefore, we take birds of a particular species, rear and keep them under fairly homogeneous conditions and test them at different ages, we find quite complex developmental changes occurring during their first year. Responsiveness, in the positive sense, at first appears to be very low; it then rises rapidly to its maximum level at about thirteen weeks, and drops again to a certain extent. Similarly, but apparently at a slower rate, there is an improvement in the capacity not to respond inappropriately or uselessly (internal inhibition). The relation between these two processes appears in Figure 7 where for the sake of clarity the trend of each curve is indicated by broken lines, although curves have not been fitted.

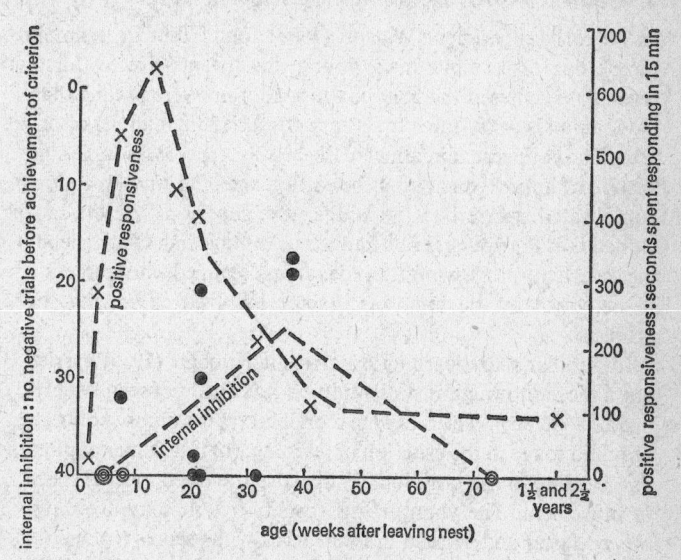

Figure 7 The relation between changes in positive and negative responsiveness in hand-reared great tits (from Vince, 1960)

The relative height of these two curves is, of course, of no significance, but the data suggest that internal inhibition is still being strengthened at an age when positive responsiveness is well past its peak.

This work, therefore, suggests the existence of developmental changes in bird behaviour of the type which must have some bearing on learning tasks. In view of the inhibitory as well as excitatory changes, these can hardly be accounted for in terms of a single factor, such as learning capacity or motivation. In addition, although these changes can be related with age, the difference between birds reared under different conditions suggests that they cannot be accounted for exclusively in this way: individual experience is at least an important element in this type of development.

The question to be discussed below is whether these results bear any relation to, or throw any light on, existing work on the development of learning capacity in other species and in man.

The relation between age and learning ability in the rat

In an early experiment Watson (1903) found that in a simple puzzle box or a simple maze young rats (twenty-five to thirty-seven days) entered the goal box in a shorter average time than older animals (sixty-three to seventy days) and than adults of one year. The youngest animals were the best, but there was some suggestion of improvement after the earliest age of testing. In a more complicated puzzle box the adults were superior. Watson concluded that the younger rats had the advantage in a task depending on activity alone while the older animals gained when direction of activity was the important factor involved in solving the problem.

In another maze-learning experiment Hubbert (1915) carried out a more thorough investigation on rats aged between twenty-five and 300 days. The rats were scored for (a) the number of trials required to reach the criterion of learning, (b) total time required for learning to this criterion, (c) distance traversed and (d) speed of movement. The younger rats (twenty-five to sixty-five days) moved faster and learned in fewer trials while scores (b) and (c) showed an optimum age at sixty-five days, when the total time spent in learning and the distance traversed was less than in other groups. In addition Hubbert came to the conclusion that learning in the younger rats was most rapid during the early trials, while for the older rats it was more rapid during the later trials.

A suggestion made by both Watson and Hubbert that there may be an improvement with age during the period immediately following weaning is supported by Biel (1940) who used a maze and rats aged between seventeen and thirty days; and by Liu (1928). Liu, in maze-learning involving seven groups of rats between the ages of thirty and 250 days, found an optimum performance in the seventy-five-day group, followed by a deterioration up to 250 days. The same trend was exhibited according to all his criteria: number of trials required to reach the criterion of learning, time and number of errors. This peak at seventy-five days is slightly less than the age at which activity in revolving and stationary cages and also nest-building activity reaches its maximum in the laboratory rat (Richter, 1922; Slonaker, 1912). It may be worth noting here that Cruze (1938) has demonstrated an improvement with age in mazes and a problem box in chickens tested from twenty-four hours to three weeks after hatching.

Maier (1932) substituted for the maze a problem involving the ability to combine two isolated experiences and found the performance of rats aged between fifty and ninety days *inferior* to that of rats aged between 120 and 300 days. Maier does not report any deterioration in the oldest rats, similar to that found by Hubbert, Liu and Watson, in maze learning. His findings may support Watson's contention that a task requiring directed rather than superabundant activity gives the advantage to older animals.

Stone (1929a and b) carried out an extended series of experiments on the age factor in learning in the rat. These experiments are frequently quoted as decisive disproof of developmental changes in learning (see, for example, Munn, 1950). Stone's conclusions were that the approximately maximum learning rate for mazes, problem boxes and a simple light discrimination is reached at thirty to seventy days and that this does not decline during the first two years of life. The differences obtained by others he regarded as spurious, due to faulty control of motivation, faulty techniques which 'provide pitfalls for the slapdash impulsive young or cater to the home cage habits which are inevitably fixed more strongly in adults than the young' and to time scores obtained from unhealthy adults.

Stone varied motivation (hunger 'drive'), age and intensiveness of training with his various learning tasks. As a result he found that younger rats learned in fewer trials than the older ones (a) when food deprivation was not too severe, (b) when an old habit had to be broken up and the opposite habit learned, (c) when early trials only were considered, (d) when training was more intensive and (e) when the task was very difficult. Under conditions of severe food deprivation or relearning, when two experiments were run simultaneously and when later trials only were considered, there were no marked differences with rats of different ages. In a single experiment in an easy maze the older rats were superior. On the whole it seems that the older rats learned more slowly and, once established, their habits were more fixed, but when hard pressed they could reach a level of performance equal to that of the younger ones.

There are two ways of looking at Stone's work.

If Stone's conclusions are correct, then there is some kind of absolute 'learning capacity' which remains approximately constant from about seventy days onwards and is revealed under particular conditions in the older animals. On the other hand, the data provided by Stone give evidence of complex behavioural change with age which he does not attempt to account for. Some of the differences, for example, that younger animals were superior in early trials only and were more flexible, are consistent with those described in birds.

However, it may not be desirable to make too detailed a comparison between the rat and the bird work. In the rat experiments mazes, problem and discrimination boxes provide situations where learning can be observed, but whose complexity makes it difficult to analyse the processes involved in the learning. Such a criticism is of course irrelevant to the experimenters concerned because they were in fact looking for something absolute in the nature of 'learning capacity' which varied with age.

These experiments on rats may be summarized as follows: learning, as measured by scores obtained in mazes and puzzle boxes, becomes more rapid up to the age of about seventy days and later becomes less rapid. The performance of older rats can, however, be raised to the level of the juveniles by increasing motivation or hunger 'drive'. In addition to these main findings it would appear that older and younger rats learn in slightly different ways. There are also experiments where a different type of situation was used which gave results of the opposite kind: the performance of the adults was superior to that of the juveniles. This lack of consistency suggests that behavioural changes occurring with development may be more complex or more delicate than can be understood either in terms of 'learning capacity' or of 'motivation'.

Some effects of experience on learning ability

There was evidence in the work on birds that individual experience was a factor affecting the process of development. Individual experience was largely ignored in the rat experiments. More recently considerable interest has been shown in the effect of experience, and especially early experience, on learning ability and behaviour in general. The work in this field has been reviewed and discussed by Beach and Jaynes (1954) and by King (1958).

Beach and Jaynes point out that there are special difficulties in this work: 'anatomical differences, nutritional requirements, sensory sensibility, motor development and previous experience are closely interwoven variables with age and cannot usually be controlled independently of each other.' They consider that early experience may influence behaviour (a) by preventing the acquisition of other types of behaviour which could compete with a habit formed in response to a particular situation; (b) because motivation may be more intense in the young; and (c) because certain types of early experience influence later behaviour by structuring the individual's perceptual capacities. They conclude also that there may be critical periods in development but that here much of the evidence may be of doubtful reliability.

Some of this work, and some published since, may be considered in more detail.

In experiments on the rat, Bingham and Griffiths (1952), Forgays and Forgays (1952) and Hymovitch (1952) have shown that animals reared in a varied environment are superior in various types of test to those reared under restricted conditions. The tests used were mazes, the Lashley jumping apparatus and the Hebb–Williams closed-field test of rat intelligence, the last consisting of a series of problem-solving situations. Hymovitch reported no significant differences in performance in an alley maze. Forgays and Forgays found that the more varied the early environment, the greater its effect on problem solving at maturity.

In another experiment reported in the same paper Hymovitch varied the age at which the 'free environment' was experienced. He reports that rats reared from thirty to seventy-five days of age in a free environment and later (eighty-five to 130 days) in 'stove-pipe' cages were superior in problem solving to animals reared at the early stage in the 'stove-pipe' cages and later in the free environment. However, they were no worse than animals reared early and late in the free environment; and again, rats reared under conditions of continued restriction up to 130 days were no worse than those given early experience of the restricted environment. He concludes that the effect of the late experience is negligible. Similarly Forgus (1956) has shown that rats which have had perceptual experience with specific two-dimensional forms are superior in discrimination and form generalization to rats which have not had such experience. He found also that rats which have this experience from nought to forty-one days are superior in form discrimination and generalization to rats which have the experience from forty-one to sixty-six days.

Thompson and Heron (1954a and b) have considered the effects of early restriction on activity and the problem solving capacity of dogs. They have interpreted 'problem solving' rather widely and some of their experimental situations are outstandingly simple. They show (1954a) that the exploratory activity of dogs reared under restricted conditions was subsequently greater than that of those reared normally, even when both groups had been living under identical, non-restricted conditions for a year or more, and younger dogs were more active than older dogs. In other experiments (1954b), they found that the animals which had been reared under restricted conditions tended to perseverate, for example, they had more difficulty than normals in breaking the habit of running straight to food when a chicken wire barrier was put between them and it, and they tended to go to the corner where they had been trained to feed even when they were shown food in a different corner. They were also virtually incapable of delayed reactions. Again, the effects of restriction were detectable after a year.

Forgays and Forgays, Hymovitch, and Thompson and Heron interpret their results largely in terms of visual experience and perceptual learning. Hymovitch has reported that rats reared in small-mesh cages where the animals could see out, and where the cages were moved every day, were superior in problem solving to rats reared in enclosed activity wheels where the opportunity for physical exercise was great, although free movement was restricted, and this particular although somewhat limited comparison supports their interpretation. Forgus (1955) has stressed that the early experience can be a hindrance or an aid to problem solving, depending on the nature of the experience and its relationship to the problem.

All this work is concerned with the rather specific problem of the effect of early restriction on later behaviour, rather than with the developmental problem as such. The animals were reared under specific conditions and tested later. Nevertheless it is of great importance in this discussion as it brings the factor of experience into the developmental problem in no uncertain way. There are, in addition, suggestions of a link between the effects of experience and the effects of age. For example, Thompson and Heron (1954a) have shown that restricted dogs and young dogs were more continuously active in an exploratory situation than normal and older dogs, respectively. This tendency to go on responding occurred in young as contrasted with older birds in the 'string-pulling' situation (see page 113). The tendency of restricted dogs to perseverate in situations requiring a change of response (presumably involving inhibition of the direct or previously trained response), as well as their failure in the delayed-response test, suggests that internal inhibition had not developed normally in the restricted animals, and is thus also consistent with the work on birds previously described. But it is not, at the moment, possible to do more than guess at what specifically may be missing from the environment of the restricted animals to produce this result.

Developmental work, mainly concerned with children

Developmental work in which the method used is most comparable with that in the bird work has for the most part been carried out on children. This raises obvious difficulties when we come to generalize from one to the other: differences of complexity, of life-span, of the presence or absence of speech, and of experience (which in the human child is almost completely beyond experimental control) have to be borne in mind.

There are two main lines of work which are relevant here, each with its characteristic approach, but as the conclusions are similar they will be discussed together.

Luria (1932) has dealt with the development of some very simple reactions in small children. His observations were made in situations which adults would normally regard as elementary: making rhythmic pressures in a pneumatic apparatus, making simple reactions such as pressing a button on receiving a signal and making 'delayed' movements, the last being a slow controlled up-and-down movement, the kymographic trace of which has a 'regular cupola form' in the adult. In testing children aged from two to seven years he found that the capacity to make these responses develops slowly. A child of two to three years was capable of making the right kind of pressure, but in successive responses the rhythm rapidly broke down. Children of four to five could make simple reactions to a signal, but each signal tended to produce many such movements so that gaps between signals were often filled with extra responses; sometimes these extra responses could be inhibited even in children younger than three or four, but this might disrupt the habit so that the occurrence of a signal inhibited the reaction. As a rule Luria found the 'delayed' movement to be impossible for a child up to seven years; in the younger children such movements were indistinguishable from rapid responses, and in older ones signs of slowing down might appear, but late, or spasmodically, giving an appearance of conflict in the trace.

Luria maintains that the excitatory aspect of behaviour presents no problem for the small child. The difficulty lies in controlling the 'intense masses of excitation' provoked by a signal. Every small child is capable of direct activity and in order to understand development it is necessary to study the regulation and control of behaviour.

In a more detailed account and a somewhat more clear-cut situation Paramonova (1955) reports that a three-year-old child can learn to press a key in response to a signal such as a red lamp; however, he usually gives the same response to other signals, such as a yellow or a green light. At this age it is beyond a child's powers to refrain from making this generalized response, even though the instructions to do so are well understood. Signs of restraint may appear, but belatedly or inappropriately as a series of negative signals may well destroy the positive response. These difficulties are usually not overcome until five or six years. Similarly Panchenkova (1956) has shown that a differentiation is established quite slowly in rats aged between eighteen and thirty-two days and breaks down rather easily, whereas the differentiation is formed more rapidly in four-month-old rats, and remains stable.

Support for the view that behaviour depending on the inhibition or control of response is weak in the very young child and develops quite slowly is also given by the work of Lambercier and Rey (1935) and by Rey (1954). Lambercier and Rey were concerned with the evolution of a manual skill involving (a) a detour and (b) the use of an intermediate agent. In younger children (four to five years) they found that a direct response to a reward which was visible but out of reach was so strong as to prevent exploration of the problem. Not until five and a half to seven years did the children pause and appear to reflect before acting. Rey (1954) gave to children of five to thirteen years, and also a group of adults, the task of drawing a line as slowly as possible across a piece of paper. The younger children were unable to make very slow movements and he concluded from his results not only that the capacity for restraint was weakest in the youngest children, but also that it was dissipated most rapidly in them in the course of making the trace. The adult level of performance was not reached until eleven or twelve years.

Certainly it would be rash to push too far any parallel between this work on children and the animal work. Nevertheless it would be difficult not to agree with Luria that regulation and control, the inhibitory aspect of behaviour, is of great importance in development; also, it appears to be weakest in the very young and to develop gradually. Apart from that, the course of development is not necessarily parallel: for instance, it is only in the bird experiments that an increase with age in the capacity not to respond appeared to be followed by a decrease in this capacity.

Discussion

The evidence suggests that we know very little about the development of behaviour in animals and in man; nevertheless it appears that there are indeed behavioural changes related with age and that these changes may have considerable bearing on what is understood as 'learning capacity'. It is also apparent that these developmental changes do not occur automatically with the passage of time, but depend to some extent at least on individual experience, that is, on environment or earlier activity. In addition, these changes may be exaggerated, or concealed, by the motivating conditions.

It is true that if the work discussed is considered in the light of traditional psychological concepts, the results appear confusing or even contradictory; they also depend too closely on particular experimental conditions for it to be possible to say whether 'learning' changes in any specific way with age. The suggestion made in this chapter is that the confusion may be produced by the concepts, which are too crudely descriptive to allow a precise analysis to be made. The work on birds presents the same difficulty if it is considered in this way. For example, if the results obtained from finches in the differentiation experiments are discussed in terms such as 'intelligence', 'learning capacity' or even 'speed of learning', the interpretation will vary according to the criterion of success chosen. In the first half of the experiment the juveniles were superior and later the adults were superior. The behaviour in fact developed and the differentiation was established in a different way at different ages.

It may well be the case that a deeper understanding of developmental change underlying what we understand broadly as learning capacity will depend on an analysis which is not only more detailed, but which is of a rather different kind from that exemplified by the concept of learning. It is clear that with the progress of adaptation – the accumulation of experience – behaviour develops as a whole. Some aspects of this development have emerged in the foregoing discussion. Firstly, there is the question of responsiveness. This appears to increase with age in the juvenile hand-reared great tit and then to decrease. Secondly, there are changes in a different type of responsiveness – internal inhibition – and here again there appears to be a rise and also probably a slight subsequent fall with age. Here the rise, as measured in a group of hand-reared great tits, occurs fairly slowly and continues for some weeks after the peak of positive responsiveness is past. Changes in these two aspects of behaviour might well give rise to inconsistent results if 'learning' is regarded as a unitary factor and different types of 'learning' tasks compared indiscriminately. It would appear, for example, that in tasks depending mainly on the level of activity the younger juveniles are likely to be superior, while older juveniles will gain in tasks depending mainly on the rather more delicate type of adaptation which involves not responding when a stimulus ceases to be reinforced.

Thirdly, there is the question of motivation in Stone's sense of hunger 'drive'. The work on birds was carried out under conditions which were normal for the individual tested; they were not starved, as some measure of food deprivation might well affect the results. Despite the difficulties involved in equating the effects of this kind of deprivation at different ages, an investigation of the kind made by Stone should prove to be of considerable value here, particularly if the effects of extreme hunger on internal inhibition were included in it. It seems unlikely, however, that the two curves given in Figure 7 could be accounted for in terms of motivation alone and indeed it might be preferable to treat motivation in the more physiological sense of excitability, the level of which changes continuously with external as well as internal factors and which is an essential part of any response, rather than as a category on its own which can be manipulated separately from behaviour coming under the category of 'learning'.

Fourthly, there are the effects on behaviour of early experience or environment. Thompson and Heron state that two-year-old dogs reared under restricted conditions behave in some respects more like young dogs than like normal adults. Some of their experiments and relevant experiments on birds may be interpreted as suggesting that internal inhibition develops more rapidly and more completely in a varied environment, presumably as a result of greater activity, stimulation, opportunity for adaptation, and so on. It could indeed be the effect of adaptive behaviour alone which is responsible for the negative changes associated with age, but we do not know enough even to guess whether the positive changes can be considered in this way. However, it is impossible to grow older without in some way adapting to and being changed by external conditions, however varied or homogeneous these may be.

We have, therefore, provisionally four aspects of behaviour connected with the problem of development of behaviour. The question which now arises is whether the traditional descriptive categories such as 'learning', 'motivation' and the like have been discarded, only to be replaced by four other separate categories, 'excitability', 'inhibition', and so on.

For the sake of clarity, positive responsiveness and internal inhibition have been treated separately, but it is not meant to imply by this that they are two separate processes or are manifested by entirely distinct elements in behaviour. It is clear that the two curves indicated in Figure 7 could represent changes in different processes or could be simply two different measures of the same process. In the work on birds the measurement of internal inhibition appeared to be a relatively simple matter, based as it was on the analysis made in existing work on conditioning; the concept of 'positive responsiveness' or 'activity' in general is, however, much less satisfactory and it might be rather difficult to say exactly what is being measured in the data given in Figure 6. The simplest view of this peak in responsiveness during the juvenile stage might well be that of Luria, who suggested that the child's cortex, being functionally weak, is unable to repress the 'large masses of excitation' provoked by a signal; the peak, it would seem, is due to the weakness of internal inhibition at this stage. It is also conceivable that the development of internal inhibition could not occur without the preliminary rise in excitability. In any case it is not likely that excitation alone can be regulated in behaviour, as the intensity of a response will be measured at all stages by inhibition of the inductive, reciprocal kind, as well as by internal inhibition. Indeed, the downward slope of the curve of 'positive responsiveness' became steeper when the stimulus was changed from one which was indifferent for the birds to one which had previously a conditioned significance, thus introducing the effect of extinction (Vince, 1960), and it is possible that families of similar curves could be obtained by varying the experimental conditions in this and other ways. Again, when measuring internal inhibition in the extinction and differentiation situations, the behaviour varies not only with the strength of internal inhibition but also with the level of excitability. It would be undesirable, therefore, to consider these two aspects of behaviour as distinct 'factors'.

Further, if motivation is considered simply as excitability it becomes not an added 'drive', but an integral part of the behaviour. Moreover, excitability, as all the conditioning work shows, is intimately bound up with the environment or with the minute-to-minute as well as cumulative effects of individual experience. The minutely controlled environmental changes in Pavlov's work, for example, with their positive and negative effects on the animal's behaviour, may be regarded as a most detailed study in 'motivation'; or, to look at it another way, in this work the maintenance of an individual's equilibrium with a changing environment is expressed in terms of excitation and inhibition. If behaviour is regarded in this way, as a ceaseless long-term as well as short-term process of adaptation to the individual's environment, it is possible to regard the four 'aspects' of behaviour described above almost as a single process, but still without abandoning the attempt at analysis.

As an example of the cumulative effects of experience, the view has been put forward that the development of internal inhibition may depend largely on experience. This is supported by Pavlov's (1927) demonstration that the rate of establishment of inhibition is improved by practice. If we consider behaviour as central nervous activity, this adds weight to a further implication of the work discussed above: that age and/or experience produce more than an increase in the individual's 'store' of sensory impressions, habits and the like, they result in actual change and development of the behavioural mechanisms. In comparing the behaviour of a very young animal or one reared under very restricted conditions with a normal adult of the same species, we may well be dealing with two mechanisms which function rather differently.

It is true that this approach produces experimental difficulties. For example, the adaptiveness of behaviour makes it difficult to separate the effects of age from those of environment or early experience. If testing is carried out at different ages, the results may be misleading because animals tested in this way will inevitably have acquired different amounts or kinds of experience. It is simpler to control age and vary experience, but still difficult to avoid or measure 'transfer' effects produced by adaptation to a particular environment in the early stages. One way of tackling this age-environment difficulty would be to consider development as adaptation to a particular environment and to compare the details of this process with those manifested by adaptation to a different environment in a comparable group of animals.

Conclusion

The view put forward is that there are behavioural changes during development which can give rise to complex, indeed confusing, age differences in traditional 'learning' tasks. It is suggested that the concept of 'learning' may be too crude, or too general, to allow an adequate investigation into these changes, and a different approach is described. Such an investigation must ultimately look for changes in the mechanisms of behaviour, which changes are likely to a considerable extent to depend on the established state of adaptation of the animal: its previous activity or experience. An approach which is concerned with the effects of experience leads, of course, to the consideration of development as an individual process.

References

BEACH, F. A., and JAYNES, J. (1954), 'Effects of early experience upon the behaviour of animals', *Psychol. Bull.*, vol. 51, pp. 239–63.

BIEL, W. C. (1940), 'Early age differences in maze performance in the albino rat', *J. genet. Psychol.*, vol. 56, pp. 439–53.

BINGHAM, W. E., and GRIFFITHS, W. J. (1952), 'The effects of different environments during infancy on adult behavior in the rat' *J. comp. physiol. Psychol.*, vol. 45 pp. 307–12.

CRUZE, W. W. (1938), 'Maturity and learning ability', *Psychol. Monogr.*, vol. 50, pp. 49–65.

FORGAYS, D. G., and FORGAYS, J. W. (1952), 'The nature of the effect of free environmental experience in the rat', *J. comp. physiol. Psychol.*, vol. 45, pp. 322–8.

FORGUS R. H. (1955) 'Early visual and motor experience as determiners of complex maze learning ability under rich and reduced stimulation', *J. comp. physiol. Psychol.* vol. 48, pp. 215–20.

FORGUS, R. H. (1956) 'Advantage of early over late perceptual experiences in improving form discrimination', *Canad. J. Psychol.*, vol. 10, pp. 147–55.

HUBBERT, H. B. (1915), 'The effect of age on habit formation in the albino rat', *Behav. Monogr.*, vol. 2, no. 6, pp. 1–55.

HYMOVITCH, B. (1952), 'The effects of experimental variations on problem solving in the rat', *J. comp. physiol. Psychol.*, vol. 45, pp. 313–21.

KING, J. A. (1958), 'Parameters relevant to determining the effect of early experience upon the adult behavior of animals', *Psychol. Bull.*, vol. 55, pp. 46–58.

LAMBERCIER, M., and REY, A. (1935), 'Contribution à l'étude de l'intelligence pratique chez l'enfant', *Arch. Psychol.*, vol. 25, pp. 1–59.

Liu, S. Y. (1928), 'The relation of age to the learning ability of the white rat', *J. comp. Psychol.*, vol. 8, pp. 75–85.

Luria, A. R. (1932), *The Nature of Human Conflicts*, Liveright.

Maier, N. R. F. (1932) 'Age and intelligence in rats', *J. comp. Psychol.*, vol. 13, pp. 1–6.

Munn, N. L. (1950), *Handbook of Psychological Research on the Rat*, Houghton Mifflin.

Panchenkova, E. F. (1956), 'The ontogenetic development of conditioned reflexes in the white rat', *Zhurnal Visshei Nerv'noi Deyatelnosti*, vol. 6, pp. 312–18.

Paramonova, M. P. (1955), 'On the question of the development of the physiological mechanism of movement', *Voprosy psichologii*, vol. 1, pp. 51–62.

Pavlov, I. P. (1927), *Conditioned Reflexes*, Milford, Oxford.

Rey, A. (1954), 'Le freinage volontaire du mouvement graphique chez l'enfant', *Cahiers de pédagogue et d'orientation professionelle*, L'Institut supérieur de science pédagogiques de l'Université de Liège, no. 2.

Richter, C. P. (1922), 'A behavioristic study of the activity of the rat', *Comp. Psychol. Monogr.*, vol. 1, no. 2, pp. 1–55.

Slonaker, J. R. (1912), 'The normal activity of the albino rat from birth to natural death, its rate of growth and the duration of life', *J. anim. Behav.*, vol. 2, pp. 20–42.

Stone, C. P. (1929a), 'The age factor in animal learning: I. Rats in the problem box and the maze', *Genet. psychol. Monogr.*, vol. 5 pp. 1–130.

Stone, C. P. (1929b), 'The age factor in animal learning: II. Rats in a multiple light discrimination box and a difficult maze', *Genet. psychol. Monogr.*, vol. 6, pp. 125–202.

Thompson, W. R., and Heron, W. (1954a), 'The effects of early restriction on activity in dogs', *J. comp. physiol. Psychol.*, vol. 47, pp. 77–82.

Thompson, W. R., and Heron W. (1954b), 'The effects of restricting early experience on the problem-solving capacity of dogs', *Canad. J. Psychol.*, vol. 8, pp. 17–31.

Thorpe, W. H. (1956), *Learning and Instinct in Animals*, Methuen.

Vince, M. A. (1958), '"String-pulling" in birds: II. Differences related to age in greenfinches, chaffinches and canaries', *Anim. Behav.*, vol. 6, pp. 53–9.

Vince, M. A. (1959), 'Effects of age and experience on the establishment of internal inhibition in finches', *Brit. J. Psychol.*, vol. 50, pp. 136–44.

Vince, M. A. (1960), 'Developmental changes in responsiveness in the great tit (*Parus major*)', *Behaviour*, vol. 15, pp. 219–43.

Watson, J. B. (1903), *Animal Education*, University of Chicago Press.

11 J. P. Scott

Early Development

Excerpts from J. P. Scott, *Early Experience and the Organization of Behavior*, Brooks-Cole, 1968, pp. 40–44, 133–41.

Validity of comparison of human development with that of other animals

Each species of animals has a unique heredity and course of development. Consequently, there is no justification for assuming that the results of any experiment done on a different species can be carried over directly to human behavior. Any such transference must always be hypothetical, but the soundness of such a hypothesis can be greatly increased by basing the comparison upon fundamental resemblances between human development and that of the experimental animal concerned. The final test of the hypothesis must always be based upon facts and experiments obtained directly from human development. Without basic developmental information which allows exact comparisons, hypotheses obtained from animal work are no more than interesting suggestions that may or may not have some application to human affairs.

Relatively slow speed of human development

In one respect, human development is entirely different from that of any of the animals on which we have detailed information. The periods of human development are measured in months instead of in weeks as with dogs, in days as with rodents or even in hours for some of the rapidly developing birds. It follows that a human infant is exposed to much more experience within a corresponding period of development, resulting in much stronger fixation of behavior by habit formation. In fact, every aspect of behavior affected by learning can be modified more strongly in human infants than in more rapidly developing animals.

This same extended experience makes much more individual variability possible in human development. Wide variation is particularly obvious in such features as motor development. The total recorded range in walking extends from eight to eighteen months, or approximately ten months difference, in children who eventually are able to walk at all. While the normal range of variation in development does not appear to be as great in the case of sensory and learning capacities as with motor capacities, there is probably at least several weeks' variation in the appearance of sensory and learning abilities in reasonably normal infants. Consequently, any interpretation of experimental results based on age from birth must always allow for variation. For example, an experiment based on the conclusion that the median time for the beginning of the motor transition period is seven months would always be affected by the fact that half of the infants of this particular age would still be in the earlier period. It would therefore be safer to choose children for comparison who were several months apart in development so that relatively little overlap would be expected. Similarly, any description of populations based on change in behavior with age would show less abrupt changes than would be seen in the individuals themselves. For example, when a child begins to walk, the change is quite sudden and abrupt, often taking place within a few days. Yet a statistical study of a population would show a gradual change taking place over a period of several months. It is well to remember that development actually takes place in individuals rather than on a population basis.

Unusual features of human development

Philosophers and scientists in the past have often tried to demonstrate that human beings are at least in some ways completely different from other animals. As we have learned more and more about animal behavior, this has become increasingly difficult, since we can find at least the rudiments of almost any human activity elsewhere in the animal kingdom. For example, human development is in many ways quite similar to that of dogs. In both species there is an early neonatal period in which behavior has evolved toward adaptation to complete maternal care, as opposed to later periods of development in which adaptation is based on adult forms of behavior with increasing independence. The same fundamental general processes of development can be observed in both, and these can be used to identify the same general periods of development. However, the human infant seems to have an unusual combination of somewhat precocious development of the sense organs and relatively delayed development of the motor capacities. In contrast, rhesus monkeys are highly precocious in learning and motor skills, and even chimpanzees, which are perhaps most similar to human beings in general development, show much more rapid changes in motor capacities than do human infants. It should be emphasized that we still do not have a thorough description of the fundamental facts of development of any primate species other than man and these conclusions may be modified by future discoveries.

Table 1 Periods and Processes in Early Human Development

Period	Approximate age limits	Major processes	Initial changes
Neonatal	0-5 weeks	Establishment of neonatal nutrition (sucking)	Birth
Primary socialization	5 weeks–7 months	Formation of primary social relationships and emotional attachments	First social smiling
Transition 1	7–15 months	Transition to adult methods of eating and locomotion	Change in response to separation; first tooth; crawling
Transition 2	15–27 months	Transition to adult method of communication	First words; first grinding tooth; walking
Verbal socialization (juvenile)	27 months– 7 or 8 years	Development of verbal communication and understanding; perfection of motor skills	Beginning to talk in sentences

The dog is unique among mammals whose development is well known in that all of its transition processes from neonatal to adult existence are concentrated in one short period. By contrast, human transitions are more extended and overlap more with other basic developmental processes and periods. The most striking difference, however, is that the human period of primary socialization comes before the transition to the adult form of locomotion. This means that human primary social relationships are inevitably formed with adult or semi-adult caretakers, usually the mother or a mother substitute. On the basis of the known facts of human development we would predict that primary social attachments should be easily formed at any time between approximately six weeks and six months of life and that these should be formed with increasing difficulty thereafter. Furthermore, any complete change of social relationships, such as that resulting from adoption, must involve the breaking off of emotional attachments, with consequently greater emotional disturbances as the child becomes older. These findings have great significance for the process of adoption. Indeed, most data on the effects of adopting children at different ages show that later emotional disturbances and maladjustments are much more common in children adopted in the second six months than in the first six months. This fact also poses the theoretical and practical problem of devising better ways of minimizing the risk of emotional disturbance in later periods.

The complexity of development of learning capacities

Such evidence as we now possess indicates that learning capacities in the neonatal period are quite limited and that consequently the results of early learning in this period are likely to have only limited effects upon later behavior. On the other hand, the risk of physical damage is greater than in later life because physiological developmental processes are still proceeding rapidly. On the basis of present information, we can say that the neonatal period is one in which the risks of physiological damage to the nervous system are much greater than those for psychological damage.

This situation changes rapidly as the child grows older. By two or two and a half months of age, the human infant can learn certain things quite rapidly, especially in the form of making simple associations and forming habits. Information received through verbal communication is not possible in any great quantity before approximately two years of age and is limited even at that time. Consequently there is a period of two years in which the infant can learn things on a nonverbal basis before he begins to learn through words. Whether this early learning is actually as lasting and permanent as later learning has never been established, but presumably it is. However, as anyone knows, what is learned in infancy is ordinarily not accessible through verbal recall. The earliest conscious memories of most people do not go back much earlier than three years.

This fact makes possible a situation not found in other species, in that what is learned on a verbal basis may conflict with what is learned on a nonverbal basis. There is every reason to suppose that while verbal learning is ordinarily dominant in the control of human behavior, the process of nonverbal learning continues throughout life. The result is that conflict is always possible between verbally learned material and that which is learned on another basis, whether in early infancy or in later life. The normal course of human development thus supports Freud's theories of the conscious and unconscious mind, to use the now rather old-fashioned language current in his day.

Of course it is also possible that preverbal learning is impermanent and has little or no effect on later behavior, or that because it is not ordinarily associated with what is learned on a verbal basis later, it is stored in such a way as to be inaccessible. Here again, we need more facts on the nature of human development.

In earlier chapters we emphasized the fact that early learning is different from later learning. Just how different it is has never been completely established, but we do know that in both newborn children and puppies the capacity for learning is quite limited. Both kinds of infants make associations much more rapidly in connection with sucking than they do with painful stimulation, and their ability to learn is greatly limited by their undeveloped sensory and motor capacities. Basic questions still to be answered are the exact ways in which learning capacities change and whether or not the simple learning which goes on in the neonatal organism has persistent effects. We can, however, draw certain conclusions from what is known about the general nature of learning processes.

Habituation

When a young puppy first reaches the end of the transition period he appears to be highly sensitive to many changes in his environment. He gives a violent startle response to any loud noise, responding to slamming doors, barking dogs and even to much milder noises. A few weeks later it takes an extremely loud and unusual sound to elicit a startle response, which is rarely seen thereafter. This process of ceasing to respond to stimuli that have no direct consequences for the animal is called *habituation*. Its nature is diagrammatically illustrated whenever a reflex is repeatedly stimulated. A young puppy will jump violently the first time it hears a loud noise. The second response is less extreme and if the noise is made four or five times in rapid succession the response may disappear entirely. After a suitable rest the reflex can be obtained again. The exact physical nature of the process of habituation is not known, but in effect it is quite similar to accommodation of the sense organs. As will be shown below, the effect of habituation can be made permanent by associative learning.

From the viewpoint of early experience, two principles are important. First, *a young child or any other young mammal is a nonhabituated animal and is much more responsive to environmental stimuli than it is in later life*. A child shows a fresh interest where an adult becomes bored and becomes hyperexcited in situations where an adult is calm and unresponsive. Second, *the kind of early experience which a child undergoes will determine the kinds of stimuli to which he becomes habituated*. Obviously, an adult cannot become habituated to all stimuli and if he moves into a quite different environment in later life he may again show the sort of fresh responsiveness typical of children. This may in fact be a partial explanation for what anthropologists call 'culture shock', the intense emotional reaction resulting from an attempt to move into a completely different social environment.

Problem solving

The general process of learning can be seen in almost diagrammatic form in a young animal like the dog. In one of our experiments (Scott and Fuller, 1965), we set up a maze problem for puppies, trying out different sorts of apparatus until we found one which worked reasonably well. This was a multiple T-maze with wire-mesh walls through which the puppies could see but which still presented a very confusing appearance from the inside. It consisted of six units, each of which had one blind alley, and the puppy had to find its way outside, where it would be given a food reward and put back with its litter mates. When first put in the maze, the puppies became very excited and moved around at random, going into many of the blind alleys and sometimes repeating mistakes over and over again. They eventually found their way out and on subsequent days began to improve, making fewer mistakes at each trial. A few of the puppies eventually discovered that they could go through the maze without mistakes if they systematically observed the next section in front of them and these animals went slowly and carefully through the maze and made no errors. However, they soon abandoned this careful method and reduced their behavior to the simple habit of making alternate right and left turns, which of course resulted in their going into some of the blind alleys.

From this example we can see that the series of events involved in problem solving includes several subprocesses. The first is variation in behavior. Without this no improvement in performance would be possible. Much learning consists of such trial and error variation in behavior accompanied by a second subprocess, the selective elimination of the kind of behavior which does not lead to results. Third, some puppies appeared to discover a general solution of the problem, learning not simply the direct path for this particular maze but a general method for staying on a direct path in all similar mazes. As a fourth subprocess, all of the puppies reduced their behavior to a simple habit, as a result of which their behavior became more and more predictable.

From the nature of these processes we may conclude that *as a young animal learns, its behavior will become more and more reliable and consistent.* This expectation was confirmed in another experiment in which puppies were trained to stay on the platform of a scale while being weighed. At first their behavior was highly variable. They adopted all sorts of postures and were either very quiet or highly active. As this experience was repeated in weekly trials, each puppy tended to adopt one posture such as standing, and one form of activity, such as attempting to escape. Another pup might consistently sit and remain quiet on the scales. The results are shown in Figure 1.

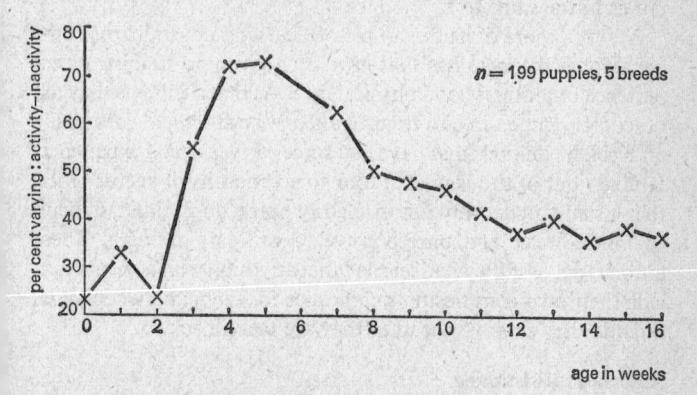

Figure 1 Development changes in variability of behavior in puppies. During the neonatal period the puppies tend to give only one reaction to being weighed, that of constant activity. As they grow older they become highly variable, switching from one activity to another, and finally they become less variable, each puppy reacting consistently with either struggling or remaining quiet on the scales

We can now draw several conclusions regarding the role of learning in early experience. The first of these is that as an individual grows older the variation in his behavior in any one situation will be reduced. Older people should be more consistent and reliable in their behavior than young children and they generally are. Second, differences in early experience will result in differences in what an individual learns or does not learn. Of particular importance is the learning of general solutions to problems, as these facilitate later learning along certain lines rather than others.

A young organism may also learn a general method of not

learning. In the simplest example, a frightening experience or repeated failure will lead an individual to avoid particular situations or to become passive in them. In one of our early maze experiments, the wall of the maze was not securely fastened, and when one of the puppies touched it, it fell down with a crash. This animal was so frightened that he would do nothing thereafter but crouch in the corner of the maze and refuse to move. His performance was consequently much poorer than those of his litter mates in the same test.

An even more drastic example of 'learning not to learn' is the behavior of kennel dogs that have been given no training or experience other than good physical care. As older animals they are practically impossible to train by the methods which work easily and well on animals that have had some early learning experience. If taken out of the kennel at four to six months of age or older, they usually make very unsatisfactory house dogs, timid, difficult to house-break and unresponsive to ordinary training. These animals act as if they had learned that anything which occurs outside their own pens has no significance for them and when taken outside they simply wait until they are taken back.

Associational learning

Of all learning processes this one has been best documented and described. We still do not know the exact physiological basis of the process, but Pavlov and Skinner and their followers have worked out the nature of the phenomenon in great detail. The results can be described in terms of a number of general laws.

The first and most basic of these is the law of association. In Pavlov's experiments a dog would associate the sound of a buzzer with the subsequent appearance of meat and begin to salivate as soon as he heard the buzzer. Similarly, Skinner's rats associated the pressing of a bar with the appearance of a food pellet and, having pressed the bar, a trained rat would go over to the food-delivery tube and wait for a pellet. In general terms, we can say that if two events occur close together in time and are repeated later in the same order, an individual will act as if the first event produced the second. Once the first event occurs, he begins to prepare for the second.

As we have seen earlier, the ability to make rapid associations is quite limited at birth in both man and dog, and the complete story of the development of learning capacities is not yet known. However, we can conclude that *the effect of any particular early experience will depend upon the state of the learning capacities of the individual at that time.*

A second law of associational learning is that of reinforcement or strength of association. If two events at first occur together but later the second one does not follow the first, the response of the animal begins to weaken. In this way it can be demonstrated that *the strength of the association depends upon the number of repetitions or reinforcements.* This might also be called the law of habit strength. From it we can conclude that *a young animal early in life will have weaker habits than an older one.* The details of this phenomenon have only been worked out in connection with food rewards, but considerable evidence indicates that the strength of an association varies considerably depending on the kind of reinforcement and the nature of the response system (that is, whether skeletal or visceral muscles are used) as well as on the genetic nature of the individual involved.

All the evidence indicates that an association, once formed, produces an extremely long-lasting effect, perhaps extending over a lifetime. In Pavlov's dogs, the salivary response could be extinguished by lack of reinforcement, but with suitable periods of rest it would reappear again. In human beings, we all know of persons who at the age of eighty can clearly remember events which occurred in early childhood. The evidence justifies the conclusion that associations, once made, are permanent. However, this is at best a well-supported hypothesis and we need to find out whether associational learning in early infancy has the same permanence as in later childhood. If learning really is permanent, it has very strong implications concerning the role of early experience. Assuming that something once learned can never be unlearned implies that if a person forms two conflicting associations, the first being based on a misleading experience, it will take about as long to make the second and correct association as strong as the first as it did to form the original erroneous one. In short, it should take about as long to break a habit as to form one in the first place. Again, we need more information on this point.

A corollary to the law of association is the law of negative association, or inhibition. Inaction as well as action can be associated with particular events. Not only will an individual learn to do nothing as a result of negative reinforcement such as fright or pain, but he can also learn to do nothing in a particular situation simply by doing nothing. *Early experience will thus determine certain patterns of inhibition or inaction that can have important consequences for later behavior.* It is perhaps no accident that young children and young animals tend to be highly active, for evolution would favor the survival of individuals who learned patterns of activity rather than of inactivity in early youth.

Finally, there is the law of discrimination and generalization. Once an association has been formed, an individual tends to give the same response in all similar situations and as a result of experience he will learn to discriminate between those situations which are truly similar and those which are not. The nature of developmental changes in this capacity is not known, but we have some evidence that the power of generalization in young animals is quite limited. For example, we gave puppies a detour test in which they learned to go around a barrier fence (Scott and Fuller, 1965). If the length of the fence was extended, they showed some carry-over from what they had previously learned, but if the barrier was turned 180° in the room, they reacted as if it were a completely new situation. If early learning tends to be specific (for the reason that very young organisms do not have the ability to generalize from special instances to whole classes of phenomena), it follows that *the effects of early experience tend to be specific rather than general.* Too severe toilet training, for example, should primarily affect eliminative behavior and should not affect sexual behavior unless the parent also punishes the latter.

We can conclude from these laws of associational learning that what an individual learns in early experience will affect what he learns or does not learn in the future. An association made with a particular event will at the very least make relearning difficult if the situation changes. Moreover, passive inhibition combined with generalization may cut off whole areas of later experience from the learning process, just as positive association combined with generalization can facilitate learning in wide areas. An individual can both learn-to-learn and learn-not-to-learn, and it is highly important for later existence that generally useful learning sets be formed.

Another implication of the laws of learning is that the results of early experience cannot be completely erased by later experience. They can be modified and even replaced to some extent, but relearning will take as long as original learning to form equally strong habits and even in this case the individual is never the same as if he had formed only one unified habit.

We would expect that the process or processes of associational learning would interact with other processes. Association should result in the 'freezing' of habituation, so that a stimulus which is repeated over and over again will eventually evoke no reaction even after rest. Thus the sounds which at first produce a startle reaction in a young puppy later produce no effect. We would further expect that the process of variation of behavior would act in opposition to associational learning and result in new solutions to problems even late in life. Long habit formation should render behavior more and more consistent, but the process of variation is always present, so that variation should never be reduced to zero. The habits established in early experience are not necessarily permanent.

Finally, we can conclude that the process of reinforcement or habit formation has major importance in determining future behavior, perhaps more so than the effect of a single traumatic experience or emotional shock. The important thing about such experiences is that they may determine the direction of a long process of habit formation rather than that they produce a tremendous effect in themselves. Indeed, this principle is now recognized in the treatment of individuals suffering from emotional shock, in that every attempt is made to treat them immediately and before the response can be set into a permanent habit pattern.

In this brief review of learning, we are obviously dealing with a group of related processes. Some of these work in opposition to each other, but all have the net effect of improving the individual's ability to adapt to an environment which may change from moment to moment and from generation to generation. It is also obvious that the behavior of an individual as he grows older becomes more and more organized. The processes of learning are organizational processes starting on very simple bases and proceeding to more complex ones.

The effectiveness of behavioral organization in any individual will depend on the nature of the organization achieved and its relevance to the world around him. An individual's behavior could be organized either for a stable world or for a rapidly changing one, but the results in either case would depend on outward circumstances. The importance of early experience is that *this is a time when organizational processes are proceeding most rapidly and hence can be modified most readily*. As an organism becomes more and more fixed, it becomes more and more difficult to modify it without destroying it.

Reference

SCOTT, J. P., and FULLER, J. L. (1965), *Genetics of the Social Behavior of the Dog*, University of Chicago Press.

12 Bettye M. Caldwell

The Optimal Learning Environment for the Young Child

Excerpt from Bettye M. Caldwell, 'What is the optimal learning environment for the young child?', *American Journal of Orthopsychiatry*, vol. 37, 1967, pp. 8–21.

A truism in the field of child development is that the milieu in which development occurs influences that development. As a means of validating the principle, considerable scientific effort has gone into the Linnaean task of describing and classifying milieus and examining developmental consequences associated with different types. Thus we know something about what it is like to come of age in New Guinea (Mead, 1930), in a small Midwestern town (Barker and Wright, 1955), in villages and cities in Mexico (Lewis, 1959), in families of different social-class level in Chicago (Davis and Havighurst, 1946) or Boston (Maccoby and Gibbs, 1954; Pavenstedt, 1965), in a New York slum (Wortis *et al.*, 1963), in Russian collectives (Bronfenbrenner, 1962), in Israeli kibbutzim (Irvine, 1952; Rabin, 1957; Spiro, 1958), in the eastern part of the United States (Provence and Lipton, 1962), and in a Republican community in Central New York (Caldwell *et al.*, 1963). Most of these milieu descriptions have placed great stress on the fact that they were just that and nothing more, i.e. they have expressed the customary scientific viewpoint that to describe is not to judge or criticize. However, in some of the more recent milieu descriptions which have contrasted middle- and lower-class family environments or highlighted conditions in extreme lower-class settings (Pavenstedt, 1965; Wortis *et al.*, 1963), often more than a slight suggestion has crept in that things could be better for the young child from the deprived segment of the culture. Even so, there remains a justifiable wariness about recommending or arranging any environment for the very young child other than the type regarded as its natural habitat, namely, within its own family.

Of course, optimizing environments are arranged all the time under one guise or another. For example, for disturbed children whose family environments seem effectively to reinforce rather than extinguish psychopathology, drastic alterations of milieu often are attempted. This may take the form of psychotherapy for one or both parents as well as the disturbed child or it may involve total removal of the child from the offending environment with temporary or prolonged placement of the child in a milieu presumably more conducive to normal development. Then there is the massive milieu arrangement formalized and legalized as 'education' which profoundly affects the lives of all children once they reach the age of five or six. This type of arrangement is not only tolerated but fervently endorsed by our culture as a whole. In fact, any subculture (such as the Amish) which resists the universalization of this pattern of milieu arrangement is regarded as unacceptably deviant and as justifying legal action to enforce conformity.

For very young children, however, there has been a great deal of timidity about conscious and planned arrangement of the developmental milieu, as though the implicit assumption has been made that any environment which sustains life is adequate during this period. This is analogous to suggesting that the intrauterine environment during the period of maximal cellular proliferation is less important than it is later, a suggestion that patently disregards evidence from epidemiology and experimental embryology. The rate of proliferation of new behavioral skills during the first three years of life and the increasing accumulation of data pointing to the relative permanence of deficit acquired when the environment is inadequate during this period make it mandatory that careful attention be given to the preparation of the developmental environment during the first three years of life.

Conclusions from inadequate environments

It is, of course, an exaggeration to imply that no one has given attention to the type of environment which can nourish early and sustained growth and development. For a good three decades now infants who are developing in different milieus have been observed and examined, and data relating to their development have made it possible to identify certain strengths and deficiencies of the different types of environments. Of all types described, the one most consistently indicted by the data is the institution. A number of years ago Goldfarb (1949) published an excellent series of studies contrasting patterns of intellectual functioning shown by a group of adopted adolescents who had been reared in institutions up to age three and then transferred to foster homes or else placed shortly after birth in foster homes. The development of the group that had spent time in the institution was deficient in many ways compared to the group that had gone directly into foster homes. Provence and Lipton (1962) recently published a revealing description of the early social and intellectual development of infants in institutions, contrasting their development with that of home-reared children. On almost every measured variable the institutional infants were found wanting – less socially alert and outgoing, less curious, less responsive, less interested in objects and generally less advanced. The findings of this study are almost prototypic of the literature in the field, as pointed out in excellent reviews by Ainsworth (1962, pp. 42–62) and Yarrow (1961).

Although there are many attributes in combination that comprise the institutional environment, the two most obvious elements are (a) absence of a mother and (b) the presence of a group. These basic characteristics have thus been identified as the major carriers of the institutional influence and have been generalized into an explicit principle guiding our recommendations for optimal environments – learning or otherwise – for young children whenever any type of milieu arrangement is necessary. This principle may be stated simply as: the optimal environment for the young child is one in which the child is cared for in his own home in the context of a warm, continuous emotional relationship with his own mother under conditions of varied sensory input. Implicit in this principle is the conviction that the child's mother is the person best qualified to provide a stable and warm interpersonal relationship as well as the necessary pattern of sensory stimulation. Implicit also is the assumption that socio-emotional development has priority during the first three years and that if this occurs normally, cognitive development, which is of minor importance during this period anyway, will take care of itself. At a still deeper level lurks the assumption that attempts to foster cognitive development will interfere with socio-emotional development. Advocacy of the principle also implies endorsement of the idea that most homes are adequate during this early period and that no formal training (other than possibly some occasional supervisory support) for mothering is necessary. Such an operating principle places quite an onus on mothers and assumes that they will possess or quickly acquire all the talents necessary to create an optimal learning environment. And this author, at least, is convinced that a majority of mothers have such talents or proclivities and that they are willing to try to do all they can to create for their children the proper developmental milieu.

But there are always large numbers of children for whom family resources are not available and for whom some type of substitute milieu arrangement must be made. On the whole, such attempts have followed the entirely logical and perhaps evolutionary approach to milieu development – they have sought to create substitute families. The same is usually true when parents themselves seek to work out an alternate child-care arrangement because of less drastic conditions, such as maternal employment. The most typical maneuver is to try to obtain a motherly person who will 'substitute' for her (not supplement her) during her hours away from her young child.

Our nation has become self-consciously concerned with social evolution, and in the past decade a serious attempt has been made to assimilate valid data from the behavioral and social sciences into planning for social action. In this context it would be meaningful to examine and question some of the hidden assumptions upon which our operating principle about the optimal environment for the young child rests.

Examining the hidden assumptions

Do intermittent, short-term separations of the child from the mother impair the mother–child relationship or the development of the child?

Once having become sensitized to the consequences of institutionalization and suspicious that the chief missing ingredient was the continued presence of the mother, the scientific and professional community went on the *qui vive* to the possibly deleterious consequences of any type of separation of an infant from its mother. Accordingly, a number of studies (Caldwell *et al.*,

1963; Gardner, Hawkes and Burchinal, 1961; Hoffman, 1961; Radke Yarrow, 1961; Siegel and Hass, 1963) investigated the consequences of short-term intermittent separation and were unable to demonstrate in the children the classical syndrome of the 'institutional child'. In reviewing the literature, Yarrow (1961) stressed the point that available data do not support the tendency to assume that maternal deprivation, such as exists in the institutional environment, and maternal separation are the same thing. Apparently short cyclic interruptions culminated by reunions do not have the same effect as prolonged interruptions, even though quantitatively at the end of a designated period the amount of time spent in a mother-absent situation might be equal for the two experiences. Also in this context it is well to be reminded that in the institutional situation there is likely to be no stable mother–child relationship to interrupt. These are often never-mothered rather than ever-mothered children, a fact which must be kept in mind in generalizing from data on institutional groups. Thus until we have data to indicate that such intermittent separation–reunion cycles have similar effects on young children as prolonged separations, we are probably unjustified in assuming that an 'uninterrupted' relationship is an essential ingredient of the optimal environment.

Is group upbringing invariably damaging?

In studies done in West European and American settings, social and cognitive deficits associated with continuous group care during infancy have been frequently demonstrated. Enough exceptions have been reported, however, to warrant an intensification of the search for the 'true' ingredient in the group situation associated with the observed deficits. For example, Freud and Dann (1951) described the adjustment of a group of six children reared in a concentration camp orphanage for approximately three years, where they were cared for by overworked and impersonal inmates of the camp and then transported to a residence for children in England. The children, who had never known their own mothers but who had been together as a group for approximately three years, were intensely attached to one another. Although their adjustment to their new environment was slow and differed from the pattern one would expect from home-reared children, it was significant that they eventually did make a reasonably good adjustment. That the children were able to learn a new language while making this emotional transition was offered as evidence that many of the basic cognitive and personality attributes remained unimpaired in spite of the pattern of group upbringing. The accumulation of data showing that kibbutz-reared children (Rabin, 1957) do not have cognitive deficits also reinforces the premise that it is not necessarily group care *per se* that produces the frequently reported deficit and that it is possible to retain the advantages of group care while systematically eliminating its negative features. Grounds for reasonable optimism also have been found in retrospective studies by Maas (1963) and Beres and Obers (1950), although in both cases the authors found evidence of pathology in some members of the follow-up sample. Similarly Dennis and Najarian (1957) concluded from their data that the magnitude of the deficit varied as a function of the type of instrument used to measure deficit, and Dennis (1960) showed that in institutions featuring better adult–child ratios and a conscious effort to meet the psychological needs of the infants, the development of the children was much less retarded than was the case in a group of children residing in institutions with limited and unsophisticated staff. It is not appropriate to go into details of limitations of methodology in any of these studies; however, from the standpoint of an examination of the validity of a principle, it is important to take note of any exceptions to the generality of that principle.

In this context it is worth considering a point made by Gula (1965). He recently has suggested that some of the apparent consistency in studies comparing institutionalized infants with those cared for in their own homes and in foster homes might disappear if it were possible to equate the comparison groups on the variable of environmental adequacy. That is, one could classify all three types of environments as good, marginal or inadequate on a number of dimensions. Most of the studies have compared children from palpably 'inadequate' institutions with children from 'good' foster and own homes. He suggests that, merely because most institutions studied have been inadequate in terms of such variables as adult–child ratio, staff turnover and personal characteristics of some of the caretakers, etc., one is not justified in concluding *ipso facto* that group care is invariably inferior or damaging.

Is healthy socio-emotional development the most important task of the first three years? Do attempts to foster cognitive growth interfere with social and emotional development?

These paired assumptions, which one finds stated in one variety or another in many pamphlets and books dealing with early child development, represent acceptance of a closed system model of human development. They seem to conceptualize development as compartmentalized and with a finite limit. If the child progresses too much in one area he automatically restricts the amount of development that can occur in another area. Thus one often encounters such expressions as 'cognitive development at the *expense* of socio-emotional development'. It is perhaps of interest to reflect that, until our children reach somewhere around highschool age, we seldom seem to worry that the reverse might occur. But, of course, life is an open system and on the whole it is accurate to suggest that development feeds upon development. Cognitive and socio-emotional advances tend on the whole to be positively not negatively correlated.

The definition of intelligence as *adaptivity* has not been adequately stressed by modern authors. It is, of course, the essence of Piaget's (1952) definition as it was earlier of Binet (Binet and Simon, 1916). Unfortunately, however, for the last generation or so in America we have been more concerned with how to measure intelligent behavior than how to interpret and understand it. Acceptance of the premise that intelligent behavior is adaptive behavior should help to break the set of many persons in the field of early child development that to encourage cognitive advance is to discourage healthy socio-emotional development. Ample data are available to suggest that quite the reverse is true either for intellectually advanced persons (Terman and Oden, 1947; Terman *et al.*, 1925) or an unselected sample. In a large sample of young adults from an urban area in Minnesota, Anderson and associates (1959) found that the best single predictor of post-high-school adjustment contained in a large assessment battery was a humble little group intelligence test. Prediction based on intelligence plus teacher's ratings did somewhat better, but nothing exceeded the intelligence test for single measure efficiency.

It is relevant here to mention White's (1959) concept of competence or effectance as a major stabilizing force in personality development. The emotional reinforcement accompanying the old 'I can do it myself' declaration should not be undervalued. In Murphy's report (Murphy et al., 1962) of the coping behavior of preschool children one sees evidence of the adjustive supports gained through cognitive advances. In his excellent review of cognitive stimulation in infancy and early childhood, Fowler (1962) raises the question of whether there is any justification for the modern anxiety (and, to be sure, it is a modern phenomenon) over whether cognitive stimulation may damage personality development. He suggests that in the past severe and harmful methods may have been the culprits whenever there was damage and that the generalizations have confused methods of stimulation with the process of stimulation *per se*.

Do cognitive experiences of the first few months and years leave no significant residual?

Any assumption that the learnings of infancy are evanescent appears to be a fairly modern idea. In his *Emile*, first published in 1762, Rousseau stressed the point that education should begin while the child is still in the cradle. Perhaps any generalization to the contrary received its major modern impetus from a rather unlikely place – from longitudinal studies of development covering the span from infancy to adulthood. From findings of poor prediction of subsequent intellectual status (Bayley, 1949) one can legitimately infer that the infant tests measure behavior that is somewhat irrelevant to later intellectual performance. Even though these behaviors predictive of later cognitive behavior elude most investigators, one cannot infer that the early months and years are unimportant for cognitive development.

Some support for this assumption has come from experimental studies in which an attempt has been made to produce a durable effect in human subjects by one or another type of intervention offered during infancy. One cogent example is the work of Rheingold (1956), in which she provided additional social and personal stimulation to a small group of approximately six-month-old, institutionalized infants for a total of eight weeks. At the end of the experimental period, differences in social responsiveness between her stimulated group and a control group composed of other babies in the institution could be observed. There were also slight but nonsignificant advances in postural and motor behavior on a test of infant development. However, when the babies were followed up approximately a year later, by which time all but one were in either adoptive or boarding homes or in their own natural homes, the increased social responsiveness formerly shown by the stimulated babies was no longer observed. Nor were there differences in level of intellectual functioning. Rheingold and Bayley (1959) concluded that the extra mothering provided during the experimental period was enough to produce an effect at the time but not enough to sustain this effect after such a time as the two groups were no longer differentially stimulated. However, in spite of their conservative conclusion, it is worth noting that the experimentally stimulated babies were found to vocalize more during the follow-up assessments than the control babies. Thus there may have been enough of an effect to sustain a developmental advance in at least this one extremely important area.

Some very impressive recent unpublished data obtained by Skeels, offer a profound challenge to the assumption of the unimportance of the first three years for cognitive growth. This investigator has followed up after approximately twenty-five years most of the subjects described in a paper by Skeels and Dye (1939). Thirteen infants had been transferred from an orphanage because of evidence of mental retardation and placed in an institution for the retarded under the care of adolescent retardates who gave them a great deal of loving care and as much cognitive stimulation as they could. The thirteen subjects showed a marked acceleration in development after this transfer. In contrast, a group of reasonably well-matched infants left on the wards of the orphanage continued to develop poorly. In a recent follow-up of these cases, Skeels discovered that the gains made by the transferred infants were sustained into their adult years, whereas all but one of the control subjects developed the classic syndrome of mental retardation.

The fact that development and experience are cumulative makes it difficult ever to isolate any one antecedent period and assert that its influence was or was not influential in a subsequent developmental period. Thus even though it might be difficult to demonstrate an effect of some experience in an adjacent time period, delayed effects may well be of even greater developmental consequence. In a recent review of data from a number of longitudinal studies, Bloom (1964) has concluded that during the first three to four years (the noncognitive years, if you will) approximately 50 per cent of the development of intelligence that is ever to occur in the life cycle takes place. During this period a particular environment may be either abundant or deprived in terms of the ingredients essential for providing opportunities for the development of intelligence and problem solving. Bloom (1964, pp. 88–9) states:

The effects of the environments, especially of the extreme environments, appear to be greatest in the early (and more rapid) periods of intelligence development and least in the later (and less rapid) periods of development. Although there is relatively little evidence of the effects of changing the environment on the changes in intelligence, the evidence so far available suggests that marked changes in the environment in the early years can produce greater changes in intelligence than will equally marked changes in the environment at later periods of development.

Can one expect that, without formal planning, all the necessary learning experiences will occur?

There is an old legend that if you put six chimpanzees in front of six typewriters and leave them there long enough they eventually will produce all the works in the British Museum. One could paraphrase this for early childhood by suggesting that six children with good eyes and ears and hands and brains would, if left alone in nature, arrive at a number system, discover the laws of conservation of matter and energy, comprehend gravity and the motions of the planets and perhaps arrive at the theory of relativity. All the 'facts' necessary to discern these relationships are readily available. Perhaps a more realistic example would be to suggest that, if we surround a group of young children with a carefully selected set of play materials, they would eventually discover for themselves the laws of color mixture, of form and contour, of perspective, of formal rhythm and tonal relationships, and biological growth. And, to be sure, all this *could* occur. But whether this will necessarily occur with any frequency is quite another matter. We also assume that at a still earlier period a child will learn body control, eye–hand coordination, the rudiments of language and styles of problem solving in an entirely incidental and unplanned way. In an article in a recent issue of a popular woman's magazine, Holt (1965) fervently urges parents to stop trying to teach their young children in order that the children may learn. And, to be sure, there is always something to be said for this caution; it is all too easy to have planned learning experiences become didactic and regimented rather than subtle and opportunistic.

As more people gain experience in operating nursery-school programs for children with an early history deficient in many categories of experience, the conviction appears to be gaining momentum that such children often are not able to avail themselves of the educational opportunities and must be guided into meaningful learning encounters. In a recent paper dealing with the preschool behavior of a group of twenty-one children from multiproblem families, Malone (1966, p. 5) describes the inability of the children to carry out self-directed exploratory maneuvers with the toys and equipment as follows:

When the children first came to nursery school they lacked interest in learning the names and properties of objects. Colors, numbers, sizes, shapes, locations, all seemed interchangeable. Nothing in the room seemed to have meaning for a child apart from the fact that another child had approached or handled it or that the teacher's attention was turned toward it. Even brief play depended on the teacher's involvement and support.

When one reflects on the number of carefully arranged reinforcement contingencies necessary to help a young child learn to decode the simple message 'No', it is difficult to support the position that in early learning, as in anything else, nature should just take its course.

Is formal training for child-care during the first three years unnecessary?

This assumption is obviously quite ridiculous and yet it is one logical derivative of the hypothesis that the only adequate place for a young child is with his mother or a permanent mother substitute. There is, perhaps unfortunately, no literacy test for motherhood. This again is one of our interesting scientific paradoxes. That is, proclaiming in one breath that mothering is essential for the healthy development of a child, we have in the very next breath implied that just any mothering will do. It is interesting in this connection that from the elementary school level forward we have rigid certification statutes in most states that regulate the training requirements for persons who would qualify as teachers of our children. (The same degree of control over the qualifications and training of a nursery-school teacher has not prevailed in the past, but we are moving into an era when it will.) So again, our pattern of social action appears to support the implicit belief in the lack of importance of the first three years of life.

In 1928, John B. Watson wrote a controversial little trade book called *The Psychological Care of Infant and Child*. He included one chapter heretically entitled 'The dangers of too much mother love'. In this chapter he suggested that child training was too important to be left in the hands of mothers, apparently not because he felt them intellectually inadequate but because of their sentimentality. In his typical 'nondirective' style Watson (1928, p. 149) wrote:

Six months' training in the actual handling of children from two to six under the eye of competent instructors should make a fairly satisfactory child's nurse. To keep them we should let the position of nurse or governess in the home be a respected one. Where the mother herself must be the nurse – which is the case in the vast majority of American homes – she must look upon herself while performing the functions of a nurse as a professional woman and not as a sentimentalist masquerading under the name of 'Mother'.

At present in this country a number of training programs are currently being formulated which would attempt to give this kind of professional training called for by Watson and many others. It is perhaps not possible to advance on all fronts at the same time and the pressing health needs of the young child demanded and received top priority in earlier decades. Perhaps it will now be possible to extend our efforts at social intervention to encompass a broader range of health, education and welfare activities.

Are most homes and most parents adequate for at least the first three years?

Enough has been presented in discussing other implicit assumptions to make it unnecessary to amplify this point at length. The clinical literature and much of the research literature of the last decade dealing with social-class differences have made abundantly clear that all parents are not qualified to provide even the basic essentials of physical and psychological care to their children. Such reports as those describing the incidence of battered children (Elmer, 1963; Kempe, 1962) capture our attention, but reports concerned with subtler and yet perhaps more long-standing patterns of parental deficit also fill the literature. In her description of the child-rearing environments provided by low lower-class families, Pavenstedt (1965) has described them as impulse-determined with very little evidence of clear planfulness for activities that would benefit either parent or child. Similarly, Wortis and associates (1963) have described the extent to which the problems of the low-income mother so overwhelm her with reactions of depression and inadequacy that behavior toward the child is largely determined by the needs of the moment rather than by any clear plan about how to bring up children and how to train them to engage in the kind of behavior that the parents regard as acceptable or desirable. No social class and no cultural or ethnic group has exclusive rights to the domain of inadequate parentage; all conscientious parents must strive constantly for improvement on this score. However, relatively little attention has been paid to the possibly deleterious consequences of inadequacies during the first three years of life. Parents have been blamed for so many problems of their children in later age periods that a moderate reaction formation appears to have set in. But again, judging by the type of social action taken by the responsible professional community, parental inadequacy during the first three years is seldom considered as a major menace. Perhaps, when the various alternatives are weighed, it appears by comparison to be the least of multiple evils; but parental behavior of the first three years should not be regarded as any more sacrosanct or beyond the domain of social concern than that of the later years.

Planning alternatives

At this point the exposition of this paper must come to an abrupt halt, for insufficient data about possible alternative models are available to warrant recommendation of any major pattern of change. At present there are no completed research projects that have developed and evaluated alternative approximations of optimal learning environments for young children in our culture. One apparent limitation on ideas for alternative models appears to be the tendency to think in terms of binary choices. That is, we speak of individual care versus group care, foster home versus institution, foster home versus own home, and so on. But environments for the very young child do not need to be any more mutually exclusive than they are for the older children. After all, what is our public education system but a coordination of the efforts of home plus an institution? Most of us probably would agree that the optimal learning environment for the older child is neither of these alone but rather a combination of both. Some of this same pattern of combined effort also may represent the optimal arrangement for the very young child.

A number of programs suggesting alternatives possibly worth considering are currently in the early field trial stage. One such program is the one described by Caldwell and Richmond (1964). This program offers educationally oriented day care for culturally deprived children between six months and three years of age. The children spend the better part of five days a week in a group care setting (with an adult–child ratio never lower than 1:4) but return home each evening and maintain primary emotional relationships with their own families. Well-child-care, social and psychological services, and parent education activities are available for participating families. The educational program is carefully planned to try to help the child develop the personal-social and cognitive attributes conducive to learning and to provide experiences which can partially compensate for inadequacies which may have existed in the home environment. The strategy involved in offering the enrichment experience to children in this very young age group is to maximize their potential and hopefully prevent the deceleration in rate of development which seems to occur in many deprived children around the age of two to three years. It is thus an exercise in circumvention rather than remediation. Effectiveness of the endeavor is being determined by a comparison of the participating children with a control group of children from similar backgrounds who are not enrolled in the enrichment program. Unfortunately at this juncture it is too early for such projects to do more than suggest alternatives. The degree of confidence which comes only from research evidence plus replicated experience will have to wait a little longer.

Effective social action, however, can seldom await definitive data. And in the area of child-care the most clamorous demand for innovative action appears to be coming from a rather unlikely source – not from any of the professional groups, not particularly from social planners who try to incorporate research data into plans for social action, but from *mothers*. From mothers themselves is coming the demand that professionals in the field look at some of the alternatives. We need not be reminded here that in America at the present time there are more than three million working mothers with children under six years of age (President's Commission on the Status of Women, 1963). And these mothers are looking for professional leadership to design and provide child-care facilities that help prepare their children for today's achievement-oriented culture. The challenge which has been offered is inevitable. After almost two decades of bombarding women with the importance of their mothering role, we might have predicted the weakening of their defenses and their waving the flag of truce as though to say 'I am not good enough to do all that you are saying I must do.'

It is a characteristic of social evolution that an increased recognition of the importance of any role leads to the professionalization of that role and there can be no doubt but that we are currently witnessing the early stages of professionalization of the mother-substitute role – or, as I would prefer to say, the mother-supplement. It is interesting to note that no one has as yet provided a satisfactory label for this role. The term 'baby-sitter' is odious, reminding us of just about all some of the 'less well trained' professionals do – sit with babies. If English were a masculine–feminine language, there is little doubt that the word would be used in the feminine gender, for we always speak of this person as a 'she' (while emphasizing that young children need more contact with males). We cannot borrow any of the terms from already professionalized roles, such as 'nurse' or 'teacher', although such persons must be to a great extent both nurse and teacher. Awkward designations such as 'child-care worker' or hybridized terms such as 'nurse-teacher' do not quite seem to fill the bill; and there appears to be some reluctance to accept an untranslated foreign word like the Hebrew 'metapelet' or the Russian 'Nyanya'. When such a word does appear, let us hope that it rhymes well and has a strong trochaic rhythm, for it will have to sustain a whole new era of poetry and song. (This author is convinced that the proper verb is *nurture*. It carries the desired connotations, but even to one who is not averse to neologisms such nominative forms as 'nurturist', 'nurturer' and 'nurturizer' sound alien and inadequate.)[1]

Another basis for planning alternatives is becoming available from a less direct but potentially more persuasive source – from increasing knowledge about the process of development. The accumulation of data suggesting that the first few years of life are crucial for the priming of cognitive development call for vigorous and imaginative action programs for those early years. To say that it is premature to try to plan optimal environments because we do not fully understand how learning occurs is unacceptable. Perhaps only by the development of carefully arranged environments will we attain a complete understanding of the learning process. Already a great deal is known which enables us to specify some of the essential ingredients of a growth-fostering milieu. Such an environment must contain warm and responsive people who by their own interests invest objects with value. It must be supportive and as free of disease and pathogenic agents as possibly can be arranged. It also must trace a clear path from where the child is to where he is to go developmentally; objects and events must be similar enough to what the child has experienced to be assimilated by the child and yet novel enough to stimulate and attract. Such an environment must be exquisitely responsive,

1. In a letter to the author written shortly after the meeting at which this paper was presented, Miss Rena Corman of New York City suggested that the proper term should be 'nurcher', a compound of the words 'nurse' and 'teacher'. To be sure, a 'nurcher' sounds nurturant.

as a more consistent pattern of response is required to foster the acquisition of new forms of behavior than is required to maintain such behavior once it appears in the child's repertoire. The timing of experiences also must be carefully programmed. The time table for the scheduling of early postnatal events may well be every bit as demanding as that which obtains during the embryological period. For children whose early experiences are known to be deficient and depriving, attempts to program such environments seem mandatory if subsequent learning difficulties are to be circumvented.

References

AINSWORTH, M. (1962), *Reversible and Irreversible Effects of Maternal Deprivation on Intellectual Development*, Child Welfare League of America.

ANDERSON, J. E., et al. (1959), 'A survey of children's adjustment over time', University of Minnesota.

BARKER, R. G., and WRIGHT, H. F. (1955), *Midwest and its Children: The Psychological Ecology of an American Town*, Row, Peterson.

BAYLEY, N. (1949), 'Consistency and variability in the growth of intelligence from birth to eighteen years', *J. genet. Psychol.*, vol. 75, pp. 165–96.

BERES, D., and OBERS, S. (1950), 'The effects of extreme deprivation in infancy on psychic structure in adolescence', *Psychoanal. Stud. Child*, vol. 5, pp. 121–40.

BINET, A., and SIMON, T. (1916), *The Development of Intelligence in Children*, trans. E. S. Kite, Williams & Wilkins.

BLOOM, B. S. (1964), *Stability and Change in Human Characteristics*, Wiley.

BRONFENBRENNER, U. (1962), 'Soviet studies of personality development and socialization', in *Some Views on Soviet Psychology*, American Psychological Association, pp. 63–85.

CALDWELL, B. M., and RICHMOND, J. B. (1964), 'Programmed day care for the very young child – a preliminary report', *J. Marr. Fam.*, vol. 26, pp. 481–8.

CALDWELL, B. M., et al. (1963), 'Mother–infant interaction in monomatric and polymatric families', *Amer. J. Orthopsychiat.*, vol. 33, pp. 653–64.

DAVIS, A., and HAVIGHURST, R. J. (1946), 'Social class and color differences in child-rearing', *Amer. soc. Rev.*, vol. 11, pp. 698–710.

DENNIS, W. (1960), 'Causes of retardation among institutional children', *J. genet. Psychol.*, vol. 96, pp. 47–59.

DENNIS, W., and NAJARIAN, P. (1957), 'Infant development under environmental handicap', *Psychol. Monogr.*, vol. 71, no. 7.

ELMER, E. (1963), 'Identification of abused children', *Children*, vol. 10, pp. 180–84.

FOWLER, W. (1962), 'Cognitive learning in infancy and early childhood', *Psychol. Bull.*, vol. 59, pp. 116–52.

FREUD, A., and DANN, S. (1951), 'An experiment in group upbringing', in O. Fenichel (ed.), *The Psychoanalytic Study of the Child*, vol. 6, International Universities Press, pp. 127–68.

GARDNER, D. B., HAWKES, G. R., and BURCHINAL, L. G. (1961), 'Noncontinuous mothering in infancy and development in later childhood', *Child Devel.*, vol. 32, pp. 225–34.

GOLDFARB, W. (1949), 'Rorschach test differences between family-reared, institution-reared and schizophrenic children', *Amer. J. Orthopsychiat.*, vol. 19, pp. 624–33.

GULA, H. (1965), Paper read at Conference on Group Care for Children, Children's Bureau, January.

HOFFMAN, L. W. (1961), 'Effects of maternal employment on the child', *Child Devel.*, vol. 32, pp. 187–97.

HOLT, J. (1965), 'How to help babies learn – without teaching them', *Redbook*, vol. 126, pp. 54–5, 134–7.

IRVINE, E. E. (1952), 'Observations on the aims and methods of child-rearing on communal settlements in Israel', *Hum. Rel.*, vol. 5, pp. 247–75.

KEMPE, C. H., et al. (1962), 'The battered-child syndrome', *J. Amer. Med. Assn*, vol. 181, pp. 17–24.

LEWIS, O. (1959), *Five Families*, Basic Books.

MAAS, H. (1963), 'Long-term effects of early childhood separation and group care', *Vita Hum.*, vol. 6, pp. 34–56.

MACCOBY, E., and GIBBS, P. K. (1954), 'Methods of child-rearing in two social classes', in W. E. Martin and C. B. Stendler (eds.), *Readings in Child Development*, Harcourt, Brace & World, pp. 380–96.

MALONE, C. A. (1966), 'Safety first: comments on the influence of external danger in the lives of children of disorganized families', *Amer. J. Orthopsychiat.*, vol. 36, pp. 3–12.

MEAD, M. (1930), *Growing Up in New Guinea*, New American Library, 1953.

MURPHY, L. B., et al. (1962), *The Widening World of Childhood*, Basic Books.

PAVENSTEDT, E. (1965), 'A comparison of the child-rearing environment of upper-lower and very low-lower class families', *Amer. J. Orthopsychiat.*, vol. 35, pp. 89–98.

PIAGET, J. (1952), *The Origins of Intelligence in Children*, trans. M. Cook, International Universities Press.

PRESIDENT'S COMMISSION ON THE STATUS OF WOMEN (1963), *American Women*.

PROVENCE, S., and LIPTON, R. C. (1962), *Infants in Institutions*, International Universities Press.

RABIN, A. I. (1957), 'Personality maturity of Kibbutz and non-Kibbutz children as reflected in Rorschach findings', *J. proj. Tech.*, vol. 21, pp. 143–53.

Radke Yarrow, M. (1961), 'Maternal employment and child rearing', *Children*, vol. 8, pp. 223–8.

Rheingold, H. (1956), 'The modification of social responsiveness in institutional babies', *Monogr. Soc. Res. Child Devel.*, vol. 21, no. 63.

Rheingold, H., and Bayley, N. (1959), 'The later effects of an experimental modification of mothering', *Child Devel.*, vol. 30, pp. 363–72.

Rousseau, J. J. (1762), *Emile*, Barron's Educational Series, Great Neck, New York, 1950.

Siegel, A., and Hass, M. B. (1963), 'The working mother: a review of the research', *Child Devel.*, vol. 34, pp. 513–42.

Skeels, H., and Dye, H. (1939), 'A study of the effects of differential stimulation on mentally retarded children', *Proc. Amer. Assn Ment. Def.*, vol. 44, pp. 114–36.

Spiro, M. (1958), *Children of the Kibbutz*, Harvard University Press.

Terman, L. M., and Oden, M. H. (1947), *The Gifted Child Grows Up: Twenty-Five Years' Follow-Up of a Superior Group*, Stanford University Press.

Terman, L. M., et al. (1925), *Genetic Studies of Genius: I. Mental and Physical Traits of a Thousand Gifted Children*, Stanford University Press.

Watson, J. B. (1928), *The Psychological Care of Infant and Child*, Allen & Unwin.

White, R. W. (1959), 'Motivation reconsidered: the concept of competence', *Psychol. Rev.*, vol. 66, pp. 297–333.

Wortis, H., et al. (1963), 'Child-rearing practices in a low socio-economic group', *Pediatrics*, vol. 32, pp. 298–307.

Yarrow, L. J. (1961), 'Maternal deprivation: toward an empirical and conceptual re-evaluation', *Psychol. Bull.*, vol. 58, pp. 459–90.

Part Four
Restriction and Enrichment of Early Experience

Experiments with animals designed to throw light on early-experience effects have commonly either (a) restricted the experiences of experimental subjects as compared with control ones or (b) provided experimental subjects with experience additional to that of control subjects. Thompson and Heron (Reading 13) studied the effects of varying degrees of deprivation of experience early in the life of dogs upon their later problem-solving abilities. Melzack and Scott (Reading 14) similarly investigated the effects of early sensory restriction on dogs' avoidance behaviour. On the other hand, Levine, Chevalier and Korchin (Reading 15) provided their subjects, young laboratory rats, with extra stimulation in the form of periodic handling and electric shocks, in order to assess the influence of such treatment upon the later learning abilities of the animals. We may well ask whether any generalizations about the effects of infantile stimulation are possible. Denenberg (Reading 16) attempts an answer to this question.

13 William R. Thompson and Woodburn Heron

The Effects of Restricting Early Experience on the Problem-Solving Capacity of Dogs

Excerpt from William R. Thompson and Woodburn Heron, 'The effects of restricting early experience on the problem-solving capacity of dogs', *Canadian Journal of Psychology*, vol. 8, 1954, pp. 17–31.

In psychological research on the nature–nurture problem, extensive work has been done on the degree to which inherited endowment can be influenced by environment. On the human side, many studies have dealt with the effects of improved environment on I Q (Jones, 1946; National Society for the Study of Education, 1940; Stern, 1949; Wellman, 1945). On the whole, these have failed to demonstrate decisively any gains in performance on intelligence tests which were administered during or shortly after the period of enriched experience. Newman, Freeman and Holzinger (1937), in their classic study of twins separated at an early age and reared apart, found in some cases differences in intelligence as great as twenty-four I Q points. But in other pairs, also raised in very different environments, they found almost no differences. Similarly, studies such as those of some Iowa investigators (National Society for the Study of Education, 1940), purporting to show losses in I Q scores due to an impoverished environment, have been by no means definitive. The rather remarkable claims made by Skeels and Dye, for example, have been challenged by Goodenough and Terman (National Society for the Study of Education, 1940) on the grounds that their study involved a highly biased sample. Thus the human data have failed to supply any clear-cut answer to the problem.

Animal experimentation on the same question has given more conclusive results. A number of authors (Bingham and Griffiths, 1952; Forgays and Forgays, 1952; Hebb, 1947; Hymovitch, 1952; Wolf, 1943) have found that adult rats, whose early experience has been restricted, do worse on tests of learning ability and intelligence than those who have had an enriched early environment. In the case of the dog, a higher genus capable of more complex behaviour, wide effects have been observed to result from limitation of early perceptual experience (Clarke, Heron, Fetherstonhaugh, Forgays and Hebb, 1951; The first of these studies by Clarke *et al.* showed that performance on intelligence tests was definitely poorer in three dogs raised in restriction; the results also indicated that restriction affected other aspects of behaviour. Although these results were based on small numbers, they agree closely with the rat experiments referred to above. Since the dog is much closer to man than the rat in the range and complexity of its behaviour, it would seem of considerable importance to check and extend the findings of Clarke *et al.* on this genus. Some light might thus be shed on the apparent discrepancy between the human and animal data.

Accordingly, the present experiment is an attempt to examine the effects of restricting the early experience of dogs on their problem-solving ability later in life.

The experiment
Animals

Twenty-six pure-bred Scottish terriers, all descendants of one litter of the Bar Harbor strain, were used. Sixteen were males and ten were females. Rearing conditions were as follows: a litter was split at the time of weaning as evenly as possible into a control and an experimental group. The control subjects, thirteen in all, were raised as pets, either in homes or in the laboratory, up to the age of eight months, so as to give them as rich an early environment as possible. After this period, they were kept in metal dog cages 24 × 32 × 72 in and exercised outside daily when weather permitted. The thirteen subjects in the experimental group were reared till they were from seven to ten months old under three degrees of restriction: severe, moderate and slight.

The two severely restricted subjects were raised in complete isolation in specially constructed boxes with solid walls, 30 × 40 × 60 in.[1] These boxes were divided in the centre by a sliding metal door into two separate compartments, so that one side could be cleaned while the dog occupied the other side. One side was

1. These boxes were designed and constructed by Mr Ronald Melzack.

always kept dark, the other lighted by an overhead bulb inside the compartment. Since the dog spent alternate days in each section, it received light on every other day. Air was circulated through the boxes by means of a fan. A small panel in the top of the boxes permitted observation.

The eight moderately restricted subjects were raised for from eight to ten months in ordinary metal dog cages. The wire-mesh fronts of these cages were covered with cardboard, but the tops were left uncovered, so that the subjects received light but were unable to see anything outside their cages except the ceiling. Two or three dogs were kept together in one cage. They had contacts with human beings for about ten minutes daily while their cages were being cleaned.

The three slightly restricted subjects were raised for seven months in similar cages, the fronts and tops of which were left uncovered. Consequently, these subjects received a considerable amount of perceptual experience, although only of the environment immediately outside their cages. They also had occasional contact with human beings and were brought into the adjoining room for grooming or medication about once a month.

At the end of the period of restriction, the experimental subjects were kept under the same conditions as the normal subjects. They were allowed to exercise outside and had frequent contact with human beings. There was no detectable difference between the two groups in health and vigour, although the mean weight of the normal subjects (15·6 lb) was greater than that of the restricted (14·7 lb).

It should be mentioned at this point that, although the total number of dogs involved in the whole study was twenty-six, the number used in any particular experiment always fell short of this. This was due largely to shortage of space for housing the animals and the consequent necessity of staggering the testing over a period of several years. Deaths and pregnancies were additional factors which reduced the total number available at any particular time. In Table 1 are shown the litters used in each experiment and their division into normal and restricted groups. Although matching in each test was not exact, variability due to genetic background was probably small, since all animals in the colony came from the same original litter of two females and one male. The order in which the subjects were tested, although not always the same within groups, was about equivalent between groups. This point will be elaborated as we deal with each test.

Table 1 Litters Used in Each Test

Litter	Preliminary tests Normal	Preliminary tests Restricted	Delayed reaction Normal	Delayed reaction Restricted	Open-field maze Normal	Open-field maze Restricted
A1	0	0	1	0	1	0
A2	1	2	1	2	1	2
B	3	3	3	3	3	3
C1	1	0	0	2	3	3
C2	1	0	0	0	1	0
D	1	3	0	0	0	0
E	1	2	0	0	0	0
F	0	0	0	0	2	0
Total	8	10	5	7	11	8

General behaviour of the restricted dogs

Restriction had gross effects which were plainly observable in the experimental animals as soon as they were removed from their rearing cages. In contrast to the reports of Clarke *et al.*, all the present animals were hyperactive after they emerged. They galloped actively about the room, often jumping at the walls. In addition, they showed a marked tendency to chase their tails and even when remaining in one spot displayed a peculiar 'marking time' behaviour, evinced by rapid movements of the legs and head. In other respects, the previous observations (Clarke *et al.*, 1951) of the restricted animals' behaviour were confirmed. The present subjects displayed a marked tendency to lick at the experimenters' hands and would become very excited when they did so. At the same time, they showed some tendency to withdraw when the experimenter approached, this withdrawal usually being accompanied by bursts of hyperactivity. These types of behaviour appear to be fairly permanent and can be noticed in animals which have been removed from restriction for over a year.

In addition, it was observed that the restricted animals at first showed marked disturbances in sensory–motor coordination.

They had great difficulty in negotiating stairs and would often skid and fall if they attempted to turn corners rapidly. In addition, they showed some tendency to bump into objects, the experimenters or other dogs. These types of behaviour, however, disappeared within a few months.

Motivational and emotional behaviour

In the measurement of problem-solving ability, the motivation and emotionality of subjects may often affect their scores. To allow for this possibility in the present experiment, a few simple tests of these traits were given to seven normal and eight restricted subjects and a comparison made between them.

The first of these involved a measurement of the amount of food eaten by each subject in four three-minute sessions. Each dog was put in a small enclosure in an experimental room and allowed to eat freely for three minutes from a dish containing 300 g of Purina dog checkers. The subject was then given its full daily ration of food and returned to its cage. Over the four sessions, the mean amounts of food eaten by the normal and restricted subjects were respectively 74·6 g and 99·4 g. These do not differ significantly.

The second test of hunger motivation was similar to one described in the Bar Harbor dog testing manual (Scott and Fuller, 1950). Subjects were required to run to food down a long corridor, approximately 9 by 90 feet. The number of seconds to get to food in two daily sessions of five trials each was used as a measure. It was found that the restricted dogs took longer than normals in both sessions, though the differences are again not significant. In session I, the means were 7·6 s for normals, 11·5 s for restricted, and in session II the corresponding means were 7·4 s and 9·7 s. However, it should be mentioned that timing was commenced only when the subject had actually started out toward the food. Some restricted subjects were very slow in this respect and sometimes had to be aided by being faced in the right direction by one experimenter and being called by the other experimenter who stood next to the goal box. None of the normal subjects behaved in this manner. Usually they had to be restrained until the experimenters were ready for them to start. This fact may not necessarily indicate a difference in motivation, however; rather it may indicate a difference in intellectual capacity to maintain attention on a specific problem. Thus, at least on the basis of these two tests, there is no reason to suppose that hunger motivation was stronger or weaker in the normal than in the restricted subjects.

Since emotionality in the two groups will be the subject of a forthcoming paper, it will not be dealt with in detail here. During the intelligence tests no systematic differences in emotionality could be detected. Some dogs in each group were more timid than others and more difficult to train. But this was by no means confined to either normals or restricted. The same applies to motivation, no differences between the groups in strength of food drive being observed during the tests.

In view of the above findings as to the normal and restricted subjects, we feel justified in attributing the differences that appeared between them in the tests of problem-solving ability to differences in intelligence or problem-solving capacity.

Preliminary tests of intelligence

Four short tests, two orientation and two barrier tests, were used initially to give some preliminary indication of the kind and magnitude of intellectual differences between the two groups of dogs. All these tests were given in an experimental room, the testing area being approximately 8 by 10 feet. Seventeen dogs were used in all tests except the first in which eighteen were used, as shown in Table 1. Of these, eight were normal, three slightly restricted, five moderately restricted and two extremely restricted. At the time of testing, their ages ranged from seven and a half to twelve months and none had been exposed previously to problem solving. All tests involved a food incentive and twenty-four-hour deprivation. All tests were conducted in the afternoon.

Orientation test I

Procedure. The situation is diagrammed in Figure 1. The four corners of the testing area are labelled A, B, C, D. Each subject was started by one experimenter at corner D and trained for ten trials to run to food at A, approximately 8 feet away. All subjects easily acquired this habit, usually in less than the full number of trials given. Then, in full sight of the subject, the food pan was switched 90° to corner C, so that, whereas it had previously been on the subject's right side, it was now on its left. The attention of the subject was drawn to the new position by banging the pan on the floor and holding the food out for it to see. Five trials were then given from starting corner D to C. After this, the pan was changed to corner B, diagonally opposite D, and five more trials given. Then another trial was given from D to C, two trials from D to A, and one final trial from B as starting point to A. There were thus ten training trials and fourteen test trials. An error was scored when, in any test run, the subject did not follow a direct path to the food. The total of possible errors was thus fourteen. Minor deviations from the direct path were not counted as errors.

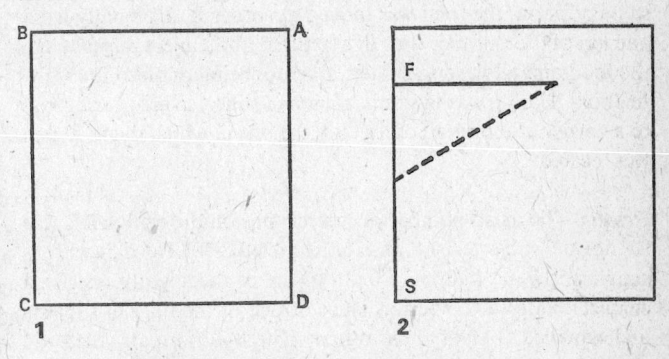

Figure 1 The testing area used in the two orientation tests

Figure 2 The testing area used in the two barrier tests

Results. The mean number of correct runs for normal subjects was 13·7 and for all restricted subjects, 5·9. There was no overlap between the groups and the difference is highly significant ($t = 8.86$, $p < 0.001$). The first few trials immediately after the ten training trials gave the most dramatic results. Without exception, restricted subjects continued to go to corner A before going to C, even though they had been shown that the food was at C and could see it there. These errors could not have been due to sensory defects, since in the training trials these dogs were able to locate the food quite easily. It is clear from the means given that the normal subjects had no difficulty in this test. Only one dog out of the seven made any errors at all, and it made only two.

Orientation test II

Procedure. The situation is essentially the same as diagrammed in Figure 1. A starting box was placed in the middle of the testing area, its entrance facing wall A B. For training purposes, food was located in the corner at point A diagonally to the right of the entrance of the starting box. Ten trials were given to the animals in this position. The starting box was then rotated so that its entrance faced, in turn, wall B C, wall A D and wall C D, one trial being given in each of these positions. It was then rotated back to the first position for three trials and, finally, with the box in the same position, the food was moved to corner B, diagonally front and left of the entrance. For this last trial, the subject was taken to the food and allowed to sniff at it before being put into the starting box. Scoring was in terms of correct runs. An error was a run to a corner of the room other than the one in which the food pan was located.

Results. The mean number of correct runs on the eight trials was for normal subjects 5·14, and for restricted 2·70. The difference is significant ($t = 4·70$, $p < 0·001$). One of the slightly restricted subjects bettered the performance of one of the normal subjects and equalled that of three others. The one normal which did poorly was one of the two which had returned to the laboratory before reaching eight months of age. As in the previous tests, restricted subjects tended to perseverate in their responses and to orientate in relation to the starting box rather than in relation to the total situation.

Barrier test I

Procedure. The situation is presented in Figure 2. The starting box was placed at point marked S, next to one wall of the testing area. Food was placed in a pan approximately six feet in front of the box at F. Each subject was given five trial runs to food under these conditions. Then a chicken-wire barrier, 5 feet in length and 4 feet high, was introduced immediately in front of the food. An error zone was marked with chalk extending from one end of the barrier to a point on the wall 2 feet from the other end. Ten trials were given to each subject; scores were the number of runs which did not involve an entry into the error zone.

Results. Mean scores for normal and restricted subjects were respectively 6·75 and 2·40. The difference is significant ($t = 6.13$, $p < 0.001$). Restricted subjects tended to have more difficulty in breaking the previously established habit of running straight to food and consequently entered the error zone much more frequently than normal subjects.

Barrier test II

Procedure. In this test, the wire barrier was placed at right angles against a wall on one side of the testing area as before and an extra piece of mesh, 2 feet long, was added to the protruding end of the barrier. This piece was arranged so that it was parallel to the wall. The whole constituted an enclosure which was open at the rear. Food was placed outside the enclosure at the mid-point of the mesh barrier. Each subject was taken to the food and allowed to sniff at it, then placed in the enclosure. To solve the problem, the animal had to turn its back on the food, exit through the rear of the enclosure and run around the barrier to the goal. The time which it took the subject to do this was used for scoring purposes. Five trials were given to each dog.

Results. Mean times in seconds from start to food, for the five trials, were 29·4 s for normal subjects and 72·10s for restricted subjects. The difference is significant ($t = 2.26$, $p < 0.05$). Only one case of overlap between the groups occurred.

In summary, the four preliminary tests clearly indicated that restricted subjects were inferior to normals in mental ability. If comparisons are made only between normal and restricted littermates, the results are exactly the same. No differences appeared between the severely, moderately and slightly restricted groups.

Delayed reaction

Procedure

Five normal and seven moderately restricted dogs were used in this experiment, as shown in Table 1. One normal and two restricted subjects were two years of age at the time of testing. All others were approximately one and a half years' old. All except one normal (litter A1) and two restricted (litter C1) had previously had the preliminary tests. These three exceptions had been run on the open-field maze (see below).

The experimental situation is diagrammed in Figure 3. The two food boxes (in front of parts marked G) were made of unpainted plywood. They measured 10 by 10 in. Their doors were suspended from a crossbar and so balanced that they would open at a touch and then remain open. On these doors were lucite frames into which stimulus cards could be inserted. In the present experiment, white cards were used on both doors. The starting box, marked S, measured $30 \times 20 \times 18$ in and was located 8 feet from the food boxes. Subjects could be released from the starting box by lifting two sliding panels, one lucite, the other wood. When subjects in either group showed any tendency to make a choice too quickly, the plywood door was lifted before the lucite one, so that the subject had an opportunity to choose the correct side before leaving the box. Beaverboard barriers, 2 feet high, were placed at the sides, as shown in Figure 3.

All subjects were put on a twenty-four-hour food-deprivation

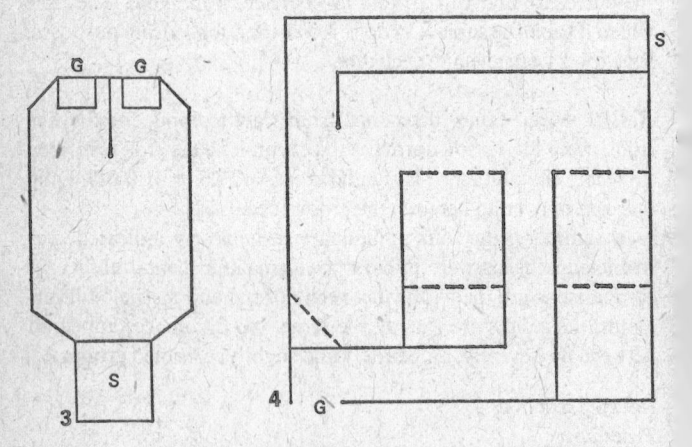

Figure 3 Ground plan of the apparatus for testing delayed reaction

Figure 4 Open-field maze, problem no. 11

schedule and were fed their full daily ration of food immediately after testing. Each was taken in turn to the experimental room and allowed to watch the experimenter placing food in one of the goal boxes. To make sure the animals were attending, they were also permitted to try to get at the food, though restrained from eating any of it. They were then taken immediately back to the starting box. For the preliminary training trials, the subject was shown the position of the food and then placed in the starting box. The door of this was then immediately opened (zero delay) and the subject allowed to make its choice. The position of the food was varied randomly, unless the subject developed a preference for one side, in which case the other side was reinforced more frequently. The wrong goal box was closed, and the subject was allowed to correct its errors. Ten trials a day were given until the subject had reached a criterion of ten correct choices in ten trials. Each dog that achieved the criterion was then tested with the following delay periods (commencing from the moment of its insertion into the starting box): 5, 10, 15, 20, 25, 30, 40, 50, 60, 70, 80, 90, 105, 120, 135, 150, 180, 240, 300 s. For each delay period, the criterion was five out of five correct runs. A total of ten trials a day was given. After a maximum of 300 trials had been given, testing was stopped.

Results

The performance of the two groups of dogs is summarized in Table 2. It is immediately apparent that there is no overlap at all between them. Six out of seven of the restricted subjects were unable to achieve criterion even at zero delay and the remaining one reached only a 25 s delay with 300 trials. Of the five normal subjects, the worst one reached a 50 s delay period within 255 trials, while the three best reached 4 and 5 min delays in less than 250 trials. There was every indication that they could have exceeded this performance if more trials had been given, but since their superiority was already plainly established, there seemed little point in continuing. The oldest subject in the normal group was the best, but in the restricted group, the two older subjects were no better than the younger ones.

A comparison between the four normal and five restricted litter-mates (litters A2 and B) that had run the preliminary tests first and the delayed-reaction test second shows exactly the same results. The other normal dog (litter A1) and the two restricted (litter C1) had the same father and their mothers were sisters. They were also run in the same order (maze followed by delayed reaction) and can, therefore, be legitimately compared. There was no overlap between them. Thus there is little doubt of the marked differences between the normal and restricted dogs.

Table 2 The Number of Trials Required by Normal and Restricted Dogs to Reach Delay Periods of Varying Lengths

Normal			Restricted		
Litter	Delay period reached	Trials required	Litter	Delay period reached	Trials required
A1	300	230	A2	25	300
A2	50	255	A2	0	300
B	240	185	B	0	300
B	240	220	B	0	300
B	135	235	B	0	300
			C1	0	300
			C1	0	300
Median	240	230		0	300

Open-field maze[2]

Procedure

This test was based on the one described by Hebb and Williams (1946) for testing the intelligence of rats, and later standardized by Rabinovitch and Rosvold (1951).

Eleven normal and eight moderately restricted dogs were used in the experiment, as shown in Table 1. Ages ranged from one to one and a half years at the time of testing. Results for six of the dogs have already been summarized in a previous paper (Clarke *et al.*, 1951), but are included here in more detail.

Nine of the subjects (four normal, five restricted) had been run previously on the preliminary tests and the delayed-reaction test, in that order. In the normal group, two subjects of litter C1, two of litter F and one of litter A1 had had none of the tests. One

2. Thanks are due to Mrs Muriel Stern who assisted in part of this test.

subject of litter C1 and one of litter C2 had taken only the preliminary tests. In the restricted group, three subjects of litter C1 had had none of the tests. It will be noted that, on the average, the restricted group had had more experience with tests than the normals.

The maze consisted of an outdoor wire enclosure, 17×17 feet, and approximately $2\frac{1}{2}$ feet high. It was divided into forty-nine square units. The adjustable barriers, also of wire, varied in length from one to six units and were arranged in various combinations, each combination forming a particular problem. Eighteen such problems were devised, each having a certain number of error zones representing deviations from the correct path. A sample problem is diagrammed in Figure 4. Barriers are marked by solid lines, error zones by broken lines.

Before formal testing commenced, a series of simple practice problems was given to the subjects, one a day, until they ran without hesitation from the starting gate to food at the other end of the maze. For most subjects this took three to five days. No difference could be detected between the normal and restricted subjects in the rate at which they adapted to the maze. The main series of eighteen problems was then given at the rate of one per day, six trials per problem. Error and time scores were taken.

The specific procedure was as follows: each dog was put on a twenty-four-hour deprivation schedule and tested in the afternoons, weather permitting. Two experimenters were necessary, one to let the subject in through the starting gate, the other to feed it at the goal (one bite of food was allowed at the end of each trial) and send it back to the starting point. All subjects readily learned to run round the side of the maze back to the start after each trial. If a subject made more than twenty errors on a trial, it was guided by one experimenter through the correct path. At the end of six trials, each subject was given the remainder of its daily ration of food in an enclosure near the maze, while the next subject was being tested.

Results

On the average, restricted subjects made more errors on all eighteen problems except nos. 10 and 17, on which the two groups were equal. The most difficult problem was no. 13 which some subjects, both normal and restricted, found impossible to solve. This is omitted in the comparison of total error scores for the eighteen problems presented in Table 3. The means of the two groups are significantly different ($t = 3.37$, $p < 0.01$) and there were only two normal subjects that did as poorly as any of the restricted subjects. One of these was a pregnant female which had some difficulty in running and quickly became tired. However, total scores of the subjects from problems 8 to 18 showed no overlap at all, indicating that the normal subjects improved more than the restricted subjects from one problem to the next. Time scores of the two groups were about equal.

Table 3 Error Totals of Normal and Restricted Dogs on Problems 1 to 18 of the Open-Field Maze Test

Normal ($n = 11$)		Restricted ($n = 8$)	
Litter	Error score	Litter	Error score
A2	218	A2	318
B	353	A2	331
B	217	B	455
B	309	B	498
C1	203	B	315
C1	218	C1	297
C1	229	C1	266
C2	262	C1	267
A1	224		
F	180		
F	192		
Mean	237	Mean	344

In this test it is possible to compare six normals and eight restricted of three litters (A2, B, C1), the members of which participated in the experiments in the same order. With these factors held constant, there was found to be only one case of overlap in error scores (in litter B).

The reliability of the test was calculated by a rank correlation of odd against even problems and was found to be 0·67 ($p < 0.01$). Application of the Brown–Spearman formula raised this to 0·80. Consequently, the maze can be regarded as a reliable test.

Although normal subjects were superior to restricted subjects in maze learning, the course of learning of the two groups during any one problem was similar. This is shown in Figure 5. The points of the curves were obtained by averaging error scores on each trial over problems 1 to 18. There is some tendency for the curves to converge gradually from the first three trials. The restricted subjects made more errors on each trial, but especially on the first few trials on a problem.

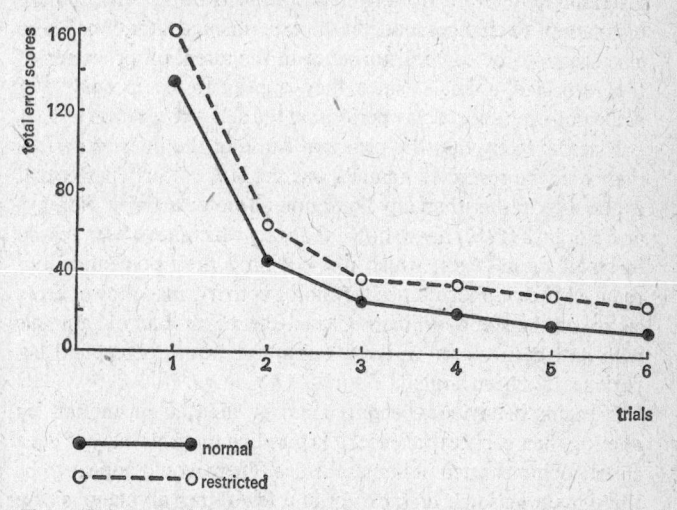

Figure 5 Intra-problem learning curve of normal and restricted dogs on the maze test

There was no indication of the development of learning sets during the course of testing. This is probably owing to the fact that only eighteen problems were used and that these were graded roughly in order of difficulty, with the easiest first and the hardest last.

In summary, it may be stated that restricted subjects showed a definite inferiority in maze learning as compared to normal subjects, particularly in the first few trials of each problem, and improved at a slower rate from problem to problem.

Discussion

The results clearly demonstrate that the limitation of early experience has adverse effects on the problem-solving ability of the adult dog. These effects appear to be fairly permanent, since they are detectable in animals which have been removed from restriction for over a year.

The exact nature of the deficit shown by the restricted dogs is not easily defined. It may be best described as a lack of ability to discriminate relevant from irrelevant aspects of the environment or to adapt to changes made in the experimental situation. There also seems to be some disturbance in the attention processes of the restricted animals, since they appear to be incapable of achieving even short delay periods on the delayed-reaction test.

It seems likely that the principal cause of the inferior performance of the restricted animals was the lack of early perceptual experience, rather than any limitation of motor activity. Forgays and Forgays (1952) have shown that rats which have been reared in small mesh cages, which did not limit their perception but reduced their opportunities for motor activity, made lower error scores on the Hebb–Williams Closed-Field Test than did animals who had been reared in large cages, but whose perceptual experience had been limited.

If major behavioural changes can be induced in animals by altering their early experience, it is puzzling that this has not been clearly demonstrated in human beings. There would appear to be three main reasons: first, except in a few rather ambiguous case studies (Davis, 1940; Hill and Robinson, 1929; Mason, 1942), there has not usually been a great contrast between the environments of the experimental and control groups. It is doubtful, for example, whether nursery-school experience is much more intellectually stimulating than the home, though it may be of benefit socially and emotionally. Secondly, enriched experience might have greater effects if commenced at an earlier age than it ordinarily is. Thus Wolf (1943) found that restricting the early experience of rats by sealing their eyes and ears induced deficits later on only if it was done during the nursing period. If introduced later than twenty-five days, it had little or no effect. Thirdly, testing for possible differences between nursery-school subjects and controls is usually carried out during the nursery-school period or soon afterwards. This may well be too soon for any effects induced to manifest themselves. There may be no point in looking for effects immediately after the nursery-school period, but a great deal of point in looking for them when the children concerned have reached maturity. Indeed, all the animal experimentation seems to suggest that this is so. This appears to be one case where the comparative method is immediately useful in interpreting and clarifying data obtained from human subjects.

References

BINGHAM, W. E., and GRIFFITHS, W. J. (1952), 'The effect of different environments during infancy on adult behavior in the rat', *J. comp. physiol. Psychol.*, vol. 45, pp. 307–12.

CLARKE, R. S., HERON, W., FETHERSTONHAUGH, M. L., FORGAYS, D. G., and HEBB, D. O. (1951), 'Individual differences in dogs: preliminary reports on the effects of early experience', *Canad. J. Psychol.*, vol. 5, pp. 150–56.

DAVIS, K. (1940), 'Extreme social isolation in a child', *Amer. J. Sociol.*, vol. 45, pp. 554–65.

FORGAYS, D. G., and FORGAYS, J. W. (1952), 'The nature of the effect of free environmental experience in the rat', *J. comp. physiol. Psychol.*, vol. 45, pp. 322–8.

HEBB, D. O. (1947), 'The effects of early experience on problem solving at maturity', *Amer. Psychol.*, vol. 2, pp. 306–7.

HEBB, D. O., and WILLIAMS, K. (1946), 'A method of rating animal intelligence', *J. genet. Psychol.*, vol. 34, pp. 59–65.

HILL, J. C., and ROBINSON, B. (1929), 'A case of retarded mental development associated with restricted movement in infancy', *Brit. J. med. Psychol.*, vol. 9, pp. 268–77.

HYMOVITCH, B. (1952), 'The effects of experimental variations on problem solving in the rat', *J. comp. physiol. Psychol.*, vol. 45, pp. 313–21.

JONES, H. E. (1946), 'Environmental influences on mental development', in L. Carmichael (ed.), *Manual of Child Psychology*, Wiley, pp. 332–69.

MASON, M. L. (1942), 'Learning to speak after six and a half years of silence', *J speech Dis.*, vol. 7, pp. 295–304.

NATIONAL SOCIETY FOR THE STUDY OF EDUCATION (1940), *Yearbook*.

NEWMAN, H. H., FREEMAN, F. N., and HOLZINGER, K. J. (1937), *Twins: A Study of Heredity and Environment*, University of Chicago Press.

RABINOVITCH, M. S., and ROSVOLD, H. E. (1951), 'A closed-field intelligence test for rats', *Canad. J. Psychol.*, vol. 5, pp. 122–8.

SCOTT, J. P., and FULLER, J. L. (1950), *Manual of Dog Testing Techniques*, Jackson Memorial Laboratory, Bar Harbor, Maine.

STERN, C. (1949), *Principles of Human Genetics*, W. H. Freeman.
WELLMAN, B. L. (1945), 'IQ changes in preschool and nonpreschool groups during preschool years: a summary of the literature', *J. Psychol.*, vol. 20, pp. 347–68.
WOLF, A. (1943), 'The dynamics of the selective inhibition of specific functions in neurosis: a preliminary report', *Psychosom. Med.*, vol. 5, pp. 27–38.

14 Ronald Melzack and T. H. Scott

The Effects of Early Experience on the Response to Pain

Excerpt from Ronald Melzack and T. H. Scott, 'The effects of early experience on the response to pain', *Journal of Comparative and Physiological Psychology*, vol. 50, 1957, pp. 155–61.

There has recently been an increase of theoretical interest in the effects of early experience on behavior, together with an increasing number of experimental studies (Beach and Jaynes, 1954). In one area, however, there is a marked discrepancy between theoretical emphasis and amount of empirical investigation: the area of avoidance behavior and pain.

Earlier clinical and theoretical formulations of the problem of early experience by Freud and his followers (Greenacre, 1945, and others there cited) have not led to any experimental studies relevant to pain perception and response, although the importance of early experience as a determinant of adult behavior was fully recognized. More recently, Scott, Fredricson and Fuller (1951) have arrived at a new hypothesis of the effects of early experience. They maintain that during the development of the organism there are specific critical periods after which sufficient maturation has occurred for various types of experience to have lasting effects on adult behavior. Although Fuller, Easler and Banks (1950) have provided evidence for a critical period in the dog for the acquisition of conditioned responses to pain, there is no direct evidence which relates early pain experience with the behavior of the mature organism.

Hebb's (1949) distinction between pain perception as a neurophysiological event and the overt response to pain, such as avoidance, has important implications for any attempt to relate early experience and pain perception in the mature organism. Hebb conceives of pain as a disruption of spatially and temporally organized activity in the cerebrum, this disruption *per se* constituting the physiological basis of pain. Since aggregates of neurons are assumed to develop their particular spatiotemporal organization as a result of prolonged, patterned sensory stimulation in early life, the theory thus suggests that the degree of pain perceived is, in part at least, dependent on the earlier experience of the organism. Pain, then, in the context of Hebb's theory, is not an elementary sensation, but a complex perceptual process in which a major role is played by all kinds of earlier perceptual learning, including both specific and nonspecific experience involving all the senses. Furthermore, as a result of direct experience with noxious stimuli, the organism tends to repeat and thus acquire any responses which decrease the cerebral disruption (i.e. pain).

That early experience does indeed play an important role in perceiving and responding to pain is strongly suggested by the study of a chimpanzee deprived of normal somesthetic stimulation during infancy and early maturity (Nissen, Chow and Semmes, 1951). After removal from somesthetic restriction, the chimpanzee appeared to have a heightened pain threshold, since 'he "panted" as chimpanzees do when they are being tickled' (ibid., p. 502) when his legs or lower ventral trunk were poked with a sharp pencil point or pin. Furthermore, the animal was found to be strikingly poor in localizing sites of noxious stimulation on its body.

The method of sensory deprivation or restriction has proved successful in ascertaining the effects of early perceptual experience on adult behavior (Melzack, 1954; Nissen, Chow and Semmes, 1951). The present experiment, then, is an attempt to study the effects of early sensory restriction, with special emphasis on the restriction of pain experience, on the adult response to noxious stimuli.

Subjects

Six litters of an inbred Scottish terrier strain were used. Each litter was randomly divided into two groups. One group, containing a total of ten dogs, was placed in restriction cages. The twelve dogs which comprised the 'free environment' or control group were raised normally as pets in private homes and in the laboratory.

Each restricted dog used in the present study was reared in isolation from puppyhood to maturity in a cage which was specially designed to prevent the dogs from seeing outside, although daylight was permitted to enter through a large air vent at the top of each cage. Each cage contained two compartments and when the sliding partition between them was opened once a day, the dog was allowed to enter a freshly cleaned compartment. In this way the dogs were deprived of normal sensory and social experience from the time that weaning was completed at the age of four weeks until they were removed at about eight months of age. After the restricted dogs were released from their cages, they received the same opportunities for social and sensory stimulation as their normally reared litter-mates.

Testing of the dogs began about three to five weeks after the restricted animals were released. Two of the restricted dogs were tested a second time about two years after their release. Since the litters used in this study were born at different times over a three-year period, it was not possible to use all the dogs for all the tests.

Experiment 1: response to electric shock
Method

Subjects. The Ss were seven restricted and nine free-environment dogs.

Apparatus. A toy car that could be maneuvered by hand through a battery and steering mechanism was connected to a variable electric shock source provided by a variac and transformer circuit. The dogs were tested with the car on a 6×3 ft sheet-metal floor surrounded by a 2 ft high wire-mesh enclosure.

Procedure. The toy car was used to pursue the dogs and deliver a 1500 V, 6mA shock when it hit them. Each shock was of 1 s duration, although the dogs could escape the full shock by moving away rapidly. The car, which had a constant speed, was kept in waiting about 2 ft from S. If S were sitting, E moved the car directly toward S. If S were moving, however, E moved the car into S's path and pursued S up to one of the far sides of the enclosure.

The E tried to hit each dog ten times during a testing period. However, if at some time during testing, the dog made five successive avoidances of the approaching car without being hit and shocked, testing was discontinued for that period, and the total number of shocks received by the dog up to that time was recorded. A dog reached the *criterion* of successful avoidance learning when it received no shock during a testing period.

Results

The restricted dogs received a mean of 24·7 shocks (range: 10 to 40) from the toy car, while the free-environment dogs received a mean of six shocks (range: 2 to 11). This difference between the two groups provided a t-value of 4·4, which is significant at the 0·001 level. By the end of the fourth test period all the free-environment dogs had reached criterion. Three of the seven restricted dogs, however, had not yet done so; and two of these had received the full forty shocks and gave no sign of learning to avoid the toy car. Testing was therefore discontinued at this time. The mean number of shocks received by the restricted dogs, then, would probably be considerably higher than it is if the restricted dogs were tested until all had reached criterion.

Characteristic differences in the behavior of the two groups were striking. The normal dogs were found to show smooth, precise movements which were oriented directly toward the toy car. They often sat looking at the car, swaying from side to side as it moved toward them, and only at the last moment, when the car was inches away from them, did they jump up and trot out of the way. Although these dogs were excited at first, their behavior after the first few shocks showed little excitement and they made only minimal, unhurried avoidance movements of a leg or the tail to avoid being hit.

This behavior stands in marked contrast with the wild, aimless activity first shown by the restricted dogs. Their typical behavior consisted of running around in a circular path with excessive, exaggerated movements of the whole body. They often avoided being hit only by virtue of the remarkable rapidity of their action. But there was no difficulty in hitting them if the car were moved into the circular path. They then ran right into it. At other times, they stood up at the side of the testing enclosure, in an attempt to climb out, and received the full ten shocks in this position.

Two years after restriction. Two restricted dogs were tested two years after they had been released from restriction and still showed the same exaggerated behavior. While one learned after nine shocks, the other received twenty-three shocks before it began to avoid successfully. This gave a mean of sixteen shocks, which differs significantly from the mean of six shocks for the normal animals at the 0·01 level ($t = 3·5$).

Experiment 2: avoidance training
Method

Subjects. The Ss were seven restricted and twelve free-environment dogs.

Apparatus. A 6×3 ft testing enclosure, bounded by wire mesh 2 ft high, was divided lengthwise into two halves by a 3 in high barrier. The steel grid floor was connected to a variable electric shock source provided by a variac and transformer circuit.

Procedure. The threshold levels at which the dogs responded to electric shock in the apparatus were first determined by raising the voltage stepwise. The voltmeter reading at which an animal first showed signs of startle or slight jumping was recorded as the threshold value. The behavior of the animals to this value of shock was then observed for two test periods during which each dog received about ten shocks on both sides of the barrier.

For the avoidance training which followed, the side which was to be 'hot' for a particular animal was the one to which it moved and which it seemed to 'prefer' when placed in the apparatus. The first shock on the training days was given 1 min after the dog was placed on the 'hot' side and a shock was given every 60 s thereafter, as long as the dog stayed on the 'hot' side, until S had received a total of ten shocks. However, when a dog jumped to the safe side during avoidance training, it was placed back on the 'hot' side and E waited 60 s before shock was again presented. If a dog made three successive jumps from the 'hot' to the safe side without receiving shock, testing was discontinued for that period for the animal, and the number of shocks received up to that time was recorded. The shock was of 1 s duration, and 1500 V, 6 mA, which was about three times the mean threshold value measured by the voltmeter. The *criteria* for successful avoidance learning were: (a) two successive days with no more than one shock on each day or (b) a training day on which a dog went to the safe side immediately and received no shock.

Results

No significant difference in the thresholds at which the two groups first responded to electric shock was obtained in this experiment. Furthermore, no behavioral differences between the two groups were observed with these minimal values of shock, either in degree of responsiveness or type of response made.

During avoidance training with 1500 V, however, differences in the behavior of the two groups were obvious. By the end of the third testing period, only two of the twelve free-environment dogs had not reached criterion; five of the seven restricted dogs, however, had not reached criterion at this stage and three of these five had received the full thirty shocks and gave no sign of learning. Because of the obvious differences between the two groups and the clearly unpleasant nature of the electric shock used, testing was discontinued at this point. Thus no dog received more than thirty shocks during avoidance training.

While the free-environment dogs received a mean of five shocks (range: 1 to 22), the restricted dogs received a mean of 20·3 shocks (range: 1 to 30) during avoidance training. The t-score of the difference between the means, 5·07, is significant at the 0·001 level.

The three dogs that received the full thirty shocks showed stereotyped forms of behavior to the shock. One dog whirled around violently in narrow circles on the 'hot' side immediately after getting the first shock in the enclosure and continued to do so until it was removed after getting ten shocks. The second dog always ran to a particular corner on the 'hot' side after the first shock and sat in a peculiar, awkward position, getting shock after shock without moving. The third dog learned a partial response to the shock, consisting of placing its forelegs on the barrier, while its hindquarters were on the 'hot' side, in this way getting repeated shocks without learning the entire response.

Two years after restriction. Two dogs that had been out of restriction for two years and were reared normally in the laboratory during that time, nevertheless received a mean of nineteen shocks during the three testing periods, which differed significantly from the free-environment dogs' mean of five shocks at the 0·02 level of significance ($t = 2·78$). One of these dogs received twenty-five shocks, and S still maintained the same awkward, 'frozen' position in the corner that it had assumed when first tested two years previously, giving little sign of learning permanently to make the appropriate response of stepping over the 3 in barrier to the safe side.

Experiment 3: response to burning
Method

Subjects. The Ss were ten restricted and eight free-environment dogs.

Apparatus. A box of safety matches.

Procedure. Each dog was allowed to roam the testing room freely for 1 min, and the amount of time S spent near E in an area which had been demarcated previously by a chalk line was recorded. The S was then called by E to this area. A safety match was struck and E attempted to push the flame into the dog's nose at least three times. Although the dog was held forcibly by E, S was able to avoid being burned by moving or turning its head away rapidly from the match. The dog was then allowed to move to any part of the room and the time spent near E in the area of the source of burning was recorded during a 2 min period. The percentages of time S spent near E before and after presentation of the flame were then compared.

Results

Of the eight free-environment dogs tested, six spent less time near E after he tried to burn them than before. Of the ten restricted dogs, however, nine spent *more* time in the area near E *after* nose-burning than before. While the restricted dogs spent 27·9 per cent of the time near E before stimulation, they spent 51·2 per cent of the time in that area following presentation of the match. The amount of time spent by the free-environment dogs near E decreased from 45·1 per cent before to 32·8 per cent after presentation of the match. The Nonparametric Sign Test (Moses, 1952) provided a chi-square value of 5·40 with Yates's correction, which is significant at the 0·02 level of confidence.

One of the most remarkable features of the restricted dogs was their behavior during and following presentation of the flame. To the astonishment of the observers, seven of the ten restricted dogs made no attempt to get away from E *during* stimulation and it was not even necessary to hold them. The sequence of behavior observed was almost identical for all seven dogs: they moved their noses into the flame as soon as it was presented, after which the head or whole body jerked away, as though reflexively; but then they came right back to their original position and hovered excitedly near the flame. Three of them repeatedly poked their noses into the flame and sniffed at it as long as it was present. If they snuffed it out another match was struck and the same sequence of events occurred. The other four did not sniff at the match, but offered no resistance nor made any attempt to get away after the first contact and E was able to touch these dogs' noses with the flame as often as he wished. Only three of the restricted dogs squealed on making contact with the flame and tried subsequently to avoid it by moving their heads. Two of these, however, made no attempt to get away from E after stimulation had stopped.

In contrast, the normal dogs moved their heads so rapidly that it was often impossible to hit their noses with the flame. The E tried to move the match in from unexpected angles or to distract the Ss in order to hit them with the flame. But the normal dogs moved their heads slightly and usually successfully, receiving only one or two very brief contacts with the flame; and they then struggled to escape from E's grasp at their sides.

Experiment 4: response to pin-prick
Method

Subjects. The Ss were eight restricted and nine free-environment dogs.

Apparatus. A large, sharp dissecting needle.

Procedure. The procedure in this experiment is the same as that used in experiment 3 except that the dogs were pin-pricked rather than burned. While the dog was held at the neck, a long dissecting needle was jabbed into the skin at the sides and hind thighs about three or four times.

Results

Of the eight restricted dogs, six spent more time near E after pin-pricking than before. These dogs increased the time spent in the demarcated area from 50·8 per cent before to 58·4 per cent after pin-pricking. The normal dogs, on the other hand, spent a mean of only 8·9 per cent of the time after pin-pricking near E, compared with 42·2 per cent before. Of the nine normally reared dogs, eight spent less time near E after pin-pricking than before. The sign test provided a chi-square value of 4·74, which is significant at the 0·05 level.

The behavior of the restricted dogs in response to pin-prick was almost identical with that observed with the flame: they appeared unaware that they were being stimulated *by something in the environment*. Four of the restricted dogs made no response whatever apart from localized reflexive twitches at the side or leg when they were pricked. The E was often able to pierce the skin of these dogs completely so that the needle was lodged in it without eliciting withdrawal or any behavioral indication that pain was being 'felt' or responded to other than spasmodic, reflexive jerks. The remaining four restricted dogs pulled their bodies aside a few inches or yipped to *some* of the pin-pricks, but when released two of them stayed right next to E, who was able to repeat the procedure and jab them with the needle as often as he wished. The noxious stimulation received was apparently not 'perceived' as coming from E and their behavior subsequently was not oriented or organized in terms of the noxious stimulus in any noticeable way.

The free-environment dogs, however, provided an unmistakable index of perceived pain. They tried to jump aside to escape the pin-prick, yelped and often struggled for release after two or three pin-pricks. They would then dash away from E's hand and take up a position in the farthest corner of the testing room.

Supplementary observations

The behavior of the restricted dogs in the four experiments just described is entirely consistent with everyday observations of their behavior. It was noted, for example, that their aimless activity resulted in some of them frequently striking their heads against water pipes that ran along the walls just above the floor of the testing rooms. One dog, by actual count, struck his head against these pipes more than thirty times in a single hour. This was never observed once in the normal dogs. Similarly, the rapid movement of the restricted dogs and their unpredictability as to direction resulted a number of times in the dogs' having a paw or the tail stepped on. Often there was no sign that the dogs 'felt' pain when this happened, though the procedure would have elicited a howl from a normal dog, and the restricted S made no attempt to withdraw from the place where injury was received.

Discussion

The outstanding feature of the behavior of the restricted dogs was their inability to respond adaptively and intelligently to the variety of stimuli which were presented to them. There can be little doubt that the restricted dogs 'felt' electric shock: their disturbance by it was marked and unmistakable. Similarly, the behavior of at least three of the restricted dogs indicates that pin-prick and contact with fire were 'felt' in some way. Nevertheless, it was obvious that the restricted dogs did not know how to make the proper avoidance responses which would have prevented further stimulation. The results permit the conclusion, then, that early experience plays an essential role in the emergence of such basic behavior as avoidance of noxious stimuli.

Sherrington has defined pain as 'the psychical adjunct of an imperative protective reflex' (1941, p. 286). And many psychologists since then (Estes, 1944; Miller, 1951; Mowrer, 1950) have interpreted pain in terms of imperative reflex responses. Such a view, however, is not consistent with the observations reported here. Most of the restricted dogs did indeed show localized reflex responses to the stimulation, yet their behavior was clearly inadequate to cope with the intense electric shocks or such grossly injurious stimuli as contact with fire or piercing of the skin. In comparison, their litter-mates which had been reared normally in a free environment exhibited the ability to avoid prolonged contact with injurious stimuli and they were able to learn with great rapidity to make highly organized, abiently oriented responses to every form of noxious stimulus that was presented. However, the capacity of the restricted dogs to acquire good, adaptive behavior to noxious stimulation was notably limited after release from restriction, even with the adequate opportunity that was provided for them to gain varied, normal perceptual experience. Maladaptive behavior like freezing and whirling also developed and they were observed as consistent responses as long as two years after release. Thus, it appears that the requisite experience must come at the correct time in the young organism's life. During later stages of development, the experience necessary for adaptive, well-organized responses to pain may never be properly acquired.

The inability of the restricted dogs to cope intelligently with noxious stimuli, however, cannot be attributed to inadequate response mechanisms alone. Their reflexive jerks and movements during pin-prick and contact with fire suggest that they may have 'felt something' during stimulation; but the *lack* of any observable emotional disturbance apart from these reflex movements in at least four of the dogs following pin-prick and in seven of them after nose-burning indicates that their *perception* of the event was highly abnormal in comparison with the behavior of the normally reared control dogs. Livingston (1953) has made the observation that experience with pain in childhood is an important determinant of the manner in which the adult perceives and responds to pain; that is, the 'meaning' involved in a perception such as pain and the attitudes of the individual in situations involving pain are largely a function of the earlier, related experiences of that individual. The results reported here are consistent with observations such as this and can be interpreted in a similar manner.

The isolation of the restricted dogs prevented them from acquiring experience early in life with severe skin damage and fire. It is evident, then, that the flame and pin-prick could not have evoked the neural 'phase sequences' (memories) acquired during earlier pain experiences (Hebb, 1949) that might have been aroused in the normal dogs. The results strongly suggest that the restricted dogs lacked awareness of a necessary aspect of normal pain perception: the 'meaning' of physical damage or at least *threat* to the physical well-being that is inherent in the normal organism's perception of pain. The observations of the restricted dogs' poking their noses into fire or permitting E to cause bodily damage by fire and pin-prick without emotional disturbance apart from localized reflexes indicates that an interpretation such as this is valid. Indeed, to say that these restricted dogs perceived fire and pin-prick as *threatening*, or even painful in any *normal* sense, would be anthropomorphism rather than inference from observed behavior.

The results which have been reported here then, make it difficult to treat behavior related to pain simply in terms of frequency and intensity of stimulations or in terms of imperative reflex responses alone (Estes, 1944; Miller, 1951; Mowrer, 1950) without regard to the earlier perceptual experience of the organism. The behavior of the restricted dogs suggests that perceiving and responding to pain, which is so fundamental to normal adult behavior and presumably so important for the survival of an individual or species, requires a background of early, prolonged, perceptual experience.

References

BEACH, F. A., and JAYNES, J. (1954), 'Effects of early experience upon the behavior of animals', *Psychol. Bull.*, vol. 51, pp. 239–63.

ESTES, W. K. (1944), 'An experimental study of punishment', *Psychol. Monogr.*, vol. 57, no. 3.

FULLER, J. L., EASLER, C. A., and BANKS, E. M. (1950), 'Formation of conditioned avoidance responses in young puppies', *Amer. J. Physiol.*, vol. 160, pp. 462–6.

GREENACRE, P. (1945), 'The biological economy of birth', in O. Fenichel (ed.), *The Psychoanalytic Study of the Child*, International Universities Press.

HEBB, D. O. (1949), *The Organization of Behavior*, Wiley.

LIVINGSTON, W. K. (1953), 'What is pain?', *Sci. Amer.*, vol. 188, pp. 59–66.

MELZACK, R. (1954), 'The genesis of emotional behavior: an experimental study of the dog', *J. comp. physiol. Psychol.*, vol. 47, pp. 166–8.

MILLER, N. E. (1951), 'Learnable drives and rewards', in S. S. Stevens (ed.), *Handbook of Experimental Psychology*, Wiley.

MOSES, L. E. (1952), 'Non-parametric statistics for psychological research', *Psychol. Bull.*, vol. 49, pp. 122–43.

MOWRER, O. H. (1950), *Learning Theory and Personality Dynamics*, Ronald Press.

NISSEN, H. W., CHOW, K. L., and SEMMES, J. (1951), 'Effects of restricted opportunity for tactual, kinesthetic, and manipulative experience on the behavior of a chimpanzee', *Amer. J. Psychol.*, vol. 64, pp. 485–507.

SCOTT, J. P., FREDRICSON, E., and FULLER, J. L. (1951), 'Experimental exploration of the critical period hypothesis', *Personality*, vol. 1, pp. 162–83.

SHERRINGTON, C. S. (1941), *Man on his Nature*, Macmillan Co.

THOMPSON, W. R., and HERON, W. (1954), 'The effects of restricting early experience on the problem-solving capacity of dogs', *Canad. J. Psychol.*, vol. 8, pp. 17–31.

15 Seymour Levine, Jacques A. Chevalier and Sheldon J. Korchin

The Effects of Early Shock and Handling on Later Avoidance Learning

Excerpts from Seymour Levine, Jacques A. Chevalier and Sheldon J. Korchin, 'The effects of early shock and handling on later avoidance learning', *Journal of Personality*, vol. 24, 1956, pp. 475-93.

Introduction

Current theories emphasize the role of infantile experience in the development of personality and behavior. Freud (1936) was one of the early theorists to place emphasis on the experiences of the infant organism and their profound effect upon adult behavior. He maintained that early trauma produces long-lasting influences on behavior. His hypothesis of primary anxiety holds early traumatic experiences to be the basis from which later anxiety develops. Numerous clinical reports tend to substantiate Freud's early observations. Greenacre (1952), Ribble (1944) and Spitz (1951) and others have reported observations on many children which indicate the importance of infantile experience on the development of behavior patterns. However, since the technique of clinical observation does not usually permit adequate control and systematic variation of relevant variables, the findings themselves have definite limitations, although the hypotheses formulated warrant rigorous and systematic study.

Hunt (1941) has suggested that in controlled studies with lower animals many parameters of infantile stimulation can be varied systematically. At the same time, rigorous control can be maintained over the genetic background and environment of the experimental Ss. Numerous animal studies (Forgays and Forgays, 1952; Forgus, 1954; Hymovitch, 1952; Melzack, 1954; Thompson and Heron, 1954) have been reported recently which indicate that experimental manipulation early in life does, indeed, have far-reaching effects on adult behavior. Many of these studies, deriving from Hebb's (1949) theory, have emphasized perceptual experience early in life. However, there have been only a few studies which have dealt with the types of infantile experiences which clinical observation indicates have the most profound effects on personality development and adult behavior, namely, deprivation and trauma. Furthermore, the majority of the experiments in this area have not dealt truly with *infantile* experience. Experimental treatment characteristically is not given until the animals are weaned, in the rat around twenty-one days of age. Unlike the extremely dependent and undeveloped infant, these animals are fully able to maintain themselves under normal laboratory conditions and are far advanced physiologically. It is possible that stimulation in infancy, the period prior to weaning, may have very different or more profound effects upon adult behavior than stimulation in the postweaning period.

The evidence to date on the effects on adult behavior of preweaning experience with noxious stimulation is sparse and equivocal. Hall and Whiteman (1951) exposed young mice, from four to seven days of age, to the stimulation of an intense sound. When thirty days old, the animals were tested for emotionality by measuring the frequency of defecation in an open field. Animals given the early stimulation were less stable emotionally when so tested. Beach and Jaynes (1954) point out the possibility, however, that the results may have been due to specific and direct conditioning to environmental cues, since both the stimulation in infancy and the later test for emotionality were carried out in the same environmental setting. Hunt and Otis (1963) report that rats handled twice daily from the seventh to the twenty-first day of age later revealed much greater emotional stability than nonhandled controls in a 'timidity' test. Griffiths and Stringer (1952) exposed infant rats to a variety of noxious stimuli from one through twenty-one days of age. These stimuli included exposure to extreme temperatures, intense auditory stimulation, rotation in a Welch stroboscope and electric shock. A control group received no noxious stimulation. No overall differences were found in either emotionality or learning ability when an F-test was used. Closer examination of the data, using a test for an extreme mean developed by Dixon (Dixon and Massey, 1951), reveals that the group that received electric shock in infancy made significantly fewer errors on the multiple-unit maze than did any of the other groups. From these studies we may gather that the demonstration of the presence of an effect of stimulation in infancy and the assessment of its magnitude and direction depend not only on the type of stimulation imposed but also on the method of measuring the effect.

The present paper reports a study of the effects of different infantile experiences with and without an unavoidable shock as measured by later avoidance learning in the rat. The different experimental treatments continued for the first twenty days of the rats' lives. After a subsequent period of forty days without further handling or treatment, all sixty animals were tested on a conditioned avoidance learning task in a modified shuttle box to establish the effects of early trauma on the behavior of adult rats. [...]

Summary of results

The major results revealed that the no-handling group was significantly inferior in its ability to learn the task as compared with the other two groups [shock and no-shock groups]. The Ss also took longer to make their first avoidance response and required more pushing during the early stages of learning. The shock and no-shock groups did not differ in their initial behavior in the test situation nor in their performance early in learning. In the overall measures of learning, the shock group was significantly poorer than the no-shock group. The shock Ss were also more resistant to extinction. [...]

Discussion

The results of this study reveal significant differences in behavior among the various groups as a function of treatment in infancy. It is our hope that the three major conditions of this experiment may be represented one day as three points along a single dimension of amount or intensity of stimulation, with a condition of minimal (insufficient) stimulation at one end and a condition of excessive (traumatic) stimulation at the other. However, the present experiment does not justify such a presentation. It is necessary for the present to consider separately the comparison of the groups whose treatment differed only in the dimension of handling (no-handling *v.* no-shock) and that of the groups differing only in the traumatic stimulus dimension (no-shock *v.* shock).

On almost all measures of performance the group which received no handling in infancy was significantly poorer than the groups which received some type of stimulation. While it is difficult to determine the precise role played by such stimulation in infancy, the data are consistent with earlier conclusions that restricted prior experience results in poorer learning (Hebb, 1949) or an increase in the animal's susceptibility to emotional disturbance (Beach and Jaynes, 1954; Hunt and Otis, 1963). That the no-handling Ss *were* more susceptible to disturbance is indicated by the fact that they took more trials than the experimental groups in making their first successful avoidance response. Much more 'freezing' behavior was also observed in these Ss.

In contrast, the comparison of the shock and no-shock groups showed no differences in initial behavior, i.e. the behavioral consequences of any initial emotional disturbance were similar for both groups. However, the tendency for the groups to become differentiated from each other later in learning, with respect to error scores and extinction, suggests that the groups were differentially affected by the earlier trials and that the effect was cumulative. Whether or not both escape and avoidance trials contributed to this effect, it still is plausible to assume that shock in infancy decreased the tolerance for subsequent stress in adulthood. Learning performance in a situation in which stress is not involved would provide a test of this hypothesis since, in the absence of later stress, equivalent performance of the shock and no-shock groups would be predicted.

Differences in any of several psychological functions might account for the differences in learning and extinction between the shock and no-shock groups. We concur in Solomon and Wynne's (1954) delineation of trauma in infancy as a situation in which the organism, confronted with noxious stimulation, is helpless and unable either to terminate or to avoid it, lacking appropriate instrumental responses in its repertoire. Viewing infantile trauma in this way leads to several hypotheses which might account for its effect on adult behavior.

It might be conceived that the observed superiority in performance of the no-shock Ss over the shock Ss reflects a difference in some cognitive function upon which learning depends (e.g. the ability to discriminate or to retain). One explanation of our data would be that shock in infancy interferes directly with such an ability. Although it cannot be specified over what range of situations performance might be impaired, the overall implication is that trauma in infancy leads to some general cognitive inability: the animals should perform less well in any situation in which this ability is required, whether or not traumatic stimuli are involved. It might well be, however, that this disruption of cognitive functioning in adulthood is limited to test situations involving noxious stimuli such as the one used in the present experiment. If we conceive that the infant S's inability to escape the trauma (i.e. his inability to make specific discriminatory responses to it) prevents him from discriminating the traumatic stimulus from the other stimuli in the environment and thus handicaps his ability to discriminate such stimuli, then we should expect poorer performance in adulthood in situations where such painful stimuli are among the discriminanda. One might also expect a higher probability of anxiety arousal in adulthood to innocuous stimuli because of their greater likelihood of being associated with the noxious stimuli of infancy. These factors would render the traumatic stimulus less distinctive for traumatized animals and it would be more difficult for such an animal to learn to differentiate the relevant aspects of the environment which lead to the reduction of anxiety.

Another hypothesis is that the early trauma leads to a heightened anxiety drive which persists into adulthood. This level may be raised further in the avoidance training situation by the reintroduction of the traumatic stimulus. There is evidence that learning is retarded by excessive intensities of drive (Kaplan, 1952; Kendler, 1945; Levine, 1956; Muenzinger and Fletcher, 1936). Thus, it can be proposed that the slow learning of the animals who received shock in the present experiment may have been a function of intense drive, resulting either from the effects of treatment in infancy alone or from the summation of the effects of the earlier and later trauma.

The fact that the shock group showed greater resistance to extinction does not aid in differentiating the hypotheses presented. Farber (1948) and Moltz (1954) both present evidence which indicates that anxiety results in response fixation. There is further evidence which indicates that greater resistance to extinction occurs when the level of drive during extinction is high (Sackett, 1939; Webb, 1949). Thus, it is possible that the shock group had greater response fixation because of their higher level of anxiety drive. However, the hypothesis of cognitive disability could also account for the shock group's resistance to extinction, since extinction depends upon a discrimination between reinforcement and nonreinforcement.

Certainly it is not possible to bring together all of the findings of this experiment into a single conceptual scheme at this time. We are still left with the question whether the types of treatment imposed here (e.g. the handling variable and the shock variable) represent quantitative variations of the same phenomenon or whether they are qualitatively different. Moreover, it is difficult to decide among the seemingly divergent explanations offered to account for the manner in which experience in infancy leads to changes in adult behavior. Since many of these decisions may be made on the basis of further experimental work, we are hopeful that a more integrated view may emerge.

Further research bearing on these questions may be concentrated fruitfully in at least three areas: (a) variables associated with the trauma in infancy; (b) treatments intervening between infant experience and adult testing; and (c) performance in various adult testing situations. Implicit in Solomon and Wynne's (1954) definition of trauma are three variables, all of which may be manipulated experimentally. The first of these, the noxious stimulus and its corresponding sensation, may be varied in intensity as well as qualitatively. The second, S's emotional response to the stimulus, can probably be varied through the use of drugs. S's ability or inability to escape from the stimulus, the third variable, may be varied by providing situations in which S *can* learn to escape. Treatments intervening between infant experience and adult testing, calculated to accentuate or reduce the effect of trauma in infancy, can throw further light on the nature of the processes involved. Finally, the demands of the adult testing situation itself may be varied to permit broad assessment of psychological functioning in such Ss.

References

BEACH, F. A., and JAYNES, J. (1954), 'Effects of early experience upon the behavior of animals', *Psychol. Bull.*, vol. 51, pp. 239–63.

CAMPBELL, B. A., and KRAELING, D. (1953), 'Response strength as a function of drive level and amount of drive reduction', *J. exp. Psychol.*, vol. 45, pp. 97–101.

DIXON, W. J., and MASSEY, F. J. (1951), *Introduction to Statistical Analysis*, McGraw-Hill.

FARBER, I. E. (1948), 'Response fixation under anxiety and non-anxiety conditions', *J. exp. Psychol.*, vol. 38, pp. 111–31.

FORGAYS, D. G., and FORGAYS, J. W. (1952), 'The nature of the effect of free environmental experience in the rat', *J. comp. physiol. Psychol.*, vol. 45, pp. 322–8.

FORGUS, R. H. (1954), 'The effect of early perceptual learning on the behavioral organization of adult rats', *J. comp. physiol. Psychol.*, vol. 47, pp. 331–7.

FREUD, S. (1936), *The Problem of Anxiety*, Norton.

GRANT, D. A. (1946), 'New statistical criteria for learning and problem solution in experiments involving repeated trials', *Psychol. Bull.*, vol. 43, pp. 272–82.

GRANT, D. A. (1947), 'Additional tables of the probability of "runs" of correct responses in learning and problem solving', *Psychol. Bull.*, vol. 44, pp. 276–9.

GREENACRE, P. (1952), *Trauma, Growth and Personality*, Norton.

GRIFFITHS, W. J., and STRINGER, W. F. (1952), 'The effects of intense stimulation experienced during infancy on adult behavior in the rat', *J. comp. physiol. Psychol.*, vol. 45, pp. 301–6.

HALL, C. S., and WHITEMAN, P. H. (1951), 'The effects of infantile stimulation upon later emotional stability in the mouse', *J. comp. physiol. Psychol.*, vol. 44, pp. 61–6.

HEBB, D. O. (1949), *The Organization of Behavior*, Wiley.

HUNT, J. McV. (1941), 'The effects of infant feeding frustration upon adult hoarding in the albino rat', *J. abnorm. soc. Psychol.*, vol. 36, pp. 338–60.

HUNT, N. F., and OTIS, L. S. (1963), 'Early "experience" and its effects on later behavioral processes in rats: I. initial experiments', *Ann. N. Y. Acad. Sci.*, vol. 25, pp. 858–70.

HYMOVITCH, B. (1952), 'The effects of experimental variations on problem solving in the rat', *J. comp. physiol. Psychol.*, vol. 45, pp. 313–20.

KAPLAN, M. (1952), 'The effects of noxious stimulus intensity and duration during intermittent reinforcement and escape behavior', *J. comp. physiol. Psychol.*, vol. 45, pp. 538–48.

KENDALL, M. G. (1948), *The Advanced Theory of Statistics*, vol. 2, Charles Griffith.

KENDLER, H. H. (1945), 'Drive interaction: I. Learning as a function of the simultaneous presence of hunger and thirst', *J. exp. Psychol.*, vol. 35, pp. 188–98.

LEVINE, S. (1956), 'The effects of a strong irrelevant drive on learning', *Psychol. Rep.*, vol. 2, pp. 29–33.

MANN, H. B., and WHITNEY, D. R. (1947), 'On a test whether one or two random variables is stochastically larger than the other', *Ann. Math. Stat.*, vol. 18, pp. 50–60.

MELZACK, R. (1954), 'The genesis of emotional behavior: an experimental study of the dog', *J. comp. physiol. Psychol.*, vol. 47, pp. 166–8.

MOLTZ, H. (1954), 'Resistance to extinction as a function of variables associated with shock', *J. exp. Psychol.*, vol. 47, pp. 418–24.

MUENZINGER, K. F., and FLETCHER, F. M. (1936), 'Motivation in learning: VI. Escape from electric shock compared with hunger-food tension in the visual discrimination habit', *J. comp. Psychol.*, vol. 22, pp. 79–91.

PAGE, H. A., and HALL, J. F. (1953), 'Experimental extinction as a function of the prevention of a response', *J. comp. physiol. Psychol.*, vol. 46, pp. 33–4.

RIBBLE, M. A. (1944), 'Infantile experience in relation to personality development', in J. McV. Hunt (ed.), *Personality and the Behavior Disorders*, Ronald Press, pp. 621–51.

SACKETT, R. S. (1939), 'The effect of strength of drive at the time of extinction upon resistance to extinction in rats', *J. comp. Psychol.*, vol. 27, pp. 411–31.

SOLOMON, R. L., and WYNNE, L. C. (1954), 'Traumatic avoidance learning: the principles of anxiety conservation and partial irreversibility', *Psychol. Rev.*, vol. 61, pp. 353–85.

SPITZ, R. E. (1951), 'The psychogenic diseases of infancy: an attempt at their etiologic classification', in O. Fenichel (ed.), *The Psychoanalytic Study of the Child*, vol. 6, International Universities Press, pp. 255–75.

THOMPSON, W. R., and HERON, W. (1954), 'The effect of early restriction on activity in dogs', *J. comp. physiol. Psychol.*, vol. 47, pp. 77–82.

WEBB, W. B. (1949), 'The motivational aspect of an irrelevant drive in the behavior of the white rat', *J. exp. Psychol.*, vol. 39, pp. 1–14.

16 Victor H. Denenberg

Critical Periods, Stimulus Input and Emotional Reactivity: A Theory of Infantile Stimulation

Excerpt from Victor H. Denenberg, 'Critical periods, stimulus input, and emotional reactivity: a theory of infantile stimulation', *Psychological Review*, vol. 71, 1964, pp. 335–51.

This paper has two purposes. The first is to question certain aspects of the critical period hypothesis (J. P. Scott, 1958, 1962). The second and more important purpose is to develop a somewhat different hypothesis: that stimulation in infancy reduces the organism's emotional reactivity; this reduction is a monotonic function of amount of stimulus input. In turn, this hypothesized change in emotional reactivity offers a useful mechanism by which one can explain a number of disparate and seemingly unrelated changes in adult performance.

The data to be considered, and the generalizations therefrom, come specifically from research with rats and mice which have received various forms of stimulation between birth and weaning. For more general reviews of early experience research and the critical period hypothesis see Denenberg (1962b) and Scott (1962).

Critical periods

Recently Scott (1962) has suggested that there are three major kinds of critical period phenomena: one for the formation of basic social relationships, a second concerned with optimal periods for learning and a third involving infantile stimulation. This discussion is concerned only with the last of these.

There are at least two different ways in which the critical period hypothesis has been interpreted. One is that the same physical stimulation at different ages has different effects upon S; this says, simply, that S's age is an important parameter and can scarcely be questioned. The second interpretation is that there are certain *limited* time periods in development during which a particular class of stimuli will have particularly profound effects and that the same stimulation before or after this interval will have little, if any, effect upon the developing organism. This approach stems directly from the embryological meaning of critical periods and it is in this context that Scott (1958, 1962; Scott and Marston, 1950; Williams and Scott, 1953) has developed and described the critical period hypothesis. The term, critical period, when used in this paper, will refer to this second interpretation.

Operationally, a test of the critical period hypothesis requires several experimental groups which receive the same stimulation at different ages and a control group which does not receive the stimulation at all. If some of the experimental groups do not differ from the control while others do, this may be construed as evidence supporting the critical period hypothesis. (On the other hand, any significant differences among the experimental groups are support for the first meaning of the hypothesis.)

Although it is obvious that the age at which S is stimulated is an important parameter, when one carefully examines experiments investigating critical periods in infancy in rats and mice, there is little evidence supporting the hypothesis that stimulation must occur only during certain delimited time intervals to affect the organism's subsequent behavior. Interestingly, the only unequivocal demonstrations of critical periods are to be found in papers which used physiological, rather than behavioral, endpoints (Bell, Reisner and Linn, 1961; Levine and Lewis, 1959a).

The general conclusion noted above might not be apparent from a casual inspection of the literature. There are several studies which, if taken in isolation, appear to support the hypothesis. For example, two early experiments on critical periods (Denenberg, 1958, 1960) seemed to support the concept. In the first study mice initially conditioned between twenty and forty days of age had essentially the same reconditioning scores at fifty days, and all these scores were significantly higher than either a fifty-day control group or a group which was initially conditioned at sixteen days. These data suggested a critical period around twenty days of age such that conditioning experience prior to that date did not affect subsequent reconditioning performance; experience after that date appeared to have the same effect upon reconditioning, regardless of the original age of conditioning or the actual amount of conditioning. A subsequent study with older Ss (Denenberg, 1960) established that it was indeed the age of the animals rather than the time interval between conditioning and reconditioning which mediated the effects.[1]

However, another study with the mouse, though not directly comparable to the two above, disclosed some complexities concerning critical period phenomena which cast doubt on the degree of generality of the hypothesis. Denenberg and Bell (1960) studied avoidance learning in adulthood as a joint function of age of infantile stimulation (i.e. critical periods), intensity of stimulation in infancy and intensity of electric shock during adult performance. These latter two parameters had been held constant in prior research. Analyses of the learning data revealed that critical periods were not significant as a main effect; but the periods × adult shock and the periods × adult shock × infantile stimulation interactions were significant. The disturbing thing was that the age variable (i.e. critical periods) was dependent upon the particular level of stimulation used in the adult learning task. By the selection of certain combinations of infantile stimulation levels and adult shock levels one could 'prove' that stimulation during certain 'critical periods' could facilitate, have no effect or interfere with avoidance learning in adulthood. The phenomena, then, appear to be far more complex than previously recognized in the generalizations afforded by the critical period hypothesis.

These data suggest that any single 'critical period' is, at least in part, dependent upon the parameter of stimulus intensity. Thus, Denenberg's prior studies (1958, 1960) should be looked upon with caution since different shock levels may have yielded very different findings.

Critical period research with the rat has generally used the procedure called *handling* rather than shock. This consists of removing the pups from the home cage and placing the young into containers (e.g. cans containing wood shavings, small wooden compartments, grid-floored boxes). The pups are left there for a

1. A number of investigators have also shown, with the rat, that stimulation in infancy has different consequences as compared to equivalent stimulation in adulthood. (These include handling in infancy and early adulthood, Levine, 1956; raising rats in groups of six or twelve during infancy or adulthood, Seitz, 1954; subjecting rats to handling and auditory stimulation in infancy and adulthood, Spence and Maher, 1962a; and temporarily blinding or deafening rats in infancy or later life, Wolf, 1943.)

short duration (generally two to three minutes though some *E*s have used intervals of eight minutes or longer) and are then returned to the home cage. This is generally done once a day for different prescribed periods.

In a series of experiments Denenberg and Karas (1960, 1961) found that rats handled for the first ten days of life were superior with respect to body weight, avoidance learning and survival capability to ones handled during the second ten days. In general, both ten-day groups were superior to *S*s which had been handled for twenty days in infancy.

These data suggested that it might be possible to handle *S*s for fewer than ten days and possibly isolate specific critical periods related to different dependent variables. Therefore Denenberg (1962a) handled different groups of rats for three- or five-day intervals at different ages during the first ten days of life. Measures of body weight, avoidance learning behavior and survival time, with one exception, did *not* support the critical period hypothesis. The exception was that *S*s handled for the first five days of life were not significantly better than controls in avoidance learning, while *S*s handled on days 6–10 were superior to controls and equal to *S*s handled on days 1–10.

Though the avoidance learning findings are compatible with the critical period hypothesis, another possibility, based upon the Denenberg and Bell mouse study, is that the failure to modify avoidance learning by handling during the first five days was because the stimulation induced by handling was not sufficiently intense to affect *S*. Denenberg and Kline (1964) tested this hypothesis by giving different groups of rats electric shock (0·2 mA) on days 1–5, 1–3, 3–5, 2 or 4. The shocked groups (with the exception of the group shocked only on day 2) were significantly better in avoidance learning than a nondisturbed control group.

In conclusion, experimental research with the mouse and rat investigating stimulation between birth and weaning has established that the critical period hypothesis is not sufficient to account for the findings. In instances where the data are consistent with the hypothesis, further study has found that the 'critical period' is a complex function of the parameter of stimulus intensity. Research to date indicates that, for the rat and mouse at least, there may be as many 'critical periods' as there are combinations of independent variable parameters and dependent variable measures (Denenberg, 1962a). Lindholm (1962) and Meyers (1962) have recently arrived at a similar conclusion.

Then should the term 'critical periods' be abandoned when discussing the effects of infantile stimulation? Not at the present time, certainly. The concept has had and will continue to have great heuristic value. However, conclusions concerning critical periods must be limited to the particular experimental operations involved until enough empirical evidence has been obtained to indicate the limits of generalization. In terms of current research strategy it appears more reasonable to study the functional relationships among various classes of independent and dependent variables between birth and weaning than to design experiments which try to isolate critical periods during this crucial stage of development.

Theory of infantile stimulation and adult performance

One approach to the problem of understanding the effects of stimulation in infancy is by means of the critical period hypothesis. A different approach is to examine the diverse research findings to see if any common factor can be discerned. Such an examination of the literature leads to the conclusion that stimulation administered between birth and weaning brings about a reduction in 'emotional reactivity'. Furthermore, the greater the stimulation in infancy, the less emotional S will be in adulthood. The central hypothesis of this paper is that *emotional reactivity is reduced as a monotonic function of amount of stimulus input in infancy*.

Before discussing this hypothesis in detail and showing some of its consequences, it is first necessary to define 'emotional reactivity' and show that this intervening variable is modified by stimulation in infancy. This will be done by showing, on the stimulus side, that different methods of stimulating S in infancy have similar consequences in adulthood; and, on the response side, by showing that different operational measures of emotional reactivity yield internally consistent results (Miller, 1959). The two most common methods of stimulating Ss in infancy have been handling and shocking. Emotional reactivity has been measured by procedures as divergent as open-field testing, consummatory behavior, behavior in a learning situation and behavior when given an opportunity to emerge from the home cage.

Handling and emotional reactivity

Open-field behavior. In two experiments Denenberg and Morton (1962a) found that rats handled daily between birth and weaning were significantly more active and had a significantly smaller defecation rate than nonhandled controls. Similar findings were obtained by Denenberg and Whimbey (1963). Rats handled for the first ten or twenty days of life were found to be significantly more active and to defecate significantly less than nonhandled controls (Denenberg, Morton, Kline and Grota, 1962). In a study relating infantile stimulation to age of testing Denenberg and Smith (1963) handled or shocked rats during the second ten days of life and tested independent groups at fifty, 100, 150 or 200 days of age. Both groups which received stimulation in infancy were significantly more active than the controls and had a significantly lower defecation percentage. The open-field test was also used by Schaefer (1963), but his index of emotionality was the amount of time spent crouching during the two minutes after presentation of a sharp click. Handled Ss crouched significantly less than nonhandled controls.

Consummatory behavior. Levine (1957, 1958) handled, shocked or did not disturb rats between birth and weaning. When adult, the Ss were deprived of water for eighteen hours and then given the opportunity to drink. Levine (1957, p. 609) 'hypothesized that since deprivation constitutes a novel internal stimulus complex for nonhandled Ss, the novelty should result in greater emotional disturbance and produce reduced water consumption following a period of deprivation'. In both experiments handled and shocked Ss consumed significantly more water than nondisturbed controls. In a similar type of experiment Spence and Maher (1962a) also found that handled Ss consumed significantly more water than controls.

Emergence-from-cage behavior. Hunt and Otis (1963) exposed their experimental rats to a variety of stimulus conditions in infancy, including handling. In their first two experiments their measure of emotionality was a 'timidity' test. The home cage of an S which had been deprived of food and water for twenty-two hours was placed on an open alley upon which were placed pellets of food. Handled Ss were found to emerge significantly further into the runway than nondisturbed controls. In their third experiment they recorded S's behavior when E opened the cage door to attach a plastic milk cup to it, scoring S with respect to the degree of 'boldness' manifested. Subjects not disturbed in infancy were found to be significantly more timid than those receiving stimulation in infancy.

Behavior in a learning situation. Several indexes of emotional behavior were recorded by Levine (1956) while testing handled and nonhandled Ss for avoidance learning. These were defecation and activity during habituation trials, percentage of Ss freezing after the first shock trial and the number of trials on which Ss showed freezing behavior. On all four measures nonhandled controls were found to be significantly more emotional than Ss handled in infancy.

Electric shock and emotional reactivity

Open-field behavior. Subjects receiving 0·25 mA of current for three minutes daily on days 11–20 were significantly more active and defecated significantly less than nondisturbed controls when tested at fifty, 100, 150 or 200 days of age (Denenberg and Smith, 1963). Rats given three minutes of either 0·5 or 0·8 mA shock on day 4 of life were significantly more active than Ss receiving the same stimulation on day 2; the latter group did not differ from nondisturbed controls (Kline and Denenberg, 1964). The effect of electric shock is measurable at weaning as well. Rats given thirty seconds of 0·2 mA current on days 1 and 2 of life were significantly less emotional than nondisturbed controls at the time of weaning as measured by time to emerge into the open field and activity in the field (Denenberg, Carlson and Stephens, 1962).

Consummatory behavior. Rat pups were given three minutes of electrical stimulation (variable current from 0·10 to 0·37 mA, disregarding S's resistance) from day 1 through day 20. These Ss consumed significantly more water in adulthood than non disturbed controls; the findings were replicated in a second experiment (Levine, 1957, 1958). A similar finding was obtained by Lindholm (1962) who shocked rats for the first ten days, the second ten days, the first twenty days of life and did not disturb a control group. No specified shock level was used; instead, the shock was set high enough to make the Ss move and squeal in the apparatus. The intensity of the shock was increased as S matured. When adult, the Ss were deprived of water for twenty-four hours and then given an opportunity to drink. The Ss shocked in infancy took significantly less time to initiate drinking and consumed significantly more water than the nondisturbed group. A subsequent analysis determined that the differences in consummatory behavior could all be attributed to the latency to approach the water tubes.

*Stimulus input and emotional reactivity:
the monotonicity hypothesis*

The data summarized above are sufficient to justify the conclusion that stimulation in infancy will result in a reduction in emotional reactivity in adulthood. It remains to be demonstrated that a monotonic relationship obtains between amount of stimulus input in infancy and emotional reactivity. Two experiments have explicitly tested this hypothesis (Denenberg and Smith, 1963; Denenberg, Carlson and Stephens, 1962). In addition, there are three other experiments in the literature which offer support for the hypothesis (Levine, 1957, 1958; Lindholm, 1962).

Amount of stimulus input was varied by Denenberg and his co-workers by handling rats for nought (control), ten or twenty days in infancy. In adult open-field testing the controls had the highest defecation rate while the group handled for twenty days had the lowest rate; all differences were significant. In the second study (Denenberg and Smith, 1963) one group of rats received three minutes of shock daily from day 11 through day 20, a second group was placed on the unelectrified grid (handled group) and a third group was not disturbed. Figure 1 shows the percentage of Ss in each group defecating before and after adult avoidance learning training. The greater the stimulus input in infancy, the smaller (significantly) was the percentage of defecators in adulthood. Furthermore, the shocked Ss were the only ones whose defecation percentage was significantly reduced following avoidance learning training.

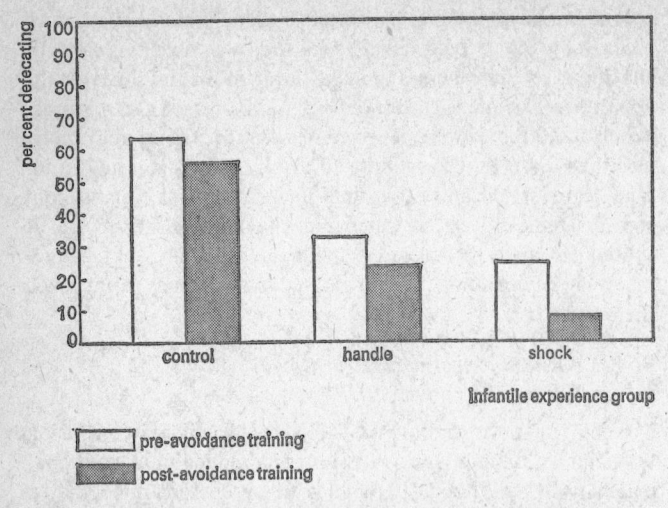

Figure 1 Percentage of rats defecating before and after avoidance learning as a function of infantile stimulation (from Denenberg and Smith, 1963)

Levine (1957, 1958) compared water consumption following eighteen hours of thirst for Ss which had been shocked, handled or not disturbed in infancy. In both experiments the shocked Ss consumed the most water, followed by the handled group, with the controls consuming the least. The difference between shocked and handled Ss approached significance in the first study ($p < 0{\cdot}10$) and was significant in the second study; nonhandled controls consumed significantly less than either experimental group in both studies.

In the Lindholm (1962) experiment rats were shocked for the first ten days of life, the second ten days or the first twenty days, while a control group was not disturbed (his postweaning experimental group is not pertinent to this discussion). Consummatory behavior following twenty-four hours of thirst found that the controls had the greatest latency and consumed the least amount of water, followed by the two ten-day groups, with the twenty-day group having the shortest latency and ingesting the greatest amount of water.

To summarize: stimulus input in infancy has been varied by number of days of handling (nought, ten, twenty) (Denenberg *et al.*, 1962), number of days of shock (nought, ten, twenty) (Lindholm, 1962) and form of stimulation (nondisturbed controls, handled, shocked) (Denenberg and Smith, 1963; Levine, 1957, 1958). Emotional reactivity has been measured by open-field behavior and consummatory behavior. In each instance the greater the amount of stimulus input in infancy the less was the level of S's emotional reactivity in adulthood. Figure 2 presents

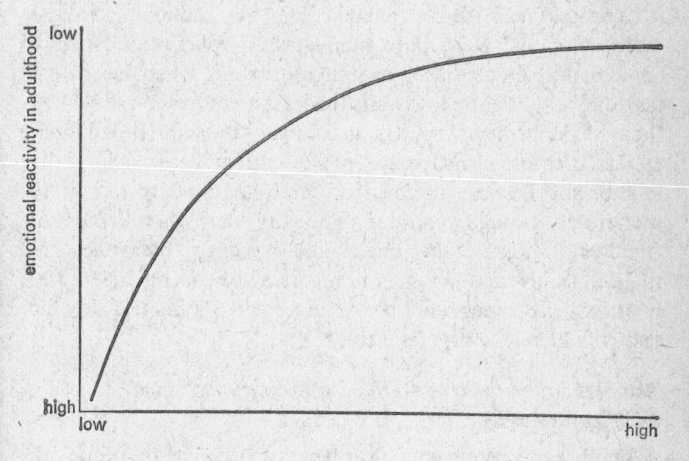

Figure 2 Theoretical curve relating stimulus input in infancy to emotionality in adulthood

an idealized curve showing this theoretical relationship. The negatively accelerated form of the curve is suggested by the findings of the five experiments cited above. In each instance the greatest change in behavior occurred between the control group and the group receiving the intermediate amount of stimulation.

Relationship between emotional reactivity and adult performance

When one examines the dependent variables used in studies of infantile stimulation, it is apparent that many of them contain some form of noxious element (avoidance learning, underwater swimming, thirst, starvation). Obviously, then, S's emotionality or level of arousal will have a significant effect upon his performance in such tasks. It is reasonable to expect that there will be an optimal level of emotionality for efficient performance. As one moves away from this optimal level, performance should drop off, thus resulting in an inverted U function (cf. Hebb, 1955).

However, another parameter is needed. The Yerkes–Dodson Law (Broadhurst, 1957) posits that the optimal level of motivation for a task decreases as task difficulty increases. Assuming that the more emotional S is more motivated, it follows that highly emotional Ss should have the best performance when the level of task difficulty is quite low while the least emotional Ss should be the best performers when the task is very difficult (Broadhurst, 1957; Karas and Denenberg, 1961). In both of these instances the relationship between performance and emotionality should be monotonic, through opposite in slope. It is only when a task is of 'moderate' difficulty that one should expect to obtain the non-monotonic inverted U function. Figure 3 presents the theoretical relationship between adult performance and S's emotionality for tasks of different levels of difficulty.[2]

Some relationships between stimulus input in infancy and adult performance

A number of experiments have been carried out, the results of which are consistent with the predictions made by the theory depicted in Figures 2 and 3. For example, Karas and Denenberg (1961) explicitly tested the theory by assuming that the greater the number of days of handling in infancy, the greater the reduction in emotional reactivity in adulthood. In addition, they assumed that 'spaced' handling would result in greater emotional reduction

---

2. Still another parameter which may be relevant is rate of development. Denenberg and Karas (1959), in comparing the effects of handling upon the rat and mouse, point out that the mouse is a more rapidly developing organism and they suggest the hypothesis that the more rapid an organism's development, the greater the effect of infantile experience.

than 'massed' handling. Experimental rats were space or mass handled for ten or twenty days while controls were not disturbed. The criterion task was an underwater discrimination Y maze similar to the one used by Broadhurst (1957) who had shown that maze performance was related to S's level of emotionality. The discrimination task was an 'easy' one (86·6 per cent correct choices, highly comparable to Broadhurst's value of 86·4 per cent errorless trials on his 'easy' task), thus leading to the deduction that the most emotional Ss should exhibit the best performance with a monotonic decline in performance as emotional reactivity decreased (see Figure 3). Analysis of the swimming time scores found that the rank order of the five groups was as predicted, thus confirming the hypotheses.

Several studies have found an inverted U relationship between amount of stimulation in infancy and later performance. In the experiments by Denenberg (1962a) and Denenberg and Karas (1960, 1961), rat pups were handled for nought (controls), three, five, ten or twenty days in infancy. One can average the data for the three-day, five-day and ten-day groups (irrespective of age of

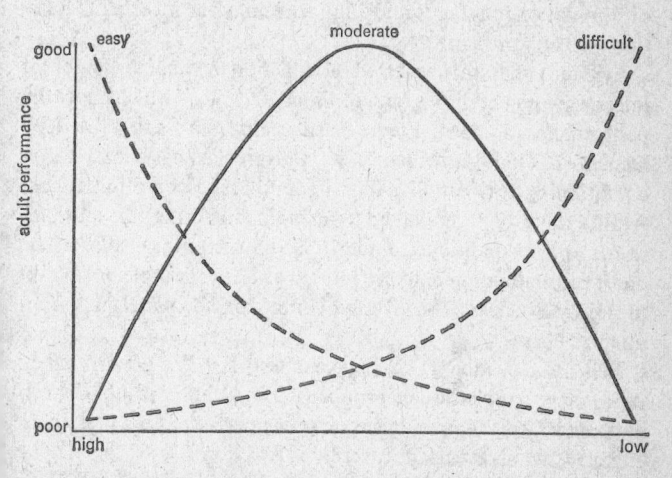

Figure 3 Theoretical relationship between performance in adulthood and emotionality level for tests of varying degrees of difficulty

stimulation), add in the findings of the control and twenty-day groups, and plot the functional relationship between number of days of handling in infancy and later performance. The averaging procedure acts to partially balance out the age of stimulation. One can, in other words, disregard 'critical periods' between birth and weaning and examine amount of stimulation within that period. Such an analysis is shown in Figure 4 for twenty-one and sixty-nine-day body weight, avoidance learning, and survival time (Denenberg, 1962a). The general function of these data may be described by an inverted U curve. Both too much and too little handling led to less than optimal performance. The optimal amount of handling varied with different dependent variables.

This same general function was obtained when electric shock was used to stimulate Ss in infancy. Rats were shocked on the second or fourth day of life using 0·2, 0·5 or 0·8 mA electricity; one group of controls was handled, another not disturbed (Denenberg and Kline, 1964; Kline and Denenberg, 1964). The Ss were given avoidance learning training between sixty and sixty-nine days of age. Figure 5 presents the relationship between intensity of stimulation in infancy and adult learning. The inverted U function is clearly present.

Evidence that this inverted U function has some degree of interspecies generality is seen in Figures 6 and 7, which show the performance of mice. Figure 6 summarizes an experiment by Denenberg (1959) in which Ss were given classical buzzer-shock conditioning at twenty-five days under 0·2, 0·5 or 0·8 mA shock. At fifty days they were taken to an extinction criterion, split into thirds and reconditioned under 0·2, 0·5 or 0·8 mA shock. The adult reconditioning data are plotted as a function of shock level at twenty-five days. The inverted U function adequately describes all three curves.

Bell and Denenberg (1963) gave mice 0·1, 0·3 or 0·5 mA shock in infancy, handled other groups (0·0 mA) and did not disturb still others. Adult avoidance learning performance, plotted in Figure 7, again reveals the inverted U function.

The relationship between stimulus input in infancy and adult performance aids in interpreting other data. For example, Levine, Chevalier and Korchin (1956) found that rats handled for the first twenty days of life performed best in an adult avoidance learning

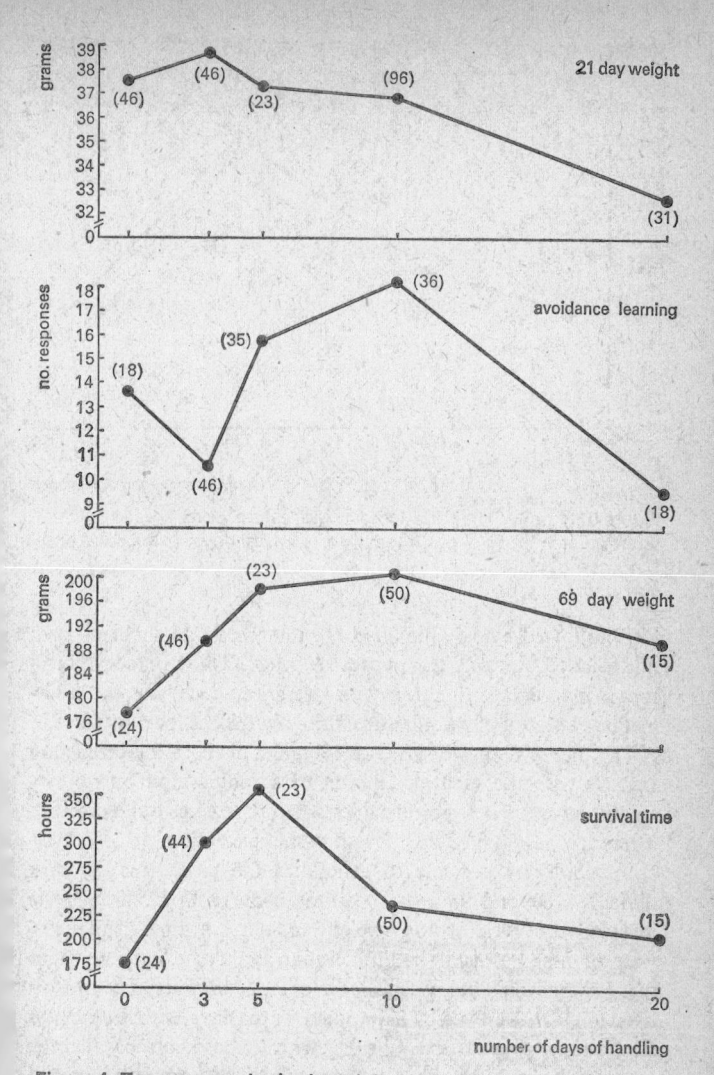

Figure 4 Twenty-one-day body weight, avoidance learning, sixty-nine-day body weight and survival time in rats as a function of number of days of handling in infancy. (Numbers in parentheses indicate *n* per point. From Denenberg, 1962a)

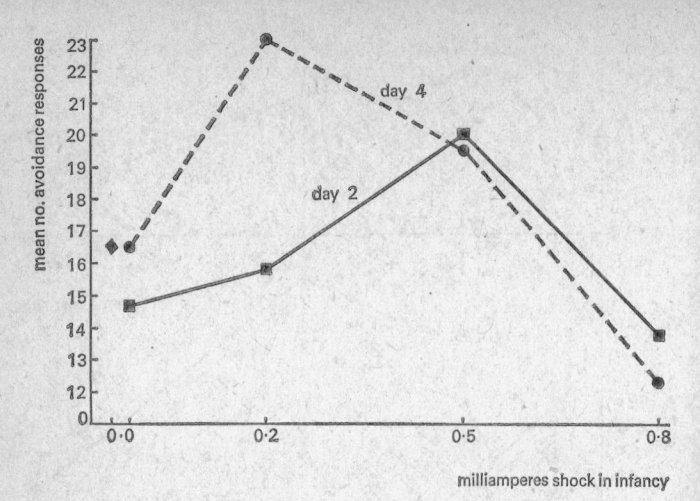

Figure 5 Number of avoidance learning responses in rats as a function of infantile shock intensity on day 2 or day 4 (from Kline and Denenberg, 1964)

task, followed by Ss which had been handled and shocked, with nonhandled controls the poorest learners. These data exhibit a rough inverted U function with the group receiving the intermediate amount of stimulation exhibiting the best performance.

The theory depicted in Figures 2 and 3 leads to the prediction that Ss with the greatest amount of stimulus input in infancy should have the best performance when the task is quite difficult. There are, as yet, no data relevant to this prediction.

It should be possible to generalize the parameter of 'task difficulty' beyond the usual learning context. For example, the inverted U curves for body weight and survival time in Figure 4 were obtained after Ss had undergone avoidance learning training. For Ss which did *not* receive avoidance training, the controls lived longest, followed by Ss handled for ten days, with the twenty-day group dying earliest. In other words, those data parallel the 'easy' curve in Figure 3 while the results of the groups which had avoidance training follow along the curve of the 'moderate' group. Since avoidance learning has been shown to be a stressor (Brady, Porter, Conrad and Mason, 1958; Denenberg and Karas,

1961), this suggests the hypothesis that stress experience, prior to a terminal stress, may act in a manner similar to the task difficulty parameter. This leads to the interesting prediction that Ss subjected to a severe, but nonlethal stress, would be best able to survive a subsequent lethal stress, if they had received a considerable amount of stimulation in infancy.

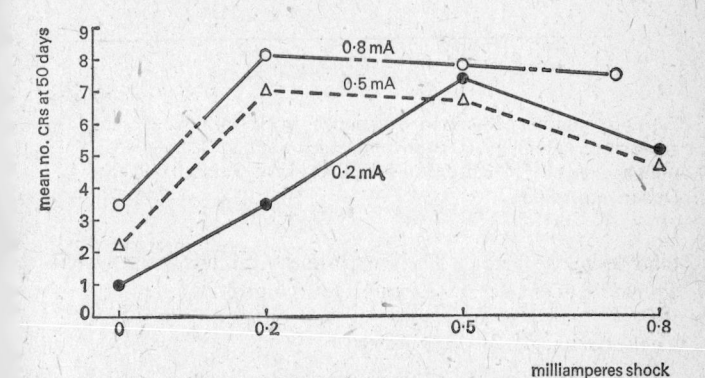

Figure 6 Fifty-day conditioning scores in mice for three shock levels as a function of infantile shock intensity (from Denenberg, 1959)

It is pertinent to ask here about the relationship between stimulation in infancy and performance on a task which minimizes the emotional component. One would expect little or no relationship between infantile stimulation and later behavior. This is exactly what Denenberg and Morton (1962b) found in a series of three experiments. Handling in infancy did not have any effect upon problem-solving behavior as measured by the Hebb–Williams Maze Test. The authors concluded that, 'These findings suggest that preweaning stimulation such as shock and handling affects emotional processes but does not have any direct effect upon perceptual or problem-solving behavior' (Denenberg and Morton, 1962b, p. 1098). Schaefer (1963) has obtained similar results.

Similarly, Spence and Maher (1962b) suggested that the obtained differences in learning performance between Ss stimulated in infancy and controls may be a function of emotional rather

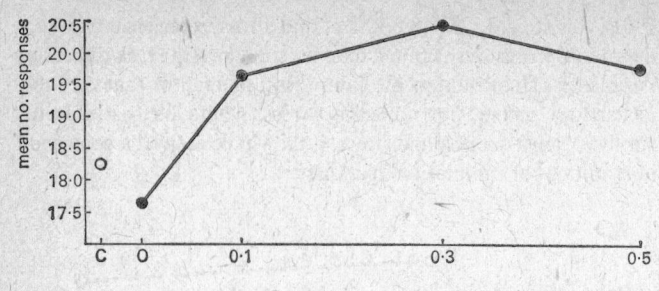

Figure 7 Number of avoidance responses in mice as a function of stimulation in infancy. (C: nonstimulated controls; O: handled, nonshocked; 0·1, 0·3, 0·5: milliamperes of shock. From Bell and Denenberg, 1963)

than learning factors. Their experiment on this point, while equivocal, does offer some support for this position.

Comparisons with Bovard's theory

Though Bovard's (1958) theory is concerned with the effects of handling upon viability, there are certain points of agreement and disagreement to be noted between his position and the one presented here. The major point of disagreement is that Bovard combines the results of preweaning and postweaning handling (the term 'gentling' has been commonly used to describe the procedure of manually manipulating postweaned rodents), while this theory has been limited to preweaning stimulation. There are logical and empirical reasons for making such a distinction. The postweaning rat is a very different organism, behaviorally and biologically, from the preweaning animal and it is not logical to assume that stimulation administered to the immature, recently born rat has the same consequences as the same stimulation administered to a weanling. The experiments cited in footnote 1 offer general support for this conclusion. Clear evidence that handling and electric shock after weaning do not affect rats in the same manner as handling and shock before weaning can be found in the monograph by Brookshire, Littman and Stewart (1961).

A paper directly relevant to this issue is the one by Levine and

Otis (1958). They either handled or gentled rats before or after weaning; a control group was not disturbed. Preweaning handling or gentling had the same effect of significantly increasing body weight and survival rate while postweaning handling or gentling had no significant effect, compared to the control group. In addition to showing that preweaning stimulation has different consequences from postweaning stimulation, the Levine and Otis (1958) paper failed to substantiate Weininger's (1953, 1956) results which Bovard used as part of the empirical base for his theory. Ader (1959) and J. H. Scott (1955) have also failed to replicate Weininger's findings. Even the Hammett (1922) reference cited by Bovard is not supportive of his position, since the experimental data reported in that paper were not concerned with the effects of gentling rats. Hammett does refer back to his 1921 paper and it is that portion of Hammett's paper which Bovard refers to in his reference to Hammett. Several other researchers have also cited the Hammett (1921) paper when discussing the positive effects of postweaning gentling. This is most interesting, since Hammett presents absolutely no data supporting such a conclusion. Hammett (1921) carried out five experiments concerning the effects of parathyroidectomy or thyroidectomy upon survival. The first three studies do not permit a valid evaluation of the effects of gentling because of lack of appropriate controls (though the experiments were valid for Hammett's purposes). The fourth and fifth experiments (see Hammett, 1921, p. 201) can be used to evaluate the effects of gentling since Hammett shifted the rats at weaning from one colony room to the other, thus balancing environmental conditions for the two different stocks of animals. The only significant effect in the fourth experiment was that the two colony stocks differed in genetic make-up; gentling failed to have any effect. And the fifth experiment contradicts this: all rats, regardless of genetic stock or whether or not they were gentled, survived the parathyroidectomy operation. One can only conclude that those who have cited Hammett's work as proof that gentling enhances survival ability have allowed their fertile imaginations to inhibit their reading comprehension. All these experiments suggest that the postweaning handling (or gentling) phenomenon is rather tenuous with respect to modification of the rat's physiology.

There is some degree of agreement between Bovard's theory and the present one concerning preweaning stimulation. In so far as behavioral indices of emotional reactivity correlate with what Bovard (1958) calls stress, then the two theories are in agreement that 'early [preweaning] handling raises the threshold for response to stress', (p. 259). Bovard, however, does not believe that handling is stressful while Denenberg (1959) and Levine (1956) have taken the opposite position. Bovard believes that 'early stress lowers resistance to later stress', (p. 260). Since electric shock – a stimulus typically considered to be stressful – and handling have similar functional properties *vis-à-vis* emotional reactivity, the Levine and Denenberg position appears to be on firmer ground. Further evidence that stressful stimulation in infancy can have beneficial results, rather than the deleterious results predicted by Bovard, is discussed in the next section.

Discussion

The hypothesis that emotionality decreases as a monotonic function of stimulus input may not appear reasonable at first glance because of our knowledge of conditioned fears, traumatic experiences in childhood, etc. It must be emphasized that this hypothesis is based upon, and is restricted to, data obtained on rodents which have been stimulated prior to weaning. Weaning has been used as a criterion point, not because of any clinical implications concerning mother–young separation, but because all of S's senses are functioning by this time and because it is only after weaning that there is any evidence of long-term retention of a learned fear response (Campbell and Campbell, 1962; Denenberg, 1958, 1959; Lindholm, 1962). Furthermore, the consequences of handling or electric shock after weaning have been shown to be very different from their effects prior to weaning (Brookshire, Littman and Stewart, 1961).

J. P. Scott (1962) has made a similar suggestion and has indicated that the transition point may occur at about sixteen days of age, when the eyes open. Up to that age the critical factor mediating infantile stimulation is hypothesized by Scott to be the adrenal cortical stress mechanism while the psychological process of reduction of fear through familiarity is presumed to predominate between seventeen days when the eyes open and thirty days.

The traditional assumption that traumatic experiences in infancy must inevitably have deleterious effects in later life is clearly not consonant with many of the studies cited above. Several other experiments, in fact, may also be noted which contradict this classical assumption. Baron, Brookshire and Littman (1957) found that rats given 1·25 mA of electric current continuously for three minutes on days 20 and 21 were better escape and avoidance learners in adulthood than controls. Infant rats either placed on a laboratory shaker which oscillated 180 times per minute or shocked with 0·1 mA electricity were found to exhibit earlier maturation of the adrenal ascorbic acid depletion response to stress (Levine and Lewis, 1959b). Using the same dependent variable Schaefer, Weingarten and Towne (1962) showed that placing rat pups into a refrigerator at 7° to 10° C also resulted in earlier maturation of the adrenal responses. Finally, Werboff and Havlena (1963) induced febrile convulsions in three-day old rats by means of microwave diathermy. The Ss so treated weighed significantly more at weaning and were significantly more resistant to audiogenic seizures.

Certain parallels may be noted between this theory and the arousal or activation theories of Duffy (1957), Hebb (1955), and Malmo (1959). All the theories are concerned with the intensity dimension of stimulation or arousal, and the inverted U function relating the intensity dimension to performance is common to all. The theory proposed here contributes to general arousal theory in two ways. First, intensity of infantile stimulation is specifically implicated as a major parameter affecting later differences in 'chronic' or general level of arousal. Brookshire, Littman and Stewart (1961) have isolated what may be a similar phenomenon with the postweaning rat. They suggest that their 'pure shock' residual factor of shock trauma may act to modify S's arousal level. The second contribution is a methodological one: the techniques used in infantile stimulation are also procedures for experimentally generating individual differences in chronic arousal level. This opens up a new avenue of attack for those interested in individual differences in arousal level.

Though the proposed theory does account for a considerable number of experimental findings, contrary data are to be noted. For example, Spence and Maher (1962a) subjected rats to intense auditory stimulation between birth and weaning, handled a second group but did not give them auditory stimulation, moved the cages of a third group and did not disturb a fourth group. Using water consumption as their index of emotionality no differences were found among the experimental groups though the stimulated Ss consumed significantly more water than the undisturbed controls. No reason can be suggested to account for the failure to find a monotonic relationship between stimulus intensity in infancy and consummatory behavior.

Finally, this theory is not meant to be a substitute for the critical period hypothesis. In fact, the functional relationships are most clearly seen when Ss are stimulated at different ages (but for the same number of days) and the date averaged so that age of stimulation is equated. Ultimately, any general theory of infantile stimulation will have to account for both age of stimulation and stimulus input and will have to relate these to the psychology and biochemistry of ontogeny (Levine, 1962).

References

ADER, R. (1959), 'The effects of early experience on subsequent emotionality and resistance to stress', *Psychol. Monogr.*, vol. 73, no. 2.

BARON, A., BROOKSHIRE, K. H., and LITTMAN, R. A. (1957), 'Effects of infantile and adult shock-trauma upon learning in the adult white rat', *J. comp. physiol. Psychol.*, vol. 50, pp. 530–34.

BELL, R. W., and DENENBERG, V. H. (1963), 'The interrelationships of shock and critical periods in infancy as they affect adult learning and activity', *Anim. Behav.*, vol. 11, pp. 21–7.

BELL, R. W., REISNER, G., and LINN, T. (1961), 'Recovery from electroconvulsive shock as a function of infantile stimulation', *Science*, vol. 133, p. 1428.

BOVARD, E. W. (1958), 'The effects of early handling on viability in the albino rat', *Psychol. Rev.*, vol. 65, pp. 257–71.

BRADY, J. V., PORTER, R. W., CONRAD, D. G., and MASON, J. W. (1958), 'Avoidance behavior and the development of gastroduodenal ulcers', *J. exp. anal. Behav.*, vol. 1, pp. 69–73.

BROADHURST, P. L. (1957), 'Emotionality and the Yerkes–Dodson Law', *J. exp. Psychol.*, vol. 54, pp. 345–52.

BROOKSHIRE, K. H., LITTMAN, R. A., and STEWART, C. N. (1961), 'Residue of shock-trauma in the white rat: a three-factor theory', *Psychol. Monogr.*, vol. 75, no. 10.

CAMPBELL, B. A., and CAMPBELL, E. H. (1962), 'Retention and extinction of learned fear in infant and adult rats', *J. comp. physiol. Psychol.*, vol. 55, pp. 1–8.

DENENBERG, V. H. (1958), 'Effects of age and early experience upon conditioning in the C57BL/10 mouse', *J. Psychol.*, vol. 46, pp. 211–26.

DENENBERG, V. H. (1959), 'The interactive effects of infantile and adult shock levels upon learning', *Psychol. Rep.*, vol. 5, pp. 357–64.

DENENBERG, V. H. (1960), 'A test of the critical period hypothesis and a further study of the relationship between age and conditioning in the C57BL/10 mouse', *J. genet. Psychol.*, vol. 97, pp. 379–84.

DENENBERG, V. H. (1962a), 'An attempt to isolate critical periods of development in the rat', *J. comp. physiol. Psychol.*, vol. 55, pp. 813–15.

DENENBERG, V. H. (1962b), 'The effects of early experience', in E. S. E. Hafez (ed.), *The Behaviour of Domestic Animals*, Baillière, Tindall & Cox, pp. 109–38.

DENENBERG, V. H., and BELL, R. W. (1960), 'Critical periods for the effects of infantile experience on adult learning', *Science*, vol. 131, pp. 227–8.

DENENBERG, V. H., and KARAS, G. G. (1959), 'Effects of differential handling upon weight gain and mortality in the rat and mouse', *Science*, vol. 130, pp. 629–30.

DENENBERG, V. H., and KARAS, G. G. (1960), 'Interactive effects of age and duration of infantile experience on adult learning', *Psychol. Rep.*, vol. 7, pp. 313–22.

DENENBERG, V. H., and KARAS, G. G. (1961), 'Interactive effects of infantile and adult experiences upon weight gain and mortality in the rat', *J. comp. physiol. Psychol.*, vol. 54, pp. 685–9.

DENENBERG, V. H., and KLINE, N. J. (1964), 'Stimulus intensity *v.* critical periods: a test of two hypotheses concerning infantile stimulation', *Canad. J. Psychol.*, vol. 18, pp. 1–5.

DENENBERG, V. H., and MORTON, J. R. C. (1962a), 'Effects of environmental complexity and social groupings upon modification of emotional behavior', *J. comp. physiol. Psychol.*, vol. 55, pp. 242–6.

DENENBERG, V. H., and MORTON, J. R. C. (1962b), 'Effects of preweaning and postweaning manipulations upon problem-solving behavior', *J. comp. physiol. Psychol.*, vol. 55, pp. 1096–8.

DENENBERG, V. H., and SMITH, S. A. (1963), 'Effects of infantile stimulation and age upon behavior', *J. comp. physiol. Psychol.*, vol. 56, pp. 307–12.

DENENBERG, V. H., and WHIMBEY, A. E. (1963), 'Infantile stimulation and animal husbandry: a methodological study', *J. comp. physiol. Psychol.*, vol. 56, pp. 877–8.

DENENBERG, V. H., CARLSON, P. V., and STEPHENS, M. W. (1962), 'Effects of infantile shock upon emotionality at weaning', *J. comp. physiol. Psychol.*, vol. 55, pp. 819–20.

DENENBERG, V. H., MORTON, J. R. C., KLINE, N. J., and GROTA, L. J. (1962), 'Effects of duration of infantile stimulation upon emotionality', *Canad. J. Psychol.*, vol. 16, pp. 72–6.

DUFFY, E. (1957), 'The psychological significance of the concept of "arousal" or "activation"', *Psychol. Bull.*, vol. 64, pp. 265–75.

HAMMETT, F. S. (1921), 'Studies of the thyroid apparatus: I. The stability of the nervous system as a factor in the resistance of the albino rat to the loss of the parathyroid secretion', *Amer. J. Physiol.*, vol. 56, pp. 196–204.

HAMMETT, F. S. (1922), 'Studies of the thyroid apparatus: V. The significance of the comparative mortality rates of parathyroid-ectomized wild Norway rats and excitable and non-excitable albino rats', *Endocrinology*, vol. 6, pp. 221–9.

HEBB, D. C. (1955), 'Drives and the CNS (conceptual nervous system)', *Psychol. Rev.*, vol. 62, pp. 243–54.

HUNT, H. F., and OTIS, L. S. (1963), 'Early "experience" and its effects on later behavioral processes in rats: I. Initial experiments', *Trans. N.Y. Acad. Sci.*, vol. 25, pp. 858–70.

KARAS, G. G., and DENENBERG, V. H. (1961), 'The effects of duration and distribution of infantile experience on adult learning', *J. comp. physiol. Psychol.*, vol. 54, pp. 170–74.

KLINE, N. J., and DENENBERG, V. H. (1964), 'Qualitative and quantitative dimensions of infantile stimulation', unpublished MS, Purdue University, Department of Psychology.

LEVINE, S. (1956), 'A further study of infantile handling and adult avoidance learning', *J. Personal.*, vol. 25, pp. 70–80.

LEVINE, S. (1957), 'Infantile experience and consummatory behavior in adulthood', *J. comp. physiol. Psychol.*, vol. 50, pp. 609–12.

LEVINE, S. (1958), 'Noxious stimulation in infant and adult rats and consummatory behavior', *J. comp. physiol. Psychol.*, vol. 51, pp. 230–33.

LEVINE, S. (1962), 'The psychophysiological effects of early stimulation', in E. Bliss (ed.), *Roots of Behavior*, Hoeber.

LEVINE, S., and LEWIS, G. W. (1959a), 'Critical periods and the effects of infantile experience on maturation of stress response', *Science*, vol. 129, pp. 42–3.

LEVINE, S., and LEWIS, G. W. (1959b), 'The relative importance of experimenter contact in an effect produced by extra-stimulation in infancy', *J. comp. physiol. Psychol.*, vol. 52, pp. 368–9.

LEVINE, S., and OTIS, L. S. (1958), 'The effects of handling before and after weaning on the resistance of albino rats to later deprivation', *Canad. J. Psychol.*, vol. 12, pp. 103–8.

LEVINE, S., CHEVALIER, J. A., and KORCHIN, S. J. (1956), 'The effects of early shock and handling on later avoidance learning', *J. Personal.*, vol. 24, pp. 475–93.

LINDHOLM, B. W. (1962), 'Critical periods and the effects of early shock on later emotional behavior in the white rat', *J. comp. physiol. Psychol.*, vol. 55, pp. 597–9.

MALMO, R. B. (1959), 'Activation: a neuropsychological dimension', *Psychol. Rev.*, vol. 66, pp. 367–86.

MEYERS, W. J. (1962), 'Critical period for the facilitation of exploratory behavior by infantile experience', *J. comp. physiol. Psychol.*, vol. 55, pp. 1099–1101.

MILLER, N. E. (1959), 'Liberalization of basic s-r concepts: extensions to conflict behavior, motivation and social learning', in S. Koch (ed.), *Psychology: A Study of a Science*, McGraw-Hill, pp. 196–292.

SCHAEFER, T. (1963), 'Early "experience" and its effects on later behavioral processes in rats: II. A critical factor in the early handling phenomenon', *Trans. N.Y. Acad. Sci.*, vol. 25, pp. 871–89.

SCHAEFER, T., WEINGARTEN, F. S., and TOWNE, J. C. (1962), 'Temperature change: the basic variable in the early handling phenomenon?', *Science*, vol. 135, pp. 41–2.

SCOTT, J. H. (1955), 'Some effects at maturity of gentling, ignoring or shocking rats during infancy', *J. abnorm. soc. Psychol.*, vol. 61, pp. 412–14.

SCOTT, J. P. (1958), 'Critical periods in the development of social behavior in puppies', *Psychosom. Med.*, vol. 20, pp. 42–54.

SCOTT, J. P. (1962), 'Critical periods in behavioral development', *Science*, vol. 138, pp. 949–58.

SCOTT, J. P., and MARSTON, M. V. (1950), 'Critical periods affecting the development of normal and maladjustive social behavior in puppies', *J. genet. Psychol.*, vol. 77, pp. 25–60.

SEITZ, P. F. D. (1954), 'The effects of infantile experiences upon adult behavior in animal subjects: I. Effects of litter size during infancy upon adult behavior in the rat', *Amer. J. Psychol.*, vol. 110, pp. 916–27.

SPENCE, J. T., and MAHER, B. A. (1962a), 'Handling and noxious stimulation of the albino rat: I. Effects on subsequent emotionality', *J. comp. physiol. Psychol.*, vol. 55, pp. 247–51.

SPENCE, J. T., and MAHER, B. A. (1962b), 'Handling and noxious stimulation of the albino rat: II. Effects on subsequent performance in learning situation', *J. comp. physiol. Psychol.*, vol. 55, pp. 252–5.

WEININGER, O. (1953), 'Mortality of albino rats under stress as a function of early handling', *Canad. J. Psychol.*, vol. 7, pp. 111–14.

WEININGER, O. (1956), 'The effects of early experience on behavior and growth characteristics', *J. comp. physiol. Psychol.*, vol. 49, pp. 1–9.

WERBOFF, J., and HAVLENA, J. (1963), 'Febrile convulsions in infant rats, and later behavior', *Science*, vol. 142, pp. 684–5.

WILLIAMS, E., and SCOTT, J. P. (1953), 'The development of social behavior patterns in the mouse, in relation to natural periods', *Behaviour*, vol. 6, pp. 35–64.

WOLF, A. (1943), 'The dynamics of the selective inhibition of specific functions in neurosis: a preliminary report', *Psychosom. Med.*, vol. 5, pp. 27–38.

Part Five The Development of Special Traits

Attention has been drawn earlier to the fact that the emphasis on the importance of early experiences for the development of adult behaviour is also a central feature of psychoanalytic thinking (see Levine, Chevalier and Korchin in Reading 15). As a matter of fact many animal studies derive directly or indirectly from Freudian theories concerning the acquisition of diverse traits as a result of various types of infantile experience. Hunt, Schlosberg, Solomon and Stellar (Reading 17), using rats as subjects, studied the long-term effects of feeding frustration in infancy. The time of weaning of babies has been said to influence markedly the development of personality in later life. This view prompted Scott, Ross, Fisher and King, (Reading 18) to inquire into the effects of early weaning on some aspects of the behavioural development of puppies. Benjamin (Reading 19) based her study of non-nutritive sucking in monkeys on the psychoanalytic proposition that children's thumb sucking has to do with the frustration of the 'infantile oral drive'. However, studies concerned with the effects of early experience on the development of characteristic modes of behaviour do not nowadays usually derive from specifically Freudian tenets. They spring more commonly from the widespread interest in the influence of upbringing on later ways of behaving. This interest is exemplified in the paper by Sackett (Reading 20) who set out to investigate the effects on the social behaviour of young monkeys of several different types of rearing conditions.

17 J. McV. Hunt, Harold Schlosberg, R. L. Solomon and Eliot Stellar

The Effects of Infantile Experience on Adult Behaviour in Rats

Excerpt from J. McV. Hunt, Harold Schlosberg, R. L. Solomon and Eliot Stellar, 'Studies on the effects of infantile experience on adult behavior in rats: I. Effects of infantile feeding frustration on adult hoarding', *Journal of Comparative and Physiological Psychology*, vol. 40, 1947, pp. 291-304.

This paper is the first of a series describing experiments designed to verify and to extend the observations on the effects of infantile feeding frustration on adult behavior reported by Hunt in 1941. It will describe the results obtained from repeating Hunt's original experiment concerning the effects of infantile feeding frustration on adult hoarding behavior of rats.

In his original paper, Hunt noted that the evidence for the stress currently placed upon infantile experience as a determinant of adult behavior derives from approaches which observe first the effect in the adult and then look backward for the causes. In the psychoanalysis, the method consists of noting the characteristics of an adult and then looking backward for the cause through his free associations into a childhood already past. In comparative study of cultures, the method consists of noting certain common behavioral characteristics of the adults in a society and then examining their method of rearing children for the causes. Hunt sought to provide a predictive, experimental test of the hypothesis that infantile experience can endure and can affect adult behavior. Using rats as subjects, because of their relatively brief span of life, he found that animals submitted to feeding frustration in infancy hoarded more than two and a half times as much as their freely fed litter-mate controls.

In one part of his experiment, Hunt split two litters when they were weaned at twenty-one days of age, putting seven animals in an experimental group (E), and retaining seven as controls (C). Starting on their twenty-fourth day, the infantile feeding frustration began. The experimental animals were fed irregularly for fifteen days, while the controls had unlimited access to food. This irregular feeding consisted of ten-minute group feedings of wet mash at irregular intervals varying from nine to thirty-six hours. Thus controlled were time of eating and time between feedings. Wet mash was continuously available in the cages of the controls. The two groups were treated alike throughout the remainder of the experiment. After five months of unlimited feeding in the colony, the experimental animals had caught up in weight with the controls. When given an opportunity to hoard pellets of food while they were satiated, none of the now-adult rats hoarded. All animals were then submitted to adult feeding frustration; food was removed from their individual cages and they were given a subsistence diet for two days and then fed a wet mash for only thirty minutes at twenty-four-hour intervals on each of three successive days. Twenty-three and a half hours following the last feeding they were tested in the hoarding alleys. Three more hoarding tests were made on successive days during which the animals were allowed unlimited food. An analysis of variance in the numbers of pellets hauled by the fourteen animals in these four tests indicated that neither sex nor litter contributed significantly to the variance in hoarding scores, but the experiment did. A t-test showed that the difference between the mean number of pellets (37·7) hauled by the experimental animals and the mean number (14) hauled by the controls could have been obtained only once in fifty trials by chance.[1]

In another part of his experiment, two other litters, weaned on their twenty-eighth day, were similarly split. The seven experimental animals in this group were submitted to the same irregular feeding schedule, beginning when they were thirty-two days old. After a second feeding frustration in adulthood, these experimental animals hauled approximately the same mean number (15·1) of pellets as did their litter-mate controls (18·0).

These results led Hunt to conclude that infantile experience can affect adult behavior and that the age of the animals is a factor in

1. See Hunt (1941, p. 354). Only an F-test appears in this paper and p for this difference is given as 0·05. Because sex and litter contributed less than the error in the analysis, degrees of freedom were, so to speak, wasted, and the t-test yields a lower p.

determining whether the effects of an infantile experience of a given intensity will endure to adulthood. He interpreted the enduring effects of infantile frustration in terms of learning. He assumed that the hunger of the infantile feeding frustration, to which the experimental animals were subjected, aroused autonomic and humoral responses which served to energize the animal. During the period of the feeding frustration, it was noted that the experimental animals were much more active than the controls. He further assumed that the cue-stimuli of any mild hunger could serve as conditioned stimuli to rearouse these energizing responses. On the basis of this assumption, the adult feeding frustration was seen to differentiate between experimental and control animals because the cues involved in this relatively mild hunger rearoused the extra energizing responses in the experimental animals while it set up only a primary hunger drive in the control animals. Thus, the experimental animals would have entered the hoarding tests energized by both the conditioned energizing responses and a primary hunger drive, while the control animals entered them with only the primary hunger drive.[2] Hunt explained the failure of the infantile feeding frustration to affect the adult hoarding behavior of the thirty-two-day group by assuming that the hunger aroused in these older animals was too slight in intensity to produce adequate conditioning of the energizing responses.

This interpretation of the obtained results, set forth for heuristic purposes, led to the conception of a research area which may be termed the *experimental control of the life history*. Immediately, it motivated a research program concerned with the adult effects of infantile feeding frustration which would determine the reproducibility of these results and determine whether effects could be shown on categories of behavior other than hoarding. The first repetition yielded results less marked than those in the original experiment. This finding led to several repetitions. The task of the present paper is limited to a description of these repetitions of the study of the effects of infantile feeding frustration on adult hoarding. In summary, they show that the effect found in the original

---

2. Such assumptions have in other settings constituted the basis of acquired drives. See Hull (1943) and Miller and Dollard (1941). The interpretation employed here is also similar to that of 'associative reinforcement'. See Mowrer and Kluckhohn (1944).

experiment is reproducible but that it is somewhat less marked than was originally indicated. A litter by litter analysis suggests that the degree of effect obtained may be determined by some condition associated with litter.

Method

The essential features of the method employed in the original experiment have been retained in the repetitions. The procedure of each experiment may be divided into the 'infantile part' and the 'adult part'. At weaning, the male and female animals in each litter were divided randomly into experimental and control groups and marked with dye. In so far as the composition of a litter allowed, an attempt was made to get equal numbers of males and females into each group. The experimental groups were kept on an irregular feeding schedule for fifteen days immediately following their weaning, in which the time between feedings and the time of eating wet mash were controlled. Although the young experimental animals were always fed as groups, the groups were small and the tin plate of food was large enough to obviate competition among the pups. A pan of wet mash was continuously available in the cages of control animals. At the end of the feeding frustration, unlimited quantities of wet mash were kept continuously available for all animals and a supply of dry pellets was added to prepare them for life in the colony where such food was used.

Approximately two weeks after the end of the feeding frustration, the animals were identified by ear-markings. Somewhat later they were caged according to size; the sexes were separated and all animals were returned to the colony where food in pellet form was continuously available.

After the animals had matured in the colony, they were housed individually in the batteries of small cages used with the hoarding apparatus (Hunt, 1941). There they were kept on an unlimited supply of food pellets for ten days to enable them to adjust in these new cages. Then, on each of three successive days, each animal was given a thirty-minute hoarding test while satiated with food (satiation hoarding). In these tests, the batteries of five cages were attached to the hoarding alleys so that each cage opened onto a separate alley one meter long. At the far end of the alley was a cage of the large pellets of dog chow. The number of pellets hauled by rat from this can to its cage during the three tests constituted its satiation hoarding score.

Following these three daily tests of hoarding while presumably satiated, the animals were subjected to the adult feeding frustration. In the repetitions, this consisted of removing all food pellets from the battery cages and allowing the animals to eat wet mash for one thirty-minute period on each of three successive days.

The adult feeding frustration was followed by the crucial hoarding tests. At the end of the fourth day, and 23·5 hours after the last feeding, the batteries were placed before the alleys for a thirty-minute hoarding test. After this first test, the animals were allowed to keep an ample supply of food pellets. With the animals thus fed, three additional daily hoarding tests were conducted. By the end of the fourth trial nearly all the animals had ceased to hoard. The hoarding scores to be reported here consist of the sums of the pellets hoarded during these four tests.

In each experiment the animals were weighed regularly: just before the feeding frustration in infancy, during its course and at its end. They were also weighed at occasional and increasing intervals thereafter, always at the time when the animals were put into the battery cages and usually just before and just after the adult feeding frustration.

In the original experiment and in the first repetition the food eaten during the adult feeding frustration was weighed. When the difference between the amounts eaten by experimental and control animals in the first repetition proved insignificant, this practice was discontinued.

The three new experiments, which we shall call Reps. I, II and III, were actually conducted as parts of experiments designed to extend Hunt's findings and they involved certain modifications of the conditions employed in Hunt's original study. The weaning age was reduced to twenty days instead of twenty-one days and the feeding schedules were begun immediately instead of when the rats were twenty-four days old. This was done with a view to increasing the effect of the infantile experience and was dictated by Hunt's finding of a greater effect in his younger group. This procedure required a modification of the feeding schedule. Probably because they lacked experience in eating wet mash, the young animals ate almost no food in the ten-minute limit allowed in the original experiment. Hence they were actually allowed several hours to eat at the first feeding and the time of eating was gradually reduced to ten minutes on about the fifth day and to five minutes on about the eleventh day. Moreover, the infantile feeding frustration in the repetitions was increased in severity in that it involved more long periods without food (two periods of thirty-six hours and six periods of twenty-four hours).

Increasing the severity of the feeding frustration resulted in loss of some experimental animals and in an increase in the weight differences between experimental and control animals at the end of the infantile feeding frustration. See Table 1.

Table 1 Mean Weights in Grams of Experimental and Control Animals in the Various Experiments and in the Litters of These Experiments Before and After the Infantile Feeding Frustration

Experiment	Litter	Before				After				% weight loss*
		No. E	E	No. C	C	No. E	E	No. C	C	
Original 24 day group	1	3	52·7	4	50·0	3	62·0	4	90·5	31
	2	4	47·5	3	46·7	4	57·8	3	74·3	22
All		7	49·7	7	48·9	7	59·6	7	83·6	29
Rep. I	1	5	28·1	5	28·2	5	44·6	5	81·4	45
	2	5	24·6	5	24·9	5	34·4	5	71·4	52
All		10	26·4	10	26·6	10	39·5	10	76·4	49
Rep. II	1	6	18·5	6	19·4	2	20·8	6	61·2	66
	2	4	30·2	4	29·8	4	37·6	2	81·7	54
All		10	23·2	10	23·6	6	34·0	8	66·3	49
Rep. III	1	3	38·5	3	37·4	3	40·9	3	106·8	62
	2	4	35·8	3	35·7	4	44·7	3	98·5	55
	3	3	34·2	3	34·9	3	35·2	3	100·3	65
	4	2	38·4	2	39·5	1	34·1	2	106·0	68
All		12	36·5	11	36·6	11	40·1	11	102·6	61

*Per cent weight loss is based on the weights of the animals at the close of the infantile feeding frustration.

$$\% \text{ weight loss} = 100 \times \frac{\text{mean weight controls} - \text{mean weight experimentals}}{\text{mean weight controls}}$$

The number of days allowed between the end of the infantile feeding frustration and introducing the animals into the battery cages of the hoarding apparatus was varied from 171 days in the original as follows: Rep. I – 190 days, Rep. II – 112 days and Rep. III – 91 days. These differences resulted from the academic schedules of the experimenters and from an effort in the last two experiments to speed up the process of getting data. As a result, weight differentials between experimental and control animals had not yet disappeared in the second and third repetitions when the hoarding tests were conducted.

The adult feeding frustrations were also varied by eliminating the first two days on which all animals in the original experiment were given two pellets each. Although this change of procedure was planned on the basis of theoretical considerations, it was probably unfortunate, because we did not make an experimental issue of the change.

Eight litters were involved in the three repetitions, two in each of the first and second and four in the third. When greater variations in the hoarding scores of control animals were found in the first and second repetitions than in the original experiment, we considered that competition for nipples during the nursing period, resulting from the accidentally large numbers of animals in the litters, might account for it. For the third repetition, we decided to reduce all litters to seven animals at birth in order to reduce the likelihood of such competition.

Results

Hoarding while satiated

As Hunt found in his original experiment, the numbers of pellets hauled by the animals when they were presumably satiated are small, and no differences, or at least no consistent differences, exist

Table 2 Mean Numbers of Pellets Hoarded per Animal in the Three Thirty-Minute Tests while Satiated by Experimental and Control Groups in the Various Experiments

Experiment	Experimentals	Controls
Original	1·6	2·0
Rep. I	1·1	0·4
Rep. II	1·3	0·3
Rep. III	1·5	3·8

between numbers hauled by experimental and control animals. The means for the two groups in the original experiment and in each of the three repetitions appear in Table 2.

Hoarding following the adult feeding frustration

In such an experiment as this, where interest in individuals may be obscured by mere statistical presentation of results, the data on the individual animals may be desired. For this reason, we present in Table 3 the number of pellets hoarded, the log hoarding scores,[3] and the grams of mash eaten or the percentage of weight lost during the adult feeding frustration by the individual animals classified according to experiment, litter, sex and experimental condition.

Cursory scanning of the individual numbers of pellets hoarded shows that the experimental animals in the repetitions tend to hoard more than their litter-mate controls, but the degree of overlapping is considerably greater than it was in the original experiment.

Comparison of the group means for each of the four experiments (see Table 4 and Figure 1) shows that the experimental animals regularly hoard more than their litter-mate controls, but only the difference obtained in the original experiment is statistically significant ($p = 0.02$ for raw scores or 0.01 for the logarithmic treatment)[4] by itself. However, since the experimental animals

---

3. Since hoarding scores are limited at zero and unlimited for higher values, frequency distributions of such scores are positively skewed to a high degree. Morgan (1945) has shown that these scores may be normalized for statistical treatment by a logarithmic procedure. He adds one to each hoarding score, then converts each score to a logarithm. Distributions of such log scores appear to be normal in that cumulative frequencies, plotted on a logarithmic grid, give a linear fit. We have substantiated Morgan's findings by means of the χ^2 test of fit with the normal function for the hoarding data from 107 of our animals. For raw hoarding scores, the value of χ^2 was 13.28 and $p = 0.01$. When these scores were treated by Morgan's method, the value of χ^2 reduced to 4.89 and p falls between 0.30 and 0.50. We shall use log scores as well as raw scores in most of our statistical treatments, in order to show the effects of the normalizing procedure.

4. Because analyses of variance have shown for each of these separate experiments that litter and sex contribute almost nothing to the variance in pellets hoarded, we have employed Student's t-test to determine the statistical significance of the differences.

regularly hoarded more than the controls and since each of these four experiments constitutes a separate event from a statistical standpoint, their p-values may be multiplied. For raw scores, the resulting product is 0·00108; for log scores, it is 0·00018. In other words, it is extremely unlikely that such results could have been obtained by chance and it is highly certain that an infantile feeding frustration will increase hoarding on the average.

Litter by litter analysis

In spite of such statistical reasoning, it has been disconcerting to find that in none of the repetitions did the difference between the experimental and control animals show up to the marked extent found in the original experiment. Had the original experiment turned out as did any one of the repetitions, there is little chance that the problem would have been pursued further. Perhaps the results from the original experiment represent luck, that one chance in fifty; perhaps the modifications of the method as employed in the repetitions may account for the smaller differences found in them. At any rate, our search for an explanation led us to examine the differences between the amounts of hoarding by experimental and control animals litter by litter.

Our first approach to the litter by litter analysis is by means of

Table 3 Individual Data for Each Animal Classified According to Experiment, Litter, Sex and Experimental Condition

Experiment	Litter	Sex	Number of pellets hoarded		Log hoarding score		Grams of wet mash eaten during adult feeding frustration*		% weight lost during adult feeding frustration	
			E	C	E	C	E	C	E	C
Original	1	M	27	10	1·45	1·04	53	45		
		F	69	8	1·85	0·95	30	33		
			55	12	1·75	1·11	36	23		
				15		1·20		27		
	2	M	32	40	1·52	1·61	49	55		
			45		1·66		48			
		F	20	9	1·32	1·00	34	37		
			16	4	1·23	0·70	43	37		

Table 3 – (continued)

Experiment	Litter	Sex	No of pellets hoarded		Log hoarding score		Grams of wet mash eaten during adult feeding frustration*		% weight lost during adult feeding frustration	
			E	C	E	C	E	C	E	C
Rep. I	1	M	5		0.78		63			
		F	14	3	1.18	0.60	38	36		
			11	4	1.08	0.70	46	53		
			15	11	1.20	1.08	41	40		
			8	8	0.95	0.95	52	20		
				13		1.15		48		
	2	M	18	6	1.28	0.85	64	38		
			8	8	0.95	0.95	54	55		
			31	62	1.51	1.80	46	44		
			57		1.76		52			
		F	56	9	1.76	1.00	36	36		
				15		1.20		45		
Rep. II	1	M		12		1.11				16
				7		0.90				16
				15		1.20				12
		F	45	12	1.66	1.11			18	18
			16	0	1.23	0.00			15	16
				66		1.83				17
	2	M	7	2	0.90	0.48			15	17
			13	2	1.15	0.48			11	10
		F	29		1.48				9	
			12		1.11				17	
Rep. III	1	M	10	11	1.04	1.08			13	14
			184	18	2.27	1.28			14	14
		F	19	7	1.30	0.90			13	24
	2	M	9	28	1.00	1.46			15	16
			14	15	1.18	1.20			16	16
		F	14	6	1.18	0.85			16	18
			16		1.23				17	
	3	M		50		17.1				16
		F	11	56	1.08	17.6			16	13
			44	17	1.65	12.6			14	13
			40		1.61				18	
	4	M	69	13	1.85	1.15			17	13
		F		4		0.70				16

*Rounded to nearest gram.

Table 4 Results from the Hoarding Tests After the Adult Feeding Frustration for Each Experiment

A. Data treated as 'raw' scores

Experiment	Mean number pellets		Ratio E/C	1	p
	E	C			
Original	37·70	14·00	2·69	2·75	0·02
Rep. I	22·30	13·90	1·60	1·02	0·30
Rep. II	20·33	14·50	1·45	0·58	0·60
Rep. III	39·11	20·45	1·91	1·16	0·30

B. Data treated as logarithms of raw scores plus one

Experiment	Mean log scores		Ratio E/C	1	p
	E	C			
Original	1·540	1·087	1·41	3·08	0·01
Rep. I	1·246	1·028	1·21	1·17	0·30
Rep. II	1·255	0·841	1·49	1·44	0·20
Rep. III	1·399	1·213	1·15	1·13	0·30

the ratios of the mean numbers of pellets hoarded by experimental and control animals. Dividing the mean for the experimental group by the mean for the control group in each litter shows readily whether and to what extent the former differs from the

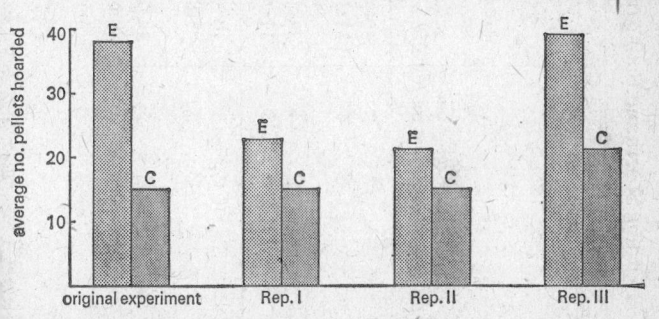

Figure 1 The effect of the infantile feeding frustration as shown by the differences between the average number of pellets hoarded by experimental and control animals in each of the four experiments

Table 5 Hoarding Scores and Eating or Weight Loss Data Arranged by Litter

Experiment	Litter	Condition	No. animals	Mean no. pellets hoarded	Ratio E/C	Mean log hoarding scores	Ratio E/C	Mean grams mash eaten during adult feeding frustr.	Ratio E/C	Mean % weight lost in adult feeding frustr.	Ratio C/E
Original	1	E	3	50.3	4.47	1.683	1.57	39.7	1.24		
		C	4	11.3		1.075		32.0			
	2	E	4	28.3	1.60	1.432	1.30	43.5	1.01		
		C	3	17.7		1.103		43.0			
Rep. I	1	E	5	10.6	1.36	1.038	1.16	47.6	1.22		
		C	5	7.8		0.896		39.1			
	2	E	5	34.0	1.65	1.452	1.25	50.0	1.15		
		C	5	20.6		1.160		43.5			

Rep. II	1	E C	2 6	30.5 18.7	1.63	1.445 1.025	1.41		16.5 15.8	0.96
	2	E C	4 2	15.3 2.0	7.63	1.160 0.480	2.42		13.0 13.5	1.04
Rep. III	1	E C	3 3	71.0 12.0	5.92	1.537 1.087	1.41		13.3 16.3	1.23
	2	E C	4 3	13.3 16.3	0.81	1.148 1.170	0.98		16.0 16.7	1.04
	3	E C	3 3	31.7 41.0	0.77	1.447 1.577	0.92		16.0 14.0	0.88
	4	E C	1 2	69.0 8.5	8.12	1.850 0.925	2.00		17.0 14.5	0.85

latter. Any ratio greater than unity indicates that experimental animals averaged more pellets hoarded than controls. Such E/C ratios (see Table 5) are fairly justified by the fact that sex contributes insignificantly to the variance in hoarding scores; inequalities in the proportions of males and females in each group do not affect the result. On the other hand, the variability of raw hoarding scores is so great and the number of animals in each group is so small that the size of a given ratio may be fortuitous to a considerable degree. Consider first the ratios for the mean numbers of pellets hoarded. The variation in these ratios appears to be great, varying from a maximum of 8·12 to a minimum of 0·77.[5] Moreover, the largest ratios appear for litters in the repetitions. This fact argues, at least weakly, against attributing the smaller differences between the hoarding scores of experimental and control animals found there to the modifications of method.

The ratios for the log scores of hoarding show a similar trend ($\rho = +0.92$), but, of course, the degree of variation is reduced.

The variability among these litter ratios suggested that some factor associated with litter might determine whether the infantile feeding frustration did or did not produce effects which persist to adulthood. If such a factor were demonstrable, one could account for the variation in the results from different experiments by means of accidental litter selection. Inspection of the E/C ratios, however, yields no information concerning their statistical significance. In order to determine their significance, we resorted to an analysis of variance of the log scores from the animals of all ten litters. This procedure lumps the four experiments together as one. The factor of sex is omitted because a trial showed that it contributed less to the variance of log hoarding scores than the error. The results of the analysis appear in Table 6.

---

5. In two of the ten litters the controls hoarded more than the experimental animals. If one treats the result from each litter as a statistical datum, considers only the fifty/fifty chance that the experimental animals may hoard more than the controls and enters the results in a two-fold table, χ^2 equals 3·6 and the resulting p-value lies between 0·10 and 0·05. Such a statistical approach would greatly reduce the certainty of the effect of infantile feeding frustration. The approach is spuriously conservative, however, for it neglects both the fact that each litter is composed of a number of individuals and the degree of the difference found in the various litters, the precise point in which we are interested here.

Table 6 An Analysis of Variance of the Log Hoarding Scores for the Seventy Animals in the Ten Litters Used in the Four Experiments

Source	Sum of squares	df	Variance	F	p
Total	10·520	69			
Litter	1·979	9	0·220	1·48	0·20–0·05
Experiment	1·492	1	1·492	13·14	0·001
L × E	1·373	9	0·153	1·34	0·20
Error	5·676	50	0·114		

Our interest in Table 6 concerns primarily the litter–experiment interaction (L times E). It is not statistically significant. With 9 and 50 df, the F-value of 1·34 yields a p-value slightly greater than 0·20. Impressive as the E/C ratios are to inspection, there is approximately one chance in five that they are simply variations in random sampling.[6] A factor associated with litter determining whether the infantile feeding frustration produces enduring effects may still be present, but the data presented here are too few to allow proof with a satisfying degree of certainty.

On the other hand, like computing the product of the p-values for the individual experiments ($p = 0.00018$), the statistical test shown in Table 6 also lends great certainty concerning the effects of the infantile feeding frustration on adult hoarding. The F-value of 13·14 indicates that there is less than one chance in a thousand that the difference between the means of the experimental (1·357 log number of pellets plus one) and control (1·065) animals is due to random sampling.

Observations concerning amounts eaten or percentages of weight lost during the adult feeding frustration

In his original study, Hunt had noted accidentally on the first day that he fed wet mash that the experimental animals appeared to eat more than their litter-mate controls. On the last two days of the adult feeding frustration, he weighed the amount of food eaten by each animal. During the last two thirty-minute feedings in the adult feeding frustration, the experimental animals in the twenty-

6. These statements are based on Croxton and Cowden (1945).

four-day group averaged five grams more of mash eaten than their controls. In the first repetition, measures of eating were incorporated in the design. The experimental animals averaged seven grams more mash eaten during the three thirty-minute feedings, but this difference fell short of significance at the 5 per cent level of certainty (see Table 7). Thus, in the original experiment and in the first repetition, there appears to be a tendency for the experimental animals to eat more during the intervals allowed than their litter-mate controls. Unfortunately, we did not weigh the food eaten in the third and fourth repetitions.

Table 7 Mean Grams of Total Mash Eaten per Animal During the Three Thirty-Minute Feeding Periods of the Adult Feeding Frustration in Rep. I

Experimentals	Controls	F	df	p
48·8	41·30	4·20	1–16	0·20–0·05
Males 51·75	Females 40·58	8·93	1–16	0·05–0·01
Litter 1 43·35	Litter 2 46·75	0·86	1–16	

In an effort to determine whether the tendency persisted, we have turned to the weight data. In these latter two repetitions, the animals were weighed both before and after the adult feeding frustration. We reasoned that if the experimental animals continued to eat more than the controls, the weight loss incurred by the adult feeding frustration should be less. It appears, if this reasoning is correct, that the tendency for the experimental animals to eat more than the controls did persist to a slight degree. At any rate, the experimental animals show a slightly smaller mean percentage of weight lost than their litter-mate controls (see Table 8).[7] The differences, however, fall far short of statistical significance.

It occurred to us that the effects of the infantile feeding frustra-

[7]. Percentage of weight lost is employed here to make the losses comparable for animals of varying size.

tion might be alternatively expressed in hoarding or eating. If an experimental animal were driven to eat relatively more rapidly during the limited feeding periods of the adult feeding frustration, this might be expected to leave it with a relatively lower primary hunger drive for the hoarding tests. Our experiments were not designed to yield a nice test of this hypothesis, but the question led us to examine the relation between the E/C ratios for the hoarding scores and the E/C ratios for eating or the inverse C/E ratios for the percentages of weight lost in the various litters. These data appear in Table 5. If the tendency for eating and hoarding to be alternative expressions of the effects of the infantile feeding frustration were strong and if the strength of the two alternatives were a function of litter, we might expect a negative correlation between these two sets of ratios. Actually, almost no relation appears between them ($\rho = +0.10$), and it is not negative. The question remains open.

Table 8 Mean Percentages of Weight Lost by the Experimental and Control Animals During Adult Feeding Frustration in the Second and Third Repetitions

Experimentals	Controls
14·17	15·22
15·35	15·45

Discussion

The new experiments described here tend to confirm Hunt's original finding that the effects of an infantile feeding frustration can endure to adulthood and influence hoarding behavior. On the other hand, the degree of the effect is less than that found in the original experiment. Why the effect is less pronounced is unclear, but the three modifications of procedure should be considered. First, the feeding frustrations were begun when the pups were four days younger (twenty days old) than those in the original experiment (twenty-four days). Secondly, the feeding frustration was made more severe. From the standpoint of Hunt's theoretical interpretation, both of these modifications were seen as ways of insuring and increasing the degree of effect. The younger age should have made the pups more vulnerable. Increasing the number of long periods between feedings should have aroused more of the intense emotional responses and thereby ensured their being conditioned to any mild cues of hunger. The fact that these modifications resulted in diminished effects suggests that they may have missed fire in some fashion. They did result in a loss of some experimental animals. It may be argued that those lost were the animals in which the effect might have been most pronounced. In the first repetition, however, no animals were lost, yet the degree of effect was reduced. It may also be argued that they passed through the highest degrees of excitement to lower levels during the longest (thirty-six hours) periods without food and this may have operated to reduce the strength of the connection between hunger cues and the autonomic responses. If one entertains an hypothesis that the traces of the infantile feeding frustration are carried in some fashion other than learning, it is difficult to see how a more severe feeding frustration can leave a diminished effect. We shall be concerned with this question in the next paper in this series.

The third modification of method involved dropping the initial two days of a subsistence ration of pellets from the adult feeding frustration. This left only the three daily, thirty-minute feedings of wet mash. From one standpoint, this also might be expected to increase the differential in the hoarding of experimental and control animals. A number of periods without food are required to instigate the hoarding response in adult animals and the number of periods varies for different animals (Morgan, Stellar and Johnson, 1943). From Hunt's interpretation, one might argue that the abbreviated adult feeding frustration would diminish the average hoarding of controls in which only the hunger drive is presumed to be operative. This would increase in the experimental animals the proportion of their total motivation attributable to the energizing responses rearoused by the hunger of the adult feeding frustration. On the other hand, one might argue that these energizing responses are indiscriminate in the response they affect. They may serve merely to facilitate any behavior involved when they are aroused. If such be the case, then it may be possible that reducing the adult feeding frustration served merely to reduce the amount of hoarding behavior on which the conditioned, energizing responses could have shown their effect. These alternatives are open to test, but they have not been examined in any of the experiments we have done.

It is interesting that both eating and hoarding appear to be affected in the same direction. This would agree with our last argument. On the other hand, there is the possibility that eating and hoarding may be alternative effects of the infantile experience. In future experiments directed toward hoarding, it would probably be wise to control the amounts eaten during the adult feeding frustration.

If future experiments bear out the suggestion that some factor associated with litter determines whether and to what degree the infantile experience affects adult behavior, a new approach to the problem will be opened. That even the suggestion of such a possibility should appear in data from our own homogeneous strain argues that it may be rewarding to use animals from a variety of strains where the temperamental characteristics are fairly well known ahead of time.

In closing it is worth noting that the vicissitudes of a war have provided examples of feeding frustration in young human beings that have resulted in the hoarding of food. *Time* (31 January 1944, p. 90) carries a report that the Nazi-besieged children of Leningrad hoarded their meager food instead of gobbling it. 'Often they crumble their bread into matchboxes to be munched furtively later.' The difficulties in the therapeutic attempts with these children argue that the effects of such experiences are difficult to eradicate. In still another report (*Time*, 5 November 1945, pp. 58–9), the former child inmates of Dachau continued to steal food from the tables at the Kloster-Indersdorf Monastery even after they had learned that plenty of food was available. These observations and those deriving from psychoanalysis and the comparative study of cultures, coupled with our own on rats, argue that we may be dealing with a phenomenon which can appear generally in mammals.

References

CROXTON, F. E., and COWDEN, D. J. (1945), *Two Extensions of the F Table*, Prentice-Hall.

HULL, C. L. (1943), *Principles of Behavior*, Appleton-Century-Crofts.

HUNT, J. McV. (1941), 'The effects of infant feeding-frustration upon adult hoarding in the albino rat', *J. abnorm. soc. Psychol.*, vol. 36, pp. 338–60.

MILLER, N. E., and DOLLARD, J. (1941), *Social Learning and Imitation*, Yale University Press.

MORGAN, C. T. (1945), 'The statistical treatment of hoarding data', *J. comp. Psychol.*, vol. 38, pp. 247–56.

MORGAN, C. T., STELLAR, E., and JOHNSON, O. (1943), 'Food-deprivation and hoarding in rats', *J. comp. Psychol.*, vol. 35, pp. 275–95.

MOWRER, O. H., and KLUCKHOHN, C. (1944), 'Dynamic theory of personality', in J. McV. Hunt (ed.), *Personality and the Behavior Disorders*, Ronald Press, ch. 3.

18 J. P. Scott, Sherman Ross, Alan E. Fisher and David J. King

The Effects of Early Enforced Weaning on Sucking Behaviour of Puppies

Excerpt from J. P. Scott, Sherman Ross, Alan E. Fisher and David J. King, 'The effects of early enforced weaning on sucking behavior of puppies', *Journal of Genetic Psychology*, vol. 95, 1959, pp. 261–81.

Introduction

Sucking behavior has attracted considerable scientific interest because of its obvious relationship to the phenomenon of early socialization in mammals, because of the supposed effects of different weaning practices upon the development of personality in different human cultures and because thumb sucking in a mildly neurotic form is a frequent occurrence in children of our own society.

The scientific literature on sucking in both human and infrahuman subjects has been reviewed in a recent paper (Ross, Fisher and King, 1957). The present research is concerned chiefly with the effects of sudden weaning on puppies of different ages. Age at weaning of human infants is an important factor in determining the amount of emotional disturbance, the greatest effect occurring between thirteen and eighteen months of age (Whiting, 1954). In puppies, which have a shorter developmental time and in which weaning normally occurs from seven to ten weeks of age, there is a possibility of defining the time element more definitely and relating it to the critical period for socialization (Scott, 1958).

The results with puppies indicate that there is a change in the reaction to weaning correlated with the onset of the critical period for socialization. Another important factor affecting the reaction of puppies to weaning is the previous state of nutrition as indicated by body weight. Finally, comparison with other experimental studies indicates that the nature of postweaning care is another important factor.

Table 1 Age at Weaning, Relative Weight and Sucking Reactions of Experimental and Control Puppies

Age at weaning	Litter no.	Litter size at weaning normal	Experimentals Wt before weaning normal %	Times tested during Sep.	Aver. sucking days 2-5	Aver. sucking days 1-14	Controls Wt before weaning % normal	Aver. sucking days 2-5	Aver. sucking days 1-14
10	14	6	99	10	4·00	4·40	66	1·00	0·42
10	14	6	96	10	5·00	5·10	79	1·00	0·42
11	13	4	58	13	5·75	5·62	—	—	—
11	13†	4	60	13	4·50	5·00	—	—	—
12	11*	6	115	10	1·25	1·00	88	0·00	0·00
12	11*	6	115	10	1·00	0·70	112	0·00	0·00
14	9	3	117	12	2·50	0·83	98	0·00	0·42
14	9	3	114	12	0·50	0·16	—	—	—
14	13†	4	46	13	5·00	5·00	—	—	—
14	13†	4	73	5	6·00	4·80	—	—	—
15	10	3	54	7	4·33	4·44	63	0·25	0·18
15	10	3	58	8	4·75	3·75	65r	0·00	0·00
15	14	6	83	11	1·66	0·90	75r	0·00	0·00
15	14	6	78	11	3·33	2·24	62	0·75	0·55
16	8	3	84	11	5·25	3·36	—	—	—
16	8	3	91	11	4·75	3·27	98	0·00	0·00
18	2	4	97	11	0·66	1·63	85	0·00	0·09
			107	7	3·00	3·00			

19	4*	4	113	13	0·25	0·46	123	0·00	0·00
19	4*	4	137	12	0·00	1·50	130	0·00	0·00
19	12	6	85	10	0·00	0·00	72	0·00	0·00
							85	0·00	0·00
19	12	6	97	11	0·00	0·00	72	0·00	0·00
21	5*	6	119	11	0·00	0·00	54	0·00	0·00
21	5*	6	119	10	1·25	0·70	88	0·00	0·00
22	6	6	96	11	0·00	0·00	95	0·00	0·00
22	6	6	96	11	0·00	0·00	78	0·00	0·00
24	5*	6	103	10	1·50	0·30	67	0·00	0·00
24	5*	6	112	10	0·00	0·00	88r	0·00	0·00
25	1	3	111	10	0·75	0·43	95r	0·00	0·00
25	1	3	91	14	0·25	0·43	116	0·00	—
26	11*	6	124	14	0·00	0·00	—	—	—
26	11*	6	131	7	0·00	0·00	121r	0·00	0·00
28	3	6	90	7	1·50	1·20	147r	0·00	0·00
28	3	6	95	10	0·25	0·16	53	0·50	0·16
				12			71	0·00	0·00
35	3	6	80	5	0·00	0·00	58r	0·00	0·00
35	3	6	69	5	0·00	0·00	72r	0·00	0·00
35	6	6	77	11	0·00	0·00	89r	0·00	0·00
35	6	6	88	11	0·00	0·00	71r	0·00	0·00
35	7	4	77	11	0·00	0·00	59	0·00	0·00
36	7	4	77	11	0·00	0·00	43	0·00	0·00

* Basenjis.   †Died during experiment (all same litter).   r = repeated control.

Subjects and materials

A total of fourteen litters and sixty-four animals were used in the experiment. Eleven litters were cocker spaniels and three were African basenjis. There were four litters of three, four litters of four and six litters of six. The puppies were weaned at ages ranging from ten to thirty-six days after birth, as shown in Table 1.

The general method was to wean the puppies, two at a time, so that isolation would not be involved and so that they would have an opportunity for body sucking if this should arise. The remaining animals were left as controls, except in the litters of six, where two pairs of puppies were usually removed at different ages. After two weeks, the weaned puppies were returned to their mothers. The larger animals in the litter were chosen for weaning, partly because they could better stand the stress of weaning and partly to weight the experiment against the hypothesis that nutritional state would produce sucking. The effect was, of course, to leave an additional milk supply for the control puppies remaining with their mothers. As Figure 4 shows, the result was an upturn in their weight curves.

In three litters (nos. 7, 10, 13), all animals were less than 90 per cent of normal weight prior to weaning, indicating that the nutrition supplied by the mother was unsatisfactory. Litter 13 was in particularly poor condition, and all members were weaned in order to increase the chances of survival, but three out of four nevertheless died. There was no other mortality in the course of the experiment.

All experiments were done in the same experimental room. This was approximately 10×18 feet in size with a large window, insulated walls, and an exhaust fan for ventilation. Observations were made through a one-way vision mirror. Few disturbing noises could be heard inside the room. Heat was provided by controlled hot air. However, the control mechanism was not efficient and the temperature varied from 67° to 87° F during the course of the experiment.

The room itself was divided into two identical halves, each with a nest box, food stand and food and water dishes. The concrete floor was kept covered with shavings and feces were removed once per day. In most cases, a pregnant female was brought into one-half of the room and had her puppies there. At the time of weaning two puppies were removed to the opposite half of the room. The partition was made of a frame covered with welded wire on both sides, so that the puppies could not come into contact with animals on the other side but could easily see them.

Before weaning, the mother and pups were given the usual routine care and feeding. Dry Purina kibbled dog meal and laboratory chow were available at all times. Once per day the mother was fed a dish of whole cow's milk prepared from powdered milk plus vitamin A and D supplement (Abbott's Haliver Malt). After weaning, the experimental puppies were fed warm Borden's Esbilac, a simulated bitch's milk, several times per day. Left-over milk was left in the room and extra feedings given if the puppies appeared hungry or not gaining weight properly. Dry food was also available as for the control puppies. No effort was made to keep the feeding on a regular schedule. In this respect the experiment is quite different from those of other authors.

The young puppies were quite clumsy in their lapping and frequently covered themselves with milk. This had to be removed by bathing, and when this happened the control puppies were treated similarly. This bathing was also necessary to make sure that any body sucking was truly non-nutritive.

The primary data were collected by daily weighing, a finger sucking test and daily observations. This routine was begun as soon as possible after the birth of a litter. Because some litters could not be moved into the experimental room until data was complete on a previous litter, the time at which this care was started varied from the first to the tenth day of life. The finger sucking test was usually omitted on weekends. At weaning the puppies were kept apart from the mother for two weeks and then returned. Testing was continued throughout this period, except in some of the older litters in which no sucking had appeared for a week or more. In a few of the litters testing was continued after the return to the mother in order to see if there was any possible disturbance of behavior at this point.

The finger sucking test consisted of placing a wet finger in the puppy's mouth for sixty seconds. A four-point rating scale was used, ranging from no sucking to sixty seconds of strong continous sucking. The actual rating scale was: 0, no sucking; 1, mild, non-continuous sucking; 2, either mild sucking continued for sixty seconds or strong sucking which was non-continuous; 3, strong sucking continued for sixty seconds. This test was given at 8 to 8·30 each morning before feeding and between 11 and 11·30 after the puppies had had an opportunity to eat. The score for each day is the mean of these two ratings. In the tables and graphs this has been presented for convenience as the sum of these two scores, giving a scale ranging from 0 to 6.

Behavioral observations were made at varying intervals throughout the day. Approximately one hour of observation was done daily, distributed in four ten- to fifteen-minute periods. The puppies were carefully watched for evidence of body sucking on themselves or litter-mates, as well as chewing, licking and sucking of other objects.

Results
General

An overall picture of the results is given in Figures 1 to 4. Figure 1 shows that the sucking tendencies of the puppies start with a high rating at birth and rapidly decline to the sixth day. This confirms Ross's (1951) original observation on a small sample of puppies. After the sixth day over half of the puppies have almost completely stopped finger sucking. During the next eight days 58 per cent of the controls and 63 per cent of the experimentals show either no finger sucking or a slight amount of sucking on one or two days.

There are a fair number of animals who continue sucking for a longer period. For these animals there appears to be actually a slight increase in the finger sucking tendency during the following week. Whether this is a maturational phenomenon or is caused by some other factor is not clear from the data.

Figure 1 also shows that the control animals originally sucked more than the experimentals, so that the selection of experimental animals was actually against the hypothesis that separation should increase sucking. As will be seen later, this effect was probably produced by selecting the larger animals in the litter for the experimental subjects.

Figure 2 shows that separation has a clear-cut effect upon sucking and that the maximum amount of sucking appears on the

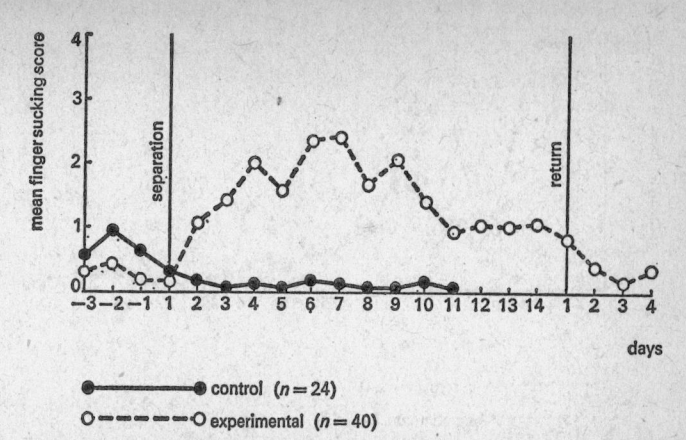

Figure 1 Average finger sucking scores for (a) control puppies and (b) experimental puppies prior to separation of the first animals. Note the rapid decline of sucking during the first week and that prior to treatment the experimental puppies show slightly less sucking than controls

sixth and seventh days of separation. Figure 3 shows that there is a clear difference between puppies separated at nineteen days and earlier and those separated from twenty to twenty-eight days inclusive. Puppies weaned after twenty-eight days of age showed no sucking whatsoever.

Figure 4 shows the relationship between weight and separation. Before separation the experimental puppies were heavier. Afterwards they tended to gain weight less rapidly than the controls and actually followed the curve formerly taken by the controls. The latter showed an upward spurt after separation, probably because of an increased available milk supply from the mother, which is the sole source of food in younger animals. This, of course, indicates that sucking is related to weight gain and, by inference, to hunger.

The effect of age

When the relative sucking scores of experimental and control puppies are graphed according to age (see Figure 5) it will be seen that there is a decline in the effect on the nineteenth day and following. The first experimental animal to show a zero score is

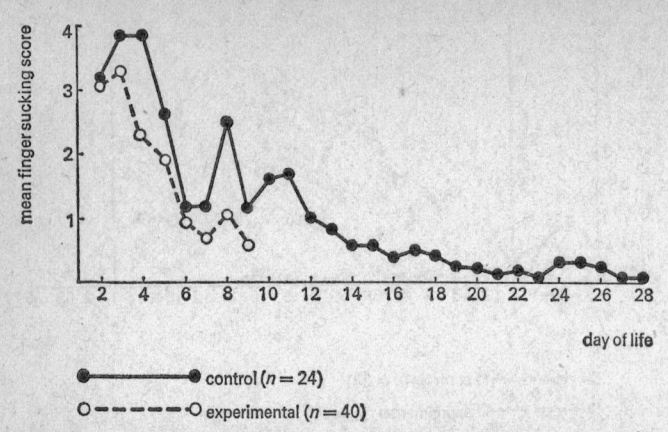

Figure 2 Average finger sucking scores for control and experimental puppies during separation, irrespective of age separation. The maximum effect on the separated pups is produced six to seven days after weaning

found on the nineteenth day. Therefore the data were divided at this point, leaving eighteen experimental animals from ten to eighteen days of age and sixteen from nineteen to twenty-eight. In relation to the beginning of the critical period of socialization, one

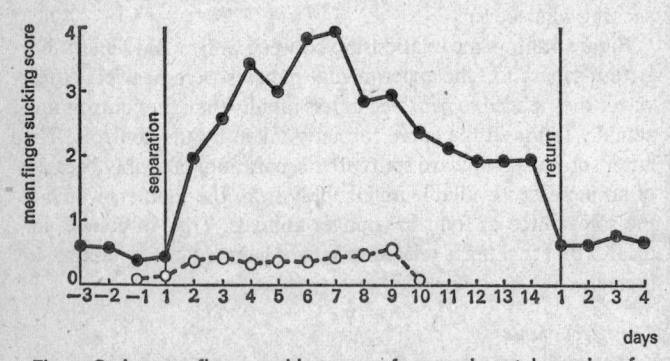

Figure 3 Average finger sucking scores for experimental puppies of different age groups. Solid line represents puppies weaned at nineteen days and earlier; broken line, puppies weaned on days 20 to 28. Puppies weaned after twenty-eight days showed no finger sucking

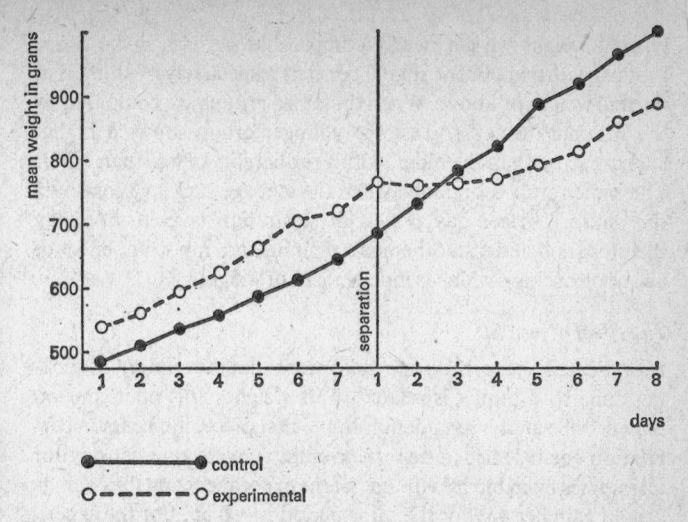

Figure 4 Average weight of control and experimental puppies, irrespective of age, before and after separation. Weaning lowered the weight of the separated animals and the additional milk supply benefited their litter-mate controls

of the most reliable measures is the appearance of the startle reaction to sound. This appears on the average at 19·5 days, with an estimated standard deviation of 2·3 days (Scott, 1958). Dividing the data between eighteen and nineteen days therefore insures that the majority of the earlier sample had not passed into the period of socialization at the time of separation.

In order to obtain the immediate effect of age of separation the sucking scores for experimental animals were calculated for the first four days following separation. Over half of the older animals received a zero score while none of the younger animals did so. The χ^2 analysis of this result gives a probability of less than 0·01 of obtaining this result by accident.

There remains the possibility that the age effect is due to an accidental selection of lighter animals in the young group. Nine out of eighteen of the younger animals were below 90 per cent of normal weight at the last weekly birthday preceding separation, while only one out of sixteen of the older animals was below this point. However, if we eliminate all animals below 90 per cent of normal weight we get nearly comparable samples in both age groups, with 55 per cent and 60 per cent respectively of animals at normal weight or above. When these two groups are compared by the Mann–Whitney U Test the younger group shows a higher sucking score than the older, with a probability of less than 0·001. The same result is obtained when the average sucking score over the entire fourteen-day period of separation is used. We may therefore conclude that there is a definite and important effect of age upon sucking which is independent of weight.

The effect of weight

As indicated above, there are indications that the amount of sucking done by a puppy is related to its weight. This phenomenon may now be analysed in detail. In the first place, the Pearson correlation coefficient between the average sucking rate per day for all puppies from birth to the end of the experiment and the average weight gain per day for the same period is $-0·55$. For the experimental puppies, the corresponding figure for the time of separation only is $-0·68$. The smaller and less rapidly growing animals

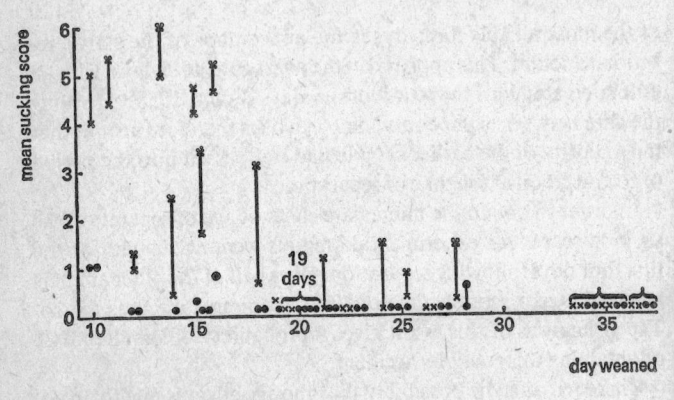

Figure 5 Average finger sucking scores for the four days immediately following separation. Note that the experimental animals first overlap their litter-mate controls on day 19. For precise data see Table 1

thus have a strong tendency to do more finger sucking than the larger ones.

This may be analysed in relation to age and previous conditions of nutrition. The mothers differ a good deal in the amount of milk which they can produce and this is the only source of food for puppies up to three weeks of age. In order to compare puppies of different ages, the weight on the weekly birthday preceding separation was compared to the mean weight at the same age of a larger number of other animals of the same breed reared under standard conditions. By accident of random selection, more of the animals in the early-weaned group from ten to eighteen days were under 90 per cent of normal weight than were the two older groups. If all animals from ten to eighteen days of age are used for a rank order correlation between per cent of normal weight and sucking, the result is -0.68. If all the animals below 90 per cent are eliminated the correlation is still -0.59. In this age group there is a strong negative correlation between weight and the amount of sucking; that is, the lighter animals suck more than the heavier ones.

If a similar analysis is made of animals between nineteen and twenty-eight days of age, there is almost no evidence of correlation and those above twenty-eight days of age show no finger sucking, in spite of the fact that these were animals which fell much below the normal weight. We may conclude that weight has an important relationship to sucking only in the early age group.

One more set of facts has some bearing on the analysis. The puppies were measured according to the time it took to equal or exceed their weight before separation. In many cases this took place on the first day, i.e. there was no loss of weight. In others it might be several days before the lost weight was regained. The third day was arbitrarily selected as a point indicating severe weight loss resulting from the fact that the puppy was not able to adjust himself quickly to the new method of feeding. As shown in Table 2, nearly four-fifths of the youngest age group had difficulty, which was slightly more marked in the lighter puppies. Only a third of the 19- to 28-day puppies showed this difficulty, while none of the older puppies showed it.

This means that in spite of every effort to keep them well fed, the puppies from ten to eighteen days of age had greater difficulty in adjusting to the new method of feeding than did the older ones.

Table 2 Proportion of Animals Showing Severe Weight Loss after Separation (Lost Weight Not Regained by Third Day of Separation)

Normal weight	Age		
	10–18	19–28	29–36
Under 90%	8/9	0/1	0/6
90% or over	6/9	5/15	0
Total	14/18	5/16	0/6

It follows that these younger animals were hungry over a longer period of time. We can conclude that the amount of finger sucking is strongly related to hunger in young puppies of eighteen days of age and younger. Hungry puppies of this age tend to suck on any available object. Beyond this age the puppies adjust themselves more rapidly to the new method of feeding and hence become less hungry. However, since there was no correlation in this group between weight and sucking, we can conclude that there is no longer a strong tendency toward non-nutritional sucking in response to hunger.

Supplementary experiment on effects of hunger

A further experiment was done in order to test the effect of hunger as separated from the possible emotional disturbances of prolonged separation from the mother. In a litter of five cocker spaniels, puppies were separated from the mother on alternate days, so that there were always at least two puppies with the mother and no puppy was exposed to prolonged food deprivation. During the first week of life the puppies were separated for periods of four hours. During the second week they were separated for eight hours and during the third and fourth weeks they were separated sixteen hours. The latter procedure was carried on at night instead of the day. The finger-sucking test was given before and after the period of brief separation.

The results showed significant differences in finger sucking and other oral activities only during the third week, the age period in which significant results were given by the experiment on sudden weaning. It may be concluded that food deprivation causes an increase in sucking up to the end of the third week, but not thereafter.

The negative results prior to fourteen days do not necessarily indicate that before this time there is no effect of hunger on sucking. During the first week the ratings on the control tests were so high that no additional effect could have been obtained by hunger. There was also a tendency in this litter for sucking activity to show a daily rhythm, with higher amounts of sucking in the late afternoon than in the morning. The scores for both experimental and control subjects tended to rise in the afternoon. If the eight-hour deprivation during the second week had been done at night, it might have given some results during the second week. Also, the period of deprivation was considerably shorter than that given later and might not have been effective.

The behavior of the hungry puppies in free situations showed some differences from week to week. During the first week the puppies showed considerable random exploratory activity and were frequently found in different parts of the room. During the second week the puppies were found huddled together in the spot in which they had been originally placed, apparently showing more responsiveness to each other. In the third week the puppies tended to locate themselves at the point in the fence nearest to the location of the control puppies. This indicates that the eyes (now open) were being used for visual localization. Finally, during the fourth week, the puppies were much more active and tended to come to the fence and yelp. All these changes are consistent with the regular pattern of maturation of sensory and motor capacities.

This experiment confirms the conclusion of the previous section that hunger increases the amount of finger sucking in animals eighteen days of age or younger but not in older animals.

Body sucking

One of the striking results of the present experiment was that no body sucking was observed between the pairs of experimental puppies. This has, however, occurred in certain other experiments and can be described as follows. Unlike the human infant, the dog has no convenient part of its own body which can be sucked. The paws are covered with hair and cannot be gotten easily into the mouth. Animals which show this type of non-nutritional sucking are most likely to suck the under parts of the bodies of other animals, either the penis of males or the vulva of females, and occasionally the tip of the tail. This seems to last for only a short period in the life of puppies, probably because as they grow older they have a tendency to fight off any puppy that nurses upon them.

In contrast to the experiment described in this paper, King and Elliot observed several cases of body sucking in an experiment involving sudden weaning. Four litters of basenjis and one litter of fox terriers were weaned at approximately four weeks of age (twenty-seven to thirty days). These sixteen animals were divided into groups of four and individually fed twice per day on a regular schedule. Two groups were given an excess of food and two a limited amount, with the result that the weights began to draw rapidly apart. The group given an excess of food had dry food available in the pen. They ate very little of this and gorged themselves on the scheduled feeding of a mixture of milk and mash.

Body sucking was observed in all four groups, at ages ranging from five to seven weeks (thirty-eight to fifty days). Body sucking was observed both before and after feeding. It occurred in four out of eleven basenjis and two out of five terriers. The two terriers were the smaller animals in the litter, both at weaning and at the time when body sucking was observed, but the basenjis which showed sucking were intermediate in size. The basenji group was unusual in that it included several unusually small litters, three litters of two and one of five, while the fox terriers came from a litter of five. Five of the cases of body sucking came from the two large litters (ten animals in all) while only one came from the small litters (six animals).

The numbers are too small to determine why only part of the animals developed body sucking. Underfeeding can be eliminated, since sucking occurred in the overfed litters. Body size may be involved but gives no significant results with the numbers used. The data suggest the possibility that animals in the two large litters were subjected to frustration previous to weaning, either through lack of opportunity to nurse, shortage of milk or both. However, the numbers are again too small to draw a definite conclusion.

The important and clear-cut result of this experiment is that the phenomenon of body sucking can be produced by sudden weaning followed by regular, scheduled feeding. This type of feeding apparently has the effect of making the animals intensely hungry at particular times of day.

During a ten-year period, careful daily observations of behavior have been kept on some five hundred different puppies raised in another experiment in which animals were left with the mother until ten weeks of age, which is beyond the normal weaning time. Beginning at three weeks the puppies were given one daily scheduled feeding of milk. Dry mash was available at all times and the puppies began eating it sometime after three weeks of age. Body sucking was observed in only one litter, following early weaning caused by the death of the mother.

This was a litter of F^1 hybrids with a basenji father and cocker spaniel mother. The litter developed in a reasonably normal fashion through the first two weeks. At seventeen days of age it was noted that the mother was not allowing the puppies to nurse freely and that they appeared hungry. The milk supply of the mother seemed to be failing and powdered solid food was made available for the puppies which were able to take some of it. The mother continued to let the puppies nurse occasionally for the next ten days. On the twenty-eighth day after the birth of the puppies she became acutely ill and died. At this point the puppies had to depend on the scheduled daily feeding of milk for their entire milk supply. Judging from the previous slow gain in weight they had been quite hungry for at least a week before death of the mother.

Two kinds of frustration were observed in this litter. The mother did not allow the puppies to nurse as long as they wished and they also were unable to obtain sufficient food to relieve their hunger.

The puppies were first observed sucking on each other's bodies when they were thirty-five days of age, which is very close to the time when this was first observed in the experiment cited directly above. These puppies would lie in a group, sucking each other's tails, ears, penises and vulvae. This activity gradually disappeared in the next few weeks as the puppies grew older.

The two cases where body sucking occurred, one experimental and one accidental, have two features in common. One is that the puppies were completely weaned at four weeks of age and the other is that the body sucking appeared approximately one week later while the puppies were given food in a scheduled fashion. The major experiment described in this paper was unlike these cases in that feeding was not done in a scheduled fashion and the puppies therefore did not become acutely hungry at particular times of day. The puppies were kept away from the mother for a period of two weeks so that there should have been opportunity for body sucking to develop.

The data in this section suggest that, in addition to the hunger produced by scheduled feeding, earlier feeding frustration and/or sucking frustration are also involved.

These observations may be compared with those of a second litter of hybrid puppies with a basenji mother, in which body sucking did not occur. This female developed a case of diarrhea which did not respond to treatment until the puppies were between four and five weeks of age. Up to this time the milk supply of the mother was deficient and the puppies were much retarded in their growth. Afterwards the mother's supply appeared to be restored to normal. Unlike the cocker mother, the basenji allowed her pups to nurse. While they showed considerable evidence of suffering from hunger, they were never seen to suck on each others' bodies either during the period of frustration or the normal period thereafter. Unlike the previous cases, these puppies were not subjected to violent hunger as they grew older, either because of periodic feeding or a short food supply.

Discussion

Comparison with other experiments on puppies

The most elaborate and detailed experiment of this sort was done by Levy (1934), with a litter of puppies which were given a great deal of individual care and attention and on which detailed measurements and observations were made over a long period. The experiment was similar to the present one in that hunger was a factor. At the end of the experiment, at thirty days of age, the control puppies left with the mother averaged three pounds heavier than those used as experimental animals, although the latter had gained approximately two pounds each over a three week period.

In Levy's experiment four out of six puppies were weaned at ten days of age. Nothing can be said about the previous state of nutrition since we have no data for normally raised puppies in the collie breeds. The treatment after weaning was to raise the animals on a bottle on regular scheduled feedings starting three hours apart, beginning at 7 a.m. and ending at 11 p.m. The care given was very similar to that given to human infants. The experimental puppies were kept in pairs in boxes up to the nineteenth day of life, after which they were separated except at feeding and testing time. The chief experimental variable was to feed one pair of puppies with bottles having small holes in the nipples, so that it took much more sucking to elicit the same amount of food than it did for the other pair who were fed with large-holed nipples.

Levy's results are reported in great detail. He observed some body sucking in both groups of animals, but it was much more frequent in the rapid-feeding pair. Body sucking was observed as early as the fourteenth day, occurring both before and after the nineteenth day. It is possible that keeping the animals in boxes instead of a large room as in the present experiment gave more opportunity for body sucking. This would be particularly important at the early age when puppies could get separated.

Levy's finger-sucking test was not begun until the fifteenth day of life. From the fifteenth to the nineteenth day he obtained more finger sucking in the slow feeders. After the nineteenth day there was much more finger sucking in the rapid feeders. Levy interprets his results in terms of the frustration of an impulse to suck, so that animals deprived of nutritional sucking tend to do more non-nutritional sucking.

Fleischl (1957) repeated Levy's experiment with three mongrel dogs, two short-time feeders and one long-time feeder. The puppies were kept in a home and their house was a dresser drawer, so that they were always in close contact. An attempt was made to raise them as much as possible like human triplets. No detailed results were given, but Fleischl reports that the rapid feeders showed more intense finger sucking throughout the experiment, in contrast to Levy's finding that slow feeders sucked more at an early age.

Lindzey, in a pilot experiment, attempted to reproduce Levy's experiment, starting with a litter of beagles at ten days of age.

Because of various difficulties the puppies were returned to the mother at sixteen days of age. No body sucking was observed at later ages.

In summary, the puppy experiments are difficult to compare because of the different techniques employed. All of them are alike in that the weaned animals were not as well fed as those kept with the mothers. Body sucking has been produced only in animals which have been fed on a regular schedule after weaning. It has been produced in late-weaned pups, when the pups are weaned to the cup or solid food (King and Elliot, etc.), and in early-weaned pups which were weaned to a bottle (Levy).

All these experiments included the factor of hunger and some evidence of sucking frustration, and it is not clear whether either of these factors or both are necessary to produce the effect.

The animal experiments lead to the conclusion that the phenomenon of non-nutritional sucking is not a simple one based on a single causal factor or situation. We can conclude that there are at least five possible factors which should be considered in any future set of experiments. The first of these is genetics. In normally raised litters of puppies there are some animals which tend to be suckers and some which do not. While we have no experimental proof for this factor, it is likely that both breed and individual differences exist in the tendency to suck non-nutritional objects. Besides this, there are differences in the care and nutrition provided by the mother before weaning.

Second, the age at weaning is an important factor, as shown by the present experiment. Puppies weaned at nineteen days and after show quite different sucking responses from those weaned earlier, and animals weaned after twenty-eight days of age show different responses again.

Third, there is the experience of the animal prior to weaning. Part of this experience is the varying amount of nutrition received from different mothers, leaving the puppies in different nutritional states. The other part of this experience is the degree of frustration which the puppy receives from the mother. Frustration due to hunger apparently has no effect by itself, but it does in combination with frustration of sucking. Frustration of sucking without hunger has not been attempted in any experiment.

The fourth variable is the treatment after weaning. Weaning to a bottle apparently produces a different effect from weaning to a cup, and weaning to regular scheduled feeding a different effect from weaning to demand feeding.

Finally, there is the factor of hunger, which has been present in all of the experiments. The question of whether sucking frustration in the absence of frustration connected with hunger would produce an effect has not yet been experimentally tested. Final and definitive results on this subject will depend on an adequate program of experimental work, using large numbers of subjects and controlling for at least the five factors outlined above.

Comparison with human data

Any comparison of the results of studies of human children with the present experimental work on puppies depends upon an accurate comparison of developmental stages. Human neonates do not have the major sensory deficiencies of puppies. In humans, both eyes and ears are responsive to stimulation at birth or shortly afterwards. On the other hand, puppies are more advanced in motor development, being able to crawl at birth and making later advances much more rapidly.

Both sorts of infants normally obtain their first nourishment by nursing. It is difficult to compare the natural times for changing over to other kinds of food, since human infants will assimilate a variety of specially prepared foods almost from birth. Under more primitive conditions it would appear that no solid food could be managed by the infant until the development of the first set of teeth. The first incisors appear at about six months of age and the complete set of deciduous teeth is usually present by one and a half to two years of age. This time may be taken to roughly correspond to the period beginning at three weeks in the puppy, when the first teeth appear. Newborn human infants can be fed successfully by a cup with careful manipulation. In this respect newborn babies resemble puppies in the transition stage (two to three weeks), which are able to eat by lapping with some assistance.

The development of human learning capacities has been reviewed by Munn (1954), who comes to the conclusion that some unstable conditioning can be obtained at birth and possibly even prenatally. Good evidence of stable conditioning does not appear until approximately one month of age. The further development of human psychological capacities is perhaps best indicated by the work of Spitz and Wolf (1946) on the smiling response, which is aroused by any human face or mask at one month of age. Discrimination between familiar and unfamiliar faces does not begin until five or six months. It may be concluded that in learning capacity the human infant from birth until one month of age is roughly equivalent to that of the puppy in the transition stage from two to three weeks. Both show unstable conditioning. From one to six months the human infant is equivalent in learning capacities to the puppy from approximately three to four weeks, in the early part of the period of socialization.

In the human experimental studies it is generally assumed that the infants are well fed, and all are fed on regular schedules. Most experiments have been done on extremely short periods of development and are frequently compared with those done at widely different ages. Two highly significant experiments have been done on babies during the first ten days of life. Davis, Sears, Miller and Brodbeck (1948) fed newborn babies by the bottle, cup and breast methods and tested their response to a finger-sucking test. They found that the breast-fed babies showed more finger sucking than the others. Like the newborn puppies, there was some tendency towards a decline as they got older. Figures are not available on the nutrition of these infants, but it is likely that breast-fed infants obtained less nourishment than the other two groups. The authors interpret the experiment as showing the results of learning, namely that the activity which is rewarding tends to be continued. This would also imply that the babies had no power of discrimination at this age.

Brodbeck (1950) has reported a second experiment which more closely parallels that described in this paper. He bottle fed a group of newborn infants for four days and then changed them suddenly to cup feeding for another four days. This would be the equivalent of sudden weaning in the transition stage of the puppy. The chief difference is that the human infants were not allowed to become hungry. The bottle-fed babies were treated in various ways, some getting less milk per feeding and others getting a more rapid flow of milk. All of the infants showed less tendency to suck the fingers when changed to cup feeding. The possibility still remains, o course, that the cup-fed infants are better fed than the bottle-fed ones and that the decline may be due to decreasing hunger. It may be concluded, however, that sudden weaning at this stage in development, when not accompanied by hunger, does not produce a tendency toward thumb sucking.

It should be pointed out that neither of these two experiments produced the persistent type of non-nutritional sucking which forms a behavior problem in older infants and which is comparable to the body sucking produced in Levy's puppies and those of King and Elliot. This early sucking of human infants may correspond to the transitory non-nutritional sucking seen in newborn puppies.

In conclusion, it is clear that there are two kinds of sucking behavior in puppies. One of these is typical of newborn puppies and consists of sucking anything resembling a nipple which is thrust into the mouth. Such behavior normally disappears during the first week, presumably because the puppies become well fed, but it can be brought back at later ages by making the animal hungry. It is difficult to elicit after eighteen days of age, presumably because the puppy is now able to discriminate between nutritive and non-nutritive objects, and it disappears entirely after twenty-eight days of age. This kind of sucking is therefore strongly influenced by hunger and age.

The second kind of sucking is the deliberate non-nutritional sucking on special objects by older animals. This is usually directed toward the bodies of litter-mates. The situation which produces it is some sort of rigid feeding schedule. This in turn produces acute hunger at special times, with the result that the animal has a tendency to eat very rapidly. As Levy showed, this kind of sucking can be greatly reduced by forcing the animals to eat more slowly, using (in his experiment) a bottle with a small-holed nipple. In all experiments in which this type of sucking has occurred there has been evidence of frustration of both eating and sucking after the age of eighteen days. Sometimes these factors have been part of the experiment and sometimes they have been accidental.

The effect of age has been thoroughly explored in the present experiment in connection with the first type of sucking. With this data and other experimental results it should now be possible to do a thorough experiment with the effect of age on the genesis of the second type of sucking.

These two types of sucking have not been hitherto distinguished either in animal experiments or in human subjects, but they are clearly and recognizably distinct. It is probable that the sucking observed in young babies in the first ten days of life belongs to the first type, which is, of course, an adaptation for biological survival. The second type of sucking can be identified with the problem thumb sucking of older children. It is to be hoped that, in the future, methods of clear diagnosis can be devised. In the case of human infants the two kinds can be easily confused because the young baby is likely to bring its thumb into contact with the mouth in the course of random movements. The recognition and diagnosis of the adaptive sucking of young infants apart from the mildly neurotic form seen in older ones may help to eliminate some of the confusion which now exists in the literature (Ross, Fisher and King, 1957).

If the same factors are assumed to develop thumb sucking as appear to produce body sucking in the dog, there are two things which may be helpful in avoiding it: (a) allowing the child to nurse or suck as long as it wishes, as suggested by Levy; (b) relaxing a rigid feeding schedule to permit demand or *ad lib* feeding. There may also be a critical age for the production of this behavior, probably a considerable time after birth. However, these possibilities should be tested by experiment before they are accepted.

References

BRODBECK, A. J. (1950), 'The effect of three feeding variables on the non-nutritive sucking of new-born infants', *Amer. Psychol.*, vol. 5, pp. 292–3.

DAVIS, H. V., SEARS, R. R., MILLER, H. C., and BRODBECK, A. J. (1948), 'Effects of cup-, bottle- and breast-feeding on oral activities of new-born infants', *Pediatrics*, vol. 3, pp. 549–58.

FLEISCHL, M. F. (1957), 'The problem of sucking', *Amer. J. Psychother.*, vol. 1, pp. 86–7.

LEVY, D. M. (1934), 'Experiments on the sucking reflex and social behavior of dogs', *Amer. J. Orthopsychiat.*, vol. 4, pp. 203–24.

MUNN, N. L. (1954), 'Learning in children', in L. Carmichael (ed.), *Manual of Child Psychology*, 2nd edn, Wiley, ch. 7.

ROSS, S. (1951), 'Sucking behavior in neonate dogs', *J. abnorm. soc. Psychol.*, vol. 46, pp. 142–9.

Ross, S., Fisher, A. E., and King, D. (1957), 'Sucking behavior: a review of the literature', *J. genet. Psychol.*, vol. 91, pp. 63–81.

Scott, J. P. (1958), 'Critical periods in the development of social behavior in puppies', *Psychosom. Med.*, vol. 20, pp. 42–54.

Spitz, R. A., and Wolf, K. M. (1946), 'The smiling response: a contribution to the ontogenesis of social relations', *Genet. psychol. Monogr.*, vol. 34, pp. 57–125.

Whiting, J. W. M. (1954), 'The cross-cultural method', in G. Lindzey (ed.), *Handbook of Social Psychology*, Addison-Wesley, ch. 14.

19 Lorna Smith Benjamin

The Effect of Bottle and Cup Feeding on the
Non-Nutritive Sucking of the Infant Rhesus Monkey

Excerpt from Lorna Smith Benjamin, 'The effect of bottle and cup feeding on the nonnutritive sucking of the infant rhesus monkey', *Journal of Comparative and Physiological Psychology*, vol. 54, 1961, pp. 230-37.

Long after the age of nursing has passed, sucking persists in the infant primate in the biologically inappropriate form of thumb sucking. Speculation on the causes of nonnutritive sucking has been plentiful (Freud, 1938; Kaplan, 1950; Klackenberg, 1949; Ribble, 1939; Woodcock, 1934), but relatively little experimental documentation of theories has been offered.

The existing research has been based on the psychoanalytic proposition that frustration of an infantile oral drive will lead to the thumb sucking fixation. Whether this oral drive is inborn or acquired has been the cause of theoretical and experimental controversy. According to innate oral-drive theory, which was first investigated by Levy (1934), too little opportunity to suck in early infancy results in the displacement of sucking energy onto the digits in the form of nonnutritive sucking. According to learning theory, the opposing point of view proposed by Davis, Sears, Miller and Brodbeck (1948), the association of sucking with food reinforcement results in an oral drive that is at least in part acquired, and thumb sucking is a secondary goal response.

Experimental tests of these theories have involved comparing the amounts of nonnutritive sucking exhibited by Ss having ample sucking during their early feeding experiences and Ss deprived of normal nutritive sucking opportunity. With humans and puppies the condition of extensive sucking has been achieved by using breast feeding and/or bottle feeding with a small-hole nipple and the condition of minimal sucking has been instrumented by one or more of the techniques of bottle feeding with a large-hole nipple, cup feeding or dropper feeding.

Findings supporting the innate oral-drive theory have been that much sucking during feeding results in little nonnutritive sucking, presumably because sucking energy has been appropriately discharged during nursing (Fleischl, 1957; Levy, 1934; Ross, 1951). In direct contrast, results in agreement with acquired oral-drive theory have been that extensive early sucking during feeding leads to much nonnutritive sucking, presumably because sucking has been strongly associated with reinforcement and has become a drive (Blau and Blau, 1955; Brodbeck, 1950; Davis *et al.*, 1948). It has been suggested that the contradictions in results may be due to methodological shortcomings (Ross, Fisher and King, 1957).

In addition to experiments, there have been surveys interviewing mothers about the thumb-sucking habits of their children. Treating a short time to weaning, a short time spent in feeding and a low frequency of feeding as independent variables indicative of deprived early sucking experience, and reports of frequency of thumb sucking as the dependent variable, has produced contradictory results. Levy (1928) and Roberts (1944) have supported innate oral-drive theory by finding a higher frequency of nonnutritive sucking under these conditions of early deprivation whereas Bernstein (1955) and Sears and Wise (1950) have supported the acquired oral-drive theory by finding a lower frequency of thumb sucking under these same conditions.

From the foregoing it is seen that there has been no resolution of the oral-drive theoretical controversy and even the experimental fact of whether extensive nutritive sucking leads to more or less nonnutritive sucking has not been clearly established.

The primary purpose of the present experiment was to determine whether there were differences in the nonnutritive sucking of bottle- and cup-raised monkeys and to obtain further information relating to the inborn or acquired oral-drive theories. There was a bottle-fed group (group B), a cup-fed group (group C), a bottle-fed and manometer group (group B-M) and a cup-fed and manometer group (group C-M). The B-M and C-M groups were allowed to suck a nipple connected to a water manometer before every feeding for the first twenty days of life and this experience was denied groups B and C.

Acquired oral-drive theory would predict that the bottle-fed monkeys would show more nonnutritive sucking than cup-fed monkeys because they have more reinforced sucking experience than cup-fed infants. Inborn oral-drive theory, by contrast, would predict that cup-fed monkeys would show more nonnutritive sucking because they would have unused sucking energy available for displacement onto thumbs and fingers.

The manometer treatments were included to provide a nutritionless sucking experience orthogonal to bottle-cup comparisons. It was reasoned that the manometer would provide an outlet for oral drive unconfounded with the primary reinforcing aspects of feeding experience.

Counterbalanced with respect to the B, B-M, C and C-M groups were two other subject variables which were expected to affect nonnutritive sucking. One such variable was sex, controlled because Kunst (1948) had reported more thumb sucking in male human infants than in females whereas Honzik (1948) had found more thumb sucking in girls than in boys. The other counterbalanced variable was type of mother surrogate (Harlow and Zimmermann, 1959), included because the Ss were simultaneously engaged in other researches.

There were a number of secondary purposes to the present experiment. First, it seemed unduly restrictive to allow the general term 'oral drive' to apply only to sucking behavior. To be more inclusive, nonsucking oral activities such as biting and licking were observed in addition to nonnutritive sucking behavior.

Second, there was a test of the assumption that variables affecting the rapidly changing infant at one time are equally relevant at a later age. This assumption has been implicit in the relatively brief experiments which have contributed to the oral-drive controversy. Observations in the present experiment extended from birth to six months of age so that the resulting body of data would trace changes in oral behavior with increased age.

Third, observations on oral behavior were supplemented by measurement of factors presumed to be related to orality, including weight, motor activity and masturbation. Differences in weight were measured because initially there was some question about the ability of cup feeding to allow adequate nourishment. Underweight infants might be expected to show more nonnutritive sucking since hunger has been shown by the present E (Smith, 1958) to increase nonnutritive sucking. Motor activity was measured to test the common belief that children suck their thumbs and fingers most when they are busy with nothing else. Measures of masturbation were made because this behavior and nonnutritive sucking have been reported to enhance each other (Freud, 1938). Two other measures were time taken for feeding and degree of postfeeding disturbance as indexed by behavior such as rocking and crouching. These were included because laboratory experience suggested they might be relevant.

Monkeys were a particularly appropriate S for the study of these problems because they are primates which will suck their digits for years in a manner strikingly similar to thumb sucking in children.

Method

Subjects

Sixteen infant rhesus monkeys that had been taken from their mothers within ten hours of birth, served as the Ss of this experiment. All animals were housed individually in wire laboratory cages, $15 \times 18 \times 24$ in. During the first fourteen days there was a heating pad covered with a cloth diaper on the floor of the cage. Attached to the cage for most of the monkeys was a separate compartment containing two of three types of mother surrogates (Harlow and Zimmermann, 1959). The first of these, the cloth mother surrogate (CM), was a cylinder inclined at 45° and covered with tan terry cloth; it has been described in detail in the Harlow–Zimmermann papers. The second type, the plane mother surrogate (PM), was a plane inclined at an angle of 15° and covered with tan terry cloth. The third was the rocking-plane mother surrogate (RM), a plane covered with tan terry cloth and rocked a full cycle between 15° and 20° every two seconds. With respect to the mother-surrogate variable, the sixteen infants of the present experiment were divided equally into four groups: (a) a control group with no mother surrogate (group CO); (b) a CM and PM group; (c) a CM and RM group; and (d) a PM and RM group. It should be noted that there was no rocking mother available for groups a and b, but that a rocking mother was available for groups c and d. Combined groups a and b are subsequently described as the nonrocking groups and groups c and d as the rocking groups.

Over all there were four groupings of these sixteen Ss according

Table 1 Variables by Animals

Variable	Animal																
	79	86	90	94	81	87	89	93	83	85	96	97	77	92	98	99
Feeding	C	C	C	C	C-M	C-M	C-M	C-M	B	B	B	B	B-M	B-M	B-M	B-M
Sex	M	M	M	F	F	M	F	F	M	F	F	F	M	M	F	M
Surrogate mother	CO	CM	CM	PM	CO	CM	PM	CM	CM	CM	PM	CM	CM	PM	CO	CO
		+	+	+		+	+	+	+	+	+	+	+	+		
	PM	RM	RM	RM	RM	RM	RM	RM	RM	RM	RM	PM	RM	RM		
Rocking–nonrocking	NR	NR	NR	NR	NR	RM	RM	RM	RM	RM	RM	NR	RM	RM	NR	NR

Feeding: C, cup-fed; C-M, cup-fed and manometer experience; B, bottle-fed; B-M, bottle-fed and manometer experience.
Surrogate mother: CO, control with no mother surrogate; CM, cylinder mother; PM, plane mother.
Rocking–nonrocking: RM, rocking plane mother; NR, no rocking mother.

to the variables (a) bottle–cup feeding, (b) manometer–nonmanometer treatment, (c) rocking–nonrocking and (d) male–female. Counterbalancing is given in Table 1. Bottle–cup feeding and manometer–nonmanometer were perfectly counterbalanced with each other and with the rocking–nonrocking and male–female variables. It was not possible to counterbalance rocking–nonrocking and male–female variables with each other and hence a predetermined correction was made in analysing those variables by omitting the data of four animals so that the remaining two groups of six animals were each perfectly counterbalanced for bottle–cup, manometer–nonmanometer, male–female and rocking–nonrocking variables.

Apparatus

All Ss were fed in the nursery on unpainted wire-mesh racks inclined at a 45° angle. The bottle-fed animals had a nipple with the smallest hole from which they would feed, projecting from the floor of the ramp near the top. Cup-fed animals had a cup suspended in the ramp at a similar location. For the first few days of life, a plastic bottom with a small depression was placed in the cup and very small amounts of milk were replaced as the infant drank. This was necessary because a pilot cup-fed animal put both its mouth and its nose into the milk and consequently developed a respiratory disorder. After about five days of age, the cup-fed animals were able to drink from the cup without this plastic device. Under these conditions the cup-fed animals developed no more health problems than the bottle-fed animals.

The manometer consisted of a nipple projecting from a wire ramp like that used for cup and bottle feeding, but painted dark green. The manometer was connected by a small rubber hose to a glass U tube 2·5 mm in internal diameter containing a double column of water 2 feet high. A sucking pressure of 0·02 g was required to deflect the manometer one unit. A recycling cam timer indicated five-second observation periods by an audiovisual signal.

A Plexiglas observation cage, 31 in in diameter and 23 in high, enclosed within a Masonite cubicle equipped with oneway-vision windows placed so that all parts of the cage could be seen was used for observing nonnutritive sucking and nonsucking oral activity. A recycling cam timer indicated ten-second observation periods by an audiovisual signal.

Procedure

All manometer testing was conducted outside the nursery. For the first twenty days of life, five times before each feeding, the mouths of the manometer Ss were placed on the manometer nipple and their heads were then left free. Every five seconds a record was made of the maximum deflection of the water column observed. There were two scores for the manometer performance: average pressure and average duration of placement. The pressure scores were the average of the maximum pressure deflections observed in the five-second periods. The duration scores were the average number of five-second periods during which the S maintained continuous oral contact with the nipple before withdrawing.

All monkeys were tested for nonnutritive sucking and nonsucking oral activity throughout a 180-day period. Observations were made at 8 a.m. seven days per week for the first thirty days of life, five days per week from days 31 through 90, and two successive days per week from days 91 through 180. All testing was done immediately after the animal had finished eating and for the first thirty days of life a record was kept of the time taken for feeding. An additional series of prefeeding observations was made in the afternoon during days 31 through 60 to test for possible reversals in bottle and cup nonnutritive sucking differences relating to feeding schedule (Brodbeck, 1950). Since no reversals were found, only the postfeeding data are presented.

The tester carried the monkey in his hands from the home cage to the circular Plexiglas observation cage and, after placing the monkey gently into this cylinder, rolled the cage into the observation cubicle. A two-minute adaptation period followed the closing of the cubicle door, during which the tester turned off the lights and took his place before a oneway-vision glass window.

The behavior of all the infants was recorded according to six categories defined as follows: (a) thumb, toe or finger sucking – closure of monkey's lips around any of these digits for one second or more; (b) body sucking – closure of the monkey's lips around any part of the body other than digit or genitals for one second or more; (c) genital sucking – closure of the monkey's lips around the penis or the scrotal sac for one second or more; (d) masturbation – active manipulation of the genitals with the hands or feet, or rubbing the legs together in rhythmic fashion; (e) body mouthing – biting or licking of any part of the body; (f) environment mouthing – biting or licking of the cage. Categories a to c are defined as nonnutritive sucking and categories e and f, as nonsucking oral activity.

During the first sixty days of life, each monkey's behavior was recorded using an Esterline-Angus polygraph pen attached to a coded keyboard with keys for the six categories. When each S reached the age of sixty days, all subsequent records were made on time-ruled observation sheets divided into twenty-five intervals of twenty seconds each. During every ten-second period, a single check was made for each type of oral behavior. The total nonnutritive sucking score for any test session was the number of ten-second periods out of a possible maximum of twenty-five which had at least one check indicating the occurrence of some form of nonnutritive sucking. Scoring for nonsucking oral activity was the same as for thumb sucking, a score of one being added for every ten-second period showing biting or licking, with a maximum of twenty-five possible. The Esterline-Angus data had also been tabulated in terms of total number of one-second periods, but nothing was gained and this procedure was dropped.

Following all observations, the tester rated the overall activity of the animal during the session on a five-point scale ranging from *very active* to *asleep*. At this same time the tester recorded whether any behaviors indicative of disturbance such as rocking or crouching (Smith, 1960, experiment 3) had occurred.

The reliability of observation was checked every fifth session by comparing scores assigned by two independent observers. The product-moment r of the total sucking scores recorded by two observers using separate Esterline-Angus keyboards from days 1 through 60 was 0·97. The product-moment r of the total sucking scores recorded by two observers using time-ruled observation sheets from days 61 through 180 was 0·99.

Results

Comparisons between bottle- and cup-raised groups

The nonnutritive sucking exhibited by the bottle-raised group far exceeded that shown by the cup-raised group. The significance of the difference was established at the 0·001 level by comparing daily group scores for the entire 180 days according to sign-test procedure (Siegel, 1956, pp. 68–75). The course of nonnutritive sucking is traced by Figure 1, where it is seen that the frequency for both groups increased progressively for the first seventy days, then stabilized for the cup-fed group and decreased for the bottle-fed group. Because of these trends, the difference between groups reached a maximum at from forty to sixty days of age and then diminished.

Although the bottle-raised group showed more nonnutritive sucking, the cup-raised group exhibited more nonsucking oral activity ($p < 0.001$, sign test of all daily group scores). The changes in nonsucking oral activities with increasing age are illustrated in Figure 2. Both bottle- and cup-raised monkeys started at comparable levels and then there was a slight, progressive decrease in the scores made by bottle-raised Ss from thirty days onward. The cup-raised group attained maximum scores at fifty to sixty days, then progressively declined. Hence, the difference between these

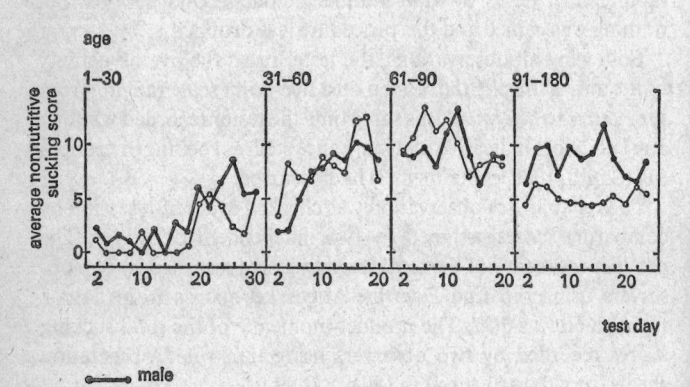

Figure 1 Mean nonnutritive sucking scores for bottle- and cup-fed groups are plotted in two-day blocks

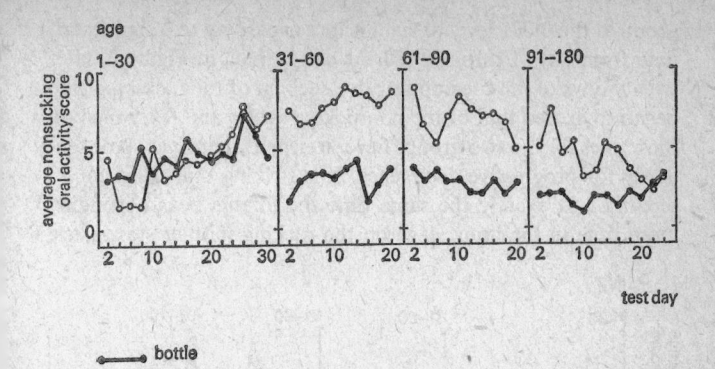

Figure 2 Mean nonsucking oral activity scores for bottle- and cup-fed groups are plotted in two-day blocks

groups was substantial from days 31 to 60 and 61 to 90, and then diminished, the curves actually intersecting by 180 days of age.

Of the monkeys given the twenty-day manometer treatment, those which were bottle-fed had manometer duration scores averaging fifteen seconds, whereas those which were cup-fed remained on the manometer only five seconds. The difference was significant at the 0·001 level according to a sign test of daily group scores. At the same time, the difference between the bottle-fed Ss and the cup-fed Ss was not significant on the manometer pressure measures, although the absolute scores favored the bottle-fed monkeys. Actually, the mean pressure scores on the manometer were extremely low for all animals, the highest daily average pressure being 0·2 g, a negligible amount. The highest manometer pressure score on a single occasion was 4 g, shown by a bottle-fed monkey. Both bottle- and cup-fed animals refused the manometer nipple within the first few days of life, showing behaviors such as vocalizing, struggling, defecating and convulsive jerking when being placed on it.

Comparisons of rocking-surrogate groups and nonrocking-surrogate groups

Daily group nonnutritive sucking scores for the monkeys raised on rocking mother surrogates exceeded those of the nonrocking group at the 0·001 level of significance according to a sign test of data from days 1 through 180. As can be seen in Figure 3, after twenty days of life the nonnutritive sucking of the rocking group began to exceed that of the nonrocking group and from then on the curves for the two groups never touched; there was some tendency for progressive divergence. It is striking that these curves separated at exactly the same time the infants began spending more time in the home cage on the rocking mother surrogates.

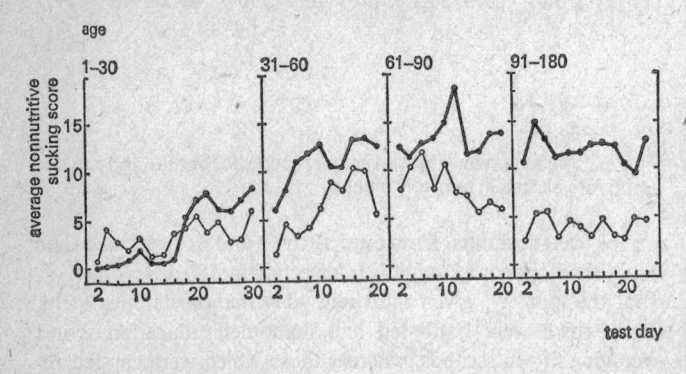

Figure 3 Mean nonnutritive sucking scores for rocking and nonrocking surrogate groups are plotted in two-day blocks

This parallel of preference for the rocking mother and increase in nonnutritive sucking persisted only until the ninety- to 180-day period. At that time, the nonnutritive sucking of the rocking group was still far greater than that of the nonrocking group, yet the preference for the rocking surrogate was disappearing. The correction for failure of counterbalance between rocking–nonrocking and male–female groups did not change the significance of the nonnutritive sucking differences. No significant difference in nonsucking oral activity appeared between the rocking and nonrocking groups.

Comparisons between sexes

The male group showed greater daily nonnutritive sucking scores than the female group ($p < 0.02$) as measured by a sign test of data from days 1 to 180. Inspection of Figure 4 reveals that the difference was slight until ninety days of age, when the females rapidly dropped in sucking level.

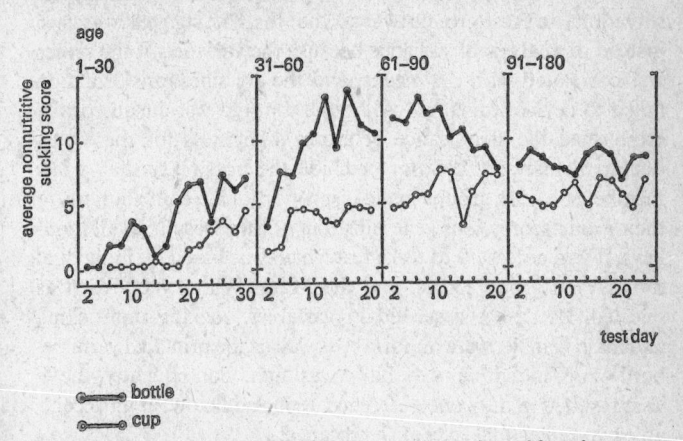

Figure 4 Mean nonnutritive sucking scores for male and female groups are plotted in two-day blocks

Females showed slightly but consistently more nonsucking oral activity than males over the entire 180 days and a sign-test comparison of group scores was significant at the 0·001 level. The two curves traveled in parallel, gently reaching a maximum from days 31 to 60 and 61 to 90 and nearly disappearing in the ninety- to 180-day period. As was the case in the comparisons between the rocking and nonrocking surrogate groups, the significance of these sex differences was not altered when the groups were reduced to six monkeys, each attaining perfect counterbalancing of all variables.

Comparisons between manometer and nonmanometer groups

Consonant with the fact that all Ss refused the manometer nipple within the first few days of life, no significant difference was disclosed by a sign test comparison of all daily nonnutritive sucking scores of the manometer group with those of the nonmanometer group. Similarly, no significant difference in nonsucking oral activity was revealed.

Tests of significance of differences using individuals' scores

The highly significant differences found between bottle- and cup-fed groups, between rocking and nonrocking groups and between male and female groups were based on sign tests of repeated observations on these groups over six months. The sign test was used instead of analysis of variance because the variance of the scores was correlated with the means, and the arc sine transformation failed to correct this fault. Although the sign test unequivocally established the significance of group differences for these particular monkeys, it did not preclude the possibility that a few members of these groups made disproportionate contributions to their group scores. For generalization of these results to all monkeys, it was necessary to use a test which was based on individual rather than group scores, and the Mann–Whitney U Test was selected. Because the secondary variables, rocking–nonrocking and male–female, were important as well as the principal variable, bottle–cup, individual variability was high. Consequently, the U Test resulted in only one difference, reported below, at an acceptable two-tailed 0·05 level of significance.

Age changes in patterns of oral behavior

Dividing the data into four age blocks (days 1–30, 31–60, 61–90 and 91–180) according to the number of observations made per week yielded nearly significant two-tail differences by the U Test at the points of maximal separation in group curves already described. It appeared that early in life, from days 31 to 60, the difference in nonnutritive sucking scores between bottle- and cup-fed individuals was at the 0·10 level, and in nonsucking oral activity, at the 0·06 level. Cup-fed individuals continued to show more nonsucking oral activity than bottle-fed Ss from days 61 to 90 and at this time the difference was significant at the 0·05 level. At this same age there was a difference at the 0·10 level in nonnutritive sucking between individuals with rocking mothers and those without; by the last three months the difference reached the 0·06 level. Also during this last age block the difference between individual males and females was at the 0·08 level.

From the location of maximal separations in group curves and from the results of the U Tests, it was concluded that bottle–cup feeding was relatively more important early in life, whereas rocking–nonrocking surrogates and male–female variables became important later.

The observation that bottle–cup feeding had an important effect on nonnutritive sucking early in life but declined in effectiveness with age, was corroborated in a B/W ratio.[1] This statistic divided the data into four feeding groups defined by the primary orthogonal variables, bottle–cup and manometer–nonmanometer. The resulting between-Ss terms were pooled (B) and compared with the pooled within-feeding-group variance (W). Dividing by W corrected for scale unit and thus gave a purer estimate of between-Ss differences than would the between-Ss term alone. As expected, the B/W ratio increased with age, being 0·53, 1·25, 1·86 and 5·63 for days 1 to 30, 31 to 60, 61 to 90 and 91 to 180, respectively. Since this ratio did not contain feeding variance, the increase in individual differences at a later age must have been due to a decline in the importance of bottle–cup feeding and to the increased importance of other variables, including rocking–nonrocking and male–female.

Relationship between individual nonnutritive sucking activities and nonsucking oral activities

An inverse relationship between individuals' nonnutritive sucking and nonsucking oral-activity scores was suggested by Kendall's rank correlation coefficients (Siegel, 1956, pp. 213–23) of −0·28, −0·12, −0·33 and −0·11 for days 1 to 30, 31 to 60, 61 to 90 and 91 to 180, respectively. Thus, there was some tendency for Ss making high nonnutritive sucking scores to engage in relatively little nonsucking oral activity, although τ was significant only for days 61 to 90 ($p < 0.04$).

Variables related to oral behavior

Comparisons of the weekly weight measures by the sign test showed small but constant and significant differences. The males were 9 per cent heavier than female ($p < 0.01$), the nonrocking

[1] For a complete description of this statistic developed especially for this problem, see appendix 2 of the dissertation, University Microfilm Service, Ann Arbor, Michigan. Sincere gratitude is expressed to D. A. Grant for his constructive comments concerning this statistic.

group 4 per cent heavier than the rocking group ($p < 0.01$) and the manometer group 3 per cent heavier than the nonmanometer group ($p < 0.01$). These weight differences did not seem directly related to oral behavior because, unlike the curves describing nonnutritive sucking and nonsucking oral activity, the weight differences were present from the first day, were very small and remained constant throughout the experiment.

The daily motor activity of bottle–cup, rocking–nonrocking, male–female and manometer–nonmanometer groups was compared by four respective sign tests of data from days 1 through 180. Paralleling daily nonsucking oral activity, cup-fed animals showed more motor activity than bottle-fed groups ($p < 0.001$) and females more than males ($p < 0.001$). This parallel may be attributed to the fact that biting and licking of the cage was usually accompanied by moving from place to place and thus motor activity ratings were necessarily increased.

The only monkeys observed to masturbate at any time in the 180-day test period were the four males with rocking mothers. They were first observed to masturbate at days 46, 75, 83 and 85, respectively. Since male groups and rocking-mother groups also showed more nonnutritive sucking, these data on masturbation provide indirect support for the suggestion that masturbation and thumb sucking enhance each other.

No significant differences were found between any groups in time required for feeding during the first thirty days of life. The bottle–cup means were the most discrepant, 11·6 min being the mean score for bottle feeding and 8·9 min for cup feeding. Other comparisons were: male, 9·7 min $v.$ female, 10·1 min; manometer, 10·0 min $v.$ nonmanometer, 9·9 min.

The measures of disturbance, including rocking and crouching, failed to show differences among any groups. In fact, there were relatively few occurrences of any of these behaviors in these animals which had been adapted to the observation cage from birth.

Discussion

The cup-fed group, for which nutritive sucking experience had been drastically and artificially lowered, showed far less nonnutritive sucking than the bottle-fed group ($p < 0.001$). This result is in direct opposition to the position that cup-fed monkeys would show compensatory sucking for their nutritive-sucking deprivation. The data support the view that thumb sucking is an expression of a need to suck which arises from the association of sucking with the primary reinforcing aspects of feeding.

The acquired oral-drive theory does not however, entirely explain the data. The association of sucking with feeding by no means had a permanent or even persisting effect on nonnutritive sucking. The greatest differences between bottle- and cup-fed monkeys appeared before sixty days of age, and by 180 days of age the differences were disappearing. Further, by days 90 to 180 other variables not associated with feeding became more important. At that time, males and infants with rocking surrogates showed far more nonnutritive sucking than females and infants with nonrocking mothers. It is clear that nutritive sucking experience was important only early in life, whereas other variables became dominant later. It would be an oversimplification, then, to conclude that all nonnutritive sucking occurs in response to a drive acquired from nutritive sucking experience at a very early age.

Further evidence that the acquired oral-drive theory is not sufficient to account for all the data is provided by the inverse relationship found between nonnutritive sucking and nonsucking oral activity. This reciprocal relation strongly indicates an underlying persistent oral responsiveness which must assume one form or another. One could apply the label 'innate oral drive' to this frequent and persistent oral responsiveness which is not wholly dependent on feeding experience. This is reasonable if 'oral drive' is broadened to include not only nonnutritive sucking, but nonsucking oral activity as well.

Such frequent and persistent oral activity is universally exhibited by infant monkeys. For example, Mason, Harlow and Rueping (1959) found the infant monkey had strong innate tendencies to manipulate chains and knobs, and a substantial proportion of the manipulatory activities was oral (personal communication).

The form which this oral activity assumes is determined by many variables – some acquired, some innate. It would seem, then, that it is not appropriate to restrict oral drive to sucking behavior and to try to determine whether it is either acquired or innate. The broader viewpoint is maintained that there is an oral responsiveness universally present in infant monkeys which is not wholly dependent on feeding experience. This innate oral drive appears either as nonnutritive sucking or as nonsucking oral activity and is affected by many variables, both innate and acquired. Some of these variables have been identified by the present experiment, e.g. sex an innate variable and feeding experience an acquired variable.

The reader is reminded that though the group differences found by repeated measurement of the oral behavior of these particular monkeys were highly significant, the generality of these results is attenuated by the fact that two-tailed nonparametric statistical tests using individuals' scores only reached significance levels between 0·05 and 0·10. This unfortunate result is undoubtedly due to the fact that there were only sixteen animals used when at least three orthogonal variables were important and individual variability, though far from random, was high.

References

BERNSTEIN A. (1955), 'Some relations between techniques of feeding and training during infancy and certain behavior in children', *Genet. psychol. Monogr.*, vol. 51, pp. 3–44.

BLAU, T. H., and BLAU, L. R. (1955), 'The sucking reflex: the effects of long feeding v. short feeding on the behavior of a human infant', *J. abnorm. soc. Psychol.*, vol. 51, pp. 123–5.

BRODBECK, A. J. (1950), 'The effect of three feeding variables on the nonnutritive sucking of new-born infants', *Amer. Psychol.*, vol. 5, pp. 292–3.

DAVIS, H. V., SEARS, R. R., MILLER, H. C., and BRODBECK, A. J. (1948), 'Effects of cup-, bottle- and breast-feeding on oral activities of new-born infants', *Pediatrics*, vol. 3, pp. 549–58.

FLEISCHL, M. F. (1957), 'The problem of sucking', *Amer. J. Psychother.*, vol. 1, pp. 86–7.

FREUD, S. (1938), 'Three contributions to the theory of sex', in A. A. Brill (ed.), *The Basic Writings of Sigmund Freud*, Modern Library.

HARLOW, H. F., and ZIMMERMANN, R. R. (1959), 'Affectional responses in the infant monkey', *Science*, vol. 130, pp. 421–32.

HONZIK, M. P. (1948), 'Biosocial aspects of thumbsucking', *Amer. Psychol.*, vol. 3, pp. 351–2.

KAPLAN, M. (1950), 'A note on the psychological implications of thumbsucking', *J. Pediat.*, vol. 37, pp. 3–8.

KLACKENBERG, G. (1949), 'Thumbsucking: frequency and etiology', *Pediatrics*, vol. 4, pp. 293–4.

Kunst, M. S. (1948), 'A study of thumb- and finger-sucking in infants', *Psychol. Monogr.*, vol. 62, no. 3.

Levy, D. M. (1928), 'Finger-sucking and accessory movements in early infancy: an etiological study', *Amer. J. Psychiat.*, vol. 7, pp. 881–918.

Levy, D. M. (1934), 'Experiments on the sucking reflex and social behavior of dogs', *Amer. J. Orthopsychiat.*, vol. 4, pp. 203–24.

Mason, W. A., Harlow, H. F., and Rueping, R. R. (1959), 'Development of manipulatory responsiveness in the infant rhesus monkey', *J. comp. physiol. Psychol.*, vol. 52, pp. 555–8.

Ribble, M. A. (1939), 'The significance of infantile sucking for the psychic development of the individual', *J. nerv. ment. Dis.*, vol. 90, pp. 455–63.

Roberts, E. (1944), 'Thumb- and finger-sucking in relation to feeding in early infancy', *Amer. J. Dis. Child.*, vol. 68, pp. 7–8.

Ross, S. (1951), 'Sucking behavior in neonate dogs', *J. abnorm. soc. Psychol.*, vol. 46, pp. 142–9.

Ross, S., Fisher, A. E., and King, D. (1957), 'Sucking behavior: a review of the literature', *J. genet. Psychol.*, vol. 91, pp. 63–81.

Sears, R. R., and Wise, G. (1950), 'Relation of cup feeding in infancy to thumb-sucking and the oral drive', *Amer. J. Orthopsychiat.*, vol. 20, pp. 123–38.

Siegel, S. (1956), *Nonparametric Statistics for the Behavioral Sciences*, McGraw-Hill.

Smith, L. J. (1958), 'Nonnutritive sucking in the infant rhesus monkey and its relation to feeding', unpublished master's thesis, University of Wisconsin.

Smith, L. J. (1960), 'The nonnutritive sucking behavior of the infant rhesus monkey', unpublished doctoral dissertation, University of Wisconsin.

Woodcock, I. G. (1934), 'Thumb sucking', *Med. Rec. N.Y.*, vol. 139 pp. 328–30.

20 Gene P. Sackett

Some Persistent Effects of Different Rearing Conditions on Pre-Adult Social Behaviour in Monkeys

Excerpt from Gene P. Sackett, 'Some persistent effects of different rearing conditions on preadult behavior of monkeys', *Journal of Comparative and Physiological Psychology*, vol. 64, 1967, pp. 263–5.

The conditions of raising infant mammals appear to have persistent effects on the development of behaviors ranging from simple exploration of novel surroundings to complex social interaction. Early social isolation, in particular, seems to play an important role in the development of rats (Rosenzweig, 1966), dogs (Scott, 1964), monkeys (Mason, 1960; Mitchell, Raymond, Ruppenthal and Harlow, 1966) and chimpanzees (Menzel, 1964). However, many early-experience studies have sampled only a small range of rearing conditions or have tested Ss only in the infant or early juvenile stages of development. The present research investigates the effects of different degrees of environmental restriction during the first year of life on social behavior through the third year, when rhesus monkeys reach the young adult level of development. It was expected that the amount of stimulation available during the first year would be linearly related to measures of social behavior at four years of age.

Method

Subjects and rearing conditions

Five groups of monkeys (*Macaca mulatta*), reared from birth in the Wisconsin Primate Laboratory, were subjected to the following conditions, presented in rank order from least to greatest amount of stimulation available during the first year of life.

1. Group 1 Y I consisted of three males and one female raised in total social isolation for one year; these Ss lived in a completely enclosed metal cage without visual, auditory or physical contact with other monkeys. The isolation environment was consistently lighted but offered no stimulus variety over time. The 1 Y I group

was hand fed by humans during the first fifteen to twenty days of life, but they could not see the human at this time or throughout the remainder of isolation. The isolation apparatus is described by Mitchell *et al.* (1966).

2. Group 6 M I, three males and one female, was raised in the total isolation situation from birth through six months and in bare-wire cages, in which other monkeys could be seen and heard, but physical contact with other animals was unavailable during the second six months.

3. Group W C consisted of seven males reared individually for one year, in bare-wire cages in which they could see and hear, but not touch, other monkeys.

4. Group M P consisted of four males and four females reared from birth to nine months with their natural mothers, all of which were born in the jungle and displayed adequate maternal behavior toward their infants. During rearing Ss had daily social contact with peers and could play with an assortment of toys in their cages.

5. Group M M P consisted of three males and one female which were also mother raised and had daily peer contact. However, the mothers of the M M P Ss had been born in the laboratory, taken from their mothers shortly after birth and reared either in bare-wire cages without peer contact or on inanimate surrogate mothers. These motherless mothers were brutal toward their infants, exhibiting a great deal of hostility and refusing to nurse. Thus, the difference between groups M P and M M P was that M P Ss experienced normal mothering, while the Ss in group M M P experienced maternal rejection and physical punishment during the first two to three months of life.

During the second and third years of life all Ss lived at some time in individual wire cages and in group cages. The Ss were all tested in a variety of social, perceptual and exploratory behavior experiments. Therefore, the experiences intervening between rearing and testing in the present study were comparable in terms of opportunity for social interaction and exposure to novel environments.

Apparatus and procedure

The social behavior test was run in the apparatus in Figure 1. Two forty-six-month-old Ss, one male and one female, were chosen as standard social stimuli during testing on the basis of their relatively neutral social behavior in other experiments; this neutral behavior was characterized by failure to initiate social interactions and by approach behavior when contacted by another monkey. To insure this neutral social behavior, the stimulus monkeys were injected with a low dose of tranquilizer (Promazine, 0·125 mg/kg) prior to each test session; each stimulus monkey was involved in a maximum of three ten-minute tests on a given day. On a test trial, with the guillotine door down, a stimulus monkey was put in the test cage and an experimental S was put in the start cage; one minute later the guillotine door was raised, starting the trial, which lasted for ten minutes. Each S was tested once with the male and once with the female stimulus monkey. Both the stimulus animal and the experimental S were free to move into or away from any part of the apparatus.

One O depressed switches activating clocks during the ten-minute tests to record durations of the following categories of behavior:

1. *Motor activity:* time S spent moving from place to place on the floor, walls, or ceiling of the apparatus.

2. *Proximity:* time S and the stimulus animal spent in the same cage.

3. *Aggression:* time the experimental S spent clasping and pulling, slapping, biting or displacing any part of the stimulus animal's body, or threatening the stimulus animal (a pattern including facial expression with brows or forehead knitted and mouth partially open, crouching posture and head movements).

4. *Fear withdrawal:* time the experimental S spent in movements away from the approaching stimulus animal in fear grimacing or screeching during or after an interaction with the stimulus animals, or in rocking, crouching or huddling after an interaction with the stimulus monkey.

5. *Contact initiation:* time spent in physical contact with the stimulus monkey that was initiated by the experimental S.

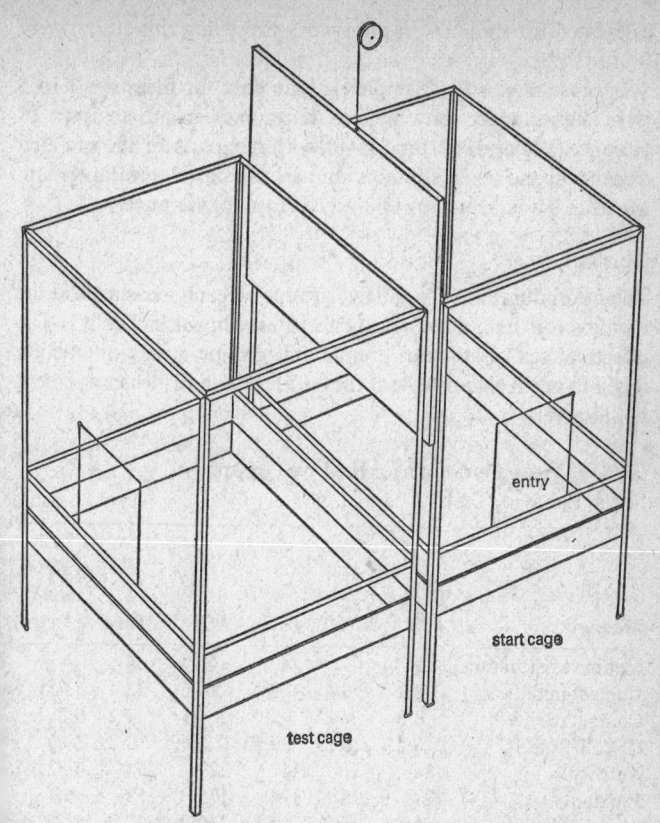

Figure 1 Dual cage apparatus used to test two-monkey social interaction. (The side and front walls were made of wire mesh, the rear walls of Masonite. The O sat in a chair in front of, and midway between, the two cages. The guillotine door was raised by pulling a cable attached to the door)

6. *Contact received:* time spent in physical contact with the experimental S that was initiated by the stimulus animal.

A seventh derived measure, the proportion of physical contact initiated by the experimental S, was calculated from the ratio of contact initiation time to contact initiation plus contact received time: $CI/(CI+CR)$. Reliability coefficients for these categories, calculated for three Os in pilot work preceding this study, were 0·91 to 0·97.

Because of unequal sample size the data for measures 1 to 5 were subjected to unweighted (harmonic) mean analyses of variance (Winer, 1962, pp. 374–8), with groups as an uncorrelated dimension and sex of stimulus animals as a correlated dimension. Measure 6 was treated by one-way analysis of variance.

Results

The mean durations for the five groups on each measure and the F-ratios for the groups' main effects, are shown in Table 1. The effects of sex of stimulus animal and groups × sex interaction failed to reach significance at the 0·05 level for all measures except withdrawal.

Table 1 Mean Durations for the Five Groups on Social Behavior Tests

Measure	Group 1YI	6MI	WC	MP	MMP	F^* for groups' main effects
Median age (months)	49	47	47	45	44	—
Contact initiation	3·1	3·4	8·5	16·6	32·4	3·71†
Contact received	8·5	7·8	7·0	4·1	4·2	0·88
CI/(CI+CR)	0·25	0·39	0·53	0·69	0·79	3·00
Activity	86	121	117	229	203	4·32‡
Proximity	227	198	174	175	158	0·67
Aggression	6·8	4·2	5·6	10·2	27·5	5·25‡
Fear withdrawal	97	25	34	12	6	5·74‡

* $df = 4/22$.
† $p < 0.05$.
‡ $p < 0.01$.

Significant group differences failed to appear on the contact received measure, suggesting that the social behavior of the stimulus animals was constant, regardless of the rearing condition of Ss. Contact initiation scores did vary with rearing conditions. A Duncan Range Test revealed that MMP Ss had the greatest contact initiation time, while MP Ss were higher than the other three groups, which did not differ from each other ($p < 0.05$). The proportion of physical contact initiated by S revealed a descending rank order with M M P Ss highest, 1 Y I Ss lowest.

The groups differed in duration of gross motor activity, with M P and M M P animals most active, W C and 6 M I lower and 1 Y I Ss least active ($p < 0.01$). Time spent in the same cage with the stimulus monkey did not vary between groups, again suggesting that the stimulus animals did not behave differentially as a function of rearing conditions.

The groups differed in the amount of fear and withdrawal. Group 1 Y I had the greatest duration of these behaviors, groups W C and 6 M I were lower and the other two groups were lowest ($p < 0.025$). On the fear-withdrawal measure, a group × sex of stimulus animal interaction appeared ($F = 3.71$, $df = 4/22$, $p < 0.02$); this was due to the 1 Y I, 6 M I and W C Ss showing more fear withdrawal when tested with the male than with the female stimulus monkey, while the M P and M M P Ss showed no differences in this measure between stimulus animals. Aggression differences also occurred between groups: M M P Ss were most aggressive and M P Ss were more aggressive than W C, 6 M I and 1 Y I groups, which did not differ from each other ($p < 0.01$).

Discussion

In this study the M P and M M P groups had been reared under the most varied early environments. The W C, 6 M I and 1 Y I Ss had been raised under successively greater degrees of social and sensory privation. In general this rank ordering of environmental restriction during the first year of life was reflected in behavior at four years of age. The more deprived the early environment, the lower was the amount of gross motor activity, the greater the amount of fearful and withdrawn behavior and the lower the amount of physical contact initiated by S. The physical contact data are of particular importance; they suggest that one effect of early isolation is to produce a monkey that avoids touching another animal. Such behavior is detrimental to the development of social interaction, which involves a great deal of physical contact such as grooming in normal animals. The data thus confirm the expectation that early isolation in monkeys produces detrimental effects on social behavior lasting through the juvenile stages of development. The results also confirm the expectation of a rank-order relationship between amount of input early in life and later behavioral development.

The aggression data suggest that experiences during the first several months of life can affect the preadult hostility responses of monkeys. The monkeys reared by motherless mothers had experienced extreme aggression during the first two to three months of life. After this time overt hostility by the mothers rarely occurred, because the infants learned to avoid attacks by the mothers This early experience with hostile mothers appears to have produced the hyperaggression exhibited by the MMP Ss, which showed more than twice the amount of aggressive behavior shown by the identically reared, but not maternally mistreated, MP monkeys.

References

MASON, W. A. (1960), 'The effects of social restriction on the behavior of rhesus monkeys: I. Free social behavior', *J. comp. physiol. Psychol.*, vol. 53, pp. 582–9.

MENZEL, E. W., Jr (1964), 'Patterns of responsiveness in chimpanzees reared through infancy under conditions of environmental restriction', *Psychol. Forsch.*, vol. 27, pp. 337–65.

MITCHELL, G. D., RAYMOND, E. J., RUPPENTHAL, G. C., and HARLOW, H. F. (1966), 'Long-term effects of total social isolation upon the behavior of rhesus monkeys', *Psychol. Rep.*, vol. 18, pp. 567–80.

ROSENZWEIG, M. R. (1966), 'Environmental complexity, cerebral change and behavior', *Amer. Psychol.*, vol. 21, pp. 321–32.

SCOTT, J. P. (1964), 'The effects of early experience on social behavior and organization', in W. Etkin (ed.), *Social Behavior and Organization among Vertebrates*, University of Chicago Press, pp. 231–55.

WINER, B. J. (1962), *Statistical Principles in Experimental Design*, McGraw-Hill.

Part Six Parental Deprivation in Infancy

A most important influence upon the growing infant is the relationship between it and its mother. Maternal deprivation has been said to affect the young adversely in many ways. It is often very difficult to assess with certainty the effects of parental deprivation, maternal and/or paternal, in children. This is not surprising in view of the many interacting influences at work at any time, where none can readily be placed under experimental control. The environment is much more easily controllable in the study of infant animals. Seay and Harlow (Reading 21) report how young monkeys reacted to maternal separation and reunion. Hinde, Spencer-Booth and Bruce (Reading 22) tackled a similar problem, observing also some rather longer-term results of separation. An assessment of the effects of maternal deprivation based on an extensive and thorough survey of research is given by Yarrow (Reading 23). There is, of course, scope for a great deal more research in this field, and such research is, in fact, continuing.

21 Bill Seay and Harry F. Harlow

Maternal Separation in the Rhesus Monkey

Excerpt from Bill Seay and Harry F. Harlow, 'Maternal deprivation in the rhesus monkey', *Journal of Nervous and Mental Disease*, vol. 140, 1965, pp. 434–41.

The present experiment was designed to study the effects of infant–mother separation on the social and emotional behavior of rhesus monkey infants. The behavior of the mothers and the infants toward each other before separation and after reunion was also investigated.

A previous study of mother–infant separation had been conducted using four infant–mother pairs denied physical contact for a three-week period but allowed auditory, visual and olfactory intercommunication (Seay, Hansen and Harlow, 1962). During the separation period these infants showed increased crying-vocalization and mother viewing, and decreased peer-directed social behavior. Immediately after reunion there were increases in mother–infant cradling, in infant–mother clinging (embracing) and infant–mother ventral contact, and a pronounced decrease in infant–mother nonspecific contact. The persistence of these effects varied among the infant–mother pairs.

Bowlby (1958, 1960) has described the behavior of human children separated from their mothers. The effects on the child occur in three phases: protest, despair and detachment, the first stemming from anxiety, the second from grief and mourning and the third from defensive reactions. The similarity of monkey (Seay, Hansen and Harlow, 1962) and human overt responses to separation from the mother is striking, particularly with respect to the first two of Bowlby's three phases. The correspondence between human and primate responses to separation may be related to similarities in the variables which produce the infant's tie to the mother in both species. There is considerable correspondence between the variables which Bowlby (1958) has described in his component instinctual response theory of the infant–mother tie and the variables producing the infant monkey's tie to its mother.

Although Harlow would attach more importance to clinging and somewhat less importance to sucking than Bowlby, and the relative importance of infant–mother affectional variables doubtless differs from macaque to man, certainly there is little fundamental difference between the two (Harlow, 1960, 1961; Harlow and Zimmermann, 1959). It is clear that clinging, which results in contact comfort, is a stronger and more persisting variable than nursing in the monkey, and any such differences in the importance of the components for monkey and man may be a function of the macaque monkey's neonatal maturity and maturational acceleration.

Seay, Hansen and Harlow (1962) prevented physical contact between infants and mothers while allowing the infants to see and hear their mothers. It is possible that their results were due to frustration induced by the mother's presence in a situation where physical contact with her was impossible. The present study involves total infant–mother separation in eight macaque monkey infant–mother pairs. The results indicate the nature of the infant monkeys' response to separation when visual presence of the monkey mother is denied throughout the separation period.

Method
Subjects

Two groups of four infant rhesus monkeys and the mothers of each served as Ss. There were two male and two female infants in each group; the within-group age span was ten days in one group and nine days in the other. The groups were otherwise identical except that the mothers of one group were primiparous and the mothers of the other multiparous. The first group was separated on 24 September 1962 and the second on 26 November 1962. The mean infant age at separation was 207 days for the first group and 208 days for the second.

Apparatus

Each group of four infant–mother pairs was separately housed in a standard playpen apparatus located in adjacent rooms. Each apparatus (Figure 1) consisted of four wire-mesh living cage $36 \times 36 \times 36$ in and a play area $60 \times 60 \times 30$ in subdivided by removable wire panels into four individual playpen units. A three and a half-inch square opening in the partition between each living cage and adjoining playpen unit allowed the infants continuous access to the playpen units but restricted the mothers, when present, to the living cage. All infant-mother pairs had lived in this apparatus since the birth of the infants and all Ss were removed from the apparatus one hour each week for cage-cleaning purposes.

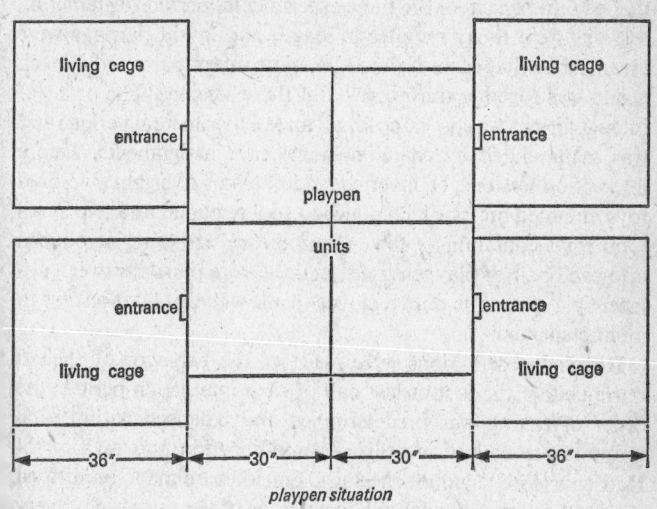

playpen situation

Figure 1 Playpen apparatus

Procedure

The study was divided into three experimental periods of two weeks each as follows:

1. Preseparation: the infants continued to live with their mothers and baseline data were obtained.

2. Separation: the infants were separated from their mothers and lived alone except for the daily test sessions with other infants.

3. Reunion: the infants were allowed to return to their mothers and to live with them throughout the remainder of the experiment.

Immediately before the first separation test session each infant-mother pair was removed from the apparatus and forcibly separated by a trained team of three men, following standard laboratory separation procedure 2. The infants were then returned to the playpen apparatus and the mothers were housed in individual cages in the breeding colony. Immediately before the first reunion test-session the mothers were returned to the home cages of the playpen apparatus.

There were twenty-one infant social interaction sessions conducted during each of the three experimental periods. Interaction sessions were thirty minutes in length and infant pairings were arranged so that each of the six possible infant pairs within each group was together during seven of these sessions. The order of infant pairings was the same for all three experimental periods and was manipulated by changing home cage assignments. Before interaction sessions, an inverted ladder, a pair of brightly colored toys mounted on four-inch plywood square panels and two small food trays containing a few grapes and raisins were introduced into each pair of playpen units, and the wire panels between adjacent playpen units were removed to allow the infant monkeys to interact in pairs.

Detailed observations were made of the behavior of each S during either the first or last half of each interaction period; the order of testing was predetermined and balanced within each group. Data collection utilized a modification and revision of Hansen's (1962) symbol checklist. Entries were made on dittoed sheets of paper divided into two columns of ten rows each. Every fifteen seconds a buzzer signaled the beginning of the next time period and symbols were placed in the next vacant row. Rows were subdivided into an upper section for recording the behavior of the mother and a lower section for the behavior of the infant. A subject's per-session score for any given category is the number of fifteen-second intervals within which that category appeared.

Three experienced observers participated, RD observing in each session and BS and BA alternating in a balanced order. Two observers seated themselves in the room during interaction sessions and recorded the behavior of mothers and infants, observing one set of interacting monkeys for fifteen minutes and the other for the remaining fifteen minutes. The order of observation was predetermined and balanced. Infant–infant pairings were changed after every seven interaction sessions by cage reassignment so that each infant combination occurred during all three experimental periods

The definitions of behavior categories used in this study are given in Table 1. Interobserver reliability was determined for each category for each tester and the procedure required each tester to test with every other tester multiple times during the six-month period preceding the study.

Product-moment correlation coefficients were computed on paired session totals with the tester in question being treated as the X variable and all other testers as the Y variable. An overall reliability index for each category was obtained by transforming individual reliabilities to Fisher's z, computing the mean and transforming back to r. These mean reliability coefficients follow each category definition.

Table 1 Definitions of Behavior Categories

Mother–infant behavior	Definition
Cradle	Encompassing or partially encompassing the body of the infant with one or both arms; $r = 0.99$
Retrieve	Bringing the infant into maternal ventral contact; $r = (0.98)$
Restrain	Active attempt to prevent the infant from breaking physical contact; $r = (0.99)$
Rejection	Termination or prevention of contact with the infant.*
Punish	Any cuff, nip, or clasp-pull directed toward the infant; $r = (0.91)$

Infant–mother behavior	Definition
Ventral contact	Gross body contact with the ventral surface of the mother; $r = 0.99$
Nipple contact	Oral contact with the mother's nipple; $r = 0.99$.
Embrace	Encompassing or partially encompassing the body of the mother with one or both arms; $r = 0.99$
Oral contact	Mouthing the mother other than nipple contact; $r = 0.93$
Nonspecific contact	Any part body contact with the mother. Not scored if a part of a gross contact or accompanying a gross contact; $r = 0.93$
Gross body contact	Any nonventral gross body contact with the mother; $r = 0.91$

Table 1 – (cont.)

Infant–infant behavior	Definition
Approach	Oriented movement of one body length or more toward another infant; $r = 0.89$
Withdraw	Oriented movement of one body length or more away from another infant; $r = 0.88$
Nonspecific contact	Any part body contact with another infant, usually very brief contact; not scored if subsumed under any other scored behavior; $r = 0.75$
Oral contact	Any social oral contact not subsumed under play, nipple contact, aggression or nipping; it is usually of a tentative nature; $r = 0.89$
Clasp–pull–nip	Any brief nip, cuff or clasp-pull directed toward another infant; $r = 0.88$
Nonmutual contact play	Wrestling, biting with head movement or shifting of position of mouth; $r = 0.83$
Mutual contact play	Contact play involving reciprocated participation of both infants; $r = 0.97$
Aggression	Extremely vigorous and intense biting, clawing and clasp-pulling. Piloerection, barking and yawning frequently accompany this behavior*
Thrust	Piston-like movement of the pelvis while in physical contact with another infant*
Present	Orientation of erect hindquarters toward another infant*

Individual behavior	Definition
Cry	Fairly high pitched tonal *Cooooo* vocalization; $r = 0.98$
Self-mouth	Any oral contact with the self which does not involve vigorous biting; $r = 0.78$
Autoerotic behavior	Any manipulation of the anogenital area; including thrusting at self or inanimate object*

An asterisk indicates insufficient cases during reliability sessions for estimation of category reliability. Coefficients given in parentheses are rough estimates based on limited occurrences.

Statistical analysis

The mean score per session for each S in each experimental period was calculated and, since the time interval count method of tabulation imposed fixed upper and lower limits on these mean scores, they were subjected to an angular (arc sine) transformation before statistical analysis. Repeated-measures analysis of variance was the primary statistical tool employed in this study. There were two separate analyses for each mother–infant and infant–mother category, one comparing scores from the last session before separation with scores from the first session after reunion, and the other comparing pre- and postseparation (reunion) mean scores over all the pre- and postseparation observation periods. The analyses of infant–infant and individual behaviors utilized orthogonal comparisons and compared (a) preseparation mean scores with postseparation mean scores and (b) separation mean scores with the combined preseparation and postseparation mean scores. The 0·05 level of significance was accepted for all tests employed.

Results

The behavior of the infants immediately after separation was characterized by disoriented running about, climbing, screeching and crying. Although the infants were paired during the separation test sessions, there was little infant–infant oriented social interaction. The two observers (RD and BS) who had also observed the previous body-contact separation (Seay, Hansen and Harlow, 1962) believed that initial infant emotional disturbance was less violent in the present study, but these infants were unquestionably disturbed.

Crying is an effective index of disturbance in the rhesus monkey and mean infant crying scores before, during and after separation are illustrated in Figure 2. The crying score was significantly higher during the separation period.

There was no increase in self-mouthing with separation, but instead a slight decrease in six of the eight infants. Decreased self-mouthing was even more evident during the postseparation period; the difference between pre- and postseparation means was significant. There were no significant effects of separation or

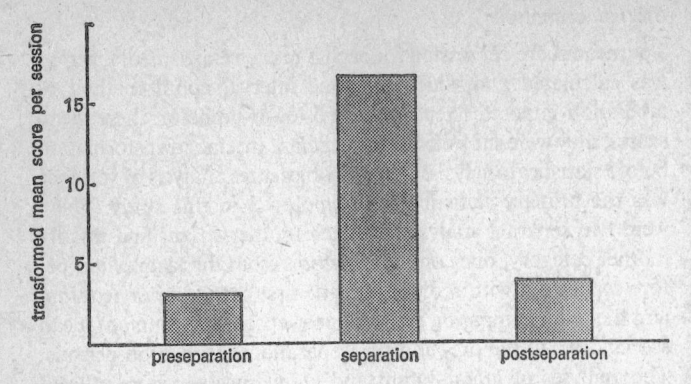

Figure 2 Infant crying

reunion on the mouthing of inanimate objects by infant monkeys.

During the separation period, the scores for complex oriented infant–infant social behaviors, including approach, withdraw, clasp–pull–nip, nonmutual contact play and mutual contact play, decreased significantly. Clasp–pull–nip and mutual contact play scores were significantly higher during postseparation than they were during preseparation. Clasp–pull–nip and mutual contact play scores before, during and after separation are shown in Figures 3 and 4. This latter difference in the scores, which have components in common with aggression, may be associated with

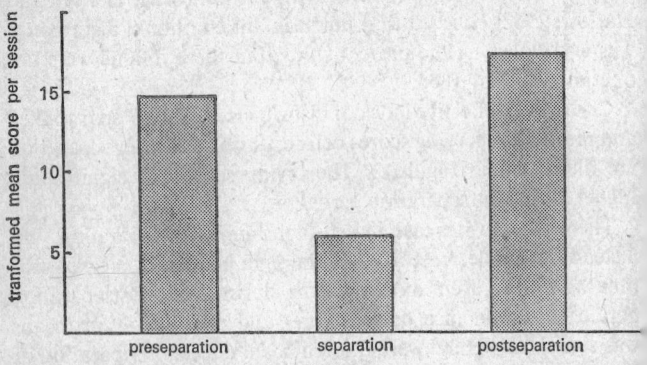

Figure 3 Infant–infant clasp–pull–nip

the appearance of aggression in the infants during and after separation. None of the infants of this study had shown aggression toward other infants before separation from the mother. Two infants received at least one aggression score during the separation period and six of the eight infants received infant-directed aggression scores after reunion with the mother. Alexander[1] is presently testing four monkeys under the same test situation, using identical scoring methods but not subjecting them to maternal separation. Only one of these monkeys, now eleven months old, has received any aggression score, and that animal has only a single aggression score.

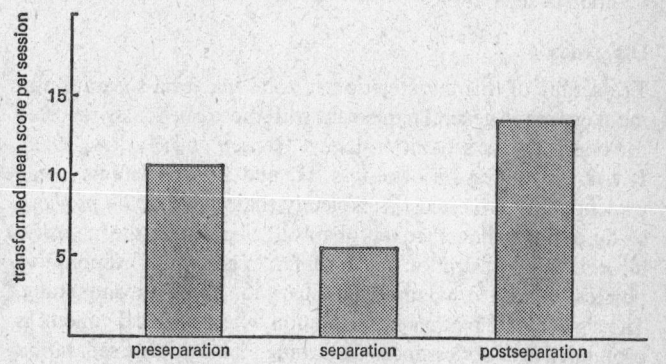

Figure 4 Infant–infant mutual contact play

Infant–infant oral contact decreased significantly during separation and remained at a lower level during the reunion period than it was during the preseparation period. Infant–infant nonspecific contact increased significantly during separation and then dropped to a level significantly lower than the preseparation level during the postseparation reunion period. This drop in nonspecific contact during the last period may be related to the higher clasp–pull–nip and mutual contact play scores during that time. Infant–infant sexual present scores were significantly lower during separation and there was a slight nonsignificant decrease in infant–infant thrusts.

1. B. K. Alexander, University of Wisconsin Primate Laboratory. Personal communication, January 1964.

Immediately after reunion with the mother there was an in-increase in positive mother–infant and infant–mother behaviors. These included initial significant increases in mother–infant cradling (Figure 5) and embracing. There was an initial significant decrease in infant–mother nonspecific contact. When the scores for the entire preseparation period were compared with the entire reunion period, the initial differences in mother–infant cradling and infant–mother embracing and ventral contact vanished. The initial decrease in infant–mother nonspecific contact was duplicated over the whole postseparation period. There were no differences in negative maternal behaviors or in nipple contact as a function of separation.

Discussion

The results of this investigation of total maternal separation in monkeys are in general agreement with those previously reported for body-contact separation (Seay, Hansen and Harlow, 1962). It was the impression of testers RD and BS that infants in the present study protested less violently than those in the previous study, and this difference is probably attributable to the intensifying effects of frustration on the infant's emotional response to physical but not visual maternal separation in the previous study. The sight of the mother in a situation where physical contact is prohibited is doubtless more disturbing than complete separation but there can be no question that complete separation from the mother was disturbing to the six-month-old monkey (Figure 2). Complete separation severely depresses play as may be seen in Figure 3 and Figure 4. This depression of play and other complex social behavior is indicative of severe emotional distress.

The infants of the present study initially responded to separation from the mother by violent protest (as shown by disoriented running about, climbing, screeching and crying). They then passed into a stage characterized by low activity, little or no play and occasional crying. The writers feel this second stage is behaviorally similar to that described as despair of children separated from their mothers. No subject of the present study exhibited behavioral correlates of Bowlby's detachment phase. This failure to show the complete pattern of Bowlby's separation syndrome is most probably related to the limited length of the separation period in the present study, and species differences in the complexity and subtlety of psychological defense mechanisms. Immediately after reunion with the mother there was a significant increase in mother–infant and infant–mother behaviors (Figure 5). When the entire reunion period is considered, the increase, shown in Figure 6, is much less striking and is not statistically significant. The result of mother–infant separation on the mother–infant relationship of these animals was transient and apparently unimportant. This does not indicate that the effects of repeated or prolonged separations would not seriously disrupt the infant–mother relationship.

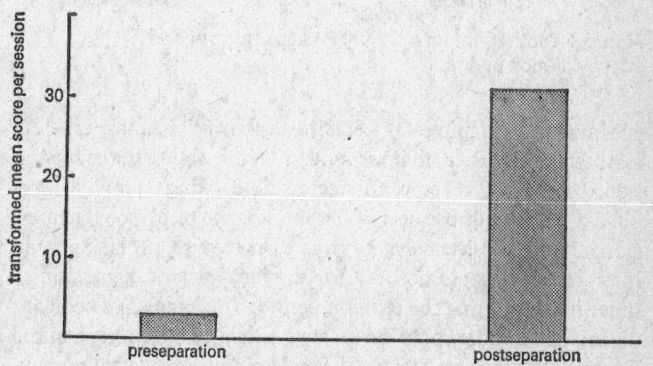

Figure 5 Mother–infant cradling. The last session before separation v. the first session after reunion

Robertson (1955) has described the responses of human children to maternal separation associated with hospitalization. One striking difference between his observations of children and the writers' previous study of monkeys (Seay, Hansen and Harlow, 1962) was that human children sometimes direct aggression to their mother after reunion, while no monkey baby was observed to do so. This species difference may be accounted for in terms of the fact that monkey mothers are not tolerant of infant aggression and the fact that aggressive responses in young monkeys are extremely rare. When aggressive behavior directed toward other infants was seen in two monkey infants during the separation period and in six infants following reunion with the mother, it was

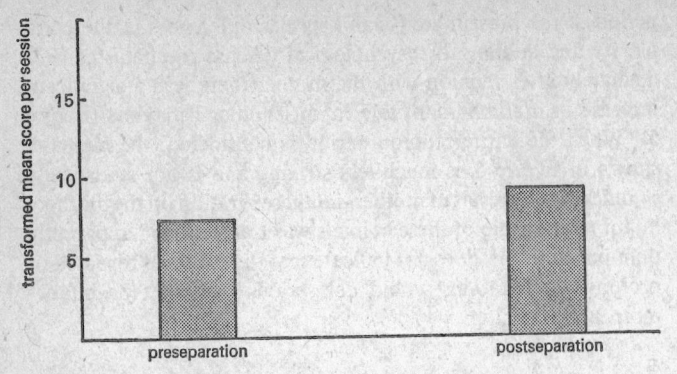

Figure 6 Mother–infant cradling. Preseparation period v. postseparation period

enormously intriguing. Dr Leonard Berkowitz[2] has suggested, in discussing these data, that the mother, as a function of the separation, may have become an aggression-evoking stimulus (Berkowitz, 1964), but because of her intolerance of personal aggression, the aggressive behavior was displaced to peers. Such an interpretation would account for the incidence of aggression to other infants during the reunion period. The aggressive behavior during separation could be related either to more generalized frustrations associated with maternal separation, normal maturational development or a combination of these and other factors. Differences between the present study and that previously reported by Seay, Hansen and Harlow (1962) are limited to heightened emotional response when the mother could be seen and heard throughout the separation period and the appearance of peer-directed aggression in the infants in the present study.

In the previous study, monkey A64 showed behavior akin to detachment in that there was considerable delay in his reattachment to the mother. It may be of importance that A64 and his mother were judged to have had a more intense infant–mother relationship prior to separation than any other infant–mother pair in either study.

2. L. Berkowitz, University of Wisconsin Department of Psychology. Personal communication, June 1964.

References

BERKOWITZ, L. (1964), 'Aggressive cues in aggressive behavior and hostility catharsis', *Psychol. Rev.*, vol. 61, pp. 104–22.

BLOMQUIST, A. J., and HARLOW, H. F. (1961), 'The rhesus monkey program at the University of Wisconsin', *Proc. anim. Care Panel*, vol. 11, pp. 57–64.

BOWLBY, J. (1958), 'The nature of the child's tie to his mother', *Inter. J. Psycho-anal.*, vol. 39, pp. 1–24.

BOWLBY, J. (1960). 'Grief and mourning in early infancy and childhood', *Psychoanal. Stud. Child.*, vol. 15, pp. 9–52.

HANSEN, E. (1962), 'The development of maternal and infant behavior in the rhesus monkey', unpublished doctoral dissertation, University of Wisconsin.

HARLOW, H. F. (1960), 'Primary affectional patterns in primates', *Amer. J. Orthopsychiat.*, vol. 30, pp. 676–84.

HARLOW, H. F. (1961), 'The development of affectional patterns in infant monkeys', in B. M. Foss (ed.), *Determinants of Infant Behaviour*, Methuen, pp. 75–97.

HARLOW, H. F., and ZIMMERMANN, R. R. (1959), 'Affectional responses in the infant monkey', *Science*, vol. 130, pp. 421–32.

ROBERTSON, J. (1955), 'Some responses of young children to loss of maternal care', *Nurs. Times*, vol. 49, pp. 382–6.

SEAY, B., HANSEN, E., and HARLOW, H. F. (1962), 'Mother–infant separation in monkeys', *J. child Psychol. Psychiat.*, vol. 3, pp. 123–32.

22 R. A. Hinde, Y. Spencer-Booth and M. Bruce

Effects of Six-Day Maternal Deprivation on Rhesus Monkey Infants

R. A. Hinde, Y. Spencer-Booth and M. Bruce, 'Effects of 6-day maternal deprivation on rhesus monkey infants', *Nature*, vol. 210, 1966, pp. 1021–3.

Bowlby (1952) concluded that if a young child is deprived of maternal care for a prolonged period, there may be far-reaching effects on his future development. His views, based in part on earlier work (Goldfarb, 1943; Levy, 1937; Spitz, 1945), have given rise to much research and some controversy. While his basic thesis is well supported (Ainsworth, 1962), it opens up many problems, such as measuring the extent of the effects produced by maternal deprivation, assessing their irreversibility and understanding the mechanisms involved.

Research on the effects of temporary maternal deprivation has depended largely on retrospective studies of individuals who have had a separation experience in the past (Bowlby, 1946) and on studies of the immediate consequences of maternal deprivation (Ainsworth and Bowlby, 1954; Burlingham and Freud, 1942; Robertson, 1955). For ethical reasons, experimental studies of maternal deprivation in human subjects are out of the question, although a few workers have taken advantage of an already existing condition to provide experimental alleviation (Rheingold, 1956; Rheingold and Bayley, 1959). Control of the deprivation circumstances, or of the post deprivation conditions, has thus nearly always been impossible and retrospective investigations are sometimes open to the criticism of possible bias (genetic or otherwise) in sample selection.

Can the symptoms of maternal deprivation seen in man be studied experimentally in animals? Monkeys are an obvious possibility, since adult behaviour is known to be markedly affected by the social conditions of rearing (Harlow and Harlow,

1962) and immediately following brief periods of separation the pattern of mother–infant interaction is disturbed (Jensen and Tolman, 1962; Seay, Hansen and Harlow, 1962). Although gross species comparisons can be misleading, whether or not maternal deprivation produces similar consequences in monkeys and men is an empirical question.

Accordingly an attempt has been made to study the effects of a period of maternal deprivation on the subsequent behaviour and mother–infant interaction of rhesus macaques. In the present experiment the age at separation was thirty to thirty-two weeks and the period of separation six days. Four infants were used, special care being taken to assess their individual pre-separation characteristics, and to study their behaviour not only immediately the mother was returned, but for several months afterwards.

The animals concerned lived in groups each consisting of a male, two or three females and their young. Each group was housed in an outdoor cage $18 \times 8 \times 8$ feet communicating with an inside room $7 \cdot 5 \times 6 \times 4 \cdot 5$ feet (Hinde and Rowell, 1962). Each infant was watched for six hours a week (birth to eight weeks) or a fortnight (weeks 9/10 to 30) to compare mother–infant relations with those of eight control infants studied previously which had no separation experience. On the three pre-separation days each mother–infant pair was watched from 10.00 GMT until the infant had been off the mother for two hours, or until 14.30, whichever was the earlier. Just before 10.00 on day 4 the mother was caught and placed out of sight of the infant in a room about sixty yards away. Further watches were made immediately the mother was removed (day 4, or first day of separation) and on days 5, 7 and 9, when the mother was returned on day 10, and on days 11, 12, 14, 16, 23, 30 and 37. Routine watches were also made for six hours a month for the rest of the first year.

The method of observation was similar to that already described (Hinde, Rowell and Spencer-Booth, 1964). In addition, during the pre-separation, separation and post-separation periods (that is, days 1 to 37) a second observer recorded the amount of locomotor activity (that is, the number of sectors of the cage entered in each half-minute period) and the type of activity shown, while the infant was off its mother. Only certain parameters of the infants' behaviour which indicate the more obvious consequences of the deprivation experience will be considered here: a more detailed analysis is in preparation.

During the pre-experimental period, the behaviour of these four infants was generally similar to that of the control subjects living under similar conditions previously studied: if anything, they spent on average rather more time off their mothers (Figure 1) and a higher proportion of that time at a distance from their mothers, than the median for the controls. During the pre-separation watches the inter-individual differences between the four subjects can be summarized as follows. Ranking the individuals with respect to one another, the amount of time spent off the mother decreased in order from Linda, Doris, Hilary to Tim: this was due to the behaviour of the infants rather than to restrictiveness by the mothers. Linda was an active infant who spent frequent short periods away from her mother, during which she did not spend long at a distance from her. The others spent less time at a distance from their mothers in the order Doris, Hilary, Tim: all had higher scores in this respect than Linda, but showed

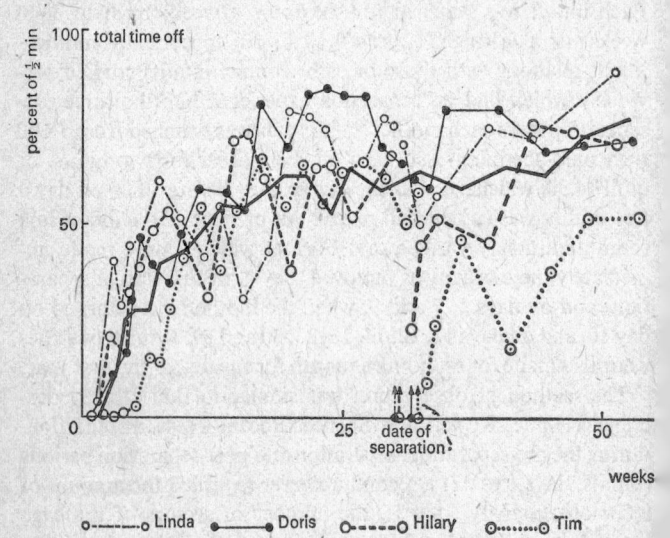

Figure 1 Percentage of half-minute periods in which infants were recorded off their mothers. Thick line – median for eight control animals which had no separation experience

(in the same order) increasing scores of social and manipulative play and locomotor activity.

During the separation period, the infants directed some of the behaviour which they had previously directed towards their mothers towards other adults in the group, but they received much less care from these than they had previously from their mothers. For example, before separation they were recorded on their mothers in 41 to 53 per cent of half-minute observation periods and on other adults for less than 1 per cent, but during the separation they were on other adults for only 0 to 24 per cent (mean 17 per cent).

When the mother was removed there was an immediate increase in 'whoo' calls – a call characteristically given by an infant separated from its mother (Rowell and Hinde, 1962). The rate of calling fell off somewhat during the rest of the separation period but in all four subjects was still higher than the pre-separation mean four weeks after the mother's return (Figure 2).

During the mother's absence, the behaviour of the infants can be described as 'depressed'. They usually sat in a characteristic

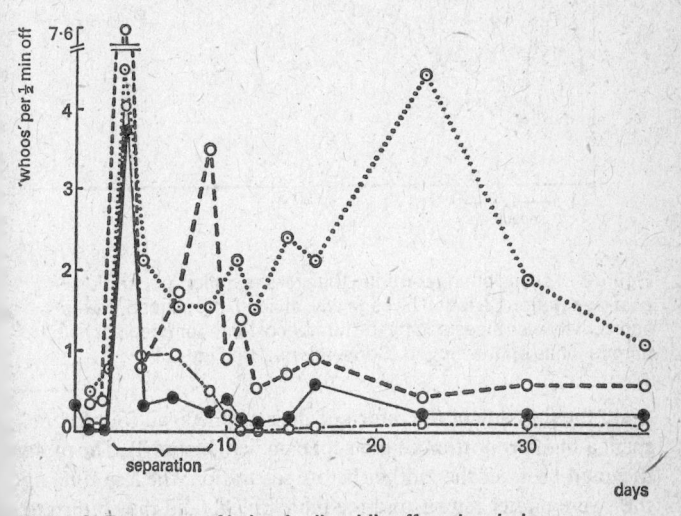

Figure 2 Frequency of 'whoo' calls while off mother during pre-separation, separation and post-separation periods. Conventions as in Figure 1

hunched posture and crept about on their hind legs. Almost immediately after the mother's removal they became less active than they had been previously when off their mothers (Figure 3). During the course of the separation period all four infants became active for more of the time (that is, they sat still less), but they became progressively less active when not sitting still. Three of the four infants returned to the pre-separation level of activity within a week of the return of their mothers, but Tim showed less activity on every watch up to four weeks afterwards. The amount of social and manipulative play shown changed in a manner generally similar to that of general locomotor behaviour.

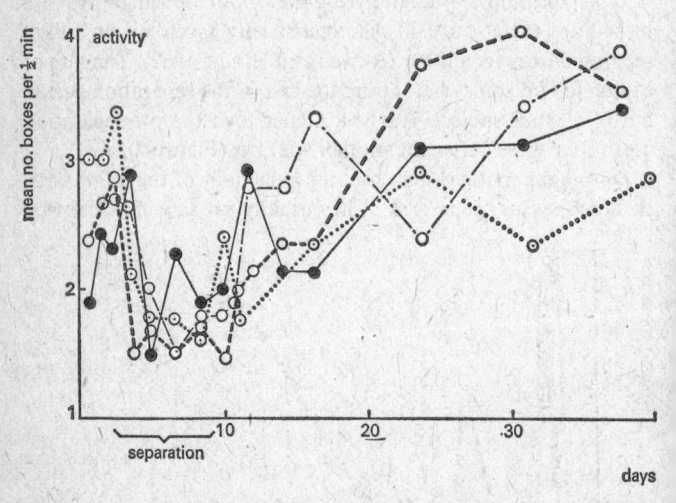

Figure 3 Activity changes during the pre-separation, separation and post-separation periods. The cage was divided into sixteen 'boxes' and activity was measured by the number of boxes entered per half minute while off the mother. Conventions as in Figure 1

On the first day of the return of their mothers, all four infants spent a high proportion of their time on her (Figure 4). The more they had been off the mother before separation, the less clinging they were on her return, and the more quickly did they return to behaviour similar to that seen before separation. Thus Linda spent only a little more time on her mother than before separation but Tim scarcely left his mother on the first day of her return. Similarly, while Linda and Doris were leaving their mothers almost as much as before separation within a week of the return of their mothers, in Hilary and Tim the effects persisted for a month or longer. When Tim was a year old he was still off his mother less than he had been before separation, although the median for the control animals was increasing during this time (Figure 1).

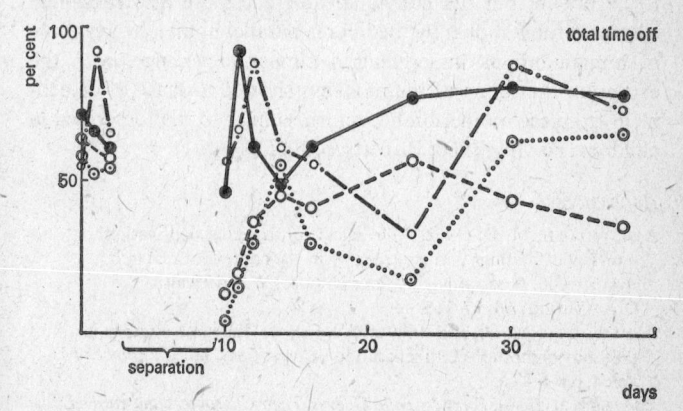

Figure 4 Percentage of half-minute periods in which infants were recorded off their mothers during pre-separation, separation and post-separation periods. Conventions as in Figure 1

In all four infants the amount of time spent off the mother recovered in the first few days after the mother's return, but then regressed for a while, the permanent recovery occurring more slowly (Figure 4). The reason for this is not apparent: although the proportion of attempts by the infant to gain the nipple which were rejected by the mother varied directly with the amount of time spent off the mother both during the pre-separation period and later in the post-separation period, it did not do so during the period in which this initial recovery and subsequent temporary regression occurred.

Not only did the infants leave their mothers less often during the post-separation period, but they went less far from her when they were off her. On this measure, all four infants recovered to their pre-separation levels about a fortnight after the return of their mothers.

These data show that some rhesus infants of this age are adversely affected by a six-day removal of their mothers, that the severity of the effects varies with the nature of the pre-separation mother–infant relationship and that they may persist for at least some weeks after the return of the mother. The consistency between individuals is adequate for conclusions of some generality to be drawn, but the individual differences are also revealing. The symptoms shown by the infants parallel in many ways those of human infants undergoing a similar experience, with the exception that none of the monkeys showed a phase of detachment from the mother on her return, similar to that described in children (Bowlby, 1960; Robertson, 1955).

References

AINSWORTH, M. D. (1962), 'The effects of maternal deprivation: a review of findings and controversy in the context of research strategy', in *Deprivation of Maternal Care*, World Health Organization, pp. 97–165.

AINSWORTH, M. D., and BOWLBY, J. (1954), 'Research strategy in the study of mother–child separation', *Courr. Cent. Int. L'Enfance*, vol. 4, pp. 1–47.

BOWLBY, J. (1946), *Forty Juvenile Thieves, Their Characters and Home Life*, Baillière, Tindall & Cox.

BOWLBY, J. (1952), *Maternal Care and Mental Health*, 2nd edn, World Health Organization.

BOWLBY, J. (1960), 'Separation anxiety', *Inter. J. Psycho-anal.*, vol. 41, pp. 89–113.

BURLINGHAM, D., and FREUD, A. (1942), *Young Children in Wartime*, Allen & Unwin.

GOLDFARB, W. (1943), 'Infant rearing and problem behavior', *Amer. J. Orthopsychiat.*, vol. 13, pp. 249–65.

HARLOW, H. F., and HARLOW, M. F. (1962), 'The effect of rearing conditions on behavior', *Bull. Menninger Clin.*, vol. 26, pp. 213–24.

HINDE, R. A., and ROWELL, T. E. (1962), 'Communication by postures and facial expressions in the rhesus monkey', *Proc. Zool. Soc. Lond.*, vol. 138, pp. 1–21.

HINDE, R. A., ROWELL, T. E., and SPENCER-BOOTH, Y. (1964), 'Behaviour of socially living rhesus monkeys in their first six months', *Proc. Zool. Soc. Lond.*, vol. 143, pp. 609–49.

JENSEN, G. D., and TOLMAN, C. W. (1962), 'Mother–infant relationship in the monkey: the effect of brief separation on mother–infant specificity', *J. comp. physiol. Psychol.*, vol. 55, pp. 131–6.

LEVY, D. M. (1937), 'Primary affect hunger', *Amer. J. Psychiat.*, vol. 94, pp. 643–52.

RHEINGOLD, H. (1956), 'The modification of social responsiveness in institutional babies', *Monogr. Soc. Res. Child Devel.*, vol. 21, no. 63.

RHEINGOLD, H., and BAYLEY, N. (1959), 'The later effects of an experimental modification of mothering', *Child Devel.*, vol. 30, pp. 363–72.

ROBERTSON, J. (1955), 'Some responses of young children to loss of maternal care', *Nurs. Times*, vol. 49, pp. 382–6.

ROWELL, T. E., and HINDE, R. A. (1962), 'Vocal communication in the rhesus monkey', *Proc. Zool. Soc. Lond.*, vol. 138, pp. 279–94.

SEAY, B., HANSEN, E., and HARLOW, H. F. (1962), 'Mother–infant separation in monkeys', *J. child Psychol. Psychiat.*, vol. 3, pp. 123–32.

SPITZ, R. E. (1945), 'Hospitalism: an inquiry into the genesis of psychiatric conditions in early childhood', in O. Fenichel (ed.), *The Psychoanalytic Study of the Child*, vol. 1, International Universities Press, pp. 53–74.

23 Leon J. Yarrow

Maternal Deprivation: Towards an Empirical and Conceptual Re-Evaluation

Excerpts from Leon J. Yarrow, 'Maternal deprivation: toward an empirical and conceptual re-evaluation', *Psychological Bulletin*, vol. 58, 1961, pp. 459–90.

The significance of early infantile experience for later development has been reiterated so frequently and so persistently that the general validity of this assertion is now almost unchallenged. An extensive literature on deviating patterns of maternal care, loosely labeled 'maternal deprivation', adds up with an impressive consistency in its *general* conclusions: deviating conditions of maternal care in early life tend to be associated with later disturbances in intellectual and personal-social functioning. It has been difficult to build on this general premise in formulating more precise research hypotheses relating specific variables of early maternal care to later developmental characteristics. If one attempts to order the empirical data from the many studies and the varied contexts, it becomes apparent that the concept of maternal deprivation is a rather muddled one. Maternal deprivation has been used as a broad descriptive term as well as an overall explanatory concept. As a descriptive term it encompasses a variety of conditions of infant care which are phenotypically as well as dynamically very different. [...]

The wide range of circumstances included under the concept of maternal deprivation stand out when the research is carefully scrutinized. Included are studies of children who have been separated from their parents and placed in institutional settings, other studies deal with children who have been grossly maltreated or rejected by their families, others are concerned with children temporarily separated from their parents because of illness and in others the maternal functions are assumed by several different persons. These experiences have occurred at different developmental stages in the children's life histories and there has been considerable variation in the length of exposure to these conditions and in the circumstances preceding and following the deviating conditions.

It is apparent that the data on maternal deprivation are based on research of varying degrees of methodological rigor. Most of the data consist of descriptive clinical findings arrived at fortuitously rather than through planned research and frequently the findings are based on retrospective analyses which have been narrowly directed toward verification of clinical hunches.

The areas of knowledge and the areas of uncertainty become more sharply delimited when we break down the complex concept of maternal deprivation into some discrete variables. For instance, in the studies on institutional care in which sensory deprivation emerges as a major variable, we can conclude that severe sensory deprivation before one year of age, if it continues for a sufficiently long period of time, is likely to be associated with severe intellectual damage. Direct observation of children undergoing the experience of maternal separation shows a variety of immediate disturbances in behavior, permitting the simple conclusion that this is a stressful experience for children. There is no clear evidence that multiple mothering, without associated deprivation or stress, results in personality damage.

With regard to the long-term effects of early deprivation or stress associated with institutionalization or maternal separation, no simple conclusions can be drawn. In the retrospective studies, significant interacting variables are usually unknown. Longitudinal studies currently underway may offer data on the reinforcing or attenuating influence of later experiences. We might hope for more pointed longitudinal studies on questions of reversibility such as studies of human or animal subjects who have been subjected to experimental deprivation or trauma, or longitudinal studies of special populations chosen because of some known deviation from a cultural norm of mothering, for example, infants who have experienced separation for adoption (Yarrow, 1955, 1956) and infants in multiple mothering situations (Pease and Gardner, 1958).

The analysis of the literature points out the need for more definitive research on the role of many 'nonmaternal' variables, variables relating to the characteristics of environmental stimulation and variables dealing with organismic sensitivities. After clarification of the influence of such variables, then perhaps systematic research can come to grips with some of the more elusive aspects of the emotional interchange in the intimate dyadic relationship of mother and infant.

References

PEASE, D., and GARDNER, D. B. (1958), 'Research on the effects of non-continuous mothering', *Child Devel.*, vol. 29, pp. 141–8.

YARROW, L. J. (1955), 'Research on maternal deprivation', paper read at Symposium on Maternal Deprivation, American Association for the Advancement of Science, Atlanta, Georgia, December.

YARROW, L. J. (1956), 'The development of object relationships during infancy, and the effects of a disruption of early mother–child relationships', *Amer. Psychol.*, vol. 11, p. 423 (abstract).

Part Seven
Early Socialization in Animals and Man

When the infant is in contact with others, mutual social bonds will tend to develop. The infant forms attachments to salient figures in the environment; and there is evidence that the attachments are established through mere exposure to these figures. The process may be regarded as imprinting, although such socialization has also been described in terms of associative learning. Taylor and Sluckin (Reading 24) have shown that the flocking of chickens depends simply on their exposure to one another. Cairns and Johnson (Reading 25) have found that social attachments of lambs are based on their exposure to other animals of the same or another species. Socialization occurs most readily in the young of certain ages; in other words, the development of social behaviour may be confined to critical periods. Scott (Reading 26) reports on critical periods for the formation of social ties in puppies. Schaffer and Emerson (Reading 27) have made a study of the growth of social attachments in human infants. Now, as the young child gets to know and becomes attached to some individuals, so it often develops a fear of strangers. The development of such fear would appear to be tied up with the process of socialization, and Schaffer (Reading 28) reports on this problem. At any rate, early socialization may be usefully studied in the broad context of early experience, including imprinting and conditioning, and with reference to such sensitive periods as there may be in the development of behaviour.

24 K. F. Taylor and W. Sluckin

Flocking of Domestic Chicks

K. F. Taylor and W. Sluckin, 'Flocking of domestic chicks', *Nature*, vol. 201, 1964, pp. 108–9.

Newly hatched nidifugous birds do not behave as if they recognized their own kind as such. On the contrary, they react in the same way to a very wide range of stimulus objects by approaching them and by giving 'pleasure' notes when near them. Thus the birds become attached to the stimulus objects. Such imprinting normally occurs to parents or parent-substitutes. However, Collias (1952) suggested that simultaneous imprinting to siblings could account for the socialization of young birds. This suggestion was also made later by Weidmann (1958) and by Gray (1958), and has been implied by other students of imprinting.

If the flocking of young birds depends not on an innate mutual recognition mechanism, but on early exposure to their own kind, then the birds' early experiences should result in their tending to return to familiar companions, be they similar young birds or any other stimulus object. This we set out to investigate, using domestic chicks hatched in the laboratory. The chicks were removed from the incubator, one at a time, to one of two circular runways. In one of these the neonates were reared in pairs. In the other, they were reared singly, but with a cardboard box which was suspended from a rotating arm so that it moved round the runway. After a day in these conditions, the subjects were isolated for fifteen minutes to improve their subsequent responsiveness (Sluckin and Taylor, 1964) and were then tested for ten minutes in a rectangular runway. This runway was divided by two mesh screens into three parts. One end-compartment contained a chick which had been reared socially, while the other end-compartment contained a rotating cardboard box identical with the one mentioned here; each subject was placed in the middle part which was three feet long. Cumulative stop-watches were used to record the times a chick spent within one foot of each mesh screen.

Eight of the ten subjects which had been reared socially spent more than half the test period near the screen which separated them from the stimulus chick, and the other two subjects stayed mainly in the neutral region of the middle compartment. The ten subjects reared with a moving box, however, were attracted in the opposite direction. One of them remained in the neutral region, but the other nine spent most of their time within a foot of the compartment containing the moving box. Table 1 gives the mean times spent in the different regions of the central compartment and shows a clear contrast between the behaviour of the two groups of chicks.

Table 1 Mean Times (Seconds) Spent in Different Regions of the Runway

	Within 1 ft of stimulus chick	In neutral region	Within 1 ft of moving box
10 subjects reared socially	442 ($\sigma = 156$)	147 ($\sigma = 155$)	11 ($\sigma = 24$)
10 subjects reared with moving box	7 ($\sigma = 18$)	131 ($\sigma = 171$)	462 ($\sigma = 171$)

The most striking feature of the behaviour of the chicks being tested was their tendency to try to 'break through' the mesh screen separating them from their earlier companion. Many repeatedly pushed their heads through the mesh and struggled energetically to approach the familiar object. Nine of the ten socially reared birds tried to get to the stimulus chick, eight of the ten box-imprinted birds attempted to reach the box and none of the birds tried to break through to the unfamiliar stimulus object.

We also tested some chicks of the same age, but without any previous experience either of another chick or of a moving box, for preference between these stimulus-objects. As Table 2 indicates, these birds failed to display any consistent behaviour except that generally they favoured the neutral region. Four of the ten subjects spent the major part of the test period there, four others stayed mainly near the moving box and the remaining two subjects spent most time near the stimulus chick. Attempts to break through one of the mesh screens were observed in only half these trials, three subjects trying to reach the stimulus chick and two to reach the moving box.

Table 2 Mean Times (Seconds) Spent in Different Regions of the Runway by Inexperienced Birds

	Within 1 ft of stimulus chick	*In neutral region*	*Within 1 ft of moving box*
10 subjects reared in isolation	144 ($\sigma = 157$)	255 ($\sigma = 127$)	201 ($\sigma = 203$)

It is quite clear that the chicks' preferences observed in the first experiment must have been acquired through experience. One way of acquiring them could have been through instrumental conditioning to the companion when associated with a reinforcing agent. This might have happened, as food and water were available in the circular runways in which each chick was kept in the company either of another chick or of a moving box. But chicks as young as these rarely eat or drink; and the troughs were left undisturbed in most cases. Moreover, it is doubtful whether such young chicks can be conditioned by positive reinforcement (James and Binks, 1963).

In order to decide whether the attachments were, in fact, acquired by imprinting free from reinforcement, rather than by instrumental conditioning, we reared six more newly hatched chicks in the circular runways as in the first experiment but without any food or water. These animals were in no way adversely affected. They were tested for choice between a chick and a moving box exactly as in the original experiment; the results are set out in Table 3.

Our findings indicated that flocking or socialization of domestic chicks may well depend largely on the learning process of imprinting.

Table 3 Time (Seconds) Spent in Different Regions of the Runway by Birds Reared without Food or Water

	Within 1 ft of stimulus chick	In neutral region	Within 1 ft of moving box
3 subjects reared socially	538*	62	—
	519*	81	—
	514*	86	—
3 subjects reared with moving box	—	53	547*
	—	61	539
	—	78	522*

*S attempted to break through mesh screen.

References

COLLIAS, N. E. (1952), 'The development of social behaviour in birds', *Auk*, vol. 69, pp. 127–59.

GRAY, P. H. (1958), 'Theory and evidence of imprinting in human infants', *J. Psychol.*, vol. 46, pp. 155–66.

JAMES, H., and BINKS, C. (1963), 'Escape and avoidance learning in newly hatched domestic chicks', *Science*, vol. 139, pp. 1993–4.

SLUCKIN, W., and TAYLOR, K. F. (1964), 'Imprinting and short-term retention', *Brit. J. Psychol.*, vol. 55, pp. 181–7.

WEIDMANN, U. (1958), 'Verhaltenstudien an der Stockente (*Anas platyrhynchos*. L.): II. Versuche zur Auslösung und Prägung der Nachfolge und Anschlussreaktion', *Z. Tierpsichol.*, vol. 15, pp. 277–300.

25 Robert B. Cairns and Donald L. Johnson

The Development of Inter-Species Social Attachments

Robert B. Cairns and Donald L. Johnson, 'The development of interspecies social attachments', *Psychonomic Science*, vol. 2, 1965, pp. 337-8.

Problem

Studies of immature mammals have demonstrated the significant effects of prolonged isolation on the development of social responses. One of the most interesting observations has been that animals reared in isolation later exhibit asocial response patterns, i.e. they remain aloof from members of their species even when opportunities for interaction become available (Harlow, 1962; Scott, 1962).

Discussions of this phenomenon have typically focussed upon the negative features of the experimentally produced environments, namely, the absence of social stimuli which are normally present. It seems reasonable to propose, however, that some attention should be given to the cues that are available in the 'isolation' setting. Not only have 'isolated' animals been deprived of interaction experiences, but equally important, they have been exposed to different patterns of environmental cues. Certain of these cues, by virtue of their saliency and constancy, might be expected to take on significant elicitory and discriminatory properties for the developing organism.

The present interspecies rearing experiment was conducted to test one implication of the above proposal. It was expected that extended isolation of a young lamb from contact with other sheep, coupled with continuous exposure to an animal of an alien species, would significantly alter the cue properties of the latter animal. After a period of continuous confinement, then, the abrupt removal of the cohabitant (alien animal) should be correlated with significant behavioral disruption; and the cohabitant's return should be associated with a cessation of disruption. It would also follow that the lamb would acquire responses which were instrumental to reinstating the presence of the cohabitant.

Method

Eight Dorset lambs served as Ss; four Rambouillet ewes and four mature female collies were cohabitants. The lambs were twelve to thirteen weeks old at the beginning of the experimental confinement.

Lambs were assigned at random to a ewe or canine. The resultant pairs were confined together for twenty-four hours a day over 105 days. Each of the eight living compartments was 8 × 10 ft, enclosed on all sides. During this period the lambs were permitted no contact with other animals. While the ewe–lamb pairs were permitted to interact without restriction, three of the four canine–lamb pairs were continuously separated: the lamb was placed on one side of a wire fence which extended down the midline of the compartment and the dog on the other. This procedure was followed because three of the canines had attacked the lambs with which they had been paired. The separations were completed during the first week of confinement.

After sixty-three ($\pm$ 2) days of confinement, the eight lambs were tested in the U maze. In the first, the noncontrast series, one goal compartment was empty and the other contained the animal with which the lamb had been housed. Prior to the first test trial, each lamb was forced twice to either goal area. The noncorrection method was used in the regular test series: as soon as the lamb entered either arm, a guillotine door was dropped and the lamb was enclosed in the goal area for sixty seconds. Testing continued until the lamb made ten consecutive runs to the goal area where the cohabitant was tethered.

A second series of learning trials was conducted on day 72 ($\pm$ 2). In this, the contrast series, a ewe was placed in one goal area and a canine in the other. One of these animals was the lamb's cohabitant. The position occupied by the cohabitant was opposite its placement in the previous series. The lambs were again given four forced runs, two to either side, prior to the first test trial. Two additional forced runs were interspersed between trials 10 and 11. Twenty consecutive test trials were run.

The final series of tests was conducted after 105 ($\pm$ 2) days of confinement. Each lamb was observed over a series of trials where the cohabitant was removed from the compartment, then reintroduced. The removal–replacement alternation sequence was continued until eleven observations of sixty seconds' duration had been obtained for each lamb. The measure of behavioral disturbance recorded was the frequency of vocalizations, i.e. number of bleats per minute emitted by the lamb.

The U maze was of plywood and wire construction. Thirty-inch wide runways were enclosed by 4 ft plywood walls, and covered by translucent netting material. The dimensions of the runway segments were: start compartment to choice point, 12 ft; choice point to turn, 7 ft; turn to goal area, 4 ft. The goal areas were 8×8 ft. Guillotine doors were located in the start compartment and on either side of the choice point.

Results

Noncontrast learning trials

All the animals learned rapidly, committing few errors prior to reaching criterion. A comparison of the error scores indicated no difference between the lambs assigned to the ewes and those assigned to the canines. Indeed, the lambs in the interspecies condition made somewhat fewer (nonsignificantly) errors than those paired with the ewes: mean errors, 3·0 and 4·8, respectively. The lambs' behavior upon reaching the empty goal compartment on 'error' trials is of some interest: the animals bleated repeatedly and vigorously and paced in an agitated fashion. These behaviors were rarely observed when the lamb entered the goal area of its cohabitant (mean bleats in goal compartment: empty = 16·08; cohabitant = 0·99). Typically the lamb approached and remained close to his cohabitant.

Contrast learning trials

Figure 1 summarizes these results. Clearly the lambs acquired responses which were instrumental to reaching the animal with which they had been housed, regardless of its species. The distributions of choices of the two groups of lambs were nonoverlapping ($t = 7·83$; $df = 6$; $p < 0·001$).

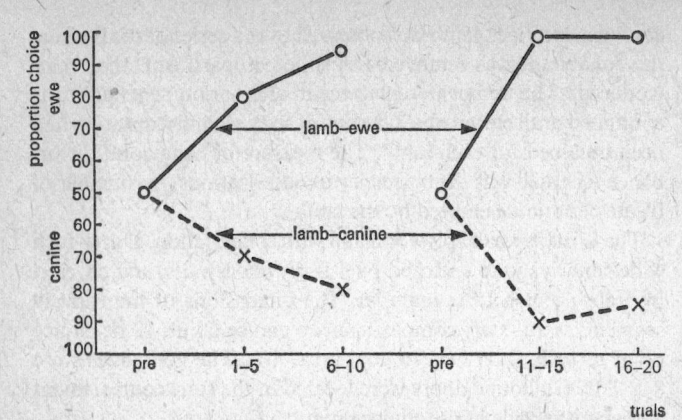

Figure 1 U maze performance of canine-paired and ewe-paired lambs in the contrast series

Removal–replacement of cohabitant

The lamb's repeated bleating formed one significant part of the general pattern of behavior disorganization that could be observed when the cohabitant was removed from the living compartment. Correlated behaviours included agitated pacing, jumping against the walls and pushing the compartment door. A perfect contingency was obtained between vocalization and the absence of the cohabitant (bleats/min present $= 0.00$; bleats/min absent $= 17.3$). The difference between pairing conditions was not significant.

Following response

One of the most striking response patterns observed was the development of a strong following response by the lambs. Scott (1945) has noted that orphaned lambs developed such a response to their human caretakers. In the present experiment, however, every lamb exhibited a marked following response with respect to its cohabitant by the ninth week of pairing.

Reversibility of interspecies preference

After 106 days of confinement, all of the lambs were returned to the breeder from whom they had been originally acquired. These animals were placed with a small flock of sheep reared under normal conditions. After four months, the three surviving canine-paired animals were returned to the laboratory and given a series of twenty contrast trials. The choice objects were the original cohabitant and another sheep. In the final block of ten trials, the lambs selected the canine on only two of the thirty trials (7 per cent). Apparently an extended cohabitation with the same species was sufficient to reverse the experimentally produced preference.

Discussion

Recent investigators (Denenberg, Hudgens and Zarrow, 1964; Hersher, Richmond and Moore, 1963) have reported the formation of interspecies attachment, e.g. mouse–rat, sheep–goat, following the animals' participation in cross-species fostering experiences. The present data extend these findings in demonstrating that remarkably strong interspecies attachments can be produced even when the animals have not been involved in extensive physical interaction. These data, it should be noted, suggest limitations on the generality of recent theoretical accounts of mammalian attachment behavior (Gewirtz, 1961; Harlow and Zimmermann, 1959).

Scott (1962) had proposed the empirical generalization that a mammal will develop an attachment toward any object to which it is continuously exposed. While our data are generally consistent with that generalization, it should be noted that the lambs in the present study became attached to the animate objects in their immediate environment and not to the equally available inanimate ones. As both the removal trials and the learning series indicate, the social preferences which developed were discriminant and specific, not general and contextual.

It seems reasonable to suggest that Scott's generalization be amended to account for the apparent selectivity of attachment behavior. It would be consistent with the available evidence, as well as with theories of associative learning, to propose that highly salient stimuli are more likely to acquire elicitory and discriminatory properties than are less salient events. Accordingly, animals, because of their relatively greater conspicuousness and prominence, would be more likely to become the focus of an attachment response than would nonliving objects. It would follow that the various stimulus characteristics of objects that have been shown to facilitate attachment formation, for example, lactation, softness and warmth, etc., are effective because they enhance the salience of the object and not because of presumed hedonic properties.

References

DENENBERG, V. H., HUDGENS, G. A., and ZARROW, M. X. (1964), 'Mice reared with rats: modification of behavior by early experience with another species', *Science*, vol. 143, pp. 380–81.

GEWIRTZ, J. L. (1961), 'A learning analysis of the effects of normal stimulation, privation and deprivation on the acquisition of social motivation and attachment', in B. M. Foss (ed.), *Determinants of Infant Behavior*, Wiley, 1961.

HARLOW, H. F. (1962), 'The heterosexual affectional system in monkeys', *Amer. Psychol.*, vol. 17, pp. 1–9.

HARLOW, H. F., and ZIMMERMANN, R. R. (1959), 'Affectional responses in the infant monkey', *Science*, vol. 130, pp. 421–32.

HERSHER, L., RICHMOND, J. B., and MOORE, A. U. (1963), 'Modifiability of the critical period for the development of maternal behaviour in sheep and goats', *Behaviour*, vol. 20, pp. 311–20.

SCOTT, J. P. (1945), 'Social behavior, organization and leadership in a small flock of domestic sheep', *Comp. Psychol. Monogr.*, vol. 18, pp. 1–9.

SCOTT, J. P. (1962), 'Critical periods in behavioral development', *Science*, vol. 138, pp. 949–58.

26 J. P. Scott

Critical Periods in the Development of Social Behaviour in Puppies

Excerpt from J. P. Scott, 'Critical periods in the development of social behavior in puppies', *Psychosomatic Medicine*, vol. 20, 1958, pp. 42–54.

As part of a program for the study of heredity and social behavior in dogs, the author and his colleagues have made a thorough study of the development of social behavior in puppies, with the idea of finding out the times at which heredity was most likely to exert its effects. As we did so, we also observed that there were certain periods in which environmental factors were particularly likely to affect behavior. As a result we have, from time to time, reported evidence on what we have called the critical period hypothesis (Scott, Fredericson and Fuller, 1951; Scott and Marston, 1950). This idea is one which is basically related to certain critical ideas concerning the effect of early experience on later mental health and behavioral adjustment. It is therefore important that it be clearly understood.

Critical period hypothesis

What is the critical period hypothesis? In the first place it is in certain respects no longer a hypothesis but a well-established generalization which can be stated as follows: All highly social animals which have been so far studied show early in life a limited period in which the group of animals with which the individual will form positive social relationships is determined. To take a few of many examples, the slave-making ants raid the nests of other species for eggs and larvae. As the captive ants grow up, they become attached to their captors and take care of their young and no longer recognize their own species. The experiments of Lorenz (1935) with the newly hatched greylag geese which quickly form a social bond with the first moving object they see, whether a goose or human, have dramatized the findings of Heinroth and others that contact with the young birds in the proper stage of development establishes a strong social relationship regardless of the species concerned. Lambs that are taken at birth and raised on the bottle form social relations with people rather than other sheep and become as a result quite unsheeplike in many respects (Scott, 1945). The dog is particularly interesting because the process of socialization with human beings is a normal part of its life as a domestic animal. Dogs are more closely attached to people than are many animals and develop a relationship which is in many ways similar to the human parent–child relationship. Furthermore, the critical period for socialization in the dog does not begin at birth but approximately three weeks later (Scott, 1953).

The existence of critical periods for the process of primary socialization can therefore be taken as established. Other parts of the critical period hypothesis, namely, that there exist certain periods of sensitivity to psychological damage, still remain as hypotheses and need a great deal more experimental evidence before they are accepted.

The existence of critical periods of any sort implies certain subsidiary hypotheses. The first of these is that the critical period has a physical basis and results from the state of anatomical, psychological and physiological development of the animal. The second is that hereditary variability between species will affect the course of development. We have found in a limited survey of different forms that such differences are great and they do not consist simply of the condensation or elongation of a standard type of development. The order of developmental events may even be reversed in different species. It does look, and this is the third hypothesis, as if the social development of any particular species is strongly correlated with the social organization of the adult (Scott, 1951). For example, in dogs there is a close association between mother and puppies during the first three weeks in life, but since the permanent social relations of the puppy are formed after this period and at a time when the mother leaves the litter for long periods, the result is that the strongest relationships are formed with the littermates. This relationship is in turn the basis of pack organization of adult dogs and wolves. A final hypothesis is that there should be genetic variability in the course of development *within a species*, which means that the time of onset of critical periods and their relative sensitivity should vary from individual to individual. This paper will be chiefly concerned with the evidence which we have been able to gather ragarding the physical basis of the critical period for primary socialization in the puppy.

Normal development

I shall first describe the normal course of social development in the puppy. The newborn pup is a very immature animal, being both blind and deaf and unable to move except in a low crawl. Its movements are slow and shaky and its reflexes sometimes occur seconds after stimulation. In spite of being deaf it whines loudly if cold or without food. Its chief needs appear to be warmth, milk and elimination, and these are taken care of by reflex behavior. If moved away from the mother the puppy will crawl, usually in a circle, throwing the head from side to side. If it comes into contact with the mother it attempts to nurse. When it succeeds it pushes with its head and forepaws and also with the hind feet. In doing this it touches and so stimulates the other puppies in the litter. Any touch will initiate exploratory movements. The mother also frequently stimulates the puppies by nosing them and licking the genital and anal areas. This produces reflex elimination as well as stimulating the pups to exploratory movement and nursing.

This is the typical behavior of puppies in the *neonatal period*. No immediate change is observed in their behavior. They gradually grow somewhat stronger and quicker until the opening of the eyes, which typically occurs just before two weeks of age. This marks the beginning of the *transition period*, one of very rapid change and development. At its beginning the eyes open and at its end the puppy gives a startle reaction to sound. It can walk instead of crawl and can move backward as well as forward. Its first teeth appear, it takes solid food and it begins to urinate and defecate without assistance by the end of the period, which typically occurs just before three weeks of age.

At approximately three weeks of age the puppy first begins to notice other individuals at a distance and shows evidence of conditioning and habit formation. This is the beginning of the period of *socialization*, in which its primary social relationships are formed. At almost the same time the mother begins to leave the puppies unattended, so that there is a tendency for the strongest relationships to be developed with the littermates rather than the mother. During the next few weeks it is easy for the human observer to form a positive social relationship with the puppy. This period of primary socialization comes to an end somewhere around seven to ten weeks of age, which is the normal period of weaning. This does not mean that the puppies are self-sufficient with regard to food. Studies of wolves show that the pups are not able to hunt at all until four months of age, and are not really independent until six months of age (Murie, 1944). In the domestic dog, food is normally supplied by man, but in the wild state it is provided by the hunting parents. This period, which ends with the sexual maturity of the puppy, is called the *juvenile* period. In some of our domestic breeds estrus of the females occurs as early as five months, but in the ancestral wolves this does not happen until the end of the second year.

We can see that there might be several critical periods affecting the development of new social relations, that of primary socialization at three weeks, the time when sexual relations are established at the end of the juvenile period and that when the parental relationships are established as a new generation of pups is born. We are here concerned primarily with the first of these periods, the period of primary socialization, because we can make the assumption that the end of the primary social relationships will strongly affect the degree of adaptation and adjustment in later relationships.

Anatomical basis for social behavior

Function is of course related to form, and form in turn to the process of growth. Let us examine the anatomical changes which accompany changes in social behavior. In the young pups there are three sorts of external changes which are easy to follow, the eruption of the teeth, the opening of the eyes and the opening of the external ear canal. The last is somewhat harder to follow and is probably less reliable than the other two.

All the following data are based on observations of purebred puppies reared under the standard conditions of our long-term experiment on genetics and social behavior (Scott and Fuller,

1950). The total numbers differ slightly from table to table because complete information was not gathered on all animals in the early part of the experiment.

The first teeth to appear are the canines, followed shortly by the incisors, which all come in together except that the corresponding upper teeth come in before the lower. No animals show teeth at two weeks, nearly half have some teeth by three weeks and nearly all have at least the upper canines through the gums by four weeks of age. An eruption of the teeth therefore coincides with the beginning of the period of socialization.

The teeth erupt the earliest in basenjis and beagles (Table 1), and wirehaired terriers are definitely slower than all the rest. The

Table 1 Eruption of Upper Canine Teeth

Breed	No.	% erupted at 2 weeks	3 weeks	4 weeks
Basenji	51	0	79	100
Beagle	54	0	74	100
Cocker spaniel	67	0	22	100
Sheltie	30	0	30	100
Wirehaired fox terrier	31	0	14	89
Total	233	0	47	99

shelties are unusual in that the lower teeth develop relatively fast and, in certain animals, the lower canines actually appear before the upper.

The eyes typically open about two weeks of age or slightly before. Very few are open at two weeks and all animals have the eyes completely open by three weeks of age (Table 2). The opening of the eye is the first external sign of the transition period. Eighty-five per cent of the purebred puppies have the eyes partly open at two weeks and we can estimate the average time at thirteen days. There is, however, individual variability and differences between breeds. The eyes open earliest in cocker spaniels and beagles, a little later in basenjis and much slower in shelties and wirehaired terriers.

The opening of the ears is a more prolonged process and comes a little later than that of the eyes. Over half the animals show the ears at least partly open at two weeks and all are completely open at four weeks. The differences between strains are not great. The shelties appear to be the most rapid and the wirehaired

Table 2 Opening of the Eye

Breed	No.	% completely open at		
		1 week	2 weeks	3 weeks
Basenji	43	0	65	100
Beagle	49	0	94	100
Cocker spaniel	51	2	94	100
Sheltie	25	0	31	100
Wirehaired fox terrier	27	0	11	100
Total	195	0·5	67*	100

*Average with equal weight for breeds = 59.

Table 3 Pupillary Reflex (Eye Open or Partly Open)

Breed	No.	% animals responding at			
		1 week	2 weeks	3 weeks	4 weeks
Basenji	42	0	57	98	100
Beagle	45	0	78	98	100
Cocker spaniel	51	0	88	100	100
Sheltie	26	0	38	96	100
Wirehaired fox terrier	24	0	13	83	100
Total	188*	0	62†	96	100

*Not observed in eight additional animals: one basenji, four beagles, three terriers.
†Average weighted equally for breeds = 59 per cent.

terriers the slowest, with the other breeds being intermediate and showing only slight differences.

The variability of any of these events which can be precisely timed, such as the eruption of the teeth or opening of the eyes, has a range of approximately one week in normal animals. The wirehaired fox terriers appear to be definitely slower in all respects, but in the other breeds the speed of development is not correlated in the different traits. It looks as if there can be separate variability in any one of these characters. One might expect that the development of all the teeth would be correlated, but even here the shelties show a relatively more rapid development of teeth in the lower jaw than do the other strains.

Function of the sense organs

Histological studies of the development of the puppy eye (Blume, private communication) indicate that the retina is not fully developed at the time of the opening of the eyes, nor even by three weeks of age (Table 3). However, it can be shown that the eye responds to light at a much earlier age. Some puppies will give a winking reflex to light at birth, long before the eyes open. This appears to happen most frequently in those breeds which have red hair color and light skin pigment.

As soon as the eyes open and the pupil can be clearly seen we can demonstrate a pupillary reflex when a strong light is shown into the eye. At the same time the nystagmus reflex can also be observed. If the puppy's head is moved slowly sideways the eyes roll or flick back and forth. This, however, is probably a reflex controlled by the nonauditory portion of the acoustic nerve rather than by sight. Incidentally, puppies do not show nystagmus in reaction to a moving object or rotating cylinder held in front of them.

Table 4 Function of the Ear:
Animals Giving Startle Responses to Some Sort of Sound

Breed	No.	Age 2 weeks	3 weeks	4 weeks
Basenji	43	0	72	100
Beagle	49	0	84	100
Cocker spaniel	57	2	61	100
Sheltie	24	0	62	100
Wirehaired fox terrier	27	4	92	100
Total	200	1	74	100

The above reflexes concerned with eye function appear early in development, but it is probable that these are responses to light and darkness, and that the capacity to perceive images is not developed until four or five weeks of age.

The onset of function in the ears is much more definite (Table 4). Only 1 per cent of the puppies give a startle reaction to sound by two weeks of age and 74 per cent give a reaction at three weeks of age. We may therefore estimate that the average time is about 19·5 days. There is considerable genetic variability between the breeds and the wirehaired terriers have the highest percentage of animals which give a definite startle reaction.

As with the eyes, there is no evidence that the puppies use their ears in finer ways at first. The tendency to startle to all sorts of loud sounds persists for a week or two.

All the puppies gave some reaction to odors at birth. They give reliable avoidance reflexes to two substances, oil of anise and a proprietary drug used as a dog repellant, which is a compound related to citronella. Eighty-three per cent of all puppies gave the avoidance response to the repellant and a smaller number to oil of anise. Harman found that the parts of the brain connected with olfaction were unmyelinated at birth and it is probable that these reactions to odor are largely connected with the sense of taste rather than true olfaction. In the human subject both substances can be detected in both the nose and throat. There is some observational evidence that hungry puppies react to the smell of milk in the neonatal stage, but we have no definite evidence on this point.

Table 5 Appearance of the 'Wink Reflex' to Touch

Breed	No.	% Responding by Birth	1 week	2 weeks
Basenji	43	86	100	
Beagle	49	96	98	100
Cocker spaniel	51	74	98	100
Sheltie	26	69	100	
Wirehaired fox terrier	27	63	100	
Total	196	80	99	100

With regard to other senses, puppies definitely react to pain and touch at birth. The majority of all newborn animals give a 'winking reflex' to touch and nearly all of them show this by one week of age (Table 5).

In general, the function of the sense organs at birth is quite limited, but all senses are at least partially functional at approximately three weeks. Prior to the beginning of the period of socialization it is impossible for the animal to be stimulated by many environmental changes. Those stimuli which are effective are ones which set off the reflexes connected with eating and other vital processes. In effect, the very young puppy is insulated from many sorts of environmental stimulation.

Development of the central nervous system

Observation of puppies in the neonatal and transition stages gives no indication that the animals learn in the way that adults do. For example, a puppy placed on the scales may crawl to the edge and fall off. When he is put in the situation repeatedly he does the same thing time and again, with no improvement in adjustment.

The only change in behavior for some time after birth is that the puppies become somewhat faster and stronger in their simple behavioral reactions. Fuller, Easler and Banks (1950) found that the avoidance behavior of puppies could be easily conditioned to sounds shortly before three weeks of age. This could not be done previously, and the change in an individual animal's behavior occurred from one day to the next. This change is, of course, related to the development of the function of hearing, but no conditioning to other sensory stimuli could be obtained at earlier ages. Responses were given to taste and touch, but did not produce conditioning. James and Cannon (1952) confirmed Fuller's results and found that the avoidance reaction to a mild electric shock is restricted to the part stimulated by twenty-eight days of age, indicating that psychological development is still going on.

Harman (private communication) has made histological examination of the brains of young puppies and finds that the newborn brain is myelinated in very few places, those corresponding to the parts associated with the observed reflex patterns of behavior. This lack of myelination may account for the slow movements of the young puppies, as contrasted with their more rapid responses at later ages.

A measure of actual function of the developing nervous system was obtained by Charles and Fuller (1956) by taking the EEG of puppy brains at different ages. At birth the puppy brain has almost no waves at all and there is no differentiation between sleeping and waking states. At three weeks, corresponding to the other differences in behavior noted above, the sleeping and waking states are differentiated and the amplitude of waves is increased. The adult form of the EEG is achieved at approximately eight weeks of age, which is shortly after the earliest time at which mothers normally wean their pups.

Another measure of nervous development is the heart rate (Figure 1). At first glance this might be considered a purely physiological response. However, the heart is actually a very sensitive indicator of both body activity and various kinds of emotions. As will be seen on the graph, the heart rate of the newborn puppies is very high and stays this way through the second week. Then it takes a very decided dip at from three to six weeks, coming back up to the early level around seven weeks of age. Thereafter the heart rate slowly declines toward the adult level. These general changes seem to be independent of breed. The first change occurs at the beginning of socialization and its end occurs at seven weeks, coinciding approximately with the time of the adult EEG. We can suppose that this is the period when complete cortical connections are established with the hypothalamus. We can conclude that the period from three to seven weeks is an especially sensitive one for emotional reactions, which corresponds to observation of overt behavior. We might also speculate that, since the cortex is not completely developed, emotional reactions during this time might be less permanently learned. On the other hand, they might be more disturbing because complete cortical control has not been established. We have here a fascinating field for further precise experiments on the effects of early experience.

The development of the nervous system and its associated psychological abilities goes through several stages. The puppy definitely does not come into the world with all its psychological abilities developed. They are, in fact, quite immature at birth and for the next three weeks. We would expect and have found (Scott, Fredericson and Fuller, 1951) that it would be extremely difficult to produce psychological trauma upon very young pup-

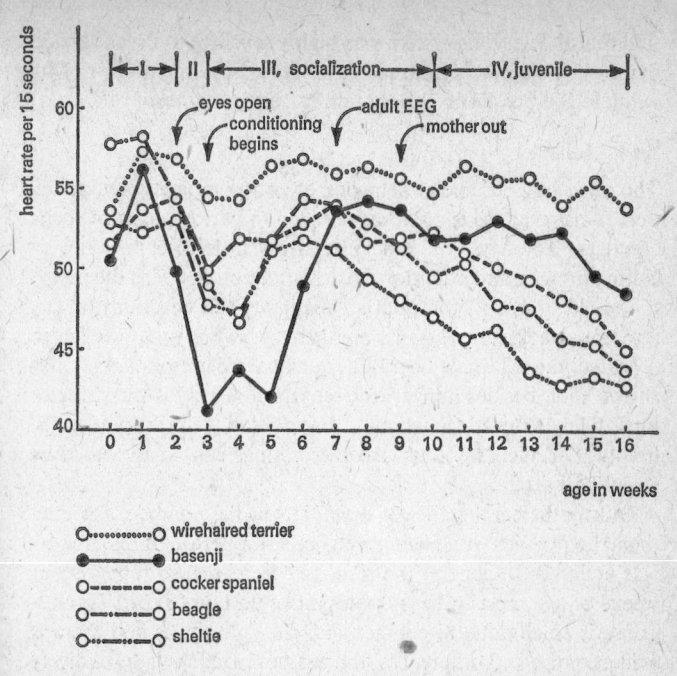

Figure 1 Average heart rates at different periods in development. Note that all breeds show a lower rate during the early part of the period of socialization than they do either earlier or later. The heart rate change probably measures the puppy's emotional reaction to being picked up and indicates unusual emotional sensitivity at this age

pies and that any future effects on their behavior produced at this time would have to be made by physiological or anatomical injury.

These results raise the question of what the situation is in the human infant. Human development is obviously different from that of the puppy, but we have every indication that the neonatal human infant has a nervous system which is decidedly undeveloped. We need to know more about the origin of learning abilities in human infants before we can talk authoritatively about the effects of early experience. It is not too much to suggest that it would be contrary to the general law of biological adaptation to find that the nervous system was highly sensitive to psychological damage at such a period as birth. This, however, does not invalidate the possibility of anatomical birth injuries.

Social behavior

The most obvious social behavior of young puppies is vocalization. This response is obviously related to various sorts of social contacts. The type of behavior involved is et-epimeletic, or calling for care and attention. In any situation in which the puppy is unable to adapt, the puppy substitutes this reaction for any attempt at adjustment on its own part. Newborn puppies whine repeatedly until they begin to nurse. Fredericson (1952) has shown that, besides hunger, the sensation of cold is the stimulus most likely to produce whining. In addition, puppies will whine loudly if accidentally hurt. All these things can be alleviated by social contact.

During the early stages of development the number of whines made by puppies while being weighed for a period of one minute was counted. In general the response decreases, so that by four weeks of age most of the puppies make no noise at all. The response is chiefly due to contact with the cold scales and there is evidence of breed differences, the beagles reacting with relatively small numbers of noises.

During the period of socialization the puppies begin to whine in response to being placed in a strange environment no matter whether warm or cold. Fredericson (1952) has shown that this response is considerably lessened if another puppy from the same litter is placed with it. We are now gathering data on the development of this response and it appears that isolation in a strange environment always produces a stronger reaction than isolation in the home pen.

This brings up another experimental problem which has been scarcely touched. There is considerable evidence (e.g. Thorpe, 1956) that there is a process of primary 'localization', in which a young animal becomes psychologically attached to a particular physical environment. There may be a critical period in development for this as well as for the analogous process of socialization.

Developmental changes in eating behavior

General changes from sucking to eating solid food have already been described. Our most objective measurement of eating behavior is an indirect one. The gain in weight of the animal reflects the amount eaten. If we chart the weekly gains of puppies we find, as we might expect, that the rate of gain declines week by week. However, there is a definite change in the nature of this curve at three weeks of age. The curve before this time is entirely dependent upon the milk supply of the mother. Afterwards the puppy has the possibility of eating solid food and we would expect that the decline in the growth would be less rapid as soon as solid food was available. However, there is probably a psychological factor involved also. Puppies pay no attention to solid food if they get plenty of milk from the mother, even beyond the age of three weeks. This was definitely the case in our F_2 hybrids which were fed by F_1 mothers having an abundance of milk, even in excess of what the pups could use. In their case also the rate of decline of growth was halted after three weeks, indicating that the animals were taking in more food (Figure 2). We may conclude that because of their ability to be conditioned the animals now learn to eat, increasing their food motivation.

This idea is supported by observations on hand-fed puppies. During the neonatal stage they are quite difficult to feed by ordinary means. It is hard to get them to take a nursing bottle and they have a tendency to stop before the stomach is filled. They can be laboriously fed by a dropper, but the easiest and most practical way to insure adequate feeding is to inject milk into the stomach through a tube. The explanation is that natural feeding is stimulated by specific primary stimuli or releasers which activate certain reflexes and simple patterns of behavior. Puppies become more active and more responsive to external stimuli if hungry, but hunger has little relation to the amount of food taken.

During the transition period, between two and three weeks, the pups are much more easy to feed. They will readily take a bottle and, if placed near a dish, they can clumsily lap the food. However, they will not take adequate amounts if the dish of warm milk is simply left with them. They still have to be stimulated by

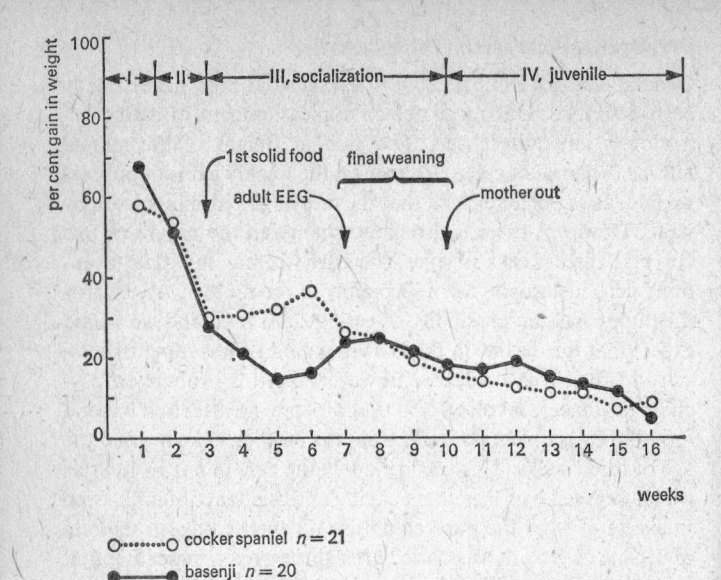

Figure 2 Weekly percentage gain in weight in male cocker spaniel and basenji pups. Note the change in the slope of the curve at three weeks. This reflects both the taking of solid food and increased food motivation resulting from learning and habit formation. The difference between the two breeds reflects a genetic difference in palatability of the food supplied

fresh food and handling several times a day in order to be properly nourished.

By contrast, puppies older than three weeks of age are relatively easy to feed, particularly because a supply of food can be left with them and they will continue to eat adequate amounts.

We can draw several conclusions from these observations. One is that puppies cannot be satisfactorily fed on a demand schedule before three weeks of age. Maternal care, together with the reflex behavior of the puppies, will provide adequate nutrition, but the puppy has not yet become a self-regulating organism with regard to eating. He needs external stimulation. Later on, when the abilty to form associations and habits is developed, the hunger mechanisms, together with motivation to eat produced by learning, are sufficient to regulate the eating of the puppy in a satisfactory way. This, of course, poses certain questions regarding the necessity for handling human infants, a problem which has been raised by Ribble (1944), Spitz (1951) and others.

Feeding and socialization

The simplest theory of primary socialization is that this relationship is built up through the association of food with a particular individual and that the relationship can develop further based on this original bond. Brodbeck (1954) tested this by rearing cocker spaniel puppies which were mechanically fed and comparing their behavior with that of puppies fed by hand. In both cases the experimenter spent an equal amount of time playing with the pups. The result was that the pups which had never been fed by people still showed strong attraction to the experimenter. This indicates that feeding is not the only element in the formation of a social bond.

On various occasions we have observed puppies which, through some accident to the mother or deficiency in her milk supply, were underfed. Young pups that are well fed are fat and lethargic. In contrast, the underfed animals are active, show more interest in people and seem to show an earlier expression of many behavior traits than do the normal ones. An opportunity to check this finding occurred recently in connection with an experiment of John A. King, in which he fed two groups of basenji puppies by hand twice a day during the period of socialization. One group was given as much as they could eat and food was left in the dish so that they could eat later. The other group was given considerably less and their weight was much lower. Both groups were given a handling test which measures responses of the puppy to a human handler.

In puppies raised in a different situation in which most of the food comes from the mother but in which there is considerable handling from five weeks on, there is a big decline of the timidity score between five and seven weeks, which may be taken as a measure of the process of socialization. In the experimental pups, whose contacts with people were started at four weeks and confined to feeding, the timidity score at five weeks averaged very nearly as low as the other animals at seven weeks. The average score stayed slightly higher in subsequent weeks than the controls, but not significantly so. At an early age, and using a genetic type of animal susceptible to the development of timidity, animals which are totally dependent for food show a greater degree of socialization than those only partially dependent.

Another obvious result was that there was a differentiation between the reaction to the person who did the feeding and another person who did not. This difference appeared more strongly as the pups grew older. All this indicates that the process of feeding does contribute importantly to social relationships but does not constitute the whole process.

The difference between the hungry and nonhungry animals was not as great as had been anticipated. There was a great deal of individual variability in behavior. However, hungry animals did show a consistently greater proportion of investigation and food begging in their responses than did the controls.

Sucking frustration

Levy's (1934) experiment on puppies indicated that the canine equivalent of thumb sucking could be produced by sucking frustration. Levy's experiment extended over a relatively long period in the development of the puppy, including the transition period and the early part of the period of socialization. Because of the importance of sucking, in early development and its disappearance later, there should be a limited period in which this effect could be produced.

Ross, Fisher and King (1959) experimented with this possibility using the technique of sudden weaning, after which the pups could obtain food only by lapping or eating solid food. The experiment was done on a group of thirty-four experimental and twenty-four control animals. None of the experimental puppies developed spontaneous body sucking, but they did show an increased tendency to suck a finger of the experimenter. When this was analysed in relation to age of the puppy, it was found that all the puppies weaned between the ages of ten and eighteen days showed more finger sucking than the controls. After this date many experimental animals were as low as the controls, although there were some indications of smaller effects. There were no effects at all by the time the animals were five weeks of age.

We can draw two conclusions. One is that there is an obvious change in the puppies' behavior with regard to sucking at the beginning of the period of socialization. Up to this time a puppy deprived of its mother will readily suck objects which are put into its mouth. After this point it shows very little tendency to suck. The simplest explanation is that the power to discriminate between objects which give nourishment and those which do not has been developed.

The other conclusion is that the simple and sudden deprivation of the opportunity to nurse does not by itself produce the neurotic form of body sucking. Whether there is a critical period for this latter phenomenon is yet to be determined.

Table 6 Estimated Developmental Ages in Days for Significant Events

Breed	Mean and standard deviation		
	Eyes completely open	Ears startle to sound	Teeth eruption, upper canines
Basenji	13·1	19·6	18·6
Beagle	11·0	18·7	19·1
Cocker spaniel	11·0±1·9	20·2±2·9	23·3
Sheltie	15·2	20·3	22·6
Wirehaired fox terrier	16·9	17·8±2·2	24·3±3·0
Total	13·0±2·3	19·5±2·3	20·8±2·9

Hereditary variability

As can be seen in Table 6, there is considerable evidence that hereditary variability in development exists, both between individuals and between breeds. For example, cocker spaniels are the first to open their eyes, are slow to develop the startle response to sound and are intermediate between the other breeds with regard to the development of teeth. The wirehaired terriers were the slowest to develop in every trait observed except the startle reaction to sound, in which they are the fastest. There is every indication that the different sense organs and anatomical characteristics vary in the speed of development independently of each other. There is no one highly correlated pattern of development which is slowed down or speeded up as a unit.

Assuming that the age of onset of each developmental event falls into a normal curve, we can estimate the average time and variability of each event. As seen by Table 6, there is approximately three days' difference between the fastest and slowest breeds. Eighty-six per cent of all animals should fall within a range of one week. If anything, these estimates of variability are probably too great, since they are based on the 1 per cent or so of animals which are as much as a week away from the normal.

The species as a whole shows a developmental pattern which is not departed from except in cases of gross abnormality. Events occur in the general order described in the early part of this paper, so that we can speak of definite periods of development. We can set the beginning of the transition period at thirteen days with a normal range of three or four days on either side. Similarly, we can place the beginning of the period of socialization at approximately 19·5 days with a similar range of variability. This means that when experimental procedures are employed in which time is the experimental variable, close attention must be paid to the breed and the state of individual development. Two litters of puppies of exactly the same chronological age could give completely different results.

Conclusions

At the beginning of this paper I stated that there is a definite critical period for the process of socialization and that it must rest on a physical basis. The data which I have just presented show that there is a definite physical basis in the dog and that there are two important points where sudden changes occur. One of these is the point just before three weeks, where there are changes in the ability to be conditioned, in the EEG, in the emotional responses indicated by the heart rate, in the ability to hear and in the growth rate and method of nutrition. The other point at seven to eight weeks is so far defined only by the adult EEG and the change in emotional reaction measured by the heart rate. Final weaning sometimes occurs as early as this date.

To summarize, the puppy before three weeks of age is highly insulated from its environment by the immature state of development of the sense organs, by the lack of ability for conditioning and by maternal care. From three to seven weeks the puppy is in an extremely interesting stage in which its sense organs and cerebral cortex are not yet completely developed but in which it has extremely sensitive emotional reactions and is capable of making associations. This is the time when primary socialization normally takes place and during which it is easiest for a dog owner to establish a strong social bond. These facts provide us with an experimental opportunity to analyse some of the theories of the effects of early experience on later social adjustment and mental health.

Comparing these with results on human babies, we see that we need more fundamental facts about human development. We know a great deal about babies from birth until ten days of age. After this time mothers and babies leave the hospital and disappear into the home where there is little opportunity for scientific study. Facts and information are very scarce until about the age of two years when the babies begin to emerge from the home and appear in nursery school. It is precisely this period in which we are most likely to find the period corresponding to the primary period of socialization in the dog, if it exists. As I mentioned above, one of the most important basic facts yet to be adequately described is the development of simple learning ability in young infants.

One of the biggest problems in predicting human development is the element of individual variability in behavior. The study of development in the different dog breeds, where we should get the maximum possible variability in development, gives us some hint as to what we might expect in human beings. There is considerable individual variability, and variability between dog strains. However, the timing does not vary a great deal in terms of the length of the period of development. The changes at three weeks of age in puppies appear to take place within a week for all animals. If we assume that the life span of a dog is one-sixth that of a human, we might expect a human range of variability of six weeks. Actually, the possible range in early development is probably considerably less than this.

J. P. Scott

The existence of a critical period for primary socialization is so widespread in the animal kingdom that there is every reason for suspecting that a similar period exists in human development. If so, we are faced with a number of questions:

1. When? In other animals, the critical period may occur immediately after birth or hatching, or fairly late in development, as it does in the puppy. The human infant is somewhat more mature than a puppy at birth, but far less so than a lamb. We would expect that the critical period would not begin immediately after birth and the evidence that we have indicates that it may begin as early as a month or six weeks or as late as five or six months. However, any social relationship depends on the behavior of two individuals and the period immediately after birth may be a critical one for the mother, although the evidence from adoptions indicates that mothers can form a strong social relationship at other times.

2. How long? The period of primary socialization certainly lasts as long as the period of complete dependency on the mother, up to one and a half or two years, and possibly even longer.

3. By what means? The positive behavioral mechanisms which establish primary social relationships, such as feeding, contact, handling and the like, are difficult to understand without experimental data. Likewise, we would expect to find negative mechanisms which prevent the socialization of infants to strangers, such as the anxiety or fear reaction to strangers described by Spitz (1950). Their understanding would be immensely important as a means for bringing about a better identification with other human beings and a broader range of tolerance.

4. Why? This brings us down to the primary data in this paper and raises the question of the physical basis of critical periods in the human infant. As I have indicated above, animal experiments indicate the type of thing we should look for: the development of sensory and motor organs, the development of the central nervous system, and the power of simple learning, the development of social behavior patterns and the development of individual hereditary differences. We have much information on the first two and far less on the rest. It is this kind of evidence which is

the easiest to get on human subjects and without this firm foundation we shall never be on safe ground.

Seen in this light, our study on the dog provides the opportunity for the experimental analysis of environmental and hereditary influence on an undeveloped nervous system. The dog is an animal which is capable of forming a type of social relationship with people very similar to the human parent–child relationship. We should be able to find out whether early emotional experiences produce lasting effects. Without evidence, it is just as logical to suppose that an immature nervous system would be less severely affected. It will take a long time and will be a laborious and expensive job to obtain the needed facts, but we should eventually be able to bring the phenomena of early social experience out of the realm of conjecture into that of established scientific fact.

References

BRODBECK, A. J. (1954), 'An exploratory study on the acquisition of dependency behavior in puppies', *Bull. Ecol. Soc. Amer.*, vol. 35, p. 73.

CHARLES, M. S., and FULLER, J. L. (1956), 'Developmental study of the electroencephalogram of the dog', *EEG clin. Neurophysiol.*, vol. 8, pp. 645–52.

FREDERICSON, E. (1952), 'Perceptual homeostasis and distress vocalization in puppies', *J. Person.*, vol. 20, pp. 472–7.

FULLER, J. L., EASLER, C. A., and BANKS, E. M. (1950), 'Formation of conditioned avoidance responses in young puppies', *Amer. J. Physiol.*, vol. 160, pp. 462–6.

JAMES, W. T., and CANNON, D. J. (1952), 'Conditioned avoiding responses in puppies', *Amer. J. Physiol.*, vol. 168, pp. 251–3.

LEVY, D. M. (1934), 'Experiments on the sucking reflex and social behavior of dogs', *Amer. J. Orthopsychiat.*, vol. 4, pp. 203–24.

LORENZ, K. Z. (1935), 'Der Kumpan in der Umvelt des Vogels', *J. Ornithol.*, vol. 83, pp. 137–213, 289–413.

MURIE, A. (1944), *The Wolves of Mt McKinley*, US Government Printing Office, Washington, DC.

RIBBLE, M. A. (1944), 'Infantile experience in relation to personality development', in J. McV. Hunt (ed.), *Personality and the Behavior Disorders*, Ronald Press, pp. 621–51.

ROSS, S., FISHER, A., and KING, D. (1959), 'The effects of early enforced weaning on the sucking behavior of puppies', *J. genet. Psychol.*, vol. 95, pp. 261–81.

Scott, J. P. (1945), 'Social behavior, organization and leadership in a small flock of domestic sheep', *Comp. Psychol. Monogr.*, vol. 18, pp. 1–9.

Scott, J. P. (1951), 'The relationships between developmental change and social organization among mammals', *Anat. Rec.*, vol. 111, p. 73.

Scott, J. P. (1953), 'The process of socialization in higher animals', in A. H. Leighton (ed.), *Interrelations between the Social Environment and Psychiatric Disorders*, Milbank Memorial Fund, New York.

Scott, J. P., and Fuller, J. L. (1950), *Manual of Dog Testing Techniques*, Jackson Memorial Laboratory, Bar Harbor, Maine.

Scott, J. P., and Marston, M. V. (1950), 'Critical periods affecting the development of normal and maladjustive social behavior in puppies', *J. genet. Psychol.*, vol. 77, pp. 25–60.

Scott, J. P., Fredericson, E., and Fuller, J. L. (1951), 'Experimental exploration of the critical period hypothesis', *J. Personal.*, vol. 1, pp. 162–83.

Spitz, R. A. (1950), 'Anxiety in infancy: a study of its manifestations in the first year of life', *Inter. J. Psycho-anal.*, vol. 31, pp. 138–43.

Spitz, R. A. (1951), 'The psychogenic diseases in infancy: an attempt at their etiologic classification', in O. Fenichel (ed.), *The Psychoanalytic Study of the Child*, vol. 6, International Universities Press, pp. 255–75.

Thorpe, W. H. (1956), *Learning and Instinct in Animals*, Méthuen.

27 H. R. Schaffer and Peggy E. Emerson

The Development of Social Attachments in Infancy

Excerpts from H. R. Schaffer and Peggy E. Emerson, 'The development of social attachments in infancy', *Monographs of the Society for Research in Child Development*, vol. 29, 1964, no. 3.

Introduction

The study of early social behavior

Although infancy has been widely considered as a formative period of great importance for development, far less is known about it than about later age ranges. This applies to every aspect of individual functioning: physiological, perceptual, intellectual and also social aspects are all as yet rarely investigated and barely understood. Those studies which have concerned themselves with the beginnings of social behavior have mostly adopted a normative approach, in that they set out to establish the age limits within which certain behavior patterns can generally be expected to appear. Thus we now know that at the age of four weeks the infant will react to social overtures by a reduction of bodily activity (Shirley, 1933); that at six weeks the first smile appears (Bühler, 1930); that from two months on the mother will be usually recognized (Griffiths, 1954); that at three months the infant may vocalize in reply to others' speech (Gesell and Amatruda, 1947); and that after eight months he will no longer smile indiscriminately at all and sundry (Spitz and Wolf, 1946). These descriptive facts are valuable, but so far they stand merely as isolated phenomena that are in no way linked together within a fully developmental framework comparable to that which Piaget (1953, 1955) has provided for early cognitive functioning. How the infant progresses from milestone to milestone, what environmental and organismic variables account for his progress, the processes that need to be postulated for the developmental trends observed: these are all problems to which there is as yet no answer.

For long, learning theory has dominated psychological thinking about the manner in which early social relationships are formed, yet curiously few empirical studies have resulted from it which shed any light on the period of infancy (the studies by Brackbill, 1958, and by Rheingold, Gewirtz and Ross, 1959, may be quoted as exceptions). The main thesis as advanced by learning theorists (see, for instance, Miller and Dollard, 1941, and Mussen and Conger, 1956) holds that the infant's emotional dependence on his mother is to be understood in the light of secondary reinforcement arising from the satisfaction of such basic physiological needs as hunger, thirst and pain. The infant's helplessness thrusts physical dependence upon him and necessitates the performance of caretaking activities on the part of the mother, who thus eventually becomes associated with drive reduction. In time her mere presence acquires reward value and through learning emotional dependence may then be said to have become a self-supporting derived drive. However, all the studies which have used this model, either in attempting to conceptualize emotional dependence more precisely (Gewirtz, 1956; Heathers, 1955) or in establishing its antecedent conditions (Baldwin, 1949; Sears, Maccoby and Levin, 1957; Sears, Whiting, Nowlis and Sears, 1953), have examined this tendency as it occurs in older (usually nursery school) children. A description or analysis of the origin and earliest stages of emotional dependence with reference to the human infant has so far failed to receive much systematic attention in empirical investigation, so that we are still largely ignorant about the developmental course which this fundamental behavior pattern takes or the manner in which it manifests itself in the first year or two.

The concept of attachment

One reason for the dearth of studies may well lie in the stranglehold which an almost universally accepted theory can sometimes exercise on research. Fortunately, controversy has now been stimulated by two developments: Harlow's intriguing work on the infant–mother relationship in the monkey, which casts doubt on the all-important role previously attributed to the infant's feeding experiences in the establishment of affectional bonds (Harlow, 1958, 1961; Harlow and Zimmermann, 1959), and the challenging theory which Bowlby (1958) has advanced to account for th nature and formation of the child's tie to the mother. In his paper Bowlby attacks the secondary drive theory of social development, suggesting instead that social tendencies are primary and that a number of inborn behavior patterns (such as following, clinging, sucking, smiling and crying) serve to bind the child to the mother from the beginning. To emphasize this change in theoretical orientation he has proposed to drop the term *emotional dependence* and substitute the term *attachment*.

The new term will, it is hoped, provide a more fertile concept for research purposes and, indeed, since the publication of Bowlby's stimulating paper, a number of investigators (Ainsworth, 1963; Caldwell, 1962b; Gewirtz, 1961) have adopted it. Some confusion still exists, however, regarding its usage and the group of phenomena to which it refers, and as the present report is devoted to a study of social attachments in infancy we feel it essential first to clarify the sense in which it will be used here.

Any attempt to conceptualize attachment soon encounters the many complexities associated in the minds of most with this term. Indeed, to the adult the manifold emotions and sentiments implied thereby are so forceful that they may well be taken to constitute the whole phenomenon, and to see it in its simplest and most basic form at the infant level is thus by no means an easy task. Our suggestion is that the core of the attachment function is represented by one of the simplest yet most fundamental elements in social behavior, namely *the tendency of the young to seek the proximity of certain other members of the species*. Approaching attachment in this way, we are dealing with a relatively clear-cut, easily identifiable behavior tendency which may be observed to occur almost universally amongst animals as well as in man. Its biological usefulness in a condition of infantile helplessness is obvious enough to need no further comment. It is likely that we are confronted here with one of the most basic requirements of the young organism to which powerful emotions are linked but to which, in the early stages of development, direct behavioral expression is generally given. Such a fundamental tendency must be isolated, named and studied, and it appears to us that the most economical usage of the term attachment is represented by this tendency.

A further advantage of this conception of attachment lies in the linkage which may be made between *proximity seeking* and *proximity avoidance*. Attachments are generally focused on certain specific individuals only, while to others fear responses may be shown. That proximity avoidance (or, as it has been more commonly labeled, fear of strangers or eight-months'-anxiety) is in some way related to proximity seeking has been widely accepted, though, apart from some preliminary suggestions by Benjamin (1959), Freedman (1961) and Spitz (1950) we are still largely ignorant about the details of such interaction.

An operational criterion for attachment

Some further examination of the attachment concept is necessary if we are to make suggestions as to how it may most suitably be recognized and assessed. It is well established that, from about the second or third month on, an infant will behave differently with his mother as compared to strangers. He may smile and vocalize at her more readily, he may visually follow her more than he would other people and he is likely to quieten sooner when picked up by her after crying. Perceptual discrimination has thus taken place: the infant is now able to recognize his mother. This is clearly a necessary *precondition* to the formation of an attachment to a specific individual, but the ability to recognize the familiar person cannot, by itself, be regarded as evidence of attachment. Thus, in a study by Schaffer and Callender (Schaffer, 1958; Schaffer and Callender, 1959) of the reactions of infants to hospitalization, evidence of separation protest did not emerge until approximately seven months of age, i.e. long after perceptual discrimination had taken place. The infant who views his mother's absence with equanimity and readily accepts a strange caretaker can hardly be said to have formed an attachment to the former, however readily he may be able to distinguish her from an unfamiliar nurse. To characterize recognition and quicker reactiveness as attachment is thus a highly doubtful supposition. Moreover, all the evidence from studies of smiling (Ahrens, 1954; Spitz and Wolf, 1946) suggests that right up to six to eight months of age the infant is not responding to the adult as another person, i.e. in a characteristic social manner, but is merely reacting to the perception of certain primitive stimulus configurations. That familiar configuration can elicit a response more speedily an intensely than an unfamiliar one can be readily understood without evoking the concept of attachment.

Another precondition appears necessary. If by attachment a particular kind of relationship to a particular kind of object is implied, then one can hardly look for such a relationship until the individual is capable of having the concept of an object. In order to form a permanent bond with another person it is necessary to conceive of this person as an entity apart from the self, with an independent existence in time and space. Attachment involves detachment, and here Piaget's (1953, 1955) demonstration of the stages through which the infant must progress before he can conserve the object becomes highly relevant to the understanding of early social behavior. Up to the third quarter of the first year, Piaget has shown, a state of 'adualism' exists, in which there is no distinction between the self and the environment. Objects do not exist in their own right but are used as functional elements for the infant's own activities. They may be recognized, but no continuity, permanence or substance are as yet attributed to them. A fundamental change in cognitive structure is required before the object becomes detached from the infant's ongoing activity and, though our knowledge of this development is still very limited, it does seem reasonable to postulate that we have here the other and more immediate precondition necessary for social attachments to emerge. It is thus no coincidence that the age when separation protests were first found to appear in the hospital study quoted above is also the period when Piaget's children began to consider objects as entities in their own right and to show an orientation towards them even in their absence.

As his criterion for object conservation Piaget used the infant's reaction to the departure of an object from the immediate perceptual field. Similarly, we propose to use the separation response of an infant as our operational criterion for the existence of social attachments. Differential behavior alone not being sufficient, the most suitable measure of attachment will be provided by the infant's reactions when he is frustrated in his attempts to remain attached by the withdrawal of the object. As Bowlby (1960, p. 14) has put it, the separation response is 'the inescapable corollary of attachment behavior – the other side of the coin'. The intensity of the infant's need for proximity may thus be gauged by the magnitude of the child's reactions and efforts (if any) to restore the *status quo*. [. . .]

Summary of empirical study

The study takes the form of a longitudinal follow-up, in which sixty infants were investigated at four-weekly intervals from the early weeks on up to the end of the first year and again at eighteen months of age. With the use of an attachment scale, based on seven everyday separation situations, the following three main parameters were explored: the age at onset of specific attachments, the intensity of such attachments and the number of objects to whom attachments are formed. A measure of fear of strangers was also included.

Results indicate that the age at onset of specific attachments is generally to be found in the third quarter of the first year, but that this is preceded by a phase of indiscriminate attachment behavior; that the intensity of specific attachment increases most in the first month following onset and that thereafter fluctuations occur in individual cases which make long-term prediction difficult; and that multiplicity of objects can be found in some instances at the very beginning of the specific attachment phase, becoming the rule in most of the remaining cases very soon thereafter. Correlations between the attachment variables, as well as with the fear-of-strangers measure, are presented and an examination is also made of the conditions eliciting protest at proximity loss, of the manner in which protest is expressed and of the conditions necessary to terminate protest.

Individual differences with regard to the three main parameters were explored in a subgroup of thirty-six infants. A number of variables were examined in relation to these individual differences and suggestions made regarding the conditions which affect the manifestation of the attachment function. [. . .]

Discussion

A number of themes arise from the results of this investigation which merit further discussion. Amongst these may be mentioned the nature of the attachment function, its developmental origins its developmental trends and the influence of the social setting. To these we shall now turn serially.

Nature of the attachment function

The picture which the present inquiry has firmly planted in our minds is not the conventional one of a socially passive infant who, when fed and free from pain, lies quietly in his cot ready to be molded by whatever social forces happen to impinge on him. On the contrary, from the early weeks on the infant appears to take an active part in seeking interaction with his social environment and it is he rather than the adults around him who is so often found to take the initiative in establishing and maintaining contact. Not only is there striving for the satisfaction of physical wants, but a considerable portion of an infant's motivational effort is also devoted to attention seeking – apparently for its own sake. The fact that, for the greater part of the first year, the infant's comparative lack of locomotor abilities precludes the use of many of the later-appearing devices employed for this end should not blind one to the power of those means with which he can signal his requirements even in the early months (crying being the most obvious and effective in this respect). In the absence of social stimulation he shows, often most forcefully, his unrest and dissatisfaction, and quiescence will only be restored when his wishes have been interpreted and met by the environment.

A directional force within the organism, of an enduring character and evoked by certain specific conditions, is thus indicated, and it appears therefore justified to postulate an *attachment need* as the motivational force behind proximity seeking. On an overt level proximity seeking is expressed by a variety of behavior patterns which may differ from individual to individual and from one developmental level to the next. It was not the aim of the present inquiry to list these, but Ainsworth (1963) has identified a large number which may be observed to 'clock in' at various ages in the course of the first year. Moreover, as the child's perceptual and conceptual horizons widen, the distance within which he regards himself as still near to the object gradually increases. A change in the manner in which proximity is defined will thus be observed: in the early months the other person may only be a few feet away and yet be regarded as lost, whereas later on even an intervening wall and the absence of visual and auditory stimulation will not prevent the child from considering himself within the required radius. Proximity, it appears, can be attained in many different ways and by the use of a wide range of different motor patterns, linked only by the common aim for which they may be used. It is this aim which provides a key concept for the study of early social behavior and permits the ordering of a highly diversified range of activities. The attachment need motivates the infant to employ a variety of responses which happen to be available to him at that particular stage of development and which have been found effective in keeping the person, towards whom they are directed, in his vicinity and thereby (incidentally from the individual's point of view though essentially from that of the species) ensuring the adequate supply of protection, love and care.

As the existence of a need can be inferred only from the responses which are designed to satisfy it, attention must be given to the conditions under which the need becomes activated. That proximity seeking is to a considerable extent a function of the total situation in which it takes place is repeatedly stressed in this report. A number of here-and-now events, organismic and environmental, may facilitate or suppress its expression, so that in certain conditions the existence of the underlying need becomes more evident than in others. The more stressful such conditions are to the infant the more intense will be his efforts of proximity seeking – hence the usefulness of the hospital situation as a means of demonstrating the existence of specific attachments. One of the infants in this sample, for instance, was hospitalized for a short period at the end of her first year and showed a considerable amount of separation upset under these circumstances; yet in the previous four-weekly period no evidence of attachment had been found at home. It appears that the longitudinal approach adopted here, though more productive in many respects than the cross-sectional study, does have to pay a price in the possibility that the tools used for evaluation may be somewhat less sensitive when they are based on assessment of behavior taking place under comparatively nontraumatic circumstances.

Individual differences in the overall intensity with which infant customarily display their attachment need are, we may assume partly a function of environmental forces and partly a function of certain inherent characteristics of the individual. That the en vironment plays a role in producing individual differences in both the manner and the extent to which the attachment need is expressed can hardly be doubted: studies of deprived infants testify most forcefully to this point and both our 'intermother' and our 'intrafamily' comparisons also lend some support to this viewpoint. The role of an inherent factor is rather more problematic and one can but speculate regarding its likely nature. However, a useful clue in this respect exists in the intercorrelations established for three of the variables investigated here, namely, attachment intensity, breadth of attachment and intensity of fear of strangers. Their association has not been found to be a consistently close one and this no doubt reflects the multi-determined nature of these phenomena. Nevertheless, the possibility must be considered that all three have in common one basic factor and that it is this which explains the otherwise somewhat puzzling relations which do exist between them. The element common to all three may be described as the degree of general responsiveness in social situations: thus some infants appear to be consistently placid in all such situations, being relatively unaffected either by the withdrawal of familiar figures or by the approach of unfamiliar figures; whereas other infants not only react violently to the loss of their principal object of attachment, but also show a similar reaction to a wide range of other familiar individuals and, furthermore, are highly responsive to any element of unfamiliarity in those with whom they come into contact, being thus more likely to manifest intense fear of strangers. A varying threshold of responsiveness in social situations generally appears indicated, in that some infants are more prone than others to react, positively or negatively, whenever the relevant stimulation is offered. The possibility must therefore be considered that, underlying the syndrome, a *social sensitivity factor* may be found. The existence of such a factor can, of course, be demonstrated only by further systematic research; in the meantime it is postulated here in order to emphasize the view that the intensity of attachments cannot be regarded in the light of environmental forces alone but that the individual's inherent characteristics must also be taken into account. Isolation of both kinds of variables is necessary before their resultant can be fully understood.

Proximity seeking is one of the two main elements in early social behavior, the other being proximity avoidance. Biphasic theories of motivation have long been popular and Schneirla (1959) in particular has emphasized the approach-withdrawal theme and its role in behavioral development. That a biological link exists between proximity seeking and proximity avoidance, in that the latter tendency effectively prevents the infant from making positive responses to inappropriate individuals, has been stressed by such writers as Collias (1952), Hess (1959) and Moltz (1960), who have demonstrated the existence of the same pair of tendencies in animals. Yet all our empirical data suggest that these response systems cannot be viewed merely as the opposite sides of the same coin, but that they represent separate functions each of which may be investigated in its own right. Some short-term interaction may occur, in that an infant, frightened by the approach of a stranger, may temporarily seek the reassuring presence of a familiar person. Moreover, infants early in developing the one are also more likely to be early in developing the other and, furthermore, a relation in the overall intensities of the two phenomena may be observed. On the other hand, their ages at onset do not coincide and it is therefore possible (though admittedly only for a short period) to find the one in the absence of the other. Also, variation in their respective intensities is by no means regular, suggesting that the conditions affecting their development are not necessarily identical. Generalizations about their interrelations must therefore be viewed with caution.

Developmental origins

The ability to form an attachment to a specific individual arises, in the majority of cases, in the third quarter of the first year. This statement can now be made with a fair degree of confidence, for it has been confirmed by two different approaches (in our previous cross-sectional study and in the present longitudinal investigation). A milestone of development with extremely important consequences for personality growth has thus been located and it now becomes essential for future research to establish the processes responsible for this development and the conditions which affect its delay or impairment. Little is known yet in this connection, though what evidence there is indicate that the onset of specific attachments is but one expression of a more general development. Of particular significance here is the previously discussed suggestion of Piaget that the beginnings of object conservation first manifest themselves in the third quarter of the first year. Similarly, studies of smiling (Ahrens, 1954; Spitz and Wolf, 1946) have shown that within the same age period this aspect of social behavior ceases to be evoked by primitive configurational properties inherent in all human faces and becomes linked to specific individuals. All these developments may be regarded as based on a fundamental change in the infant's cognitive structure, i.e. in the manner in which perceptions are organized and related to each other and to their external sources. However, only further research can illuminate the details of the processes involved.

One point our data have definitely indicated, namely, that proximity seeking can be found long before the emergence of specific attachments. The need appears to be present even in the first six months and to give rise to behavior patterns that are identical to those found later on. In the second half-year, however, these responses become channeled into certain directions and are no longer indiscriminate in object choice. A striking parallel with the smiling response is thus indicated: in both cases two developmental stages (an indiscriminate one and a specific one) are found and the evidence from both suggests that truly social behavior (in the sense of being object – rather than stimulus – oriented) only begins with the second stage.

If proximity seeking is present from the early weeks on, must we regard the attachment need as primary, i.e. as an inborn motivational tendency to seek the presence of other people for its own sake and not, in the first place, for the satisfaction of other needs? In this study we have not only failed to find any relation between attachment intensity and socializing severity, but we have also observed attachments to be formed to individuals who have never participated in routine care activities. Taken in conjunction with Bowlby's (1958) theory, Harlow's (1958) findings and Ainsworth's (1963) similar observations, the view that social behavior arises primarily in the context of the feeding situation must now be seriously questioned. Satisfaction of physical needs does not appear to be a necessary precondition to the development of attachments, the latter taking place independently and without any obvious regard to the experiences that the child encounters in physical care situations.

Another possibility must, however, be considered. We were impressed by the extent to which in the early months the occurrence of protest in the various separation situations depended on the supply not only of specifically *social* stimulation but of stimulation of almost any kind. All the mothers in our sample, to varying degree, quite naturally used a wide range of 'stimulators' in the hope of preventing or minimizing the infant's crying when they had to leave him to his own devices: toys, radio and television, vividly patterned curtains and wallpaper, the branches of trees moving in the wind, passing traffic, pram rocking, water pouring out of a tap, a dog playing on the floor or a bird hopping around its cage, the sight of leaping flames, the feel of a sheet of paper – these and very many other similar means were described to us in the course of our interviews. They were generally considered as forms of 'distraction', it being assumed that the infant's need was, from the beginning, for the kind of stimulation provided solely by humans but that, when this requirement could not be met, a diversion into other channels could take place. There is, however, another interpretation which suggests itself, namely that the infant's need for the proximity of other people is not primary but arises, in the course of development, from his need for stimulation in general.

The notion that environmental stimulation is necessary for full development to take place is now widely accepted. In early infancy in particular, as studies of deprivation (Casler, 1961; Spitz, 1945) have shown, this requirement must be met. According to Rheingold (1961), one of the most prominent characteristics of the young infant is his constant searching of the environment for stimulation – not only is his *responsiveness* well developed by three months of age, but by this time he is also already actively *seeking* for the arousing properties of his surroundings. But, as Rheingold further suggests, the most interesting object in his environment is the human object, with its high arousal potential and most varied stimulation propensity. In time, one may add, the infant learns that other human beings are particularly satisfying objects and that, moreover, the provision even of nonsocial stimulation is usually associated with their appearance. A need for their presence may thus be said to develop: the other person's proximity is initially sought as only one source of stimulation amongst many but will eventually be required in its own right once the infant has had the opportunity of learning about its special functional characteristics.

A three-stage development of early social behavior is thus envisaged. In the first stage, an asocial one, the individual seeks optimal arousal equally from all aspects of his environment, in time he learns to single out human beings as particularly satisfying objects and makes special efforts to seek their proximity. Thus we have the second stage, a presocial one, which is characterized by indiscriminate attachment behavior. Finally, a further narrowing down occurs and, in the last and only truly social stage, attachments are formed to specific individuals.

Whether the attachment need is to be regarded as innate or not becomes, according to this formulation, a meaningless question. Biologically, the infant's characteristics at birth are such that, given an 'average expectable environment', he is bound to go through the sequence of events indicated and develop an attachment need. From the point of view of the individual, however, this is not a *necessary* sequence, for under certain conditions (such as social deprivation) an infant may not have the opportunity of exposure to the required environmental stimulation and will thus fail to develop the attachment need. The same argument applies, of course, to other aspects of social behavior: the following response in young birds, for instance, can initially be elicited by all moving objects and not only by the mother; sucking occurs in response to any nipple-shaped object and not only to the maternal breast; the infant monkey will at first cling to any furry object that provides contact comfort; and a mask containing but two eyes will, in the early months, evoke a smile from the human infant as readily as the mother's face. In all instances the particular key stimulus, though a property of the parent figure, covers a very much wider range and, while under normal circumstances a narrowing down to the 'right' object will eventually take place, the individual organism must first be guided into that particular direction by a learning process. Thus the innate behavior propensity is in the beginning not a truly social activity, but becomes so only through its contact with a particular kind of environment.

From this formulation we would expect that the previously mentioned social sensitivity factor is related developmentally to individual differences in the stimulus need. That differences in responsiveness to environmental stimulation can already be isolated in neonates has been demonstrated on a behavioral level by Graham (1956) and on an autonomic level by Richmond and Lustman (1955). Bell (1960) too has described an 'arousal factor' in newborn infants and it may well be that in this fundamental characteristic the forerunner of the social sensitivity factor is to be found, providing the constitutional element that drives some infants to seek stimulation more eagerly and to react more intensely in social as well as nonsocial situations.

Developmental trends

Despite short-term consistency in attachment intensity, fluctuations over wider spans are marked in this parameter, making prediction difficult. In this respect our data parallel findings on other behavior systems in infancy: Hindley (1960), for instance, reviewing studies on early intellectual functioning, concludes that predictions based on existing infant tests are very uncertain within the first eighteen months, and similarly Winitz and Irwin (1958), in a study of early verbal development, found that rank order correlations for a number of measures of speech were so low between the various age levels that prediction was all but impossible.

A number of reasons for the instability of proximity seeking may be advanced. One of these may be ruled out with a fair degree of confidence, namely, the possibility that purely temporary, situational conditions produce diverse effects on an infant's scores as obtained at different times. By assessing behavior across a variety of situational contexts and by basing this assessment on wide time spans rather than on one particular test session, this factor has been minimized to a considerable extent.

However, the multidetermined nature of the intensity score does produce difficulties. As has been shown, the various separation situations do not all make an equal contribution at every age period, being affected by the rate of growth of perceptual range and possibly (though much more controversially) by the change from predominantly tactual-kinesthetic to visual-auditory means of interpersonal relating. In so far as such functions are not necessarily equally represented on the attachment scale, the total score of different individuals is likely to be affected to varying degree according to the developmental progress made in these abilities. Intragroup fluctuations in attachment intensity may thus be a function of the method of assessment rather than of the individual child.

Consideration must also, however, be given to the possibility that genuine irregularity in developmental rate occurs. Though it would be difficult to produce conclusive evidence on this point, it is at least conceivable that a lack of stability is an inherent feature of the attachment function in its early stages and that constancy in the intensity with which the need is manifested cannot therefore be expected. Such an interpretation would appear to contradict the findings of Chess, Thomas and Birch (Birch, Thomas, Chess and Hertzig, 1962; Chess, Thomas and Birch, 1959), according to which the persistence of stable and consistent reaction patterns from the early months on is a definite feature of personality development. The focus of these studies, however, in terms of both the nature and the frequency of the measures employed, is considerably cruder than used here and can hardly serve for purposes of comparison. Although the notion of an intrinsic factor underlying a particular response tendency, as advanced by these authors, is, as we have seen, echoed in this report, it does not follow that stability and consistency in expression is guaranteed thereby. Quite apart from the vicissitudes which result from interaction with the environment and the varying extent to which an infant may receive reinforcement in the manifestations of the attachment need, the fluctuations that have been found to occur in the absence of any obvious change in external conditions indicate that consistency is by no means an essential feature of this particular function. Further work may succeed in isolating the variables responsible for such fluctuations, but until this has been done the possibility of an inherent instability must be borne in mind.

Influence of the social setting

One of the more controversial findings of this investigation arises from the examination of the breadth dimension. This suggests that the choice of attachment object, even at the very beginning of the specific phase, is not necessarily confined to one person only, but that straightaway attachments may be formed to a number of different (though discriminated) individuals. While many infants did select just one object in the first month following the emergence of specific attachments, the substantial minority in whom attachments were focused on more than one person at this time indicates that this is neither a necessary nor an inherent feature in the development of this function. Moreover, although the mother was generally at the top of the hierarchy of the infant's objects, this choice was again not an inevitable one, for the importance of other people in the child's environment, particularly that of the father, was strongly emphasized throughout. To focus one's inquiry in the child's relationship with the mother alone would therefore give a misleading impression of the attachment function.

That attachments are, for intrinsic reasons, initially confined to one object, that subsequent attachments are formed only gradually after the first relationship has become firmly established and that these other attachments are always subsidiary in intensity compared with that to the mother – these are all assumptions that are widely and firmly held, despite the fact that no empirical studies have concerned themselves with this point. Gewirtz (1961, p. 237), for instance, expresses the usual point of view with his statement that 'It is unlikely that the child of the typical family, during his earliest years, would develop more than a very few all-encompassing attachments in addition to the one to his constant caretaker-interactor, i.e. mother-figure.' Investigators have thus generally isolated the child's relationship with the mother from his total social behavior and studied it without reference to any other relationship also formed by him. A wider focus is needed, however, in order to appreciate that the usual view is too simple.

There appear to be three reasons for the failure to consider the infant's other social relationships. In the first place, the widely held belief that a child's social behavior is initially associated with the alleviation of physical wants has excluded from consideration all those individuals who have little or no part in routine care activities and has directed attention almost exclusively to the child's caretaker. Consequently the notion, for instance, that a young sibling, whose interaction with the infant is confined to play or general stimulation, can become an object of attachment may at first sight seem somewhat strange despite its by no means infrequent occurrence. In the second place, there is the assumption that availability is a crucial variable in determining choice of attachment object and that the mother is therefore bound to take priority over all other individuals. This, as we have seen, is not so: a person's constant presence in the infant's immediate environment is no guarantee that interaction will occur and the necessary stimulation be offered. The most available person has, of course, the best opportunity of providing such stimulation and for this reason the mother is, more often than not, the infant's principal object. Yet not every mother will avail herself of this opportunity: personality factors and practical considerations may prevent her from doing so and thus allow other people, more responsive if less available, to become the child's principal attachment objects.

A final reason for the exclusive preoccupation with the child–mother relationship is historical. The emphasis on this relationship stems very largely from the writings of the early psychoanalysts, who viewed the child's development against the background of the typical European family of fifty years ago. In such family a rather strict division of labor existed which confined childrearing almost totally to the mother, giving her a near-monopoly of interaction with the child in his early years and thus minimizing the latter's opportunities of forming anything but shallow and fleeting relationships with others. Now, however, and especially in the Anglo-Saxon countries, family roles have changed and a far greater sharing of family tasks may generally be observed. On the one hand, mothers are more likely to have interests (including part-time jobs) that take them away from the child's side and, on the other hand, fathers are no longer the stern and rather distant figures of Freudian days but tend to take a far greater part in the bringing up of their children. The latter are thus exposed to a wider range of interpersonal contacts and to more opportunities of forming multiple attachments.

Social practices have changed but psychological theories have not, with the result that the current view of the beginnings of social behavior in childhood tends to assume a type of family which is no longer prevalent. Whom an infant chooses as his attachment object and how many objects he selects depend, we believe, primarily on the nature of the social setting in which he is reared and not on some intrinsic characteristic of the attachment function itself. This view receives strong support from anthropological data: Margaret Mead (1956, 1962), on the basis of her observations of different types of family structure, has seriously questioned the view that exclusiveness of attachment to one mother-figure is biological in origin and that attachments cannot be safely distributed amongst several figures. In certain societies multiple object relationships are the norm from the first year on: the relevant stimuli which evoke attachment behavior are offered by a number of individuals and not exclusively by one person, and a much more diversified system of attachments is thus fostered in the infant. While anthropological material has the advantage of great diversity in the types of social setting that one may study, in our society, too, variation, though less extreme, may be found and investigated. Whether a child has one caretaker or many, the identity of these caretakers and the distribution of tasks among them, the extent to which the family is an 'open' or a 'closed' system in its relationship with the rest of the community: these are all aspects of the social dimension about whose influence on the growing child little information is as yet forthcoming. Hoffman and Lippitt (1960), in a review of this topic, find a paucity of empirical research connecting family variables with child variables, and in similar vein Young and Willmott (1957) point out that we can at present hardly even guess which kind of family produces which kind of person. The assumption in most psychological writings of a type of family which is not only stereotyped but also largely outmoded has led to the neglect of a wide range of variables with potentially important influence on personality development. Yet the data of the present report suggest strongly that such individuals as fathers, grandmothers and even siblings need not play quite the minor subsidiary role generally allotted to them, but that from the beginning they may assume important positions in the infant's world. Once the view has been accepted that the child–mother relationship does not necessarily exhaust the infant's attachment behavior, a linkage becomes possible between the family setting and one aspect of personality growth. The details of this linkage still require to be investigated; our concern here is to emphasize the possibility of making it by questioning the assumption that attachment in infancy is of necessity unidirectional in form.

The purpose of these remarks is not to challenge the importance of the mother *vis-à-vis* her children, but to stress the fact that other people in the infant's environment may also play important roles. The mother is usually in a particularly good position to make a powerful impact on the child and understandably most infants select her as the principal object. Yet greater availability and prime responsibility for physical care are not by themselves a sufficient guarantee of monopoly over the infant's attachment behavior. This may assume a very much more complex form, the details of which will depend to a considerable extent on the nature of the social setting in which the infant is reared.

References

AHRENS, R. (1954), 'Beitrag zur Entwicklung des Physiognomie und Mimikerkennens', *Z. Exp. Ange. Psychol.*, vol. 2, pp. 412–54.

AINSWORTH, M. D. (1963), 'The development of mother–infant interaction among the Ganda', in B. M. Foss (ed.), *Determinants of Infant Behaviour*, vol. 2, Methuen.

BALDWIN, A. L. (1949), 'The effect of home environment on nursery school behavior', *Child Devel.*, vol. 20, pp. 49–62.

BELL, R. Q. (1960), 'Relations between behavior manifestations in the human neonate', *Child Devel.*, vol. 31, pp. 463–77.

BENJAMIN, J. D. (1959), 'Prediction and psychopathological theory', in L. Jessner and E. Pavenstadt (eds.), *Dynamic Psychopathology in Childhood*, Grune & Stratton.

BIRCH, H. G., THOMAS, A., CHESS, S., and HERTZIG, M. E. (1962), 'Individuality in the development of children', *Devel. med. child Neurol.*, vol. 4, pp. 370–79.

BOWLBY, J. (1958), 'The nature of the child's tie to his mother', *Inter. J. Psycho-anal.*, vol. 39, pp. 350–73.

BOWLBY, J. (1960), 'Separation anxiety', *Inter. J. Psycho-anal.*, vol. 41, pp. 1–25.

BRACKBILL, Y. (1958), 'Extinction of the smiling response in infants as a function of the reinforcement schedule', *Child Devel.*, vol. 29, pp. 115–24.

BÜHLER, C. (1930), *The First Year of Life*, Day.

CALDWELL, B. M. (1962a), 'Mother–infant interaction in the monomatric and polymatric families', *Amer. J. Orthopsychiat.*, vol. 32, pp. 340–41 (abstract).

CALDWELL, B. M. (1962b), 'The usefulness of the critical period hypothesis in the study of filiative behavior', *Merrill–Palmer Q.*, vol. 8, pp. 229–42.

CASLER, L. (1961), 'Maternal deprivation: a critical review of the literature', *Monogr. Soc. Res. Child Devel.*, vol. 26, no. 2.

CATTELL, P. (1940), *The Measurement of Intelligence of Infants and Young Children*, Psychol. Corp.

CHESS, S., THOMAS, A., and BIRCH, H. G. (1959), 'Characteristics of the individual child's behavioral responses to the environment', *Amer. J. Orthopsychiat.*, vol. 29, pp. 791–809.

COLLIAS, N. E. (1952), 'The development of social behaviour in birds', *Auk*, vol. 69, pp. 127–59.

DAVID, M., and APPELL, G. (1961), 'A study of nursing care and nurse–infant interaction', in B. M. Foss (ed.), *Determinants of Infant Behaviour*, Methuen.

FREEDMAN, D. G. (1961), 'The infant's fear of strangers and the flight response', *J. child Psychol. Psychiat.*, vol. 2, pp. 242–8.

GESELL, A., and AMATRUDA, C. S. (1947), *Developmental Diagnosis*, Hoeber.

GEWIRTZ, J. L. (1956), 'A program of research on the dimensions and antecedents of emotional dependence', *Child Devel.*, vol. 27, pp. 205–21.

GEWIRTZ, J. L. (1961), 'A learning analysis of the effects of normal stimulation, privation and deprivation on the acquisition of social motivation and attachment', in B. M. Foss (ed.), *Determinants of Infant Behaviour*, Methuen.

GRAHAM, F. K. (1956), 'Behavioral differences between normal and traumatized newborns: the test procedures', *Psychol. Monogr.*, vol. 70, pp. 1–16.

GRIFFITHS, R. (1954), *The Abilities of Babies*, University of London Press.

HARLOW, H. F. (1958), 'The nature of love', *Amer. Psychol.*, vol. 13, pp. 673–85.

HARLOW, H. F. (1961), 'The development of affectional patterns in infant monkeys', in B. M. Foss (ed.), *Determinants of Infant Behaviour*, Methuen.

HARLOW, H. F., and ZIMMERMANN, R. R. (1959), 'Affectional responses in the infant monkey', *Science*, vol. 130, pp. 421–32.

HEATHERS, G. (1955), 'Acquiring dependence and independence: a theoretical orientation', *J. genet. Psychol.*, vol. 87, pp. 277–91.

HESS, E. H. (1959), 'The relationship between imprinting and motivation', in M. R. Jones (ed.), *Nebraska Symposium on Motivation*, University of Nebraska Press.

HINDLEY, C. H. (1960), 'The Griffiths Scale of infant development: scores and prediction from 3 to 18 months', *J. child Psychol. Psychiat.*, vol. 1, pp. 99–112.

HOFFMAN, L. W., and LIPPITT, R. (1960), 'The measurement of family life variables', in P. H. Mussen (ed.), *Handbook of Research Methods in Child Development*, Wiley.

LEVY, D. M. (1960), 'The infant's earliest memory of inoculation: a contribution to public health procedures', *J. genet. Psychol.*, vol. 96, pp. 3–46.

MEAD, M. (1956), Comments in J. M. Tanner and B. Inhelder (eds.), *Discussions on Child Development*, Tavistock.

MEAD, M. (1962), 'A cultural anthropologist's approach to maternal deprivation', *WHO pub. Health Pap.*, no. 14, pp. 45–62.

MILLER, N. E., and DOLLARD, J. (1941), *Social Learning and Imitation*, Yale University Press.

MOLTZ, H. (1960), 'Imprinting: empirical basis and theoretical significance', *Psychol. Bull.*, vol. 57, pp. 291–314.

MUSSEN, P. H., and CONGER, J. J. (1956), *Child Development and Personality*, Harper & Row.

PIAGET, J. (1953), *The Origin of Intelligence in the Child*, Routledge & Kegan Paul.

PIAGET, J. (1955), *The Child's Construction of Reality*, Routledge & Kegan Paul.

REGISTRAR-GENERAL (1960), *Classification of Occupations*, HMSO.

RHEINGOLD, H. (1960), 'The measurement of maternal care', *Child Devel.*, vol. 31, pp. 565–75.

RHEINGOLD, H. (1961), 'The effect of environmental stimulation upon social and exploratory behaviour in the human infant', in B. M. Foss (ed.), *Determinants of Infant Behaviour*, Methuen.

RHEINGOLD, H., GEWIRTZ, J. L., and ROSS, H. W. (1959), 'Social conditioning of vocalizations in the infant', *J. comp. physiol. Psychol.*, vol. 52, pp. 68–73.

RICHMOND, J. B., and LUSTMAN, S. L. (1955), 'Automatic function in the neonate', *Psychonom. Med.*, vol. 17, pp. 269–75.

SCHAFFER, H. R. (1958), 'Objective observations of personality development in early infancy', *Brit. J. med. Psychol.*, vol. 31, pp. 174–84.

SCHAFFER, H. R. (1963), 'Some issues for research in the study of attachment behaviour', in B. M. Foss (ed.), *Determinants of Infant Behaviour*, vol. 2, Methuen.

SCHAFFER, H. R., and CALLENDER, W. M. (1959), 'Psychologic effects of effects of hospitalization in infancy', *Pediatrics*, vol. 24, pp. 528–39.

SCHNEIRLA, T. C. (1959), 'An evolutionary and developmental theory of biphasic processes underlying approach and withdrawal', in M. R. Jones (ed.), *Nebraska Symposium on Motivation*, University of Nebraska Press.

SEARS, R. R., MACCOBY, E. E., and LEVIN, H. (1957), *Patterns of Child Rearing*, Row, Peterson.

SEARS, R. R., WHITING, J. W. M., NOWLIS, V., and SEARS, P. S. (1953), 'Some child-rearing antecedents of aggression and dependency in young children', *Genet. psychol. Monogr.*, vol. 47, pp. 135–236.

SEWELL, W. H., MUSSEN, P. H., and HARRIS, C. W. (1955), 'Relationship among child training practices', *Amer. sociol. Rev.*, vol. 20, pp. 137–48.

SHIRLEY, M. M. (1933), *The First Two Years: A Study of Twenty-Five Babies: II Intellectual Development*, University of Minnesota Press.

SPITZ, R. A. (1945), 'Hospitalism: an inquiry into the genesis of psychiatric conditions in early childhood', in O. Fenichel (ed.), *The Psychoanalytic Study of the Child*, vol. 1, International Universities Press.

SPITZ, R. A. (1950), 'Anxiety in infancy: a study of its manifestations in the first year of life', *Inter. J. Psycho-anal.*, vol. 31, pp. 138–43.

SPITZ, R. A., and WOLF, K. M, (1946), 'The smiling response: a contribution to the ontogenesis of social relations', *Genet. psychol. Monogr.*, vol. 34, pp. 57–125.

TANNER, J. (1951), 'Some notes on the reporting of growth data', *Hum. Biol.*, vol. 23, pp. 93–159.

WINITZ, H., and IRWIN, O. C. (1958), 'Infant speech: consistency with age', *J. speech hear. Dis.*, vol. 1, pp. 245–9.

YOUNG, M., and WILLMOTT, P. (1957), *Family and Kinship in East London*, Routledge & Kegan Paul.

28 H. R. Schaffer

The Onset of Fear of Strangers and the Incongruity Hypothesis

Excerpt from H. R. Schaffer, 'The onset of fear of strangers and the incongruity hypothesis', *Journal of Child Psychology and Psychiatry*, vol. 7, 1966, pp. 95–106.

Introduction

The beginnings of social development in the human infant may be understood in terms of two general behaviour tendencies, namely proximity seeking and proximity avoidance (Schaffer and Emerson, 1964). The former underlies the formation of social attachments, whereas the latter, which concerns us in the present paper, has also been described as fear of strangers or (after its approximate age of onset) as eight-months' anxiety. The phenomenon has been recognized and described by many writers (e.g. Bridges, 1932; Bühler, 1930; Freedman, 1961; Meili, 1955; Preyer, 1888; Spitz, 1950; Tennes and Lampl, 1964) and has also been reported in a wide range of animal species (Sluckin, 1964).

In both human and animal development there is an initial period following birth during which no fear reactions to strangers can be found. The subsequent onset of fearful behaviour was at one time explained in purely maturational terms (Gesell and Thompson, 1934), but largely due to Hebb's (1946) theorizing is now more often considered as a function of the individual's preceding perceptual experience. According to Hebb, fear arises when an object is seen which is like familiar objects in enough respects to arouse habitual processes of perception, but is also sufficiently dissimilar to arouse incompatible processes and thereby disrupt the central neural patterns laid down by previous stimulation. An initial period of experience is thus a necessary prerequisite in order to establish the notion of the familiar and give rise to the feeling of discrepancy with new patterns of sensory stimulation. Support for this view comes from studies which show that in perceptually naïve subjects such as chimpanzees blindfolded from birth (Hebb, 1949), chicks brought up in isolation

(Collias, 1950) and individuals operated on for congenital cataract (Dennis, 1934), no fear of strangers can be observed until exposure to relevant perceptual learning experiences has taken place. The considerable evidence which has accumulated on the avoidance behaviour of animals confronted by novel objects differing to a certain degree from familiar objects (Fiske and Maddi, 1961) also points in the same direction.

In a recent series of papers Hunt (1963, 1964, 1965) has proposed a theoretical framework which sets out to account for a wide range of motivational and developmental phenomena and which, by incorporating the Hebbian position, also has special relevance to the understanding of fear of strangers. Motivation and the direction of behaviour (approach or withdrawal) are, according to this view, regarded as inherent within the organism's informational interaction with its environmental circumstances. Behaviour is instigated by the degree of incongruity between sensory input and some standard within the organism, representing information already coded and stored within the brain as a result of previous encounters with the category of circumstances concerned. At a certain optimum degree of incongruity, interest is aroused and approach behaviour results, whereas deviation in either direction will give rise to avoidance and withdrawal responses. Thus, when the inputs from a situation are too similar to the information already in storage, boredom ensues and the organism withdraws in order to seek incongruity, stimulus-change, novelty or dissonance elsewhere. If, on the other hand, the discrepancy between input and centrally present storage is too great, the organism finds itself unable to deal with the situation and is impelled to flee. The feared object is therefore one which excites receptors in a fashion which is incongruous with the central pattern accrued as a residue of the individual's past experience. Until the central pattern has been learned, however, incongruous stimulation is impossible.

Both Hebb and Hunt indicate that fear cannot be explained in terms of sensory events alone, but that it must be related to the discrepancy between what is expected on the basis of past experience and what is observed. A period of previous relevant experience must first occur in order to establish a central standard with which new sensory patterns may then be compared. It follows that the nature of the individual's previous experience will, through a process of perceptual learning, determine the nature of the central standard and thus the parameters of the fear response subsequently manifested. It is to this problem that the present paper is addressed, its purpose being to assess the adequacy of the incongruity hypothesis in the light of data obtained in the course of a longitudinal study on the development of the fear-of-strangers response system in human infants.

The incongruity hypothesis, when applied to the development of fear of strangers, is based on two propositions. In the first place, it suggests that fear cannot develop until a central pattern has been laid down by the individual's previous learning experiences in social situations, which defines the familiar person and with which strangers can then be compared. In the second place, the speed with which fear develops depends, on the one hand, on the extent to which the child has had opportunities to establish the central pattern (i.e. the amount of contact with the mother) and, on the other hand, on the range of people other than the mother with whom he has come in contact (i.e. the diversity of his social relationships). As to the first of these propositions, we shall offer some descriptive material designed to illustrate the natural history of the infant's response to strangers and to indicate the manner in which fear first manifests itself. As to the second proposition, various writers have expressed opinions on this matter; Freedman (1961), for instance, regards the relative exclusiveness or intensity of the mother–infant relationship as a crucial variable, so that infants with intense relationships exhibit fear of strangers earlier than the average. Freedman has also indicated his belief that in large families where the mother attends the infant minimally and where a number of people come and go, fear is rather less likely to be manifested, and similarly Hunt (1960) has suggested that fear of strangers does not occur in children who have always been exposed to a large number of persons and that multiple mothering acts therefore as an inoculation against social shyness or fear. We shall therefore examine how far age at onset of the fear-of-strangers response system is a function of different kinds of social interaction experienced by infants.

Method

Subjects

The sample is composed of thirty-six infants (eighteen boys and eighteen girls) who took part in a short-term longitudinal investigation of early social behaviour (see Schaffer and Emerson, 1964, for further details). The infants were selected from the files of a maternity and child welfare clinic as living at home with their own parents, having been born full-term, showing no evidence of any congenital abnormality and having had no illnesses or hospitalizations prior to contact. Cattell developmental quotients (Cattell, 1940), obtained at six months of age, gave a mean of 112·7 and a range of 92 to 143. The initial contact with the infants was made at a point varying from six to fourteen weeks of age, and thereafter contacts took place at regular four-weekly intervals until the end of the first year, after which each child was seen once more at the age of eighteen months. All contacts occurred in the family's own home and, for this particular sample, were made by a female investigator.[1]

Procedure

The fear-of-strangers measure. Right at the beginning of every visit, the investigator related to the infant in a series of steps involving progressively greater proximity, as follows:

1. The investigator (E) appears in the infant's visual range and remains standing still, looking at the infant, but not in any other way stimulating him.

2. E smiles and talks to the infant without as yet moving any closer.

3. E approaches the infant, smiling and talking.

4. E makes physical contact with the infant by taking his hand or stroking his arm.

5. E offers to pick up the infant by holding out her hands.

6. E picks up the infant and sits him on her knee.

---

1. I am most grateful to Mrs Peggy Emerson for help in the execution of this project.

Age at onset of fear of strangers was defined as the age at which the infant for the first time showed a fear response towards the investigator at some step during the interaction sequence. Fear reactions were specified as whimpering, crying, lip trembling, screwed-up face, looking or turning away, drawing back, running or crawling away and hiding face. Not included are all instances where the child merely failed to respond positively, e.g. when he stared solemnly without smiling or vocalizing, or when he quietly watched the adult without moving. The procedure was terminated as soon as the infant showed his first fear response. During the procedure the mother stood just by the infant, who thus had ready access to her. As well as noting the particular step in the experimental procedure which elicited the fear response (if any), a detailed observational record was kept of all responses shown by the subject to the investigator throughout the proceedings. In addition, reports were obtained each visit from the mother as to the infant's behaviour towards strangers met with in the course of his everyday life.

How far the use of the same investigator as the 'stranger' at each visit affected the obtained results is problematic. The rather sparse evidence available about memory functioning in infancy (Levy, 1960) indicates that this is too poorly developed in the first year to bridge a four-weekly gap and thus produce a familiarization effect. The nature of the infant's reaction to the first sight of the investigator during each visit certainly did not suggest such an effect, nor does the 92 per cent agreement between the occurrence of fear in the experimental procedure with the mothers' reports about the infants' behaviour to strangers met with in the usual course of his life. Nevertheless, the possibility that a more pronounced fear reaction might have been shown had different adults confronted the infant at each visit cannot be overlooked.

The social interaction variables. The following variables were used in order to investigate the extent of the child's opportunities to learn the familiar mother:

1. Maternal availability. In order to measure the amount of time which a mother spends with her child, two measures were obtained at the eighteen-month visit. The mothers were asked to

note both the number of times on which they left their infants for more than half an hour during the subsequent seven days and the total time in hours which these absences involved. An extra visit was paid one week later in order to collect this information.

2. Maternal responsiveness. The degree of the mother's willingness to respond to the infant's crying and other signals for company and attention was rated on a six-point scale, ranging from 'leaves infant to cry indefinitely, mostly refuses to respond at all', to 'always responds quickly, goes almost at once'.

3. Maternal interaction. This variable refers to the extent to which the mother herself initiates interaction with the infant. The relevant information was again categorized according to a six-point rating scale which ranged from 'mother follows a policy of "leave well alone", avoids interaction outside routine care situations, tends to ignore infant to a considerable extent' to 'fairly continuous stimulation of infant, often of a rather intense form, mother highly demonstrative'.

4. Number of children in family.

As measures of the child's opportunities to become acquainted with a range of people other than the mother, the following variables were investigated:

1. Number of caretakers. This variable refers to the number of people customarily participating in the child's care. Included here were not only those who helped in such physical routines as feeding and bathing but also those who regularly took the infant for walks, played with him, and generally amused him.

2. Number of people contacted. At the eighteen-month visit the mothers were asked to note the number of people with whom the child came into contact during the subsequent seven days, either as visitors to his own house or when visiting other homes.

Results

The mean age at onset of fear of strangers in this sample was 35·94 weeks. This bears out the findings of others, that this phenomenon tends to be manifested first around eight months of age. Behind this mean figure, however, lies a considerable range of individual differences, which is expressed in a standard deviation of 8·97 weeks and may be appreciated from the distribution given in Table 1.

Table 1 Distribution for Age at Onset of Fear of Strangers

Age in weeks	25–8	29–32	33–6	37–40	41–4	45–8	49–52	over 53
n (total=36)	7	7	11	3	4	2	0	2

There was a tendency for the girls in the group to reach this developmental milestone somewhat earlier than the boys (34·72 weeks and 37·06 weeks respectively), but this difference did not reach statistical significance. On the other hand, the seventeen first-born children in the sample were considerably younger at showing fear of strangers than the nineteen later born children (32·50 weeks and 39·28 weeks respectively, $t = 2·73, p < 0·01$).

The onset of the fear-of-strangers response was often sudden and dramatic. At one contact with the investigator there was no evidence of negative responses; at the next visit the fear response was present in its full intensity. Mothers' reports corroborate this finding, in that they usually pointed to some one particular episode in the course of the child's daily life when quite suddenly he showed fear towards a particular stranger.

However, this apparent suddenness of onset is, in a sense, somewhat misleading. Although negative responses towards the investigator were not in evidence until this point, positive responses towards her did change in the preceding months by gradually diminishing and becoming increasingly difficult to elicit. In the initial weeks of life all infants showed automatic responsiveness, i.e. they smiled almost immediately at the stranger and gave no indication of any awareness of unfamiliarity. At ages varying from thirteen to nineteen weeks, however, a lag in the smile appeared, and while the mother continued to elicit an immediate positive response from the infant, the stranger was in all cases greeted with a 'sobering of the features' (as Gesell and Thompson, 1934, refer to it) which only gradually in the course of the contact gave way to more positive responses. Sometimes an ambivalent pattern of behaviour was observed, in that the infant would alternately stare, smile and then stare again, repeating this a number of times. With increasing age the lag grew longer in duration, until in the month just before the onset of fear a period of complete unresponsiveness occurred in fourteen of the group, when neither fear nor positive responses were observed and the infant remained 'frozen' throughout the contact.

A further qualification that must be made in relation to age at onset refers to the reports made by a number of mothers of fear towards other people occurring already in the early months – long before age at onset as defined here. Such early instances of fear have also been reported by other writers (Benjamin, 1963; Morgan, 1965) and have been characterized as referring only to certain exceptional incidents rather than being consistently evoked by all unfamiliar individuals, as well as by being responses to intensity or unexpectedness of stimulation rather than to strangers as such. Thus, in the thirteen cases in the present sample where fear responses were reported, on at least one occasion before age at onset it was found that not only strangers but also familiar persons (e.g. a grandmother, an uncle and even the mother herself) were involved. The cause appeared to refer to such stimuli as a loud voice, rough handling and (in the case of the mother who elicited fear) a pair of spectacles not previously worn. As soon as the appearance or behaviour of the individual involved was changed, the fear responses disappeared. They may thus be regarded as isolated occurrences rather than as consistent reactions to encounters with strangers.

It must not be thought, however, that once an infant has reached the age where he is capable of showing fear of strangers, he will inevitably show fearful responses the moment he is confronted by a stranger. A number of observations may be quoted in this respect. For one thing, as may be seen from Table 2, the first step in the experimental procedure (the confrontation of the infant with the silent and inactive adult) hardly ever elicited fear in the initial months following onset. Contrary to what one might expect, the sight of an immobile stranger looking at the infant without smiling or speaking did not appear to be a fear-provoking stimulus situation. It was rather the active impinging of the stranger on the infant, particularly through physical interaction, that elicited the fear response. Thus the very type of stimulation which, when it emanates from familiar individuals, will give rise to positive social responses, resulted in proximity

Table 2 Procedural Steps Eliciting Fear Response at Different Intervals Following Onset of Fear of Strangers

Procedural step*	Lunar months from age at onset							
	1		2		3		4	
	n†	%	n	%	n	%	n	%
1	0	0	1	3	0	0	1	4
2	2	6	2	7	0	0	0	0
3	3	8	4	14	3	12	1	5
4	14	39	3	11	5	19	6	25
5	0	0	3	11	2	8	2	8
6	17	47	5	18	4	15	2	8
No fear	—	—	10	36	12	46	12	50
Total	36	100	28	100	26	100	24	100

*See page 390 for a description of the various steps comprising the fear-of-strangers procedure.

†The number of subjects at each age period varies (a) because the number of fear-of-strangers scores obtained by an infant in the course of the first year depends on his age at onset and (b) because of the non-availability of some infants on account of illness, absence from home, etc.

avoidance when offered by unfamiliar individuals. Moreover, it was repeatedly observed that, even when the stranger began to approach the infant, the latter would not immediately withdraw or cry at this point but would first several times look to and fro between the stranger and the mother – as though comparing one with the other. In four instances the infant, after such initial comparison, visually fixated the mother and continued to stare at her despite the investigator's attempts to attract the child's attention – as though, one might interpret, to preserve the familiar and thereby avoid the unfamiliar sight. Finally, it is interesting to note from Table 2 the considerable proportion of infants who, following the onset of this phenomenon, did not in subsequent months show any fear whatever in the course of the whole experimental procedure. This applies to between 30 and 50 per cent of the subjects observed at any given point and supports the observation also made by Morgan (1965) that fear is far from being an inevitable response to strangers. In three cases fear appeared to a marked degree in the course of one contact with the investigator at around eight months of age, but was never observed again on any subsequent occasion. In most other cases inexplicable variations took place from month to month, in that the infant would sometimes show fear and sometimes not. Maternal reports confirmed such fluctuations without being able to throw any light on their causes.

Turning to the relation between age at onset and the variables defining the infant's social interaction experiences, we find from Table 3 that only two of the relationships examined are of significance. Number of children in family is one of these, indicating

Table 3 Relationship between Age at Onset of Fear of Strangers and Social Interaction Variables ($n = 36$)

Maternal availability		
Number of absences	$r =$	-0.04
Hours of absence	$r =$	-0.14
Maternal responsiveness	$r_{bis} =$	0.16
Maternal interaction	$r_{bis} =$	0.02
Number of children in family	$C =$	$0.41*$
Number of caretakers	$r =$	0.07
Number of people contacted	$r =$	$0.35†$

*Significant at 1 per cent level.
†Significant at 5 per cent level.

that the more siblings a child had the later he was in reaching age at onset. This appears at first sight to bear out the above quoted suggestion by Freedman (1961), that infants who have to share the mother with other children will be less likely to manifest fear. Yet when one examines directly the variables which would presumably be responsible for this difference, i.e. those which define the intensity of the relationship with the mother, no supporting evidence can be found. In fact, none of the indices used to describe the amount and kind of contact with the mother, and therefore the extent of the child's opportunities to learn her, showed any relation to age at onset. On the other hand, the diversity of the child's social experiences did show some relationship to age at onset, indicating that the greater the number of people that were normally encountered by the infant in the course of his daily life, the later he tended to develop fear of strangers.

Discussion

It is to the credit of the incongruity hypothesis that the onset of fear of strangers is not treated as a 'magical' event, i.e. one solely due to maturational processes which defy further explanation, but that it stipulates the conditions which lead up to the emergence of fear in terms which permit empirical inquiry. These conditions refer to the infant's perceptual experiences in social situations and are based on the ability to distinguish familiar from unfamiliar individuals. That such distinction develops in the months preceding the onset of fear, that it gradually builds up from a slight lag in smiling at the stranger to a complete failure to evince any positive responses at all and that, when fear eventually emerges, it is frequently manifested in such a way as to indicate the infant's perception of the stranger in terms of his distinction from the familiar person – these findings obtained within the present longitudinal context are in accord with the view advanced by the incongruity hypothesis that the development of fear is dependent on the ability to perceive the stranger as 'different'.

There are, however, three respects in which the hypothesis appears in need of emendation. In the first place, writers concerned with the development of fear in animals (e.g. Moltz, 1965; Scott, 1962) appear to regard the ability to differentiate perceptually between known and unknown stimulus patterns as the only condition required for such a development to take place. Moltz (1965, p. 39), for instance, believes that what is necessary for the appearance of fear of strange, though innocuous, visual stimuli, is 'commerce with a structured sensory environment – commerce in which the very fact of exposure seems sufficient to establish the visually familiar.... Once early contact delimits the perceptually typical, presentation of an incongruous stimulus combination is all that is necessary to evoke an emotional response.' The adequacy of this statement must, however, be questioned. It is the advantage of human development that it affords the opportunity of observing processes in comparative slow-motion and we are thus made conscious of the fact that the human infant shows signs of being able to differentiate between known and unknown persons as early as three or four months of age, yet does not show fear until several months later. An unexplained age gap exists, when the stranger is experienced as different, yet not as frightening. It must be concluded that the ability to make the distinction is a necessary but not a sufficient condition and that the incongruity hypothesis is therefore in need of extension in this respect.

As has been pointed out elsewhere (Schaffer, 1963), an analogous situation is to be found in the development of attachment behaviour. Here too, the ability to establish attachments to specific individuals first occurs at a point several months subsequent to the appearance of differential recognition, thus necessitating the stipulation of a further condition for this development to take place. This, it has been suggested, is to be found in the change in cognitive structure which takes place in the second half of the first year and which results in the establishment of the object concept. As Piaget (1955) has pointed out in considerable detail, an infant of this age will no longer apprehend the world in terms of fleeting images unrelated to one another and only responded to on the basis of their functional properties, but will now begin to organize his perceptions around permanent objects with an independent existence in time and space. Whereas in the earlier stage the infant is said to experience only a series of images which may be recognized, but which have no continuity or substance, in the second six months of life objects become divorced from the subject's immediate perception of them and from his own ongoing activities. One result of such a change is that the child now becomes capable of forming permanent relationships to others: in the early months attachments assumed an indiscriminate form in that the proximity of anyone prepared to supply attention and stimulation was sought, while from six or seven months on proximity seeking is confined to certain specific individuals who are not only recognized but actively sought in their own right. The child, in brief, has become object-oriented rather than stimulus-oriented.

It is suggested that the development of fear follows a similar course. Here, too, initially it is certain stimulus properties, such as intensity, suddenness and unexpectedness that evoke fearful behaviour. Morgan (1965), for instance, found evidence of fear of other people in forty of his eighty subjects before the age of seven months, but concluded that these involved relatively iso lated incidents which were the result of loud talking or sudden movements rather than the newness of the person. Indeed, as in the present sample, several of the mothers reported negative reactions towards themselves and their husbands under such conditions. Similarly Benjamin (1963) has concluded that 'there can be a fearful or anxious response to a stranger at an early age that has nothing to do with his human attributes as such, but rather with his belonging to a subclass of the general class of strange things' and that this is dependent on such factors as suddenness and speed of movement and noises. In so far as the infant will respond with fearful behaviour to certain stimulus situations irrespective of whether these involve familiar or unfamiliar individuals, one may regard this early phase as socially indiscriminate in nature. Certain minimal signs, such as differential lag in smiling, indicate an ability to distinguish known from unknown persons, but the dramatic bifurcation into positive and negative social responses cannot take place until other people are no longer responded to on the basis of isolated stimulus characteristics but are instead conceived *in toto*. Only at this point will the infant's social responses be determined by the perceived identity of the other person and only then can he be said to have the ability to compare one individual with another in terms, for instance, of familiarity. Thus fear responses in relation to the unexpected can already be found in the early months of life, but it is not until the second half of the first year that such responses become linked to a particular class of person rather than to certain more primitive stimulus events. The establishment of the object concept is, therefore, a precondition to the onset of fear of strangers over and above the appearance of differential recognition. Only when this additional condition has been met can the indiscriminate phase of fearful behaviour give way to a specific phase in which responses are based on the identity of the particular person and no longer merely on certain aspects of his behaviour or appearance.

A further modification of the incongruity hypothesis arises from the finding that, in the early months following age at onset, fear was rarely evoked by the mere sight of the stranger. Simply to be confronted by a stationary, immobile adult, who did not in any way interact with the infant except by visual regard, did not appear to be an emotionally provoking event. It was rather the stranger's active impinging on the infant that produced fear and withdrawal responses. There are several possible explanations for this finding that one might consider, e.g. that the crucial factor lay in the distance between adult and child or that it was the occurrence of movement that was the essential stimulus – both possibilities that receive some tentative support from studies of fear in animals (Hess, 1958). The role of such factors in the production of fear will have to be determined by future experimentation. In the meantime, however, a further explanation should be considered, namely, that a crucial factor in the perception of unfamiliarity lies in the speed and intensity with which the novel stimulation impinges on the infant in relation to the latter's ability to process and adjust to such information. In his statement of the incongruity hypothesis, Hunt (1963, p. 67) has shown awareness of this additional precondition when he wrote that 'not only degree of incongruity but also abruptness or rate at which incoming information appears to demand reorganization of information in the storage will be factors determining the degree of emotional arousal'. This may well account for the fact that fear of strange inanimate objects is reported far less frequently and appears to assume a very much less dramatic character than fear of strange animate objects – human or animal. With an inanimate object the child can himself regulate the speed and manner of stimulation to which he is exposed and under these conditions exploration and approach may eventually take place rather than fear and avoidance. Similarly an immobile adult, despite the infant's perception of his unfamiliarity, does not present stimulation of the intensity and temporal complexity provided by the stranger who actively impinges on the infant. In the latter case the manner and amount of stimulation is determined by the adult without reference to the subject's ability to assimilate the information and is thus far more likely to be experienced as a disruptive force and hence to produce fear. It must be concluded that the perception of strangeness in itself does not necessarily bring about avoidance behaviour, but that the manner of interaction between subject and stranger must also be taken into account.

The third emendation of the incongruity hypothesis arise

from the attempt to define the parameters of the social learning process responsible for differential age at onset of fear of strangers in terms of antecedent social interaction variables. Only two of the variables examined reached significant levels and even in these cases the coefficients are not very high. It is, of course, possible that the measures used here were not sufficiently sensitive or that relationship variables other than those examined represent the crucial determinants. However, it is noteworthy that both Ainsworth (1963) and Dennis (1940), in the case of the Ganda of East Africa and Hopi Indians respectively, have found fear of strangers to occur at the usual time despite the prevalence of child-rearing practices that in many respects differ appreciably from those adopted in Western countries. Morgan (1965), in his study of a sample of infants in the USA, has also reported insignificant correlations between previous experience variables and parameters of the fear response, and his explanation that the sample studied by him was too homogeneous to highlight any relationships that do exist may well apply to the present sample too. That variations in upbringing can influence the timing of early social phenomena is indicated by the failure of deprived infants to develop differential smiling (Ambrose, 1961) or fear of strangers (Spitz and Wolf, 1946) at the usual time, but it seems likely that these variations must be of a more extreme form than those found here if they are to produce systematic differences in the emergence of distinctive responses to strangers. The possibility must, therefore, be considered that the individual differences observed in the present sample relate less to environmental and more to genetically determined factors. Freedman (1965), on the basis of greater concordance found in identical than in fraternal twins, has suggested that heredity plays an important role in the development of fear of strangers, with reference both to the timing and the intensity of the response. To accept his proposition does not, of course, involve an abandoning of the view that the onset of fear can only take place if certain relevant learning experiences have taken place: rather, the position is similar to that discussed elsewhere in relation to age at onset of specific attachments (Schaffer and Emerson, 1964), which also showed little relation to experience variables. In both cases it is likely that the social conditions in the sample studied happen to meet minimal learning requirements, so that the new milestone will be reached at a rate that is primarily determined by the individual's genetic endowment. Under more extreme conditions, on the other hand, such as may be found in institutionalized settings, delay or even complete developmental failure can occur.

However welcome the emphasis of the incongruity hypothesis on the individual's previous perceptual experience may be, it is apparent that the manifestation of fear of strangers is a multi-determined event. The perception of unfamiliarity alone, it appears, is not sufficient to bring about fear: other variables, referring both to organismic and to stimulus characteristics, must also be taken into account.

References

AINSWORTH, M. D. (1963), 'The development of mother–infant interaction among the Ganda', in B. M. Foss (ed.), *Determinants of Infant Behaviour*, vol. 2, Methuen.

AMBROSE, J. A. (1961), 'The development of the smiling response in early infancy', in B. M. Foss (ed.), *Determinants of Infant Behaviour*, vol. 1, Methuen.

BENJAMIN, J. D. (1963), 'Further comments on some developmental aspects of anxiety', in H. Gaskill (ed.), *Counterpoint*, International Universities Press.

BRIDGES, K. M. B. (1932), 'Emotional development in early infancy', *Child Devel.*, vol. 3, pp. 324–41.

BÜHLER, C. (1930), *The First Year of Life*, Day.

CATTELL, P. (1940), *The Measurement of Intelligence of Infants and Young Children*, Psychol. Corp.

COLLIAS, N. E. (1950), 'Social life and the individual among vertebrate animals', *Ann. N.Y. Acad. Sci.*, vol. 51, pp. 1074–92.

DENNIS, W. (1934), 'Congenital cataract and unlearned behavior', *J. genet. Psychol.*, vol. 44, pp. 340–51.

DENNIS, W. (1940), 'Does culture appreciably affect patterns of infant behavior?', *J. soc. Psychol.*, vol. 12, pp. 305–17.

FISKE, D. W., and MADDI, S. R. (1961), *Functions of Varied Experience*, Dorsey.

FREEDMAN, D. G. (1961), 'The infant's fear of strangers and the flight response', *J. child Psychol. Psychiat.*, vol. 2, pp. 242–8.

FREEDMAN, D. G. (1965), 'Hereditary control of early social behaviour', in B. M. Foss (ed.), *Determinants of Infant Behaviour*, vol. 3, Methuen.

GESELL, A., and THOMPSON, H. (1934), *Infant Behavior: Its Genesis and Growth*, McGraw-Hill.

HEBB, D. O. (1946), 'On the nature of fear', *Psychol. Rev.*, vol. 53, pp. 259–76.

HEBB, D. O. (1949), *The Organization of Behavior*, Wiley.
HESS, E. H. (1958), '"Imprinting" in animals', *Sci. Amer.*, vol. 198, pp. 81–90.
HUNT, J. McV. (1960), 'Experience and the development of motivation: some reinterpretations', *Child Devel.*, vol. 31, pp. 489–504.
HUNT, J. McV. (1963), 'Motivation inherent in information processing and action', in O. J. Harvey (ed.), *Motivation and Social Interaction*, Ronald Press.
HUNT, J. McV. (1964), 'The psychological basis for using pre-school enrichment as an antidote for cultural deprivation', *Merrill–Palmer Q.*, vol. 10, pp. 209–48.
HUNT, J. McV. (1965), 'Traditional personality theory in the light of recent evidence', *Amer. Sci.*, vol. 53, pp. 80–96.
LEVY, D. M. (1960), 'The infant's earliest memory of inoculation: a contribution to public health procedures', *J. genet. Psychol.*, vol. 96, pp. 3–46.
MEILI, R. (1955), 'Angstentstehung bei Kleinkindern', *Schweiz. Z. Psychol.*, vol. 14, pp. 195–212.
MOLTZ, H. (1965), 'Contemporary instinct theory and the fixed action pattern', *Psychol. Rev.*, vol. 72, pp. 27–47.
MORGAN, G. A. (1965), 'Some determinants of infants' responses to strangers during the first year of life', unpublished Ph.D. thesis, Cornell University.
PIAGET, J. (1955), *The Child's Construction of Reality*, Routledge & Kegan Paul.
PREYER, W. T. (1888), *The Mind of the Child*, vol. 1, Appleton-Century-Crofts.
SCHAFFER, H. R. (1963), 'Some issues for research in the study of attachment behavior', in B. M. Foss (ed.), *Determinants of Infant Behaviour*, vol. 2, Methuen.
SCHAFFER, H. R., and EMERSON, P. E. (1964), 'The development of social attachments in infancy', *Monogr. Soc. Res. Child Devel.*, vol. 29, no. 3.
SCOTT, J. P. (1962), 'Genetics and the development of social behavior in mammals', *Amer. J. Orthopsychiat.*, vol. 32, pp. 878–88.
SLUCKIN, W. (1964), *Imprinting and Early Learning*, Methuen.
SPITZ, R. A. (1950), 'Anxiety in infancy: a study of its manifestations in the first year of life', *Int. J. Psycho-anal.*, vol. 31, pp. 139–43.
SPITZ, R. A., and WOLF, K. M. (1946), 'The smiling response: a contribution to the ontogenesis of social relations', *Genet. psychol. Monogr.*, vol. 34, pp. 57–125.
TENNES, K. H. and LAMPL, E. E. (1964), 'Stranger and separation anxiety in infancy', *J. nerv. ment. Dis.*, vol. 139, pp. 247–54.

Further Reading

J. A. Ambrose (ed.), *Stimulation in Early Infancy*, Academic Press, 1970.

P. P. G. Bateson, 'The characteristics and context of imprinting', *Biol. Rev.*, vol.41, 1966, pp. 177–220.

S. J. Dimond, *The Social Behaviour of Animals*, Batsford, 1970.

D. A. Goslin (ed.), *Handbook of Socialization Theory and Research*, Rand McNally, 1969.

R. A. Hoppe, G.A. Milton and E. C. Simmel (eds.), *Early Experiences and the Processes of Socialization*, Academic Press, 1970.

G. Newton and S. Levine (eds.), *Early Experience and Behavior*, C. C. Thomas, 1968.

H. R. Schaffer (ed.), *The Origins of Human Social Relations*, Academic Press, 1970.

J. P. Scott, *Early Experience and the Organization of Behavior*, Brooks-Cole, 1968.

W. Sluckin, *Imprinting and Early Learning*, Methuen, 1964.

W. Sluckin, *Early Learning in Man and Animal*, Allen & Unwin, 1970.

H. W. Stevenson, E. H. Hess and H. L. Rheingold (eds.), *Early Behavior: Comparative and Developmental Approaches*, Wiley.

Acknowledgements

Permission to reproduce the Readings published in this volume is acknowledged to the following sources:

1. Einar R. Siqueland and Louis P. Lipsitt, Academic Press, Inc.
2. J. Cock and S. Karger, Basel
3. D. F. Caldwell, J. Werboff and the American Association for the Advancement of Science
4. Walter C. Stanley and the American Psychological Association
5. *The Quarterly Journal of Experimental Psychology*
6. P. P. G. Bateson and *Animal Behaviour*
7. *Nature*
8. Howard S. Hoffman and the Society for the Experimental Analysis of Behaviour
9. John Wiley & Sons, Inc.
10. Cambridge University Press
11. Wadsworth Publishing Company, Inc.
12. Bettye M. Caldwell and the *American Journal of Orthopsychiatry*
13. William R. Thompson and the *Canadian Journal of Psychology*
14. Ronald R. Melzack and the American Psychological Association
15. S. Levene and Duke University Press
16. Victor H. Derenberg and the American Psychological Association
17. J. McV. Hunt and the American Psychological Association
18. J. P. Scott and the Journal Press
19. Lorna Smith Benjamin and the American Psychological Association
20. Gene P. Sackett and the American Psychological Association
21. B. Seay and Williams Wilkins Company
22. *Nature*
23. Leon J. Yarrow and the American Psychological Association
24. *Nature*
25. Psychonomic Press
26. J. P. Scott and Harper & Row Inc.
27. H. Rudolph Schaffer and the Society for Research in Child Development
28. Pergamon Press Ltd.

Author Index

Ader, R., 227
Ahrens, R., 368, 375
Ainsworth, M. D., 12, 151, 320, 367, 371, 375, 401
Aldrich, C. A., 17
Alexander, B. K., 315
Amatruda, C. S., 365
Ambrose, J. A., 11, 401
Anderson, J. E., 153
Andrew, R. J., 75

Baer, D. M., 21, 62
Baldwin, A. L., 366
Banks, E. M., 44, 189, 351
Barker, R. G., 149
Baron, A., 229
Bateson, P. P. G., 11, 49, 71, 89–91, 93, 95
Bayley, N., 156, 157, 320
Beach, F. A., 118, 125, 189, 203, 205
Bell, R. Q., 378
Bell, R. W., 211–13, 222, 226
Benjamin, J. D., 368, 394, 399
Benjamin, L. S., 235
Beres, D., 154
Berkowitz, L., 318
Bernstein, A., 281
Biel, W. C., 36, 122
Bijou, S. W., 21
Binet, A., 155
Bingham, W. E., 125, 173
Binks, C., 11, 335
Birch, H. G., 17, 20, 379
Blau, L. R., 281
Blau, T. H., 281
Blauvelt, H., 17, 18, 20
Bloom, B. S., 158

Blume, D., 349
Bovard, E. W., 226–8
Bowlby, J., 12, 97, 307, 308, 316, 320, 326, 366–7, 369, 375
Boyd, H., 52
Brackbill, Y., 366
Brady, J. V., 224
Bridges, K. M. B., 387
Broadhurst, P. L., 220, 221
Brodbeck, A. J., 276, 280, 281, 286, 357
Bronfenbrenner, U., 149
Brodbeck, A. J., 276, 280, 281, 286, 357
Bronfenbrenner, U., 149
Brookshire, K. H., 226, 228, 229
Brown, J., 54–6
Bruce, M., 305
Bühler, C., 365, 387
Burchinal, L. G., 153
Burlingham, D., 320

Cairns, R. B., 96, 331
Caldwell, B. M., 101, 149, 152, 162, 367
Caldwell, D. F., 15
Callender, W. M., 368
Campbell, B. A., 228
Campbell, E. H., 228
Cannon, D. J., 44, 351
Carletti, A., 61
Carlson, P. V., 216, 217
Carmichael, L., 105
Casler, L., 376
Cattell, P., 390
Charles, M. S., 352
Chess, S., 379

Chevalier, J. A., 171, 222, 235
Chow, K. L., 190
Clarke, R. S., 172, 174, 182
Cofoid, D. A., 89
Collias, N. E., 52, 75, 333, 374, 388
Conger, J. J., 366
Conrad, D. G., 224
Corman, R., 164
Cornwell, A. C., 15, 39, 44
Cowden, D. J., 251
Croxton, F. E., 251
Cruze, W. W., 123

Dann, S., 153
Davis, A., 149
Davis, H. V., 276, 280, 281
Davis, K., 186
Denenberg, V. H., 12, 169, 210–26, 228, 341
Dennis, W., 154, 388, 401
Dimond, S. J., 12
Dixon, W. J., 203
Dollard, J., 239, 366
Duffy, E., 229
Dye, H., 155, 171

Easler, C. A., 44, 189, 351
Elmer, E., 161
Emerson, P. E., 331, 387, 390, 401
Estes, W. K., 188, 202

Fabricus, E., 51, 52, 57, 58, 66
Farber, I. E., 206
Fetherstonhaugh, M. L., 172, 174, 182
Finch, G., 108
Fisher, A. E., 235, 259, 278, 281, 358
Fiske, D. W., 388
Fleischl, M. F., 273, 281
Fletcher, F. M., 206

Forgays, D. G., 125, 126, 171, 172, 182, 186, 202
Forgays, J. W., 125, 126, 171, 186, 202
Forgus, R. H., 126, 127, 202
Fowler, W., 156
Fredericson, E., 189, 343, 352, 354
Freedman, D. G., 368, 387, 389, 396, 401
Freeman, F. N., 171
Freud, A., 153, 320
Freud, S., 189, 202, 235, 280, 283
Fuller, J. L., 39, 44, 142, 146, 175, 189, 343, 346, 351, 352

Gardner, D. B., 153, 329
Gentry, E. F., 17
Gesell, A., 365, 387, 393
Gewirtz, J. L., 18, 341, 366, 367, 380
Gibbs, P. K., 149
Gibson, J. J., 67, 68, 105
Goldfarb, W., 151, 320
Goodwin, D., 65
Gordon, E. W., 17, 20
Goslin, D. A., 12
Gottlieb, G., 71, 90, 97
Graham, F. K., 378
Grant, D. A., 293
Gray, P. H., 62, 90, 333
Greenacre, P., 189, 202
Griffiths, R., 365
Griffiths, W. J., 125, 171, 203
Grota, L. J., 215
Guiton, P., 51, 55–9, 62, 65, 66, 71, 79, 89, 90
Gula, H., 154
Gunther, M., 18

Hafez, E. S. E., 97
Halikas, N., 63

Hall, C. S., 203
Hammett, F. S., 227
Hansen, E., 307, 308, 310, 313, 316–18, 321
Harlow, H. F., 11, 97, 108, 282, 283, 295, 298, 299, 305, 307, 308, 313, 316–18, 320, 321, 337, 341, 366, 375
Harlow, M. F., 320
Hass, M. B., 153
Havighurst, R. J., 149
Havlena, J., 229
Hawkes, G. R., 153
Heathers, G., 366
Hebb, D. O., 11, 51, 101, 107, 125, 171, 172, 174, 182, 186, 189–90, 199, 202, 205, 220, 225, 229, 387–8
Heron, W., 126, 127, 131, 169, 172, 174, 182, 202
Hersher, L., 341
Hertzig, M. E., 379
Hess, E. H., 11, 51, 54, 56–9, 61–3, 71, 72, 93, 95, 374, 400
Hilgard, E. R., 9, 36, 37
Hill, J. C., 186
Hinde, R. A., 9, 52, 57, 65, 66, 89, 305, 321, 323
Hindley, C. H. 378
Hoffman, H. S., 49
Hoffman, L. W., 153, 382
Hogan, H. P., 105
Holmes, H., 11
Holt, J., 159
Holzinger, K. J., 171
Honig, W. K., 89
Honzik, M. P., 282
Howard, K. I., 62, 90
Hubbert, H. B., 122, 123
Hudgens, G. A., 341
Hull, C. L., 239
Hunt, H. H., 203, 205, 215
Hunt, J. McV., 103, 202, 235, 237–41, 243, 251, 253, 254, 388, 389, 400
Hymovitch, B., 125, 126, 171, 202

Irvine, E. E., 149
Irwin, O. C., 378

James, H., 11, 52, 335
James, W., 104
James, W. T., 44, 351
Jaynes, J., 51, 55, 57–62, 66, 71, 89, 90, 118, 125, 189, 203, 205
Jensen, G. D., 321
Johnson, D. L., 96, 331
Johnson, O., 254
Jones, H. E., 171
Joos, M., 75

Kaplan, M., 206, 280
Karas, G. G., 213, 220, 221, 224
Kaufman, I. C., 89
Kaye, H., 17, 95
Kempe, C. H., 159
Kendler, H. H., 206
King, D., 259, 278, 281, 358
King, J. A., 118, 125, 357
Klackenberg, G., 280
Kliavina, M. P., 39
Kline, N. J., 213, 215, 216, 222, 224
Klopfer, P. H., 11, 55
Kluckhohn, C., 239
Kobakova, E. M., 39
Koch, J., 15
Koffka, K., 105
Korchin, S. J., 169, 222, 235
Kozma, F., 49
Krechevsky, I., 105
Kunst, M. S., 282

Lambercier, M., 129
Lampl, E. E., 387
Lashley, K. S., 109, 125
Leeper, R. W., 105
Levin, H., 366
Levine, S., 169, 206, 211, 212, 215–19, 222, 226–30, 235
Levy, D. M., 272–4, 277, 278, 280, 281, 320, 358, 391
Lewis, G. W., 211, 229
Lewis, O., 149
Lindholm, B. W., 214, 217–19, 228
Linn, T., 211
Lippitt, R. 382
Lipsitt, L. P., 11, 15, 17
Lipton, R. C., 149, 151
Littman, R. A., 226, 228, 229
Liu, S. Y., 122, 123
Livingston, W. K., 199
Lorenz, K. Z., 51, 65, 66, 71, 93, 343
Luria, A. R., 128, 129, 132
Lustman, S. L., 378

Maas, H., 154
Maccoby, E., 149, 366
McGeoch, J. A., 103
McKenna, J., 17, 18, 20
Maddi, S. R., 388
Maher, B. A., 212, 215, 225, 229
Maier, N. R. F., 123
Malmo, R. B., 229
Malone, C. A., 159
Marquis, D. G., 9, 36, 37
Marston, M. V., 39, 211, 343
Mason, J. W., 224
Mason, M. L., 186
Mason, W. A., 11, 295, 298
Massey, F. J., 203
Mead, M., 149, 382
Meili, R., 387
Melzack, R., 169, 172, 190, 202

Menzel, E. W., Jr, 298
Meyer, C. C., 49
Meyers, W. J., 214
Miller, H. C., 276, 280, 281
Miller, N. E., 198, 200, 214, 239, 366
Miner, J. B., 108
Mitchell, G. D., 298, 299
Moltz, H., 51, 63, 71, 89, 90, 206, 374, 397
Moore, A. V., 341
Morgan, C. T., 244, 254
Morgan, G. A., 394, 395, 398, 401
Morton, J. R. C., 215, 225
Moses, L. E., 195
Mowrer, O. H., 103, 198, 200, 239
Muenzinger, K. F., 206
Munn, N. L., 123, 275
Murie, A., 346
Murphy, L. B., 156
Mussen, P. H., 366

Najarian, P., 154
National Society for the Study of Education, 171
Nelson, A. K., 17
Newman, H. H., 171
Nissen, H. W., 190
Nowlis, V., 366

Obers, S., 154
Oden, M. H., 155
Otis, L., 203, 205, 215, 227

Panchenkova, E. F., 128
Papousek, H., 11, 17, 20, 21
Paramonova, M. P., 128
Pavenstedt, E., 149, 161
Pavlov, I. P., 114, 133, 144, 145
Pease, D., 329
Peiper, A., 17

Pfaffmann, C., 41
Piaget, J., 155, 365, 369, 375, 398
Poggiani, C., 15
Porter, M., 11
Porter, R. W., 224
Pratt, K. C., 17
Prechtl, H. F. R., 17, 18, 20
President's Commission on the Status of Women, 163
Preyer, W. T., 387
Provence, S., 149, 151

Rabin, A. I., 149, 154
Rabinovitch, M. S., 182
Radke Yarrow, M., 153
Ramsay, A. O., 51, 57
Raymond, E. J., 298, 299
Reisner, G., 311
Rey, A., 129
Rheingold, H. L., 11, 156-7, 320, 366, 376
Ribble, M. A., 202, 280, 357
Richmond, J. B., 162, 341, 378
Richter, C. P., 123
Riesen, A. H., 106, 108
Roberts, E., 281
Robertson, J., 317, 320, 326
Robinson, B., 186
Rosenblatt, J. S., 11
Rosenblum, L. A., 51, 63
Rosenzweig, M. R., 298
Ross, H. W., 366
Ross, S., 235, 257, 262, 278, 281, 358
Rosvold, E. H., 182
Rousseau, J. J., 154
Rowell, T. E., 321, 323
Rueping, R. R., 295
Ruppenthal, G. C., 289, 299
Ryall, R. W., 61

Sackett, G. P., 11, 235

Sackett, R. S., 207
Salzen, E. A., 11, 49, 51, 52, 71, 90-91, 93, 95
Schaefer, T., 215, 225, 229
Schaeffer, H. H., 71
Schaffer, H. R., 331, 368, 387, 390, 398, 401
Schein, M. W., 96
Schlosberg, H., 235
Schneirla, T. C., 11, 374
Schutz, F., 11
Scott, J. H., 227
Scott, J. P., 11, 39, 101, 142, 146, 175, 189, 210-11, 228, 235, 257, 265, 298, 331, 337, 340, 341, 343, 344, 346, 352, 397
Scott, T. H., 169
Searle, J. L., 49
Sears, P. S., 366
Sears, R. R., 276, 280, 281, 366
Seay, B., 305, 307, 308, 313, 316-18, 321
Seitz, P. F. D., 212
Semmes, J., 190
Shirley, M. M., 365
Sidman, M., 46
Siegel, A., 153
Siegel, S., 288, 293
Simon, T., 155
Siqueland, E. R., 115
Skeels, H., 157, 171
Skinner, B. F., 46, 144
Slonaker, J. R., 123
Sluckin, W., 11, 49, 51, 52, 71, 93, 95, 97, 331, 333, 387
Smith, F. V., 52, 53
Smith, L. J., 282, 287
Smith, S. A., 215-19
Solomon, R. L., 205, 207, 235,
Spence, J. T., 212, 215, 225, 229
Spencer-Booth, Y., 305, 321

Spiker, C. C., 11
Spiro, M., 149
Spitz, R. A., 276, 357, 365, 368, 375, 376, 387, 401
Spitz, R. E., 202, 320
Stanley, W. C., 15
Steller, E., 235, 254
Stel'makh, L. N., 39
Stephens, M. W., 216, 217
Stern, C., 171
Stern, M., 182
Stettner, L. J., 71
Steven, D. M., 65, 96
Stevenson, H. W., 11
Stewart, C. N., 226, 228, 229
Stone, C. P., 112, 123–4, 131
Stringer, W. F., 203
Sun, K. H., 17

Taeschler, M., 61
Taylor, K. F., 331, 333
Tennes, K. H., 387
Terman, L. M., 155, 171
Thomas, A., 379
Thompson, H., 387, 393
Thompson, W. R., 126, 127, 131, 169, 172, 202
Thorpe, W. H., 51, 52, 57, 64–6, 68, 113, 354
Tinbergen, N., 12, 103, 107
Toffey, S., 49
Tolman, C. W., 321
Towne, J. C., 229
Trattner, A., 15
Troshikhin, V. A., 39
Turkewitz, G., 17, 20

Vince, M. A., 52, 57, 65, 66, 101, 114–21, 132
Volokhov, A. A., 39, 44
von Senden, M., 105

Walter, A. A., 105
Warren, R. P., 41
Watson, J. B., 112, 122, 123, 160
Webb, W. B., 207
Weidmann, U., 52, 57, 58, 333
Weingarten, F. S., 229
Weininger, O., 227
Wellman, B. L., 171
Werboff, J., 15, 229
Whimbey, A. E., 215
White, R. W., 156
Whiteman, P. H., 205
Whiting, J. W. M., 257, 366
Wickens, D. D., 36
Williams, E., 211
Williams, K., 125, 182, 186, 225
Willmott, P., 382
Winer, B. J., 302
Winitz, H., 378
Wise, G., 281
Wohlwill, J. F., 67
Wolf, A., 171, 186, 212
Wolf, K. M., 276, 365, 368, 375, 401
Woodcock, I. G., 280
Woodrow, H., 104
Woodworth, R. S., 105
Wortis, H., 149, 161
Wright, H. F., 149
Wynne, L. C., 205, 207

Yarrow, L. J., 151, 153, 305, 329
Young, M., 382

Zangwill, O. L., 105
Zarrow, M. X., 341
Zimmermann, R. R., 97, 282, 283, 308, 341, 366

Subject Index

Adult behaviour, 169–256
Aggression, 300, 304, 317
Altricial species, 15
Ants, 343
Anxiety, 202, 307, 368, 387
Appetitive conditioning, 39, 41–6
Approach responses, 333
Arousal, 220, 229, 377–8
Associative learning, 144–8, 331, 341
Attachment, 64, 67, 139, 331, 337–42, 366–70
   function, (need), 371–7
   scale, 370, 379
Aversive conditioning, 39, 43–6
Aversive stimuli, 98–9
Avoidance
   learning, 192–209, 212–13, 222–4
   responses, 74, 78–80, 84–90, 198, 351, 388

Behavioural control, 97–9
Behavioural development, 101, 112–34, 303–4, 331, 343–6, 387
Body sucking, 269–75, 286
Bottle feeding, 280–96
Bovard's theory, 226–8
Breast feeding, 280–81

Canaries, 115–17
Chicks, 52–66, 71–91, 93–6, 331–6, 387–8
Children, 127–9, 132, 137–40, 149–67, 202, 305–7, 317, 328–30, 366, 380–83, 389–96
   see also Infants

Chimpanzees, 106–9, 138, 192, 298, 387
Classical conditioning, 35–8, 39–47, 222
Cognitive development, 151, 155–6
Conditioned head-turning, 17–22, 23–34
Conditioned leg flexion, 35–8
Conditioned orienting reactions, 23–34
Configurationists, 108
Consummatory behaviour, 215–18
Contact comfort, 308, 377
Critical periods, 57–9, 93–6, 189, 210–30, 257, 331, 343–64
Cup feeding, 280–96

Discrimination learning, 19–21, 51, 107, 186, 276
Dogs, 126–7, 131, 137–9, 144–5, 171–87, 190–200, 298, 338, 344–6
   see also Puppies,
Drive reduction, 366
Ducklings, 52, 61, 63, 66, 97–9

Early conditioning, 10, 15, 17–22, 275–6
Early development, 136–48, 365–6
Early experience, 9–12, 117, 131, 141–8, 156–8, 171–207, 237–55, 298–304, 328–31, 343–63
Early learning, 9–11, 17–22, 101–10, 140–41

Subject Index 413

Early socialization, 257, 331–3
Early trauma, 202–5, 229, 329
Eating behaviour, 355–8
Effectance, 156
Emotional dependence, 367
Emotional development, 155–6, 307, 360
Enforced weaning, 257–8
Environmental restriction, 173–87, 190–200, 298–304
Exploratory behaviour, 298–9, 345

Fear, 58–9, 64, 300–303, 331, 368, 370–73, 387–403
Feeding frustration, 235, 237–55, 271–2
Finches, 113–17
Flocking, 331–6
Following responses, 51–60, 74–5, 84–90, 340, 377

Goslings, 343
Great tits, 117–21
Greenfinches, 115–17
Group upbringing, 153–5

Habit formation, 147
Habituation, 19–20, 58, 141, 147, 216
Handling (gentling) in infancy, 202–7, 212–20, 226–30
Heart rate, 352–3, 360
Heredity and behaviour, 343–4, 359–60, 401
Hoarding behaviour, 240–51
Hospitalization, 319, 368

Immobility (freezing) responses, 74, 79–80
Imprinted stimulus, 97–9
Imprinting, 11, 49, 51–70, 71–92, 93–6, 97–9, 331–3

effort, 61–2
primacy, 93–5
reversibility, 65–6, 93–6
Incongruity hypothesis, 387–403
Infantile stimulation, 202–30
Infants, 17–34, 138–9, 275–8, 331, 353, 357, 362, 365–86, 389–96 (*see also* Children)
Inhibition, 114–18, 127–9, 130–33, 146
Institutional environment, 151–8, 328–30
Instrumental learning, 17–22, 335
Inverted U function, 220–24, 229

Kibbutzim, 154

Lambs, 331, 337–42, 344
Later learning, 103–10, 140
Learning
 capacity, 101, 108–9, 112–34, 139–40, 275–6
 environment, 149–67
 in primates, 105–6
 theory, 280, 365–6
Learning to learn, 144, 146
Learning to perceive, 105
Longitudinal studies, 329, 372, 389

Maternal deprivation, 305, 320–30, 376
Maternal separation, 152–3, 305–26
Maze learning, 122–4, 142, 182–5, 221
Mice, 203, 210–13
Monkeys, 137, 235, 280–96, 298–327, 377
Monotonicity hypothesis, 217–20, 228–30

Mother surrogate, 283, 289–90, 295
Motivation and learning, 105–6, 112, 123, 131–3
Motor development, 137
Multiple mothering, 329, 382, 389

Neuronal model, 93–6
Non-nutritive sucking, 235, 269–78, 280–96
Novel stimuli, 71–91, 388
Noxious stimuli, 190, 199, 203–7
Nystagmus reflex, 349

Object conservation, 369, 375
Open-field behaviour, 215
Operant conditioning, 18–22, 46, 97–9
Operational criterion, 368–70
Oral-drive theory, 280–83, 295–6
Orienting reflex, 23, 31

Pain, perception and responses, 189–201, 350
Parental deprivation, 305
Peeping (distress) calls, 75, 87, 98
Perceptual learning, 51, 67–8, 93, 126, 388–9
Personality development, 257, 374
Phylogenesis, 106–10
Precocial species, 15, 49
Primary socialization, 138–9, 344–6, 353–63
Problem solving, 142–4, 171–87
Proximity
 avoidance, 368, 374, 387, 394–5
 seeking, 367–9, 371–8, 387
Psychoanalysis, 235, 237, 280

Puppies, 39–47, 140–46, 257–78, 280, 331, 343–64
 see also Dogs

Rats, 35–8, 106–9, 122–7, 144, 171, 203–4, 210–18, 222, 227–55, 298
Reactivity, (emotionality), 210–30
Rearing conditions, 173–87, 190–200, 298–304, 334
Reinforcement, (reinforcers), 17–33, 44–6, 97–9, 114, 145–7, 159, 335
Responsiveness, (activity), 119–22, 130–33, 141, 376
Restriction of experience, 173–87, 190–200, 298–304

Secondary drive, 367
Secondary reinforcement, 366
Sensitive period, 57–9, 71–92, 93
Sensory deprivation, 190–200, 203, 298–304, 329–30, 376
Sensory stimulation, 151, 190, 210–30, 298–304, 376, 387
Smiling response, 276, 375–7, 393, 401
Social attachments, 337–42, 365–87, 398
Social behaviour, 298–304, 307, 333, 343–64, 365–6, 381–3, 387
Social interaction, 310–16, 391–2, 396
Social isolation, 298–9, 337
Social setting, 380–3
Social stimulation, 376
Sucking behaviour, 257–78, 358–9, 377

Tactile stimulation, 17–21
Thumb sucking, 235, 257, 278, 280–83, 286, 295

Transfer of training, 103–5
Twin studies, 171
Twittering calls, 75, 80

Unfamiliarity, 397–403

Verbal development, 378
Verbal learning, 140

Wolves, 344, 346

Yerkes–Dodson, law 220